Employment, wages and income distribution

Whilst there is widespread agreement about the goals of economic policy, consensus about how best to achieve them can be harder to obtain. No issues are more contentious than employment and income distribution. In recent years full employment and a just distribution of incomes have been downgraded as policy objectives, as greater priority has been given to price stability and balance of payments objectives. This emphasis has been supported by a mainstream economic theory which has an unswerving belief in the ability of market forces to achieve a satisfactory regulation of employment and income distribution.

Other economists have remained more sceptical, and none more so than Kurt Rothschild. This new volume collects together his twenty-two most important essays in the area, many of which are appearing in English for the first time. Throughout pure theory is linked to relevant practical investigations. The book will provide stimulating reading for students of labour markets and distribution theory and policy, and for macroeconomic theorists in general.

Kurt W. Rothschild studied law and economics in Vienna before coming to Britain in 1938 following Hitler's invasion of Austria. After studying economics and lecturing at Glasgow University, he returned to Austria in 1947 where he worked first in the Austrian Institute of Economic Research and then became Professor of Economics at the University of Linz. He retired in 1985.

His theoretical and research interests were wide and included labour market analysis, economic growth, unemployment, income distribution, disequilibrium theory and forecasting. His major publications include *The Theory of Wages* (1954) and *Power in Economics* (editor, 1971).

Employment, wages and income distribution

Critical essays in economics

Kurt W. Rothschild

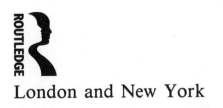

London and New York

First published 1993
by Routledge
11 New Fetter Lane, London EC4P 4EE

Simultaneously published in the USA and Canada
by Routledge
29 West 35th Street, New York, NY 10001

Typeset in Times by
Mathematical Composition Setters Ltd, Salisbury, UK
Printed and bound in Great Britain
by Mackays of Chatham PLC, Chatham, Kent

British Library Cataloguing in Publication Data

A catalogue record for this book is available from the British Library

ISBN 0–415–08579–9

Library of Congress Cataloging in Publication Data

Rothschild, Kurt W. (Kurt Wilhelm), 1914–
    Employment, wages, and income distribution : critical essays in
economics / Kurt W. Rothschild.
      p. cm.
    "Half of the papers were originally published in German and are
here presented in English translation"—Introd.
    Includes bibliographical references and index.
    ISBN 0-415-08579-9
    1. Employment (Economic theory) 2. Wages. 3. Income
distribution. I. Title.
HD5701.5.R67 1993
331.12′5—dc20
                                         92-37260
                                           CIP

Contents

Figures

Tables

Preface

The publication of a collection of previously published papers always demands an apology and an explanation. The easiest way out for me would be to offer the excuse that Routledge's economics editor was so kind to ask me whether I would be willing to prepare such a collection. And who can resist such a proposal? But there is a bit more that can be said in defence of my action.

First of all there is the usual explanation that some of the papers might still be (so one hopes) of interest today but might not be easily accessible. This is particularly true in the present case because half of the papers, chapters 1, 2, 3, 4, 5, 8, 9, 13, 15, 16, 22 were originally published in German and are here presented in English translation for the first time.

More important, however, is the fact that the various papers – though published at different times and for different occasions – do hang together via a basic and pervasive perspective. This requires a short biographical explanation. My early studies of economics as a law student at Vienna University in the 1930s were mainly an indoctrination with undiluted Austrian marginal utility theory which contrasted strangely with a mass unemployment of 25 per cent in the surrounding environment. When the arrival of Hitler turned me into a refugee I had the good luck to obtain a scholarship at Glasgow University where I had the first opportunity to come into touch with Keynesian economics. It immediately impressed me as an obvious key to the pressing employment problems which I had previously missed. This macroeconomic perspective was challenged a few years later when I was asked (as assistant-lecturer in economics in Glasgow University) to deliver a course on wage theory. My main source was Hicks's famous 'Theory of Wages' written before Keynes's General Theory. This forced me back to the old microeconomic equilibrium approach which had proved so unsatisfactory and which could not be easily fitted into the Keynesian perspective. These confrontations and contradictions between theory and reality, between Keynesian macroeconomics and neoclassical micro-economics mixed with the experience of unemployment as a major social problem, 'pushed' me into a continuing critical argument with various aspects of employment and wage theories and their interrelations. This is the background which provides a common bond for the diverse papers contained in this volume.

Papers 1 to 4 all serve to stress the uniqueness and peculiarities of the labour market which make it inappropriate to analyse it in neoclassical fashion in analogy to goods markets. In each paper certain aspects of this 'uniqueness' are considered. Papers 5 to 7 deal with special employment problems. Paper 5 shows how disguised prejudices (against women, foreigners, etc.) can lead to protracted unemployment, paper 6 refers to difficulties for employment chances in a globalized economy, and paper 7 indicates that an explanation of the changes in the supply of female labour has to move beyond a purely economic analysis.

From employment it is only a short step to wages, the latter being the main (or sole) determinant of employment in neoclassical theory. Paper 8 provides for wages what the earlier papers did for employment: it stresses the theoretical diversity of wage aspects which are connected with the peculiarities of the labour market. Paper 9 is a summary of the fundamental Keynesian proposition that macroeconomic changes in nominal wages have no unequivocal effects on the level of employment. The fact that nominal wages have no unique equilibrium market level and the existence of an oligopolistic environment makes bargaining an important element in wage formation. This is the subject of paper 10. An empirical paper (number 11) shows that contrary to neoclassical expectations wage differentials do not compensate for various risks and disadvantages. The Phillips curve revolutionized traditional ideas about wage dynamics. Its contents and problems are treated in papers 12 and 13. Paper 14 critically examines Weitzman's ambitious proposal to kill inflation and unemployment through a system of profit-sharing (instead of fixed wage contracts).

Wages represent a dominant part of national income. Their level (together with the level of employment) leads directly to the economically and socially important questions of income distribution some of which are treated in the third section. Paper 15 surveys the empirical and theoretical aspects of the famous Kaleckian wage share hypothesis, while paper 16 deals with different interpretations of wage share formulas. In the wake of Keynes's macroeconomics new distribution theories emerged; their differences and special features are treated in papers 18 to 20. Finally papers 21 and 22 turn to normative aspects which are almost unavoidably connected with the income distribution theme.

Part I
Employment

1 Microeconomics of the labour market

(Translation of (1986) 'Mikroökonomik des Arbeits marktes' in H. Schelbert-Seyfrig et al. (eds), *Mikroökonomik des Arbeitsmarktes*, Bern: Verlag Paul Haupt, pp. 431–8)

The conference of the last two days has enabled us to obtain a good idea of the impressive research carried out by the Bale project on labour market problems. There can be no doubt that the themes treated are important and that valuable, new empirical material has been provided. We can expect that the ensuing discussion will have a lot to say on the interpretation of the results and on the conclusions and recommendations which can be derived from them for Switzerland's economic policy.

In the introductory remarks to the discussion which I have been asked to make I shall refrain from dealing with these important concrete policy consequences, mainly because as a foreigner I am not sufficiently acquainted with the historical and institutional background of the Swiss labour market processes, which is of considerable importance particularly in this field. So my remarks will be restricted to some observations on the theoretical background which – explicitly or implicitly – underlies the prescribed studies and those in other countries as well. Even where the studies seem to be 'purely' empirical some rudimentary theory must exist because without 'theoretical' ideas no orderly concept can be developed. Since this conference was dedicated to the microeconomics of the labour market I shall also restrict myself to this sphere. I shall try to consider quite generally what role microeconomics can play, its possibilities and its tasks, when labour market problems are under discussion. I hope that this can be of some service to the ensuing discussion. Needless to say that my considerations are necessarily incomplete and not free from some subjective bias.

Let us start with the question: why should it be necessary to have a special *microeconomic* theory of the labour market? Why is it not sufficient to have a general theory of the labour market? After all, there is such a thing as a real labour market which we can observe and study. We do not distinguish between a micro- and a macro-market. Why, then, two separate theoretical approaches? Let me begin with some general remarks before dealing with this question in more detail.

For several years now it has become fashionable to ask for a micro-economic foundation of macroeconomic theory. Differences between neoclassical and Keynesian approaches suggested such a demand and difficulties in aggregation pointed in the same direction. How important is such a demand?

One answer would probably be that we want to achieve consistency between various theoretical approaches. With regard to the labour market this sentiment was very clearly expressed in the paper of Wolfgang Franz, when he says: 'The necessity of a (revised) microeconomic foundation of economic paradigms should be undisputed in view of the breakdown of prominent macroeconomic relations in the past decade.' But this conclusion is not quite convincing. Are we not also faced with competing micro-theories which do not fit properly? And could the answer to unsatisfactory macro-theories not be found in a revised macro-theory? And, third, why do we not just demand better theories? After all, each and every theory is at best only a partial analysis which tries to provide a logical structure for certain parts of a complex reality. All of them can only claim relative validity for certain aspects and problems. Seen from this perspective a sharp division between micro- and macroeconomics is not immediately self-evident.

But the distinction between micro and macro becomes more meaningful when we deal with the labour market. The special conditions there provide two good reasons for making a microeconomic foundation an issue. The first is that in this field the general micro–macro problem is very pronounced. Keynes's *General Theory* gave pride of place to labour market and employment questions in the framework of a theory which was deliberately and wholeheartedly a macro-theory. It provided some startling results which in many ways contradicted traditional classical ideas about employment and unemployment. Counter-arguments appeared now and then but the fundamental backlash occurred round about 1970. The traditional theory hit back, quite generally but also and in particular in relation to labour market issues. The well-known collection of papers issued by Phelps in 1970 was a landmark of this development (Phelps 1970).

This literature of the neoclassical backlash which in the meantime has reached considerable proportions has been excellently treated in the paper by Franz. It tries to stick as far as possible to the traditional assumption of utility maximization as the optimal strategy. In the centre we have optimal information strategies, optimal search strategies, the never-ending comparisons of utility and costs. To some extent this approach presents an attempt to incorporate 'unpleasant' facts in such a way that the basic structure of the traditional theory is not endangered. We get an example for Kuhn's remarks about the defence of traditional paradigms. Some of these novelties are not much more than a translation of some neglected events into the homely language of habitual theories.

The other source for a microeconomic view of the labour market has a far longer history. Much more than is usual in other spheres we have an old tendency in labour market approaches − be they descriptive or theoretical, neoclassical or unorthodox − to take a micro-view of relevant processes. Special works in Labour Economics have existed for a long time, but nothing comparable is written about Good Economics, Service Economics, etc. Good books on Labour Economics always presented a mixture of general theories and numerous micro-elements and studies. Many well-known names come to mind, including Douglas, Dunlop, Reynolds, Phelps, Brown, Kerr and others. Hicks was rather exceptional with his strong theoretical orientation.

Why has this tendency for a specialized presentation and a micro-analysis been so concentrated in this branch of economics? The reason has certainly to be found in the peculiarities of the labour market. These peculiarities − among others − consist of the facts that the 'goods' supplied on this market are firmly linked to a person; that income from work constitutes − far more than the income from the sale of commodities − the main source of personal income; that the type of work one supplies has a strong influence on social status; that labour supply is characterized by a specially high degree of heterogeneity; that mobility problems are more serious than in other markets; and last but not least, peculiarities follow from the long-term nature of incompletely determined labour contracts.

It was probably a mistake from the very beginning to treat the labour market in comparison to goods markets and to press it into the usual demand−supply scheme. It would have been far better to look for a special approach to labour market questions. This would probably have led to quite different theories characterized by interdisciplinary analyses in which psychological and sociological elements would play an important role side by side with economic factors. As Franz shows very clearly in his paper, the new microeconomics of the labour market start off with the question: why is the labour market not a spot auction market with continuous market clearing? It is quite obvious that the problem is approached under the perspective of a model which takes general equilibrium as the 'normal' case. This is as if a person whose views are firmly based on the Bible took the sentence that people should propagate like the sand at the sea as a basis for a research agenda asking why some families have fewer than fifteen children.

Many questions which are nowadays attacked by micro-analyses, be they classical or unorthodox, are nothing but troublesome attempts to find a way out of the difficulties which were created by a misdirected start of labour market theory. It is not surprising that in this attempt to come into closer contact with the peculiarities of the labour market a multitude of microeconomic approaches are presented. Many subjects have to be considered: differing and changing behaviour patterns, political actions, institutional and other non-economic influences, etc. In this respect it could be fruitful to look for an enrichment of economic theory with sociological and political elements rather than to follow the fashionable path of extending economic methodology to the other social sciences.

There can be no doubt that the new approaches in the classical microeconomic tradition offer an important addition to our understanding of labour market processes and problems. But I believe that more attention should be paid to the contemporary non-orthodox approaches dealing with segmented labour markets, job rationing, screening, discrimination, etc. and to distributional conflicts. These are elements which tend to be neglected in theories which derive their perspective from harmonious equilibrium models. The schizophrenia which this perspective can cause for some theorists is illustrated by the well-known and very useful survey-article by Glen Cain (1976). Although Cain is fully aware of the limitations of the neoclassical approach ('Neoclassical research can become terribly inbred and out of touch with policy makers...', p. 1248) and regards modifications in line with the alternative non-classical theories as important, he nevertheless hesitates to grant to the latter full status as labour market theory. He seems to be unable to accept the idea that these non-orthodox approaches can be seen as equally 'valid' attacks on a very complex phenomenon.

What seems certain is that all the diverse microeconomic approaches can only be partial explanations. The multi-faceted events in the labour market cannot be gathered in one single comprehensive approach. When different microeconomic theories and studies are compared and judged, the criteria to be used will frequently not be the question whether a theory is 'right' or 'wrong' but rather whether and when it can be useful. This is not a purely theoretical question; an answer also requires some acquaintance with local and historical conditions. More than elsewhere is it true for labour market questions that the theory is a toolbox which has to be used with care and with a grain of salt.

I should like now to say a few words about possibilities in this area and about the future. Let us return once more to the macro–micro problem. I think that for quite a time we shall have to be content with a more or less peaceful coexistence of the two perspectives without being able to obtain a perfect fit between them. Macro-theory is certainly better suited to find answers when questions regarding total employment and the general level of wages are raised and when we want to see the labour market as a subsystem of the entire economy. In this task the macro-analysis can gain a lot by incorporating some of the elements and insights which the new micro-studies have produced. But if this is to be done in a manageable way it will be necessary to look for radical simplifications of these various approaches in order to find ways to combine them in some sensible analytical apparatus. All this, however, will not prevent a continuation of confrontations between conflicting macro-theories which will tend to form 'schools' with diverging prescriptions for economic policies.

The micro-theory cannot offer an alternative for finding better answers to aggregative questions dealing with the economic system as a whole. But as has been said already it can provide many valuable building blocks for a better analysis of different labour market situations, allowing more consideration for local and institutional specificities. Micro-theory cannot yet play a decisive role in judging the qualities and relevance of competing macro-theories; but it can modify them and can help to make their limitations and their relative usability more transparent. Since microeconomic approaches are under less pressure to conform to a given total theoretical structure they can accept their special limitations and assumptions more openly and can thus pay more attention to neglected details and niches. This means that many of these theories look at problems from a special perspective or that they do not necessarily contradict each other but are rather overlapping or supplementary. Peaceful coexistence can be established far more easily than in the case of macro-theories.

Let me summarize my views on the present situation. The literature and research on the microeconomics of the labour market has grown rapidly over the past fifteen years. Survey articles are becoming necessary and have themselves to be surveyed further. Very useful surveys concerning the 'new (neoclassical) microeconomics' of the labour market are available (e.g. Cain 1976; Magoulas 1982).

These new studies have sharpened our insights into many peculiarities of the labour market and have led to important empirical investigations with interesting new quantitative information. Even where the results look somewhat trivial or self-evident the studies have provided better foundations for traditional opinions and have provided more detail with regard to data, lags, etc. Further studies may also lead us to new and unexpected perspectives. What becomes obvious, however, is that in this area where traditions, institutions, social structures, etc. play such a prominent role, research on a national scale is particularly needed. Neither with regard to methods nor to results would it be wise to accept blindly the research from other countries: without an addition of domestic know-how one cannot expect to obtain satisfactory conclusions.

What about the future? Spectacular breakthroughs on the theoretical front are unlikely; too complex are the conditions in view of the constantly changing behaviour patterns of individuals, institutions and governments. There will be a continuous need for further and diversified micro-studies – ranging from interviews and descriptive case studies to extensive theoretical and statistical analyses – just in order to keep in touch with a quickly changing environment. We shall probably have to learn to be content to live for a long time in a world where different theories and approaches exist side by side. As Professor Franz rightly observes at the end of his paper, 'the demand to combine the various detailed studies into one single theoretical structure is understandable, but its realization under the present state of research (and I would add: under present circumstances) must be regarded as hopeless'.

REFERENCES

Cain, G. C. (1976) 'The challenge of segmented labor market theories to orthodox theory: a survey', *Journal of Economic Literature*, 14, 4, 1215–57.
Magoulas, G. (1982) *Probleme und Ansätze der Arbeitsmarkttheorie*, Bern: Haupt.
Phelps, E. S. ed. (1970) *Micro-Economic Foundations of Employment and Inflation Theory*, London: Macmillan.

2 Full employment – a special situation?

(Translation of 'Vollbeschäftigung – eine Aushnahme situation?',
Politik und Zeitgeschichte, no. B31, 1983)

INTRODUCTION

More than twenty years ago Gunnar Myrdal, the famous Swedish economist and Nobel prize winner, wrote an essay on the welfare state in which
he pointed out that the greatest step so far on the path to a real welfare state
had been the achievement of full employment. And he continued that the
people in the Western industrial nations would never permit a reappearance
of high unemployment.[1] And as late as 1969 a representative international
conference of economists discussed in London the question whether business cycles are a thing of the past.[2] Only a few years later these ideas and
questions had been overtaken by reality. Unemployment as a serious economic and social problem is omnipresent; with more than thirty million
unemployed in Western Europe and North America it has reached a level
which would have been regarded as unbelievable ten years ago.

'What can be done to fight unemployment?' has once again become an
urgent question with which economists are confronted. But it seems that
neither satisfactory nor unanimous answers are forthcoming. There is no
lack of suggestions and recommendations but they are usually contested or
prove to be not practicable. In the meantime unemployment continues to
grow or to remain at the high levels already reached.

What are the causes of these difficulties? Is economic theory incapable of
getting a hold on the problem or are political conditions to blame that no
'solution' can be found? What are the possibilities and the limits of a
realistic employment policy?

UNEMPLOYMENT AS THE RULE

A realistic assessment of possible therapies against unemployment will
depend on the view one takes regarding the 'normal behaviour' of the

economic system of the Western industrial states. If we look at this system, which can be classified as 'developed capitalist market economies', from a historical perspective we see that for almost two hundred years it has been characterized by disturbances and cycles which were always accompanied by considerable degrees of unemployment. Great economists like Marx, Schumpeter, Keynes and diverse trade cycle theorists have made this susceptibility for disturbances and crises a central element in their theories.

If we accept the historical perspective and the theories connected with it we shall have to admit that the difficult situation of stagnation and unemployment with which we are faced just now cannot be called an *exceptional* situation. Even though the younger generation experiences its first contact with mass unemployment, the events represent more or less a return to the 'normal' rhythm of capitalist economies. If we want to talk about exceptional situations it is not the present state of affairs we should think of but rather the 'golden sixties' with their historically almost unique prosperity. A similar exceptional situation in the other direction was probably the depression of the 1930s, with its abnormally high and prolonged decline. In both cases it seems that an atypical concentration of several factors pointed in one direction – expansive in one case, depressive in the other. The mutual stimulation of these factors created a basis for the unusual intensity and duration of these abnormal periods.

Background of the boom period

Though we do not want to deal in detail with the boom period of the 1960s it will be useful to give a short account of the main influences which were responsible for this high-level achievement. This will help us to see more clearly the difference in conditions under which an employment policy has to act today.

In most countries the years after the Second World War demanded enormous efforts for readjustment and reconstruction. Many economists had feared that the transition to a peacetime economy would be connected with serious disturbances and unemployment. And in fact many countries experienced unemployment in the 1940s and early 1950s. But its level was far lower than in pre-war days and it was quickly absorbed in the following years. This quick and resounding employment success was the result of a whole group of strong expansive factors.

The destruction caused by the war, together with the neglect of investment in the preceding depression and war years, led to a practically unavoidable investment push in private and public sectors to get production going and to repair and provide the necessary infrastructure. This push was intensified by a broad, formerly repressed, demand for consumption goods which was backed by more or less forced savings in previous years. Moreover, investments were not very risky because the quickly growing consumer demand was at first concentrated on easily foreseeable essential goods. An intensified demand for better food was followed by consumption waves for clothes and housing. A further incentive for investment was provided by the existence of a considerable pool of usable new technologies whose introduction had been neglected or postponed in the depression and war years. Japan and the European states had the additional advantage of being able to learn from American experience, which had been less interrupted by the political events. Finally, an accommodating, slightly inflationary monetary policy eased the push for a broad investment stream.

These different investment and demand forces intensified each other and so created a climate which contributed to the high levels of production and employment in the 1950s and the 1960s. This position was further consolidated by the revival of world trade (which had fallen back so badly in the depression) and last but not least by an economic policy which allotted a high priority to the employment target. The employment policy was not always very efficient and benefited from favourable circumstances. But the employment measures – more or less of the Keynesian type – had some importance in some countries at certain times. The least one can say is that the economic policy did not erect barriers in the path towards high employment.

Changed conditions in the 1970s

At the beginning of the 1970s the unique combination of several expansive forces had lost its impact. A 'trend turn' set in and with it a return to 'normality'. The relatively light recession of 1967–8 had been a first warning. In contrast to some small disturbances in the years before, this was the first time when most countries were hit by a (light) recession at the same time so that increased exports could not provide a way out of the difficulties. Then other events followed in quick succession: the years 1970–2 saw the breakdown of the Bretton Woods system with some negative effects on international trade and payments relations; unemployment began to rise in most countries; in 1973 the rise in oil prices shook the world; and finally the first proper post-war world recession materialized in 1975. Since then unemployment has grown almost continuously; a permanent economic recovery has not returned so far.

If we look at the world as it presents itself since the 'trend turn' we recognize that all the factors which had favoured the 'golden sixties' have disappeared or have been reversed. The basic investment urge flowing from reconstruction and modernization has come to an end. New and interesting technological changes are of course occurring all the time but the breadth of choice which existed after 1945 is no longer available. Also, some of the new technologies – microelectronics in particular – may have strong labour-saving effects. On the demand side we no longer have the strong effects of pent-up desires. With incomes increasing demand becomes more fickle. It must be 'created' and is open to diverse influences of fashion and chance. All this means that investment has become more risky.

In the international sphere the expansive effects of trade liberalization and reconstruction have run their course and the new alignment of currencies has led to new risks. Further problems for Europe and the US are added by the export drives of the new industrial states such as Japan, Taiwan, Hong Kong and Singapore, and by the strategies of multinational firms to transfer employment into these and other regions. This creates structural adjustment problems which – in connection with the unemployment problem – promote protectionist tendencies with negative effects on trade and expectations. A certain intensification of the problems comes also from the increased integration of the world economy which has led to a close synchronization of cyclical movements so that exports can no longer be an easy national remedy in a recession and none at all for the world as a whole.

The confrontation of present-day conditions with the very different special conditions of the 1950s and 1960s stresses the fact that the creation and maintenance of a high employment level has become *objectively* much more difficult than it was in the earlier years; and this is quite apart from the additional problems connected with the (transitory) increase in labour supply which we experience at present as a consequence of the 'baby boom' in the 1950s and early 1960s. The main conclusion following from these considerations seems to be that with the trend turn of 1970 the need for employment-orientated policies has grown considerably.

Ruling 'philosophies'

The weight that is attached to the above conclusion will depend decisively on the 'philosophies' and perspectives under which the economy is seen and analysed. A first and most decisive line divides economists with regard to the question whether employment policies in principle make sense or not. In contrast to the conclusion stated at the end of the previous section we find today a growing tendency among economists and politicians to take a completely different view, which reflects the ideas of traditional equilibrium theories and can therefore be labelled 'neoclassical'. Some of the presently fashionable currents in economic theory, such as monetarism, supply-side economics or the theory of rational expectations, are expressions of this tendency.

The basic ideas of these theories rest on the assumption that 'free' markets with fully flexible prices and wages constitute a mechanism for an efficient and comparatively smooth economic process in which all markets – including the labour market – will normally be 'in equilibrium'. In so far as disturbances occur, they are not so much failures of the market system but rather a consequence of preventing the market system from functioning properly. Monopolies and unions are responsible for price and wage rigidities which hamper adjustment processes; governments and banking systems interfere in the market process with negative effects on private investment activities.

Under this perspective the increased economic difficulties since 1970 are mainly interpreted as *abnormal* developments due to interferences of the sort just mentioned. Special blame is put on the growth of inflationary tendencies in the 1960s. Though a decisive source for their acceleration was the Vietnam war, more stress is laid on the links which – doubtlessly – exist between inflation and full employment policies. Fighting inflation thus becomes the main task for economic policy. Employment policy has to take second place or can be neglected altogether because the return to 'properly' functioning markets would automatically solve the employment problem. These ideas, which by now have guided the economic policies of conservative governments for more than a decade, have added considerably to the recessionary tendencies flowing from objective difficulties and have thus contributed to the size and persistence of contemporary unemployment.

TASKS FOR AN EMPLOYMENT POLICY

Employment policy as top priority

A first precondition for an effective strategy against unemployment seems to be that one acknowledges fully that we have entered a changed and 'normalized' crisis-prone situation which does not admit easy hopes for quick solutions by way of market automatisms. Employment policies with high priority are more needed than before. But acknowledging this is not enough. Today's conditions differ in many respects from earlier recessions and depressions and this forbids an uncritical application of simple Keynesian prescriptions which had been developed for a different environment. The hope that one could cut down unemployment by an expansion of global public expenditure of one sort or another and could then keep cycles under control by a policy of 'fine tuning' the budget can hardly be maintained under present conditions. Though some regularities in business cycles certainly exist it remains true that each cycle has an individuality of its own. Particularly in the present situation we find a number of new elements which have to be taken into account if employment policies are to be effective.

Of course, some instruments from the Keynesian tool-kit remain essential. Increased public expenditure will still be necessary to prop up a weak private investment activity and to prevent cumulative demand reductions. But in contrast to the depression period of the 1930s this can no longer be achieved by *undifferentiated* public spending (or tax reductions). Fifty years ago the situation was one of mass unemployment in practically all sectors of the economy and with a deflationary background. It did not really matter where additional demand was mobilized. Whichever line was chosen one could reckon with some expansion of production and employment which would then spread to other sectors.

Today we are faced with a far more differentiated situation. Though general unemployment exists it is very unevenly distributed among sectors, regions, skills and personal attributes (young people, women, invalids, etc). A second decisive difference is the influence which many years of inflation have had on the distributional conflict. The practice of inflationary price—wage races has created an ever-present danger that additional demand will result in price increases rather than in additional output. *Global* demand stimulation is therefore no longer a suitable prescription. What is needed is a targeted tax and expenditure policy which tries to avoid demand stimulation in bottleneck sectors where inflationary consequences would be particularly virulent. Measures should be concentrated on sectors and regions where free capacities and unemployment are clearly in evidence and they should aim at strengthening competition in order to weaken inflationary tendencies. Policies of this sort need not be restricted to the *additional* public and tax-induced private expenditures but could also be supported through reallocations of existing spending patterns.

Public demand stimulation and differentiated labour market policies

A stimulation of effective demand through public measures (fiscal and monetary policy) seems to be an essential precondition for the success of any employment policy whatsoever. In view of the recessive climate expansionary tendencies have hardly a chance of survival without the creation of a credible basis for higher sales expectations. But the traditional Keynesian policy — even when applied in a differentiated form — is not enough. The present unemployment has various roots and therefore requires a variety of therapies. A demand policy which takes *present* capacity reserves and unemployment rates as signposts for a differentiated policy runs into the danger of perpetuating outdated structures and thus to foster present and future *structural* unemployment. It prolongs demand for occupations and skills that will not be needed in the future.

A differentiated demand stimulation must therefore be modified and supplemented by a differentiated labour market policy. In so far as bottlenecks exist even now in obtaining certain skills, an active labour market policy can make an immediate contribution to a reduction of unemployment by providing appropriate training and retraining opportunities and by subsidizing regional mobility. Equally important is the training of the unemployed in general and of unemployed youngsters in particular in skills and occupations which are likely to be needed in a coming recovery. This can help to improve the chances of a quicker and more lasting absorption of unemployed persons at some future date.

Quite a lot could probably be done in this direction though the difficulties should not be overlooked. First, such a policy is expensive. But when looking at the costs one should not forget that the benefits derived from such measures in terms of maintaining and expanding qualifications and of reducing psychological stress and social conflicts are very great indeed. A second difficulty arises from the fact that in a prolonged recession it becomes increasingly difficult to forecast the structures and the employment needs in a coming recovery. But certain steps are possible and a lot might be gained by a co-ordination of long-term investment plans, training programmes, infrastructure developments, etc. Furthermore, the more successful the general policy is in reducing unemployment levels the quicker and more clearly the structural weaknesses and requirements will become visible, thereby enabling the active labour market policy to make 'correct' decisions.

CONSTRAINTS FOR AN EMPLOYMENT-ORIENTATED ECONOMIC POLICY

The concept of an employment-orientated policy which has been indicated in the previous section can come up against three constraints which play an important role in public discussions: the problem of public debt, inflation, and – in the case of some countries – the balance of payments problem.

Public debt

The problem of a high and growing public debt occupies a prominent place in present-day discussions. Though the public debt can cause genuine economic problems, the reason for its retarding effects on employment measures is more often than not the dominance of erroneous beliefs in public discussions. If government policy is called upon to take action against cumulative demand reductions in recession periods then it is a *conditio sine qua non* that the government does not restrict its expenditures at the same rate as the private sector. This means that the state should run into debt. If the government refrains from doing this by scaling down its expenditures in line with the stagnating revenues it will contribute to an intensification of the recession. When a recession lasts for a longer period then an employment-orientated policy will require a readiness to permit budget deficits for several years. This necessarily means that the *level* of the public debt will continuously rise during this period.

A growing public debt in recession periods is thus a necessary and desirable concomitant of an employment-orientated policy. Even governments which are not particularly employment-orientated but want to avoid deep depressions cannot escape deficits and debt accumulation as has been amply proved in all industrial states over the past ten years. This situation finds its *raison d'être* and justification in the special situation of the state which has to see the budget policy in relation to the stabilizing or destabilizing effects it can have.

The extent of the debt and the way it is managed are, however, problems which are not negligible; they call for a considered and intelligent debt policy. But the path to what is seen from the employment perspective as an efficient and sustainable deficit and debt policy is often obstructed by psychological and political factors. In the public debate deficit-financed employment policies are often equated with private prodigality. This leads to completely misleading ideas. One of these is, for instance, the thesis that the debts of today will be a burden for future generations. Though this is true as far as external debts are concerned, it is not so simply applicable to the domestic debt. The deficit-financed expenditure leads – in recessive periods – to additional outputs today which otherwise would not have been produced at all. It does *not* mean that one lives on the output of future generations, though debt problems will arise in connection with the distribution problems which are caused by the repayment arrangements. But the main problem consists of the misconceptions, the prejudices and the political-tactical misinformation which prevent an unemotional and informed discussion about the pros and cons of a balanced policy of deficits and debt repayments over longer periods.

Inflation

The inflation question is a serious problem for every kind of employment stimulation. The oligopolistic and monopolistic structure of the economy and the wage policies of the unions can cause prices and wages to rise long before the additional demand has resulted in full employment. If one regards this tendency as an unshakeable fact and at the same time makes price stability a top target for economic policy, then employment will fall by the wayside and we get underemployment equilibrium or – worse still – stagnation. The challenge one has to face is to find combinations between employment promotion and other measures which will see to it that the expansionary forces will *above all* be reflected in additional employment with relatively mild inflationary effects. This means that one has to try – in spite of many disappointing experiences – to develop some sort of incomes policy, i.e. attempts to keep the distributional conflict between the industrial contestants within certain bounds by such means as increased contacts, 'big' bargains covering several items in addition to wages, co-determination, etc. This would probably not stop the price–wage escalation but could slow it down. If the incomes policy could be linked to a credible employment policy the chances for a consensus would certainly rise.

Balance of payments problems

If in a world-wide recession only a few countries are prepared to fight unemployment on a bigger scale they are likely to run into balance of payments difficulties. With rising economic activity imports will increase while the exports will suffer under the continued stagnation abroad. Integration into a recessive environment sets severe limits to an isolated national employment policy. In principle this difficulty could be circumvented by introducing fully flexible exchange rates which could overcome the problem of foreign exchange scarcity. But the isolated expansionary policy would cause a permanent tendency towards devaluation which would aggravate the inflation problem. It would therefore be desirable to reform the rules for international trade in such a way that employment policies have a better chance. The undiluted free trade dogma – the guiding principle of the international trade regime – was derived for international economic relations in a fully employed world. When unemployment is a frequent problem the rules should be so modified that national expansionary programmes, which in the end will benefit other underemployed countries too, become possible. Some sort of regulated consensus procedure could provide possibilities for mutually agreed measures to make employment policies in individual countries possible without endangering their balance of payments but also without leading to protectionism and a shrinkage of international trade. If nothing is done in this direction an unhindered spreading of recessive tendencies could lead to secretive and mutually damaging protectionist actions. Beginnings of such developments are already visible.

THE PRESENT DEMAND FOR SHORTER WORKING TIME

As far as the question of a shorter working time is concerned it is first of all necessary to stress that this is an aim which has always been regarded as desirable quite irrespective of the employment question. Leisure time for freely chosen personal activities and for rest and recuperation is an essential element for a higher standard of living. From this point of view, further shortenings of the work week (month, year, lifetime) can certainly be advocated. At the present time they could also contribute – in the framework of a more general employment policy – to ease the unemployment problem. But it is not likely that a moderate reduction of working time by itself could make sharp inroads into the state of the labour market. If, however, it should turn out that for one reason or another the aforementioned employment policies cannot be applied even if the stagnation tendencies continue, then a more radical shortening of working time and/or reorganization of the production process could become topical if the unemployment problem is not to become continually more severe in a world of growing labour productivity and lagging production.

CONCLUDING REMARKS

The developed capitalist industrial nations which dominate the world economic scene are now in the midst of a more or less 'normal' recessive period with the corresponding increase in unemployment. A decisive victory over unemployment is hardly possible under these circumstances and even modest improvements are difficult and require determined efforts. There are no patent medicines which could be applied and they cannot be expected because we live in a period of quick and dramatic changes (world monetary system, multinational firms, new industrial stages, microelectronic revolution, inflation and interest rate fluctuations, etc.) which have an unsettling influence on investment behaviour and consumption patterns making both of them more fickle and less calculable. Since the 'trend turn' the uncertainties have probably grown further and this makes it difficult to design an efficient and balanced economic policy. Past experiences and theoretical views are not useless, but they must be modified and corrected in a continuous learning process.

In such a situation an employment policy that takes its tasks seriously has to keep in mind certain basic principles, quite irrespective of the concrete measures that are ultimately chosen. Probably the most important point is that the employment perspective should penetrate the entire economic policy since most measures with global effects have an impact on the employment situation. The increased uncertainty suggests a policy which remains open in several directions and displays flexibility and a readiness for experiments so that learning processes are furthered and facilitated. This implies the use of a multi-dimensional strategy, i.e. the use of various employment-relevant instruments in varying proportions (depending on the situation) and the avoidance of narrow dogmatic blinkers. Such a strategy cannot be reduced to a ready-made and coherent concept which can then be simply applied; it is rather a basis for a progressing pragmatic policy, thoroughly dedicated to its task, understanding the past, and with an open mind for the future.

NOTES

1 Myrdal, G. (1960) *Beyond the Welfare State*, London: Duckworth.
2 Bronfenbrenner, M. ed. (1969) *Is the Business Cycle Obsolete?*, New York: John Wiley.

3 Is there such a thing as unemployment?

(Translation of 'Arbeitslose: Gibt's die?', *Kyklos*, vol. 31, no. 1, 1978, pp. 21–35)

The intensification of many economic and social problems in the past ten years, the uncertain and not always hope-inspiring future, as well as a tendency towards economies in the funding of research should induce scientists to look more critically at their research activities. How they occupy themselves and with what subjects is regarded more sceptically today than was the case in the euphoric years of economic miracles.

In this situation the ever-present demand for relevant themes in social and economic research gains importance, and the same is true for the desire to obtain as far as possible a transparent and relevant treatment of the main questions. Now there can be no doubt that it is not easy to find an objective answer to the question what constitutes a relevant problem now or in the long run. Like people in general economists will have different opinions regarding the relevance and the urgency of various questions. This is unavoidable. Nevertheless one can retain the 'demand' that a theme, once it has been chosen as relevant, should be analysed as clearly as possible. Its relevance and its *problematique* should not be sacrificed to ideological blinkers or to theoretical niceties with a life of their own.

To a not inconsiderable degree contemporary research violates already the first demand mentioned above. Non-existing or artificially inflated problems are the subjects of sophisticated theoretical structures whose practical relevance remains questionable even under a very wide and sympathetic interpretation of 'basic research'. This is one of the reasons why we meet so many doubts regarding the value of academic economic research. But even more questionable is – in my opinion – the practice of choosing a highly relevant theme and then treating it in such an oblique way that it creates more confusion than understanding – thus violating the second 'demand'. I think that there is a danger that a practice like this is at present spreading in the field of the highly topical theme of unemployment.

While in the 1930s the depression and the Keynesian revolution saw to it that unemployment suddenly moved into the centre of economic research, notable change set in after 1945. The fast growth of the post-war economies and the success of employment policies induced theorists to turn to other questions which could now be treated under assumptions of full employment or neglecting the employment question altogether. A turning point was reached when Phillips published his famous paper (Phillips 1958) in which he presented the problem of a trade-off between inflation and unemployment. This paper set off lively theoretical and policy discussions which, however, consisted mainly of attempts to explain and expand the Phillips curve. A further impulse – the one which will be treated in this paper – occurred in the wake of the monetarist and neoclassical 'counter-revolution'. Its birth can be ascribed to critical papers by Friedman and by Phelps and his 'microeconomics school' round about 1970 (Friedman 1968; Phelps 1968, 1970).

As we know Friedman, Phelps and their followers try to show that the Phillips curve is only a transitory phenomenon and that in the long run no 'choice menu' exists permitting a trade-off between unemployment and inflation. In the end there can only be a state of voluntary or 'natural' unemployment whose level depends on the behaviour and intentions of the workers concerned. A case for many of these neoclassical theories is provided by a job-search model of one sort or another. The essence of this approach can be summarized as follows. Workers look for jobs, but are only prepared to take a job when a certain real wage ('acceptance wage') is paid. Since preferences among workers differ we obtain a rising supply curve of labour (with rising real wages). Demand for labour on the other hand is – in line with marginal productivity theory – a falling function of real wages. Since the labour market is modelled in analogy to competitive commodity markets the assumption is that it is characterized by flexibility and capacity for adjustment. 'Rational' employers and workers will then arrive – under 'normal' circumstances – at an equilibrium wage where everybody who wants to work at this wage will find employment.

But at any moment we find that there are vacancies and unemployed persons. It is at this point that the 'new' theory steps in: this 'disequilibrium' is explained as a consequence of the lack of transparence and homogeneity which is typical for labour markets. Neither workers nor employers have full knowledge about conditions in different regions and firms. In their desire to maximize their income chances some workers will always prefer to remain unemployed for a while in order to look for a good (or better) job. Unemployment is seen exclusively or at least predominantly as a frictional phenomenon in a world of imperfect information. Unemployed persons, who could get a job, prefer to stay unemployed for some time in order to gather more information. This idea can be easily fitted into the traditional 'rational' optimizing calculus of marginal theory: the additional costs of unemployment (lost wages minus unemployment benefits) and of information gathering are set against the additional gains which can be expected from finding a better-paying job (discounted value of future wage differentials). [1]

Thus some workers will be completely unwilling to work under present conditions, while some others will be out on job search: this is the 'natural' unemployment. It is 'voluntary' in nature; there is no room for 'involuntary' unemployment in the sense of Keynes or as used in ordinary language. [2] The Phillips curve, with its 'deviations' from the natural unemployment rate, is interpreted as a transitory phenomenon caused by uncertainty in times of shifting inflation rates. Rising inflation rates cause mistaken beliefs that real wages have gone up and this means that search periods are shortened as workers enter – by mistake – lower-paid jobs (in real terms). The opposite is true in cases of falling inflation rates (or growing deflation); this is regarded as a real wage deterioration with consequent extensions of the search period. Thus a short-period Phillips curve connecting inflation and unemployment is created. After a while the workers will recognize that they were victims of a money illusion and will once again be able to orientate themselves on real wages irrespective of the degree of inflation: unemployment will return to its 'natural' level, the sloped Phillips curve will disappear.

Nobody will deny that the theory of 'job search' represents an interesting and valuable contribution for an explanation of short-term unemployment even though the main ideas were already contained in a much earlier paper by Stigler (1962). What makes this new development suspect both from a theoretical and methodological point of view is the inclination to present this model as *the* theory of unemployment. In addition criticism is provoked because some principal considerations as well as empirical results raise serious doubts about the basic assumptions of the new theory.

Let us look very briefly at some of the more important and obvious doubts and objections. We can begin with the assumption that a worker has very clear ideas about real wages (or wage changes) which will determine exactly whether and how much labour he is going to supply. The fact, however, is that for a majority of primary employees the main desire is directed towards a steady job with (normally) fixed hours of work. Wage levels, working conditions and career opportunities certainly play an important role in the choice between different job opportunities, but they are far less important when it comes to a choice between employment and voluntary unemployment. It is also important to see that in view of the heterogeneity and incomplete information typical for labour markets most workers have difficulties in developing clear ideas about 'realistic' acceptance wages just as firms cannot have very fixed ideas about 'proper' profits. Orientation is afforded by ruling wages on one's own and neighbouring sectors of the economy, combined with rough ideas about probable changes in money and real wages (Rothschild 1971: 266; Tobin 1972: 12–13).

Thus the assumption of a flexible labour supply responding more or less smoothly to flexible real wages is contradicted by many experiences and field studies. Similar difficulties exist with the assumption that search unemployment is the typical form of unemployment. The 'new theory' bases its admittance of a short-term Phillips curve on the assumption that in times of falling inflation rates, search unemployment increases because the *illusion* of falling real wages induces workers to prolong their search for jobs which pay the 'necessary' wage. This would mean that in recession periods, when money wages rise less than before or even fall, the number of quits from among the employed workers would have to rise. But the opposite is true. On the other hand we find that voluntary quits increase – in contradiction to the theory – in times of boom even when inflation rates are rising. To this must be added the general objection that a search for a better job does not necessarily require quitting one's job and many workers do in fact change from one job to another without intermediate unemployment (Tobin 1972; Mattila 1974; Hines 1976). As an example we might mention the results of an investigation in the Austrian micro-census which showed that more than 80 per cent of the workers who had changed employment over a given past period had conducted their search on the job, i.e. without unemployment (Bartunek 1976: 110).

And so we come to the question that forms the central part of this paper. How is it that a theoretical structure which suffers from such obvious weaknesses and question marks can find such a rapid acceptance among economists leading to widespread discussions and proliferations of ever new variants of the model? I think that it is not difficult to find reasons for this development. They can be found in the realm of theory and in that of ideology.

One of the big advantages which economics has to offer in contrast to other social sciences is the existence of a comprehensive and widely accepted theoretical structure. This theory, which has achieved a high degree of formal perfection and elegance on the basis of some simple assumptions regarding rational optimizing behaviour and equilibrating tendencies, has proved to be a fruitful starting point and co-ordinating framework for many theoretical considerations in spite of several obvious weaknesses (too far-reaching abstractions, too much reliance on unrealistic models of full competition, fascination with the methods of mechanical physics, neglect of sociology and psychology, etc.). Such a coherent theoretical structure can become dangerous and a brake for further progress when thinking in its categories blocks the access to reality and when most efforts are directed towards fitting this reality into the traditional theoretical scheme. Such a situation seems to me to be characteristic of the 'new' microeconomic theory of unemployment.

The existence of unemployment always presented a nuisance for strong 'model believers' among economists. Since markets – labour markets included – are said always to tend towards equilibrium and market clearing we should expect that unemployment and unfilled vacancies are normally non-existent. A certain low level may exist in both cases as a frictional adjustment problem; but if these low levels were surpassed this would have to be either voluntary unemployment or the consequence of 'false' behaviour on the part of the government or the unions who disturb the market mechanism through fixing minimum wages.

The deep and persisting unemployment after 1929 undermined the credibility of this model. Nevertheless it could maintain its hold for a while over non-Marxist economists; even such an outstanding and sensitive economist as Pigou could not get free from it right away (Pigou 1933). Keynes's achievement[3] in the field of employment theory lay not only in his resolute attempt to establish contact with the real world but also in his endeavour to show how the phenomenon of high and persisting unemployment can be related to positive elements of the traditional theory if one is prepared to admit important modifications of the equilibrium concepts.

Though we know today that simple realistic assumptions about wage and price rigidities in combination with the principle of effective demand are capable of providing for Keynesian underemployment equilibria (with involuntary unemployment) the same formal-theoretical status as that of the neoclassical equilibrium model (Morishima 1976: ch. 7), the Keynesian approach nevertheless remained 'unsavoury' for many economists dedicated to the neoclassical theory. Their research seems less directed towards a continuous improvement of our knowledge of labour market processes than towards the invention of increasingly sophisticated models which would permit a smooth inclusion of the undeniable unemployment problem into the framework of the traditional market and equilibrium theory. The stress on information, search and related problems should open a path which would allow all unemployment to be explained as voluntary and as a consequence of friction and money illusion. The model of general equilibrium could thus be saved.

It is probably not a mere accident that these theories, which after all are just revivals of pre-Keynesian unemployment theories in refined forms (Hines 1976: 70; Robinson and Wilkinson 1977: 8), gained importance in the course of the 1960s. The long period of relatively low unemployment rates (achieved in part on the basis of Keynesian policies) in the developed industrial nations made it easier and less grotesque to view unemployment as a voluntary phenomenon than had been possible when the depression of the 1930s was still in everybody's mind. But once one has started on this road the appetite grows and one is prepared to see even the mass unemployment of those years (and possible future repetitions?) as a special constellation which can be covered by the term 'voluntary unemployment'.[4]

How strong the moulds of the traditional theory are in shaping and limiting research can most clearly be seen when we look at some contributions which deplore and criticize the lack of realism in the 'new' unemployment theory but nevertheless find it difficult to free themselves from the common neoclassical shackles. Instead of trying to find out how and why workers, employers, trade unions, employers' organizations and governments act on labour markets in certain ways in order to find an adequate basis for a labour market theory, they, too, start with the assumption that 'rational' action must always be guided by individual wealth-maximizing behaviour along neoclassical lines. For other motives which can be regarded as 'rational' in our oligopolistic class society, like solidarity, defence of acquired standards, etc. there seems to be no room. Thus – to take an example – we see that Donald Gordon, who develops an interesting model of involuntary unemployment by stressing the importance of the uncertainties and the long-term nature of labour contracts, insists on staying within the confines of a theory which is compatible with 'maximizing behaviour' *because of which*(!) the Phillips curve cannot be accepted: 'the Phillips curve is a contradiction of traditional price theory as it has developed over some two centuries. For that theory suggests that it is irrational (*sic*!) for both workers and employers to permit extended periods of non-equilibrium wages' (Gordon 1976: 66).

While the 'new' theory of voluntary unemployment does at least display some new elements as compared with older models, another element has remained unchanged: the ideological element. Unemployment is seen by many people as one of the worst economic and social evils and experience has shown that it tends to be a recurring phenomenon in free, unregulated market economies. Economists who – for whatever reasons – want to defend and support such a system have an understandable bias for theoretical approaches which deny the existence of an inherent connection between a market economy and unemployment. As far as the latter exists it should be attributed to 'non-systemic' elements and interventions.

Such apologetic undertones are clearly noticeable in the new unemployment literature. The frontal attack consists in sweeping the *problematique* of an unemployment which cannot be denied altogether under the carpet by declaring all existing unemployment as 'voluntary' or 'natural'. As Keynes said nearly half a century ago: 'Many people are trying to solve the problem of unemployment with a theory which is based on the assumption that there is no unemployment' (Keynes 1933).

A similar 'strategy' is contained in a series of new efforts (resting on old traditions) which do not deny the existence and growth of unemployment but try to show that this is mainly due to the influence of unemployment benefits and minimum wage regulations. It is these that make employment less attractive or impossible so that in this case, too, one can speak of – individually or collectively chosen – 'voluntary' unemployment. In addition to such general arguments a number of empirical studies have in recent times tried to prove the existence of such links between levels of unemployment benefit and unemployment rates (e.g. Bailey 1974; Marston 1975; Grubel, Maki and Sax 1975; Maki and Spindler 1975; Grubel and Maki 1976; König and Franz 1976; Hamermesh 1977).

Quite apart from the fact that the results of these investigations are not very rich and are partly due to wrong specifications (Cubbin and Foley

1977) the attempt to use them for an apologetic 'de-problemization' of existing unemployment as 'voluntary' is not convincing, and that for several reasons. Research about concrete cases of unemployment and individual unemployment histories have shown that refusals to accept reasonable job offers because of benefit payments can be shown to apply only in the case of a very small percentage of unemployed persons.[5] This is supported by the fact that in an economic recovery the unemployed are quickly absorbed in the expanding employment. This is even true for those unemployed who were regarded as 'difficult cases' and for the 'hidden' unemployed (discouraged workers) whose unemployment can hardly be regarded as voluntary. But if it is only a small percentage of the unemployed who prefer to draw unemployment benefit rather than to take a job then their existence will only affect the question *who* among the unemployed will move into the available vacancies which are limited in number. The size of the unemployment problem will still be well represented by the given unemployment totals.

Similarly the attempts to regard existing unemployment rates as voluntary at least on a collective plane because they are due to minimum wage regulations (e.g. Friedman 1972; Phelps 1972: 64–6) are strange and neglect historical factors. One could, of course, even doubt whether an abolition of minimum wages – seen as part of the circular interdependence of an oligopolistic-oligopsonistic system – would always result in more employment. More important, however, is the fact that we do not live in an abstract model but in a world where certain institutions determine the frame within which we can act and set our targets. When workers in the course of history have been able to institute minimum wages as a protection against certain badly felt disadvantages in 'free' wage bargains, then 'involuntary unemployment' has of course to be understood as being willing to work *under the given legal and institutional conditions* but not being able to get a corresponding job. To call such unemployment 'voluntary' and to place responsibility for it on the unemployed themselves is the same as if we said that the poor starve 'voluntarily' because they acknowledge private property rights rather than breaking them and still their hunger from the plentiful stores.

The considerations in this paper are meant to point out the dangers which can arise when research is too much under the influence of certain theoretical perspectives or ideological ideas. These dangers are particularly prominent when one has to deal with a problem which is socially and economically as important as the unemployment problem. When it comes to wrong orientations in such a field the consequence can be either serious practical difficulties and/or a loss of confidence in the achievements and possibilities of economic science.

One must admit, however, that it is easier to attack some mistaken approaches than to offer alternative, satisfactory solutions. That is a task which at present can hardly be hoped for. A realistic labour market research, which today seems more needed than has been the case for a long time, will have to start from a basic insight that labour markets differ in many respects from markets for goods (Rothschild 1969; Gordon 1976: 94) and that therefore the ideas of a stylized market theory can only be of limited use. One task for the research will be to extend the study of the phenomena of recent labour market theories in addition to the traditional macroeconomic analysis of season, cycle and structure. Rigidities, fluctuations, duration of unemployment, frequency of unemployed periods, problems of special groups (women, young people, etc.) are candidates for additional research and should be integrated into the economic process as a whole. This could lead to a more realistic view of the unemployment problem even though it is unlikely that it could result in such 'rounded' elegant theoretical structures as one obtains from the 'new' microeconomic theory of the labour market.[6]

Such a more open research strategy could make sure that the path to a better knowledge of the unemployment problem and its mitigation will not be hindered by theoretical and ideological prejudices as has been the case in the past. As yet it is still true, as Bombach says, that:

> We may need again courageous men who are to give proper advice against hardened dogmas. It is obvious that this advice will have to be different from past prescriptions. . . . That the unemployed today are far better off than in former times is a positive fact and not least a success of more efficient economic policies; but it also carries the danger that it weakens the efforts for resistance.
>
> (Bombach 1976: 8)

NOTES

1 For examples of such an approach see Lucas and Rapping (1970) and Mortensen (1970).
2 The 'classical' definition of Keynes runs as follows: 'Men are involuntarily unemployed if, in the event of a small rise in the price of wage-goods relatively to the money-wage, both the aggregated supply of labour willing to work for the current money-wage and the aggregate demand for it at that wage would be greater than the existing volume of employment' (Keynes 1936: 15). But – as Kahn (1976) has rightly stressed – this is an unnecessarily complicated formulation which probably originated in some thought experiments which occupied Keynes in those days. The essence of the idea which is current among most economists and the general public was expressed much more simply by Keynes in the same book: 'The population is seldom doing as much work as it would like to do on the basis of the current wages. . . . More labour would, as a rule, be forthcoming at the existing money-wage if it were demanded' (Keynes 1936: 7). Contrasted to this we have the new theory: 'Measured unemployment. . . is then viewed as consisting of persons who regard the wage rates at which they could currently be employed as temporarily low, and who therefore choose to wait or search for improved conditions. . . . The view that nonfrictional unemployment is in this sense "voluntary" does not, of

course, imply that high measured unemployment rates are socially costless' (Lucas and Rapping 1970: 285).

3 Similar achievements – but with less effect – were produced by Kalecki in Poland, Föhl in Germany and to some extent by the Swedish school.

4 Thus Malcolm Fisher writes *in connection with the inter-war depression period*: 'I would maintain that involuntary unemployment as a phenomenon still lacks confirmation.... . Involuntary unemployment is a theory which as yet lacks adequate empirical support' (Fisher 1976: 53–4).

5 In an intensive socio-economic investigation of the unemployment problem in three English towns Hill *et al.* come to the following conclusion: 'There seems to be no evidence from this survey to substantiate the view that many men remain unemployed because it is more lucrative than working. It is very doubtful that more than a very small number of men fall into this category, and secondly, it cannot be conclusively proved that longer periods of unemployment are due to high unemployment income, rather than the possession of other characteristics such as a low level of skill' (Hill, Harrison, Sargeant and Talbot 1973: 130).

6 The unavoidable difficulties which at the present time prevent the construction of well-formulated rigid theories unfortunately induce economists who have grown up with such comprehensive theories to be extremely sceptical *vis-à-vis* the attempts of a more realistic labour market research. Thus we find that Glen Cain, who has no illusions about the poor explanatory qualities of the job search theories ('It is my view that the new job-search models of unemployment are not yet tractable for empirical work and, therefore, cannot yield useful predictions'), nevertheless attacks the realism-orientated approaches of dual and segmented labour market theories (SLM) for not being sufficiently 'theoretical' ('My brief summary judgement of the SLM challenge is that it does not begin to offer a theory of the labour market that can replace neoclassical theory, despite our various degrees of dissatisfaction with the empirical corpus of that theory'). (Cain 1976: 1241, 1247–8.)

REFERENCES

Arndt, H. (1969) *Lohnpolitik und Einkommensverteilung*, Berlin: Duncker u. Humblot.

Bailey, M. N. (1974) *Unemployment and Unemployment Insurance*, New Haven: Yale University Press.

Bartunek, E. (1976) 'Dienstgebersuche bei Arbeitsplatzwechsel', *Österreichische Statistische Nachrichten*, vol. 31, pp. 105–12.

Bombach, G. (1976) 'Einleitung' in Bombach, G. (ed.) (1976), pp. 1–8.

Bombach, G. (ed.) (1976) *Der Keynesianismus II: Die beschäftigungspolitische Diskussion vor Keynes in Deutschland*, Berlin: Springer.

Brunner, K. and Meltzer, A. H. (1976) *The Phillips Curve and Labor Markets*, Amsterdam: North-Holland.

Cain, G. C. (1976) 'The challenge of segmented labour market theories to orthodox theory: a survey', *Journal of Economic Literature*, 14, 4, pp. 1215–57.

Cubbin, J. S. and Foley, K. (1977) 'The extent of benefit-induced unemployment in Great Britain: some new evidence', *Oxford Economic Papers*, 29, 1, pp. 128–40.

Fisher, M. R. (1976) 'The new micro-economics of unemployment' in Worswick (1976), pp. 35–57.

Friedman, M. (1968) 'The role of monetary policy', *American Economic Review*, 58, 1, pp. 1–17.

—— (1972) *An Economist's Protest*, Glen Ridge, NJ: Thomas Horton.

Gordon, D. F. (1976) 'A neo-classical theory of Keynesian unemployment' in Brunner and Meltzer (1976), pp. 65–97.

Grubel, H. G., Maki, D. and Sax, S. (1975) 'Real and insurance-induced unemployment in Canada', *The Canadian Journal of Economics*, 8, 2, pp. 174–91.

Grubel, H. G. and Maki, D. (1976) 'The effect of unemployment benefits on U.S. unemployment rates', *Weltwirtschaftliches Archiv*, 112, 2, pp. 274–99.

Hamermesh, D. (1977) *Jobless Pay and the Economy*, Baltimore: Johns Hopkins.

Hill, M. J., Hannison, R. M., Sargeant, A. V. and Talbot, V. (1973) *Men out of Work: A Study of Unemployment in Three English Towns*, Cambridge: Cambridge University Press.

Hines, A. G. (1976) 'The micro-economic foundations of employment and inflation theory: bad old wine in elegant new bottles' in Worswick (1976), pp. 58–79.

Kahn, R. (1976) 'Unemployment as seen by the Keynesians' in Worswick (1976), pp. 19–34.

Keynes, J. M. (1933) *The Means to Prosperity*, London: collected writings, vol. IX.

—— (1936) *The General Theory of Employment, Interest and Money*, London: Macmillan.

König, H. and Franz, W. (1976), *Unemployment compensation and the rate of unemployment in the Federal Republic of Germany*, Mannheim.

Lucas, R. and Rapping, L. (1970) 'Real wages, employment, and inflation' in Phelps (1970) pp. 257–305.

Maki, D. and Spindler, Z. (1975) 'The effect of unemployment compensation on the rate of unemployment in Great Britain', *Oxford Economic Papers*, 27, 3, pp. 440–54.

Marston, S. (1975) 'The impact of unemployment insurance on job search', *Brookings Papers on Economic Activity*, 1, 13–48.

Mattila, J. P. (1974) 'Job quitting and frictional unemployment', *American Economic Review*, 64, 1, pp. 235–9.

Morishima, M. (1976) *The Economic Theory of Modern Society*, Cambridge: Cambridge University Press.

Mortensen, D. T. (1970) 'A theory of wage and employment dynamics' in Phelps (1970), pp. 167–211.

Phelps, E. S. (1968) 'Money-wage dynamics and labour market equilibrium', *Journal of Political Economy*, 76, 4, pp. 678–711.

Phelps, E. S. (ed.) (1970) *Microeconomic Foundations of Employment and Inflation Theory*, London: Macmillan.

Phelps, E. S. (1972) *Inflation Policy and Unemployment*, London: Macmillan.

Phillips, A. W. (1958) 'The relation between unemployment and the rate of change of money wage rates in the United Kingdom', *Economica*, 25, 100, pp. 283–99.

Pigou, A.C. (1933) *The Theory of Unemployment*, London: Macmillan.

Robinson, J. and Wilkinson, F. (1977) 'What has become of employment policy?', *Cambridge Journal of Economics*, 1, 1, pp. 5–14.

Rothschild, K. W. (1969) 'Unterschiedliche Dimensionen der Lohntheorie' in Arndt (1969), pp. 53–81.

—— (1971) 'The Phillips curve and all that', *Scottish Journal of Political Economy*, 18, 3, pp. 245–80.

Stigler, G. (1962) 'Information in the labor market', *Journal of Political Economy*, 70, supplement, pp. 94–105.

Tobin, J. (1972) 'Inflation and Unemployment', *American Economic Review*, 62, 1, pp. 1–18.

Worswick, G. D. N. (1976) *The Concept and Measurement of Involuntary Unemployment*, London: Allen & Unwin.

4 Is structural unemployment an alibi for economic policy?

(Translation of (1983) 'Ist strukturelle Arbeitslosigkeit ein Alibi für Wirtschaftspolitik?' in H. Schelbert-Syfrig *et al.* (eds), *Arbeitsmarkt strukturen und prozesse*, Diessenhofen, Verlag Rüegger, pp. 29–50)

Ten years of growing unemployment in the developed capitalist countries have induced economic theory and economic policy to turn – after the usual time lag – more massively than in the years before to problems of unemployment and to labour market questions in general. There is no lack of investigations nowadays dealing with types and forms of unemployment and with possibilities of fighting it. The present paper does not pretend to be able to offer any fundamental new insights into the problems under discussion. All that is attempted is to throw some light on the question indicated by the title of the paper, viz. whether structural problems on the labour market demand or obstruct an active employment policy and what connections there are between structural problems and current economic policy.

This question tends to remain permanently on the agenda, first because it can be judged differently depending on political conditions and targets and second because the phenomena to be discussed are not sharply defined and not easily pinned down. I shall take up this second point first. Alternative attitudes regarding economic policy and its targets will be treated later when they come up in connection with concrete problems.

The 'fuzziness' of the subject matter which has just been mentioned has first of all important roots in the absence of a clear notion regarding the meaning of 'structure'. Machlup once even suggested – in a slightly ironic mood – that the term 'structure' should be abandoned altogether because of its 'sponginess'.[1] This would certainly be a mistake and would remove an important dimension in economic discussions and particularly in discussions about labour market problems. But the fact remains that hard definitions and delineations of 'structure' are not easily obtained. This can be very clearly seen in the use of different notions of 'structure' in the labour market literature. I want to draw attention to three of the most important definitions of structure which can be found in the discussion of unemployment.[2] Later we shall take up each type separately.

Probably the most common meaning of structural unemployment refers to a mismatch between the skill requirements (in the widest sense) on the demand side and the quality of labour supply. Demand and supply on the labour market do not fit; vacancies and unemployment exist side by side but cannot be married. Let us call this definition of structure S1. A second notion of structure (S2) emerged in connection with the Phillips curve and is based on macroeconomic ideas and aims. Structural unemployment is defined as that level which could only be reduced by (further) global policy measures at the cost of higher inflation rates. These are regarded as a barrier for taking employment action. A third idea of structure (S3) is related to the theories of segmented labour markets. Like these theories themselves this definition of structure can take on a variety of forms. But the general idea is that sociological and institutional barriers and traditions reduce the access to and the mobility between certain economic branches and jobs and can thus cause structural unemployment. Many well-known specific unemployment problems like youth unemployment, female unemployment, etc. are related to this group, though skill elements also play a part.

Thus some confusion can arise from the variety of definitions and the practical impossibility of exact measurements. These difficulties are enhanced by the fact that interdependencies exist between structural and some other types of unemployment which are not easily diagnosed and separated. Hardly any difficulties arise from seasonal unemployment, which can be easily separated from other forms of unemployment. But with frictional unemployment we meet some question marks. Thus an increase in the number of coexisting vacancies and unemployed workers can follow from changed search strategies of unemployed persons or from changed quality demands on the part of the employers. In the first case we could speak of frictional unemployment, in the second it would be structural unemployment. To make the proper distinction in practice would not always be easy.

Even more problematic are the interdependencies between cyclical and structural unemployment. Since the branches of the economy are hit very unevenly by a recession we necessarily observe rather different disequilibria in the various sectorial labour markets. These will look very much like structural disequilibrium. On a purely definitional level it is not difficult to draw a line between such cyclical deviations and those caused by structural shifts: the first are short- and medium-term phenomena while structural disequilibria tend to be long-term and frequently irreversible. But in practice it is not always easy to separate cyclical and structural elements when divergent unemployment trends are analysed.[3]

Finally, when dealing with structural unemployment and economic policy we should not forget that public and private economic activities are not only confronted by structural problems but are themselves causing structural change or shifts in the perspective under which it is seen. If, for instance, a society regards commuting over very long distances (perhaps with weekly absences from home) as acceptable it will show fewer problems of regional unemployment than if such movements are regarded as oppressive. Or to cite another example: in recessions employers often increase their skill requirements for given jobs. This creates a structural (occupational) problem which is closely interlinked with the cyclical aspect.

Yet in spite of all these difficulties to obtain sharp contours or exact measurements for structural unemployment (mark 1, 2 or 3) it remains a notion which has to be used for two reasons. First there is no doubt that some real problems are covered by this definition (however vague) and second it has to be treated because it plays such an important role in economic policy discussions and strategies. In the following discussion of some links between structural unemployment and economic policy I shall on the whole refrain from pointing out the 'fuzziness' of the structural definitions. When dealing with the *basic* questions of the position of economic policy *vis-à-vis* the structural problem this fuzziness is only of secondary importance. It can become more troublesome when decisions have to be taken about forms and extent of interventions in concrete situations.

Before we turn to the question whether and how economic policy should react to structural unemployment it will be useful to remember a discussion of the 1970s which was particularly lively in Germany. It addressed the question of whether the quickly rising unemployment in those years had its main roots in cyclical or structural elements or whether it should be regarded as a general stagnation phenomenon. The answer to this question is not immediately relevant to our considerations. But it is not without interest to see how different approaches to this question can influence the attitude about the chances and uses of economic policy.

After what has been said earlier about the vagueness of the term 'structure' and its interlinkage with other forms of unemployment it will be obvious that there can be no easy answer to the above question of the 'main' roots of the unemployment growth in the 1970s. As far as I can see – dealing with structural unemployment S1 and the situation in Germany (though things were probably similar in other countries) – there was no intensification of structural disequilibria in the critical decade. This conclusion was reached in a study by a group of authors in the Institut für Arbeitsmarkt- und Berufsforschung (Institute for Labour Market and Occupational Research) in Nuremberg in 1976 and is also supported by the simple comparison of demand and supply for different occupational groups in 1971 and 1981 which is given in the appendix to this paper. It shows that the variance of the disequilibria (weighted by unemployment figures) declined between 1971 and 1981. These results make it difficult to accept the arguments which maintained that the growing unemployment of the 1970s and early 1980s could not be successfully overcome because of its structural nature and the absence of possibilities or of the required policy instruments to deal with this type of unemployment.[4]

We can now turn to the principal question: what role can economic policy play in the face of structural unemployment (its existence and/or intensification)? As a first observation we must point out the fundamental difference in perspective connected with the obvious schism in theoretical approaches and economic ideologies which affects the attitude to all types of structural unemployment. Ideas of structural change and imbalance normally imply that we have to deal with some deeper influences which can only be overcome – if at all – by long-term adjustment processes. This immediately brings us face to face with the differences of opinion regarding the possibilities for efficient action. The main dividing line concerns the views regarding the problem-solving capacities of markets and state (regulation) respectively. If one adheres to the view that market signals and market processes are highly efficient and that rational expectations can recognize and foresee structural developments and if one adds to this a sizeable portion of scepticism regarding the motives and capabilities of government action then one arrives at a model in which there is neither room for structural policy nor for cyclical measures. Models of this sort can be covered by the term 'new neoclassics'.

This is certainly an extreme position and it would be difficult to assume that belief in this model is the sole and compelling reason for opposition to structural employment measures. A few modifications of the above-mentioned assumptions suffice to permit also a 'confessing' neoclassical economist to take a more compromising view with regard to structural policies even if he regards markets and non-intervention as ideal for frictional and cyclical unemployment.

Two reasons are particularly obvious. First, it is doubtful whether prices and other market signals are really suited for steering long-term adjustments in the right direction and at an adequate speed; and second some actions by the state are unavoidably connected with structural consequences (e.g. infrastructure, educational policy) so that a rational policy should aim at a consistent concept for private and public adjustment processes.

Active measures against *structural* unemployment should therefore not constitute a separation between neoclassical market believers and Keynesian market sceptics. If such measures are none the less resisted we must look for other reasons. One source of opposition is a liberal philosophy à la Hayek. Structural change affects events which lie mainly in the future. But the complexity of the economic system does not allow to obtain reliable knowledge about the future. Neither markets nor economic policy can 'solve' this problem. But market processes seen as a continuous search strategy are regarded as a more efficient adjustment process than government intervention. Structural unemployment becomes an unavoidable predicament in a dynamic world, public remedial action will lead to a deterioration of the situation rather than to an improvement.

This point of view can only be shared if one accepts fully – in addition to the doubtlessly existing basic *problematique* of an uncertain future – the two very strong supporting premises of the argumentation, viz. a *complete* impossibility of making usable forecasts *and* an *absolute* superiority of markets over public policy in steering adjustment in such a situation. If one is prepared to discount the strict validity of these two assumptions then this argument against structural policies can no longer be regarded as a general principle.

But more important for an oppositional stance is a political position. If fears that policy measures which go beyond global signals and which intervene into more detailed processes could be the thin end of a wedge threatening the existing economic 'system'. Conservative status quo ideologies will therefore tend to resist structural interventions, which by necessity may have to deal with concrete details, even if they might benefit from such policies in specific cases.

An exact opposite to the last-mentioned conservative ideology is a reformist perspective which (on the basis of its fundamental views) is bound to look positively on structural policies. Particularly when social reformers want to deal with the question of segmented labour markets and the structural unemployment they produce (S3) then some political action is quite obviously on the agenda. These structures are traditionally and institutionally usually so rigid that market processes by themselves cannot be expected to overcome them. On the contrary, they may intensify the problems when for instance repeated unemployment in secondary labour markets leads to (further) real or imagined disqualifications of the workers concerned. Changes can only be expected from economic and social policies which over a longer period try to reduce barriers and to provide more room for equality of opportunity.

But let us leave now these very general considerations and turn to the question of structural unemployment and economic policy in the concrete situation of the present. How important is a structural policy now, what role can it play, what are the prevailing attitudes?

Let us start with the structural type S2, not because it is the most important or the most frequently discussed type – in this respect S1 would have to be chosen – but because it is the one which has a direct bearing on the policy problem. S1 and S3 unemployment can be dealt with in a purely descriptive way without having to touch the question of economic policy (whether and how it should be used). This is not the case for S2 unemployment. Here structural unemployment is counted as that which remains in existence when further global employment policies would lead to 'inadmissible' inflationary tendencies. Economic policy is here directly linked with the problem of structural unemployment and the policy conflict regarding employment and price stability becomes articulated.

To begin with the question has to be raised whether the above approach has a realistic basis, i.e. whether one accepts (or has to accept) the existence of a short- or medium-term Phillips curve with its trade-off between unemployment and inflation. If such a trade-off is absent then the whole approach and the definition of S2 structural unemployment break down.

But conditions approximating a (not necessarily stable) sloped Phillips curve are probably not atypical over certain periods and we shall assume that such conditions exist. Then the S2 problem can lead to various policy conclusions. An obvious first aspect is that this approach gives prominence to the conflicting targets of employment and price stability. Depending on the inflation levels that one regards as 'acceptable' one can obtain more or less structural unemployment by allowing less or more room for *general* employment policies which are particularly required in times of high unemployment.

In addition to this demarcation of the problem in line with political targets one has to decide how to deal with the structural unemployment so defined. Here the ideological inclinations discussed earlier come into play. A conservative view will tend to regard the structural problem as intractable and will stop short of further measures when the inflation barrier is reached. Solutions will be expected from changes in behaviour patterns. Reduced wage demands in particular will be seen as a possible weapon in the fight against structural unemployment. Thus the employees themselves are to be held responsible for the level and persistence of structural unemployment.[5] A more reform- and employment-oriented regime will react differently. It will regard the inflation barrier as a signal that the traditional Keynesian-type global tool-box has reached its limits and that other, more differentiated measures have to be added as, for instance, an active labour market policy or steps in the direction of an incomes policy.

It would seem that the problems just discussed have some relevance for the extreme deterioration of the unemployment situation in recent years in most countries and particularly in Great Britain. The structural problem we have in mind (S2) had been intensified with the inflationary developments of the 1960s (i.e. the Phillips curve shifted to the right) and parallel to this the influence of monetarism caused a shift in priorities from employment to price stability. This meant that the threshold for the appearance of structural unemployment was lowered. The switch to more conservative neoclassical perspectives added a general reluctance to look for remedial action suited to the changed circumstances.

But let us now turn to the more important themes of S1-unemployment which corresponds to the structural definition that is most prominent in theoretical and practical discussions. Since structural problems of this sort − mismatch between demand and supply profiles − can exist even in boom times it is interesting to pose the question whether a structural employment policy becomes more or less urgent when a recession sets in.

To begin with we should remember that a recession causes a *definitional* increase in S1-unemployment. Knowing that there exists a great and diversified pool of unemployment induces employers to ask for higher skills at the labour exchange or at the factory gate than they expected to get when the labour market was tighter. They are less prepared to accept – and train on the job – workers with lower skills or less experience. The consequence is that new unemployment criteria are created ('insufficient qualification') and adjustment processes inside the firms (training of employees, adjusting work processes to skills, etc.) are reduced which means that the burden of matching demand and supply is shifted more to the employees and to public bodies. The latter may well respond to these new requirements by 'structural' policies like retraining, extended education, etc. But it should be seen that this recession-dependent *additional* structural problem could be better solved by means of a *general* employment policy. With the approach of higher employment and more labour scarcity the nature of skill demands would change and some of the structural unemployment would disappear.

Leaving behind these somewhat speculative remarks we can turn to the core of the structural problem which is not dependent on the stage of the cycle. We can see that – as far as our figures for Germany show – the regional and the occupational mismatch has not deteriorated after 1970. This is shown for Germany but things are probably similar in other countries.[6] What does this imply for economic policy in the face of the rapid increase of general unemployment? Since the *absolute* levels of structural disequilibria have gone up with the general increase in unemployment the question arises whether more attention and more effort should now be directed towards structural policies or whether the old policy mix (or an improved one) should be continued (or renewed) because the *relative* size of structural imbalance (the relative deviations) has remained constant or has even declined.

I want to advance two points of view, a short-term one and one concerning a somewhat longer period. In the short run with recession and mass unemployment prevailing I would argue that structural measures become less important as compared to policies directed towards a general recovery of employment. The reason for this is very simple. When we look at the rough comparisons in Germany's occupational labour market structures in 1971 and 1981 (in the Appendix) we see that the relative variation of the imbalances (in terms of the relation between vacancies and unemployment) for twenty-six occupational groups is approximately unchanged in both years when we use unweighted data and has fallen when weighted data are used. But a very deep difference exists in another respect: in 1971 there existed on average two vacancies per unemployed person while in 1981 the relation had changed to six unemployed for each vacancy. While in 1971 the statistical mismatch consisted of a surplus of unfilled vacancies in twenty-one of the twenty-six occupational groups[7] we find in 1981 a surplus of unemployed in all groups without exception.

Even when one takes into account the limited reliability of labour market data in general and of vacancy statistics in particular one cannot deny that a dramatic reversal of the structural problem had taken place. In the boom period the difficulty lay in finding urgently needed labour for the expanding branches of the economy. An index showing the relation between vacancies and unemployed persons for different branches or occupations could be accepted as a rough indicator for the *intensity* of the structural (mismatch) problem and could thus serve as a guiding post for a national active labour market policy (retraining, mobility subsidies, foreign workers, etc.).

Things, however, look very different in a period of stagnation. No meaningful indices for a differentiated structural policy exist nor can one expect any notable effects from such a policy. Once there is a *general* shortage of vacancies the *relative* surplus of unemployed persons in different sectors does not tell us anything about the relative urgency of specific structural measures.[8] Also, training and related measures lose their plausibility and effects when the persons concerned are likely to face renewed unemployment after the termination of their training – though possibly in a different sector. The instruments of an active labour market policy which in many respects approximates a structural approach have few chances of working efficiently in times of recession[9] and often cannot do much more than mitigate (through training courses, etc.) the psychological and financial burdens of unemployment and reduce the level of statistically recorded unemployment.[10]

The fact that during a recession the structural characteristics are not clearly definable and that no reliable indicators for a structural policy exist does not provide an excuse for policy abstinence. It only suggests that *specific* actions which are added to the necessary global measures may have to be orientated towards problems that are not structural ones. Thus social elements may deserve more attention than a traditional structural policy would indicate. Examples would be wage subsidies for particularly needy groups or special policies for reducing youth unemployment, etc.

The situation looks different when one takes a longer perspective. Then the structural aspect comes into view. Whatever may be said in favour of certain employment-intensive short-term measures (e.g. support for certain groups, regions, branches) there is always a danger that they may prove to be misallocations in the longer run. This would act as a brake in later recovery phases. Thus, while a structural policy *as such* can offer little in the form of orientation and immediate help in the depth of recession, it seems advisable that the structural perspective should be kept in mind whenever policy measures *of any sort* are designed. But we must be aware that this desideratum presupposes something which both theory and practice find very difficult to deliver: a somewhat concrete idea about structural developments in the medium- and long-term future.

Table 4.1 Vacancies and unemployment by occupation, Germany 1971 and 1981 (end of month)

Occupational group	1971 (January)				1981 (Annual average)			
	Vacancies	Unemployed	Vacancies per unempl.		Vacancies	Unemployed	Vacancies per unempl.	
1 Agricultural occupations	8,253	23,556	0.35		5,048	26,075	0.19	
2 Mining	8,376	5,163	1.62		894	5,956	0.15	
3 Building materials, glass etc.	5,374	13,378	0.40		974	10,371	0.09	
4 Chemical workers	7,614	3,501	2.17		1,780	21,102	0.08	
5 Paper and printing	8,458	3,182	2.66		2,466	13,612	0.18	
6 Wood-working	15,075	5,477	2.75		603	8,324	0.07	
7 Metal-working	54,012	11,181	4.83		6,361	30,256	0.21	
8 Engineers	74,433	8,043	9.25		20,047	140,715	0.14	
9 Electricians	29,121	6,570	4.43		6,271	20,708	0.30	
10 Textiles and clothing	27,967	10,733	2.61		4,029	40,901	0.10	
11 Leather and furs	5,959	2,865	2.08		1,175	8,401	0.14	
12 Food and drink	24,539	6,319	3.88		12,315	40,468	0.30	
13 Joiners, painters, decoration	55,480	43,179	1.29		22,071	117,965	0.19	
14 Warehouse personnel	7,827	7,426	1.05		1,780	46,958	0.04	
15 Unskilled workers	34,256	47,264	0.72		1,443	41,696	0.03	
16 Machinists	5,125	5,575	0.92		1,502	10,688	0.14	
17 Physicists, chemists	19,409	3,498	5.55		9,853	12,557	0.78	
18 Technical specialists	8,573	877	9.78		7,863	24,255	0.32	
19 Sales personnel	36,697	13,415	2.74		15,664	102,705	0.15	
20 Transport	22,839	15,894	1.44		10,303	111,427	0.09	
21 Office workers	68,602	18,725	3.66		22,581	161,526	0.14	
22 Order and security	3,617	3,314	1.09		2,546	21,580	0.12	
23 Writers and artists	1,353	2,941	0.46		1,332	14,446	0.09	
24 Health	17,189	2,479	6.93		14,599	34,215	0.43	
25 Education	8,366	2,800	2.99		7,247	51,094	0.14	
26 Various service occupations	62,601	15,586	4.02		27,181	113,553	0.24	
Total	621,169	282,941	2.20		207,928	1,231,563	0.17	

Source: German Statistical Yearbooks 1971 (p. 130) and 1981 (p. 106) and own calculations

APPENDIX

Vacancies and unemployment by occupation (Germany 1971 and 1981)

In Table 4.1 the data for the occupational groups had to be slightly adapted to make the two years comparable. It has to be noted that the data of 1971 refer to end of January only while the 1981 data represent an annual average. 1971 has therefore a seasonal bias. To take account of the worst effects of this influence the statistical indicators given below were calculated not only for the total of twenty-six groups but also for twenty-three groups only with the exclusion of agriculture, building and building materials occupations (groups 1, 3 and 13) which are the occupations with the strongest seasonal fluctuations in unemployment.

On the basis of the data given in the statistical table an index of *vacancies per unemployed person* was calculated for each occupational group and for these 26 (23) indices the following values were obtained for X (average), Y (standard deviation) and − as an indicator of structural imbalance − for V (variation coefficient). The calculations are shown for the unweighted indices and for the indices weighted by the number of unemployed in each group.

Table 4.2 Index of vacancies per unemployed person

		Unweighted		*Weighted*	
		1971	1981	1971	1981
26 occupational groups	X	3.06	0.19	2.20	0.17
	Y	2.49	0.15	1.95	0.10
	V	0.81	0.80	0.89	0.59
23 Occupational groups[a]	X	3.38	0.19	2.72	0.17
	Y	2.47	0.16	2.06	0.11
	V	0.73	0.84	0.76	0.65

Note: [a] = without groups 1, 3 and 13

NOTES

1 Machlup (1958), p. 298: 'In general, the term ('structure') is more often used as an unnecessary jargon and as a plain weaselword than it is as a technical term with a clearly defined meaning. This should be reason enough for avoiding it.'
2 See on this, for instance, Schmid (1980), Brinkman (1981) and the literature given there. The simple notion of structure which just refers to any subdivision of some aggregate is not mentioned because it is as such not related to any problem. In ordinary language and as a descriptive device it plays an important role, including studies of the labour market.
3 'A fully satisfactory concept for a quantitative answer to the question whether and at what rate a structural change has occurred has not yet been discovered. A particular problem is presented by the cyclical influences.' (Autorengemeinschaft 1976: 83)

4 The discussions about changes in the extent of structural unemployment were mostly concerned with S1-unemployment and it is this type which is referred to in the text. When S2 is considered changes may occur when inflationary tendencies are intensified as soon as the demand for labour increases. Arguments of this kind have found more attention in Anglo-saxon studies. We shall return later to this aspect of structural unemployment.

5 'Questions about "structural unemployment" have in fact always been questions regarding the causes of *and* the responsibility for unemployment' (Schmid 1980: 13).

6 With regard to the United Kingdom see, for instance, Bosanquet (1979)

7 Since data for 1971 refer only to January the labour surplus in five occupational groups is partly a seasonal phenomenon.

8 The notion of structural unemployment loses importance in times of recession. Thus Bosanquet (1979: 300) says: 'Structural unemployment is more likely to appear when there is strong demand for labour'. Similarly, Perlman (1969: 168): 'Structural unemployment is more a product of good times than of bad.'

9 In boom periods when labour shortages are typical in most branches an 'active labour market policy' (as originally developed in Sweden in the 1960s) is introduced in order to reduce inflationary pressure, particularly that emanating from rapidly expanding sectors. Under these circumstances it has a structural but no employment target. As a *combination* of structural and employment policy aims it has probably its best opportunities in times of an interim phase between boom and recession when additional jobs are required in the midst of expanding and declining developments of various sectors.

10 It is true that in times of high unemployment people who have attended retraining courses find it easier to get a job. But this fact should not be overestimated. The choice of participants of such courses on the part of the labour exchanges as well as the individual preparedness to take part in retraining are not free of some bias in the direction of motivated persons making such limited measures more successful than would be true in cases of wider application.

REFERENCES

Autorengemeinschaft (1976) 'Zum Problem der strukturellen Arbeitslosigkeit', *Mitteilungen aus der Arbeitsmarkt- und Berufsforschung*, 9, 1, pp. 70–83.

Bosanquet, N. (1979) '"Structuralism" and "Structural unemployment"', *British Journal of Industrial Relations*, 17, 3, pp. 299–313.

Brinkmann, G. (1981) *Ökonomik der Arbeit. Vol. 2: Die Allokation der Arbeit*, Stuttgart: Klett-Cotta.

Machlup, F. (1958) 'Structure and structural change: weaselwords and jargon', *Zeitschrift fur Nationalökonomie*, 18, 3, pp. 280–98.

Perlman, R. (1969) *Labor Theory*, New York: John Wiley.

Schmid, G. (1980) *Strukturierte Arbeitslosigkeit und Arbeitsmarktpolitik*, Königstein: Athenäum.

5 Disguised discrimination and search unemployment

(Translation of (1986) 'Versteckte Diskriminierung und Sucharbeitslosigkeit' in *European Journal of Political Economy*, 2, 1, pp. 99–114)

ALTERNATIVE APPROACHES FOR A THEORETICAL TREATMENT OF DISCRIMINATION ON THE LABOUR MARKET

It can be regarded as an established fact that at least at certain times and/or in different countries discrimination in labour markets has been exercised. But it is equally true that until recently economists (in contrast to sociologists and political scientists) have not given much attention to this phenomenon. As an exception we should name the United States, where the race problem had always made the discrimination question a topical theme. This paper is intended to make a small contribution to the discrimination literature. To indicate its place within this literature I start off with a short summary of the most important approaches in this field.

First a few words about terminology. Discrimination on the labour market should cover all cases where individuals or (typically) groups are disadvantaged in comparison to comparable individuals or groups *and where these disadvantages are not due to any of the traditional economic criteria*. Such discrimination can affect wage levels, working conditions, job security, etc. and it can be direct or indirect discrimination. We speak of direct discrimination when certain groups are worse off (lower wages, fewer career opportunities) than others although they have the same qualification and do the same type of work. Indirect discrimination, on the other hand, refers to a situation where equal pay for equal work applies to all groups but some groups are denied access to the 'better' jobs.

The neoclassical approach to a theoretical explanation of discrimination, represented by the pioneering work of Becker (1957, 1971) and Arrow (1974), concentrates on direct discrimination with special stress on wage differentials. This can be easily understood. First, the problem of wage differences between white and Afro-American workers (and to a lesser degree between men and women) was (and is) an old and burning question which had been neglected by economic theorists for too long a time. Second, neoclassical theorists are naturally particularly irritated by the phenomenon of unequal market prices (wages) for a homogeneous good (work of a given quality). This does not fit at all into their basic theoretical model. Their research is therefore not so much motivated by an attempt to analyse the discrimination problem in all its different forms and details, but rather by a desire to make this theoretical 'nuisance' compatible with the traditional paradigm. This becomes very obvious when Arrow pleads that discrimination should be explained without regress to social factors as a rather uninformative category of 'imperfections', because this could lead to a precipitate rejection of neoclassical theory with its analytical efficiency. And he recommends an extension of Becker's neoclassical theory which should be linked more closely to the theory of competitive equilibrium (Arrow 1974: 4/5).

What is the essence of the neoclassical approach? This will be shown in outline by a simple description of Arrow's basic model, which in many respects builds on Becker's ideas. Both of them want to explain wage discrimination within the framework of traditional utility theory. Employers aim not only at maximum profits, they also have a 'taste for discrimination' (Becker). They prefer to employ white workers and are prepared to pay a price for it; alternatively, they have a dislike for black workers and demand a 'premium' for letting them have a job.[1] This leads to the following 'model'.

The employer has a utility function (U), whose arguments, in addition to profits (P), also contain the structure of employment subdivided into whites (W) and blacks (B):

$$U = U(P, W, B) \tag{1}$$

Total labour input is given by L

$$L = W + B \tag{2}$$

Assuming that labour is the sole variable factor and wage costs the sole variable cost and making the production function $f(L)$ dependent on labour inputs only we obtain for gross profits (everything measured in units of output)

$$P = f(L) - wL$$

with w for the real wage rate. Under discrimination we have a split wage with w_w and w_B as wage rates for whites and blacks respectively. The profit equation correspondingly becomes

$$P = f(W + B) - w_w W - w_B B \tag{3}$$

We now introduce a 'taste for discrimination':

$$MP_w = w_w + d_w; \qquad d_w < 0 \qquad (4)$$

$$MP_B = w_B + d_B; \qquad d_B > 0 \qquad (5)$$

where *MP* stands for the marginal productivity of the employed workers and *d* is the discrimination index. Both arguments are applied separately to each group. When $d = 0$ (no discrimination), equations (4) and (5) yield the usual condition for profit maximization. In the given case (with non-zero *d*'s) the employer is willing to pay an additional sum of d_w for getting a white worker while he requires a 'compensation' of d_B if a black worker is to be installed. Or in other words: the black worker must deliver a marginal product which is higher than his wage while the white worker's marginal product can lie below his wage.

We now assume that all workers are of the same quality so that the marginal product of all workers is the same:

$$MP_w = MP_B = MP_L \qquad (6)$$

From (4), (5) and (6) we get

$$w_w - w_b = d_B - d_w > 0 \qquad (7)$$

which is the condition for a 'discrimination equilibrium' where the employer is indifferent between employing a white or a black worker.

Direct discrimination with regard to wages is also in the centre of the so-called 'statistical discrimination theories' for which Phelps (1972) can be seen as an example. In this case the starting point is not utility maximization under the influence of a 'taste for discrimination' but the existence of imperfect information. In a labour market with homogeneous jobs employers are faced with an inhomogeneous labour force. Skills and qualities differ and the 'economic' wage must be fixed in relation to individual capacities. These must be tested before a contract is made. But reliable tests which give full information are not available or would be very costly. If under these circumstances employers have a prejudice (a statistical presumption) that *on average* white workers are better qualified than black workers then they will assume that *with equal test results* the white worker will probably be more efficient than the black worker. Wage differentials will be the consequence. 'Tastes for discrimination' are here irrelevant. Only a *presumption* about objective facts (averages and variance of qualifications) is important. Exact tests are too expensive; it is more profitable to use incomplete tests and then pay higher wages to whites to cash in on the statistical presumption. But the question is whether such prejudices can survive if in reality no such differences *between* the groups exist. One reason may be, as Arrow has stressed, the effects of cognitive dissonance; the execution of discrimination may contribute to a rationalization of the prejudice.

While the two approaches just mentioned try to incorporate discrimination into the traditional model of price formation through modifications of the utility function and/or the extent of information, another group of theories looks for an explanation of discrimination to the specifities and incompleteness of labour markets. These are the theories of dual and segmented labour markets and related approaches as propounded among others by Doeringer and Piore (1975), Sengenberger (1978) and Thurow (1975).[2] A typical characteristic of all these theories is that they – as far as the discrimination problem is concerned – deal predominantly with indirect discrimination and that they consider several aspects of discrimination in addition to wages: job security, working conditions, career ladders, etc. The unified labour market is replaced by labour market segments, which are separated through historical and institutional influences and between which relatively few opportunities for mobility exist.[3] 'Primary' sectors or jobs offer good wages, comparatively secure employment and good chances for advancement, while in the 'secondary' segment all these conditions are less favourable. On given special labour markets (sector, job) equal wages are paid for equal work; discrimination arises from limited access to better jobs. There are typical jobs for male workers, for white workers, etc., and parallel to this female jobs, jobs for black workers, etc. The consequence is a discrimination in the average conditions of various groups but not in their special field of employment.

DISGUISED DISCRIMINATION

In the following paragraphs I want to present a simple discrimination model which has a number of characteristics in common with the usual model but differs in so far as discrimination is not openly shown and may in fact be denied by those who practise it. This is more typical for Europe than for the United States because in Europe there is no stark white–black problem and both public opinion and legal provisions make it difficult to apply explicit discrimination. But this does not mean that 'tastes for discrimination' against minorities, women, etc. do not exist. The model which follows takes this situation into account; in spite of its simple structure it may contain some degree of realism.

We look at a specific labour market where perfectly homogeneous workers (as far as their qualifications are concerned) are employed or looking for work in firms which have completely homogeneous work places (as far as required qualifications are concerned). With regard to non-economic characteristics the labour force can be divided into two groups (e.g. men and women). We assume that the market is in equilibrium in the sense that there is an equal number of jobs and of workers. In the long run every vacancy can be filled and every worker finds employment. But there are frictions in the short period. New persons enter the labour market, old persons leave; some firms expand, some shrink. There are dismissals, quits, hirings, new contracts, etc. Assuming incomplete information and limited transparence, search (frictional) unemployment becomes possible. This will be the only type of unemployment in the model.

As far as the firms are concerned we assume that every firm pays exactly the same wage to all its employees (with identical qualifications!), but that wages differ between firms because of incomplete information and trans-action costs. These differences can be a consequence of various factors: differing costs of training newcomers, differences in internal wage struc-tures and perks, lacking knowledge of other firms' wage offers, etc. These 'imperfections' on the side of the firms in the wage-setting process are paralleled by an ignorance on the side of the workers regarding the exact wages paid by different firms.[4] This constitutes an environment where job search and search unemployment come into existence.

Next we introduce some simple assumptions about search behaviour without entering into discussions about other possible (and more sophisti-cated) search strategies. As far as the firms are concerned we assume that they stick to their set wages for the entire (medium) period which is covered by our analysis. When new workers are needed, one chooses them from the job seekers who call at the factory gate every now and then.[5] According to our assumption all workers are equally qualified to accept an open job. But some may refuse to accept it in a specific firm if the wage offered there does not correspond to their expectations.

If the firms have no preferences or idiosyncrasies with regard to the per-sonal (i.e. non-economic) characteristics of the job applicants then they can apply a very simple decision rule: 'Take on the first applicant who is willing to take the job'. But if the firms have a (not openly admitted) 'taste for dis-crimination' this rule is no longer self-evident. Let us assume that employers prefer the group of N-persons (non-discriminated group) and have a certain prejudice against D-persons (discriminated group). Then an employer may hesitate to accept a willing D-applicant in the hope that an N-person will soon turn up. But since the labour market is basically in equilibrium so that no big unemployment pool exists he cannot rely on the appearance of a willing N-person and cannot afford to reject D-applicants for too long a period. This will also be avoided because one does not want to be accused of discriminatory behaviour. Under these circumstances a simple and 'satisfying' rule could take the following form: 'If a willing N-applicant arrives engage him/her at once; if the first two applicants refuse the job because the wage is too low or if they belonged to the D-group (and were therefore sent away) accept the next willing applicant irrespective of his group characteristic.'[6]

Turning to the job seekers we assume that they know the existing range of wage offers but do not know (without search) what specific wage is paid by the various firms. They are also not informed (without search) of the firms at which vacancies exist (though they know that sufficient vacancies exist to ensure full employment). Every job seeker starts her search with a certain aspiration level; she aims at an 'acceptance wage' which she places somewhere within the total wage range which is known to her. This acceptance wage will vary between persons depending on such factors as time preference, risk aversion, optimism, pessimism, etc. But for all individuals we assume the same decision rule, which reads as follows: 'If a firm offers a wage which corresponds to my acceptance wage or lies above it, accept the job; after two unsuccessful applications (either because the wage is too low or no vacancies exist or one is rejected by the firm) reduce your acceptance wage by one unit and continue to do this after *every* following failure to get a job'.

These decision rules on the side of employers and employees are compatible with 'disguised discrimination' because the discrimination will find no explicit reflection in its final results: most firms will employ N- and D-workers who will be paid equal wages (varying from firm to firm) and both N- and D-workers will experience a certain variance in wages and in the duration of search unemployment. The discrimination that consists of a hesitation to engage D-workers *right away* need not cause alarm because it is not unusual that firms send away applicants with the remark that they would like to sample several applicants. This type of discrimination can therefore remain 'invisible'; but it is not without consequences. These will now be shown more concretely with the aid of a simple example.

Simplifying (but without loss of generality) we assume that at the beginning of a period the number of job-seeking persons in the N-group and in the D-group is the same. We also assume that the psychological factors that determine the individual acceptance wages have an identical distribution in both groups. From this it follows that under the conditions mentioned above the D-workers will have fewer chances than the N-workers to land a job in a high-wage firm and that over time − with new workers replacing old ones and workers shifting between firms − the N-workers and the D-workers will be unequally distributed over the firms arranged by wage levels. Though our full employment assumption guarantees that ultimately all workers will find a job, the N-workers have a better chance of getting a good job without, however, excluding D-workers from such jobs altogether.

The resulting situation is shown schematically in Figure 5.1, and a numerical example follows in the next section. On the abscissa the wage rates (w) paid by the various firms are located which reach from a minimum w_b to a maximum w_c (w_a will be explained later). The ordinate shows the number of workers (n) which are employed at differently paid work places. The N- and D-curves show the different distributions of N- and D-workers following from discrimination, the T-curve gives the distribution of the total labour force. The illustration in this figure assumes an approximately normal distribution of jobs arranged by wage levels. In the ensuing simple numerical illustration we shall use a rectangular distribution (equal frequencies over the whole range of wages).

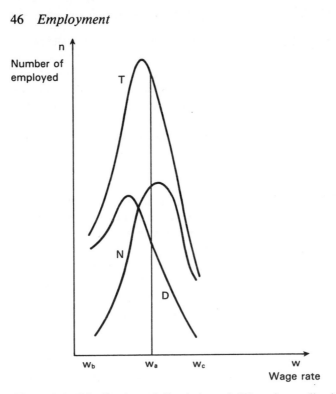

Figure 5.1   Distribution of discriminated (D) and non-discriminated (N) workers and total labour force (T) by wage rates.

I now come to the central point of this paper. If the fact of discrimination remains disguised (and is denied) then both N- and D-workers will form their ideas about a 'reasonable' acceptance wage not on the basis of their specific group chances (the *N*- and *D*-curves in Figure 5.1) but on the basis of the observed total situation (*T*-curve). Let us now look at the two persons – one N- and one D-worker – who go out to find a job. With an equal degree of information and identical psychological foundations they will – considering the shape of the *T*-curve – arrive at the same acceptance wage as a starting point, say w_a in Figure 5.1. But their *objective* chances to find an acceptable job are different. They are shown by the areas between w_a and w_c under the *N*-curve and the *D*-curve respectively (with the total area under the curves normalized to 1). The chances for D-persons are smaller and their unemployment will therefore last longer *on average*.[7] The discriminatory element of this higher average unemployment will not be immediately obvious because part of it takes the form of *voluntary* search unemployment. (Some part is 'involuntary' when the willing D-worker is rejected by the firm. A further disadvantage arises because with prolonged search the chances of finding a firm where there are still vacancies will be reduced. On this see the next section.)

A complete change in the situation can occur when a recession sets in and firms have to dismiss workers. If they stick to their discriminatory prejudices (rather than to a last-in-first-out rule or something of this sort) they will at first dismiss D-workers only before firing any of the N-workers. The discriminatory taste which was disguised before would be revealed. Whether such policies can take place will depend on the general attitudes towards discrimination and on the bargaining power of the groups concerned.

A NUMERICAL ILLUSTRATION

In this section the general ideas presented in the last section will be illustrated in a very simple simulation model. We shall analyse the results of five independent search periods (say five 'months'). In each period there are twenty firms, F_1 to F_{20}, which have vacancies. Their wage offers range from 91 to 110, with a wage of 91 in F_1, 92 in F_2, 93 in F_3 and so on up to 110 for F_{20}. The average wage is 110.5. At the beginning of each period there is just one vacancy in each of the twenty firms. There are also exactly twenty workers starting a job search in each period, ten of which are N-workers ($N_1, N_2...N_{10}$) and ten D-workers ($D_1, D_2...D_{10}$). All workers know the ruling wage range. Depending on their individual preferences they start with different acceptance wages. These are identically distributed over the two groups and range from 96 for N_1 and D_1 up to 105 for N_{10} and D_{10} (N_2, D_2: 97, $N_3 D_3$: 98, and so on).

To find a job the workers choose randomly one of the twenty firms, knowing that they had vacancies at the beginning of the period. But they do not know whether the vacancy is still open nor do they know what wage the particular firm pays (within the range 91 to 110). We assume that workers can visit only one firm per day and that firms wait passively for applicants. The workers – as long as they are unemployed – go out every day to a randomly chosen firm but without repeating an unsuccessful visit.

Every contact between a worker and a firm can result in one of the following four constellations:

1 the worker accepts and gets the job (he/she leaves the search queue and is no longer unemployed);
2 the worker refused the job because the wage is too low;
3 the vacancy is no longer available; or
4 the firm postpones a contract decision with a willing D-worker ('disguised discrimination').

In cases (2) to (4) the worker remains unemployed and continues the search on the following day. The previously mentioned adjustment patterns remain valid:

a) each worker reduced his/her acceptance wage by one unit after two unsuccessful applications (because of (2), (3) or (4)) and by a further unit for every further failure of obtaining a job;

b) every firm gives up discrimination (i.e. takes on willing D-workers) if two contacts with applicants have been unsuccessful (for reasons (2) or (4)).

For each of the five 'experimental' periods a search process along the lines just described was simulated for ten consecutive days. After ten days fifteen to eighteen of the twenty job seekers had found a job. On the eleventh day the remaining unemployed were randomly distributed over the remaining unfilled vacancies.[8] Full employment is reached. In each period unemployment of an individual cannot last longer than ten days; the minimum duration is zero days (when a contract succeeds on the first day of search). This minimum can be fairly easily achieved by N-workers when they happen to pay their first visit to a firm which meets their wage aspiration. For D-workers such immediate successes will be very rare because they will normally meet with rejections in the early periods; but success can happen when a D-worker is the third visitor on the first day in a firm which had already two visitors before which could not be taken on because the wage was insufficient or because of their D-characteristic.

The following two tables present the combined results of the five period simulations. In these five periods a total of 100 vacancies were filled (five for each firm) with fifty N-workers and fifty D-workers. Table 5.1 shows the distribution of the 100 workers over the twenty firms arranged by wage levels. It shows very clearly why we are justified to talk of 'disguised discrimination'. The discriminatory bias of the firms certainly has effects. The N-workers are more concentrated in better-paid jobs, the D-workers in the less attractive jobs. The median wage is 103 for N-workers and 97 for D-workers. But D-workers can also be found in the high-wage firms and the distribution of D-workers over the various firms is sufficiently wide to

Table 5.1 Distribution of N- and D-workers by wage rates after five search periods

Wage rate	N	D	Wage rate	N	D
91	0	5	101	5	0
92	2	3	102	3	2
93	0	5	103	2	3
94	1	4	104	3	2
95	2	3	105	3	2
96	4	1	106	5	0
97	0	5	107	4	1
98	2	3	108	3	2
99	2	3	109	3	2
100	3	2	110	3	2

Note: N = non-discriminated; D = discriminated

permit the impression that one deals with a non-discriminatory labour market, particularly when discriminating intentions are strictly denied. Under these conditions it is not unrealistic to assume (as we did) that both groups take the *total* distribution with a median wage of 100.5 as their bench-mark when deciding their acceptance wages.

Table 5.2 contains the information about the different impact of unemployment in the two groups. It shows the average duration of unemployment (measured in days) per worker (fifty N- and fifty D-workers in five periods) within the given limits of 0 and 10 days. The total search unemployment is subdivided by causes: *r* means that a job was refused because of low wages, *n* means that the vacancy is no longer available, and *d* refers to discriminating rejection.

From Table 5.2 we see that D-workers experience significantly higher average unemployment (6.72 days) than N-workers (2.44 days). But of the difference of 4.28 days only 26 per cent (1.12 days) are caused by *direct* discrimination. The remaining difference follows from two causes:

1 because D-workers find jobs already occupied more often than N-workers because of the time lost when rejected (+ 2.44 days) and
2 because D-workers fail to adjust their acceptance wage to their (non-perceived) lower objective chances.

This means that they are more often in the position of rejecting a job than N-workers (+ 0.72 days). Thus even in the case of *r*-unemployment, where we have truly 'voluntary' unemployment, D-workers are disadvantaged when they are not aware of their true situation.

In conclusion I want to show how the situation changes in the given model when the workers become aware of the discrimination and its effects. Both N- and D-workers now know that their 'true' ex-post situation is different from what they believed on the basis of the total figures. We assume the same 'rectangular' distribution of acceptance wages as before but with the difference that now each group takes its own *group-dependent* median wage as a bench-mark. Initial acceptance wages range consequently

Table 5.2 Average duration (in 'days') of search unemployment per unemployed worker by type of unemployment

| | *Unemployment* | | | |
	r	*n*	*d*	*Total*
N-workers	1.34	1.10	0	2.44
D-workers	2.06	3.54	1.12	6.72

Notes: N = non-discriminated, D = discriminated
r = applicant refuses because of low wages
n = vacancy is no longer open
d = discrimination by firm

Table 5.3 Average duration (in 'days') of search unemployment per unemployed worker by type of unemployment (open discrimination)

| | Unemployment | | | |
	r	n	d	Total
N-workers	1.62	1.60	0	3.22
D-workers	1.14	2.42	1.40	4.96

Note: See Table 5.2

from $98(N_1)$ to 107 (N_{10}) for N-workers and from 92 (D_1) to 101 (D_{10}) for D-workers. All other assumptions and decision rules remain unchanged. We analyse again the results of five simulation periods.

The new initial position has the obvious consequence that the D-workers get still more concentrated in low-wage firms than before because they are now more willing to accept such 'bad' jobs. Their median wage falls from 97 in the previous case (*disguised* discrimination) to 96.5. The median wage of the N-workers, on the other hand, rises from 103 to 104. The wage discrimination becomes more pronounced. But the unemployment differentiation narrows down considerably and the situation of the D-workers improves as a comparison between Tables 5.3 and 5.2 shows.

Unemployment of D-workers is, of course, still higher than that of N-workers because of the discriminating rejections which they still experience and which prolong their search time. But the 'voluntary' element of unemployment (rejection of a contract) is now much lower – 1.14 days compared to 2.06 days before – and lies below that of the N-workers. This greater readiness to accept 'bad' jobs also reduces the probability of finding jobs already occupied as a consequence of prolonged search behaviour. Thus N-employment also declines for D-workers (from 3.54 to 2.42 days). Altogether we get the result that the duration of D-unemployment surpasses N-unemployment by 175 per cent when discrimination is disguised, but only by 54 per cent when its working is recognised and taken into account.

NOTES

1 The preferences ('taste for discrimination') need not necessarily be those of the employers. They can also have their origin among the foremen or the white workers whose behaviour then influences the decisions of the employer. This fact is stressed by Arrow but will not be specially mentioned in what follows.
2 Good surveys are given by Cain (1976) and Marshall (1974).
3 This idea was already propounded in the nineteenth century by Cairnes in his 'non-competing groups'.
4 'It has been shown that in a market like that of labor, where new individuals are continually entering with imperfect information about wages being offered by different firms, there exist equilibrium wage distributions where individuals who

have identical productivities receive different wages simply depending on their luck in sampling firms' (Stiglitz 1973: 291). About the different factors which influence the wage setting strategies of firms and the search strategies of firms and workers see the basic work edited by Phelps (1970).

5 This means that we assume that all firms fix a wage which is acceptable to at least some workers since we stipulated the *possibility* of full employment once the search activities have been concluded.

6 In our case there is uncertainty whether and when an N-worker will turn up. But as far as qualification and wages are concerned all workers in the firm are treated equally. In the statistical theory of discrimination uncertainty consists in incomplete knowledge about the qualification of an N- and a D-worker (when test results are imperfect) and this leads to differentiated wages.

7 Since both N- and D-workers erroneously regard the *T*-curve (rather than the *N*- and *D*-curves) as the relevant information about their chances, the N-workers will in the end *on average* fare better than expected and the D-workers worse. But averages are not explicit individual experiences and the actual wage obtained will be partly ascribed to personal luck or misfortune.

8 A realistic assumption could be that unemployment benefit is only paid for ten days and that afterwards the worker relies on the recommendations of the (better informed) labour exchange.

REFERENCES

Arrow, K. J. (1974) 'The Theory of Discrimination' in Ashenfelter, P. and Rees, A. (eds), *Discrimination in Labor Markets*, Princeton: Princeton University Press.

Becker, G. S. (1957 and 1971) *The Economics of Discrimination*, Chicago: Chicago University Press.

Cain, G. G. (1976) 'The challenge of segmented labour market theories to orthodox theory: a survey', *Journal of Economic Literature*, 14, 4, pp. 1215–57.

Doeringer, P. B. and Piore, M. J. (1975) 'Unemployment and the "Dual Labor Market"', *The Public Interest*, 38, 67–79.

Marshall, R. (1974) 'The economics of racial discrimination: a survey', *Journal of Economic Literature*, 12, 3, pp. 849–71.

Phelps, E. S. (ed.) (1970) *Microeconomic Foundations of Employment and Inflation Theory*, London: Macmillan.

Phelps, E. S. (1972) 'The statistical theory of racism and sexism', *American Economic Review*, 62, 4, pp. 659–61.

Sengenberger, W. (1978) *Der gespaltene Arbeitsmarkt*, Frankfurt: Campus.

Stiglitz, J. E. (1973) 'Approaches to the economics of discrimination', *American Economic Review*, 63, P & P, pp. 287–95.

Thurow, L. C. (1975) *Generating Inequality*, New York: Basic Books.

6 The neglect of employment in the international economic order

The post-Second World War international economic order obliged the nation-states to conduct their foreign economic policies according to binding rules. As employment continued to be a purely national responsibility of the individual countries, international obligations turned into serious constraints on the pursuit of national employment policies. International agreement should provide the possibility that countries disengage themselves from the restrictive influence of foreign obligations. In addition, international employment policies would be desirable. They should focus on a common commitment to the goal of full employment rather than on concrete policy measures. But broad international strategies, such as the assumption of locomotive functions by strong economies or massive financial support for Third World development, can – depending on various conditions – also be positive.

When it came to the question of economic reconstruction after the end of the Second World War, the developed capitalist industrialized countries of Western Europe and North America were overwhelmingly influenced by the traumatic experience of the 1930s' depression. The two phenomena from these earlier times that appeared particularly threatening were mass unemployment and the restriction and departmentalization of international trade through a network of protectionist and currency controls. The question of how a new world economic order might prevent a return to these conditions was therefore already at the centre of public interest and official thinking in the democratic countries, above all Britain and the United States, long before the end of the Second World War. Sir William Beveridge's book *Full Employment in a Free Society*, published in Britain in 1944, found more of an echo in public opinion than almost any economics book that preceded it. Writers of the time, such as Clarence Streit and others, who emphasized not only the political but also the economic significance of the fact that we all have to learn to live in one crowded world, also found a similar interest.

These sentiments soon found their way into official texts, statements and actions, partly out of a genuine desire for reform and partly for fear of pressure for revolutionary change. It was in this fashion that employment objectives became almost obligatory in the government statements and legislation in Britain and America, which then acted as examples for other countries.

International conferences led to the establishment of the International Monetary Fund (IMF), the World Bank and ultimately, after the failure of the Havana Charter, the first effort to establish a comprehensive regime for foreign trade, the General Agreement on Tariffs and Trade (GATT). Thus an institutional framework was created that was to prevent a relapse into the double catastrophe of the 1930s, mass unemployment and the progressive strangulation of international trade. It was also seen as a basis from which to make further progress.

From the very beginning, however, there was a significant difference between the way the two problems were addressed, a difference that could be only partly attributed to the different nature of the problems of unemployment and trade. The employment problem has from the start been seen as essentially a national problem to be resolved by national effort. Apart from relatively inconsequential summit and other declarations, there have been no significant international agreements on – or commitments to – employment objectives. In total contrast, there is an expansive network of – admittedly, not always effective – consultations, co-ordination and regulations aimed at preventing the slide into protectionism, currency controls, and export subsidization. Included in this network are, among others, the IMF, the Organization for Economic Co-operation and Development, the GATT and the European Economic Community.

As already mentioned, this difference is partly due to the nature of the problems and would exist whatever national policies were pursued or whatever international agreements were reached. Foreign economic policy inevitably involves numerous players and is therefore amenable to mutual agreement and quid pro quo agreements. In contrast, employment policies always appear to be seen as a domestic concern.

Things are obviously not always quite so simple. One could, after all, always adopt a totally unilateral standpoint in foreign economic policy. One could, for example, argue – as I do not – that, according to the widely represented free-trade equilibrium model, every move towards free trade improves productivity and resource allocation even when it is not reciprocated. Above all, however, although it seems hardly credible that employment is an isolated problem that can be resolved by national means alone, it is largely treated as such in the discussion and practice of economic policy. This phenomenon requires more detailed analysis.

From a theoretical point of view there is little call to distinguish, in principle, between employment and international economic policy problems. Both could be seen to have national and international components. The well-developed macroeconomic models and theories of the global economy do indeed suggest that there is a high degree of interdependence between all parts of the economy and that there is a circular chain of causal links between them. The degree and form of interdependence vary according to circumstances and theoretical approach and thus provide scope for differences of opinion and debate. But no model denies the existence of a direct and indirect – that is, inter- and intrasectoral – interdependence between changes in domestic and foreign employment and trade and capital flows. This is true whether or not there is labour mobility.

There are therefore no theoretical grounds for drawing a dividing line between domestic employment policies and the presumably necessarily global foreign economic policy. Employment policy measures of an expansionary or deflationary nature affect trade flows and therefore affect trade and employment in other countries. Equally, foreign economic policy measures also influence both international trade as well as employment in a number of countries, regardless of whether they are national/unilateral measures or global/ multilateral measures. The subsequent knock-on effects can then have further – multiplier – repercussions in all countries and sectors. Therefore, the difference between macroeconomic models does not concern so much the question of whether domestic or internationally agreed-upon policies are appropriate for individual sectors. It refers far more to the possibilities in principle of an active employment policy, be it a national or an international one. We need not concern ourselves further here with this conflict, which runs under the slogan of 'monetarism or rational expectations versus Keynesianism', because we shall work under the premise that an employment policy is possible and makes sense.

THE NATIONAL–INTERNATIONAL DICHOTOMY

How can one then explain why, despite the ease with which both theoretical and common-sense views of the world point to interdependence, such a widespread dichotomy exists between national employment policies and international foreign economic policy? There are a number of explanations that, as will be shown, all have serious consequences. The fact that theoretical and policy discussions prematurely and almost totally accept the existence of such a dichotomy is largely due to the origins of the modern theory of employment policy. These were decisively influenced by Keynes's famous book *The General Theory of Employment, Interest and Money*, which was published in 1936. Keynes wrote the book during the depression, when world trade was already shattered, and concentrated on the possibilities of expanding employment in what was a relatively large country under relatively strong controls on the balance of payments. While he did not neglect foreign questions, his approach was largely geared to a relatively closed economy that therefore had to pursue its own employment objectives. This approach meant a national employment policy and thus influenced the discussion for a long time.

Ten years later, during preparations for the establishment of the IMF, Keynes saw the coming open world economy and was thoroughly aware of the links between domestic and international employment and economic policies. He had ideas on how to address the question of such links, which can be found in the so-called Keynes Plan and which were presented to the

IMF but got nowhere due to American opposition. In both theory and practice, therefore, employment policies remained constrained to the national model. External factors – in particular, the importance of exports for employment – were recognized but usually only as exogenous factors beyond national control that could either increase or decrease employment. In addition, politicians, bending to the forces of political expediency, tended to ascribe good results on the employment front to domestic policies and negative results to uncontrolled external influences. Little attention was paid to the common ups and downs in employment and to the mechanisms of transmission from one country to another, which might make common policy approaches advisable. [1]

Things are very different when one turns to what was happening on the foreign economic policy front. Although there is a good deal of scope for unilateral actions in foreign economic policy, such as in the form of open or disguised protectionism or exchange rate policies, the philosophy of mutual and binding agreements is still seen as normal. This philosophy is supported above all by the trauma of the 1930s, when every country tried to improve its own economic and employment position at the expense of others by adopting protectionist measures in the pursuit of competitive beggar-thy-neighbour policies. The result was that world trade declined or stagnated while unemployment persisted. A repeat of such a self-destructive process was to be prevented by mutual commitments to open trade.

A second factor promoting bi- or multilateral approaches is the idea that unilateral action should be avoided. The trade and currency policy instruments that can discriminate against other countries are retained as bargaining chips, even when their unilateral removal is possible or even preferable for purely economic reasons, and are only negotiated away in return for reciprocal concessions. In principle, such an approach is also conceivable for employment policies. As every country is interested in higher employment, and demand, in other countries, a country could use its own employment measures as a bargaining chip in order to get other countries to introduce similar measures in international agreements. Of course, the analogy does not hold in practice because employment is much too explosive an issue politically for such a policy to be practicable. The use of increased tariffs in retaliation against foreign protectionism and as a means of bringing pressure to bear on another country is not unknown, even when these initially damage the domestic economy. But it is unheard of to use the threat of increased domestic unemployment in an effort to bring about a change in another country's restrictive economic policies.

Whatever the causes of this nationalization of employment policy and globalization of foreign economic policy might have been, we are faced with the reality that the discrepancy between them remains and has become more entrenched. That this should have happened at all is significant and must be discussed, at least briefly, before the question of a global employment policy is addressed.

There appear to be two important issues. The first concerns the interests involved. It is in the interests of the ever more important and powerful multinational companies that countries should enter into internationally binding agreements requiring relatively free trade and capital flows that are not qualified by any international or national requirements concerning socioeconomic objectives such as employment, living standards and the like. In contrast to the earlier pressure for protective tariffs from the ruling national monopolies and oligopolies, the multinationals seek a freedom to reallocate resources through their global transactions that is secure from sociopolitical interference. This is a political-economic fact of life that helps explain why the institutional hierarchy favouring economic or trade policies over employment policies has been so stable despite significant changes in the economic climate.

The implications of this hierarchy bring us to the second reason why employment objectives have remained nationalized while foreign economic policy objectives are global. As already emphasized, it is not possible to compartmentalize employment and foreign policy. The objectives of foreign economic and employment policy are interdependent and cannot be carried out in isolation from each other. Therefore, when the foreign economic components of a policy are subject to international commitments without there being similar commitments to employment, there is clearly a hierarchy of policy objectives and thus of what can be achieved in pursuit of these objectives for every single country. A clear asymmetry prevails. Commitments in the field of foreign economic policy – free trade, free flows of capital, and so forth – impose constraints on national employment policies, while the globally conceived rules for foreign economic policy – as in the GATT, IMF, OECD, the European Economic Community and others – are scarcely constrained by specific commitments on employment.

In other words, while there is an internationally sanctioned effort to prevent efficiency losses due to the uneconomic allocation of resources resulting from protectionist measures, there is no equivalent provision for losses due to underemployment and insufficient capacity utilization. Nothing illustrates the harsh reality of this hierarchy better than the way the IMF uses its internationally agreed-upon rules to prescribe national policies for indebted countries in order to get the current debt crisis under control. Monetary, credit and trade criteria take precedence, with catatrophic consequences for employment, living standards and social cohesion in the countries concerned. In the end, this has implications for the balance of the international economy.

This all suggests that, given the continued high levels of unemployment in many parts of the world, more attention should be given to the question of global employment strategies. In what follows, a modest attempt is made to describe what these might look like.

GLOBAL EMPLOYMENT STRATEGIES

First of all, one should consider the consequences for national employment policies if, as is quite likely, a move towards global employment policy measures is politically infeasible and the expectations of various countries with regard to employment policy become strongly divergent. In such a situation a country wishing to improve prospects can face a real conflict between respecting international treaties and the need to expand its domestic economy. A degree of disengagement from restrictive foreign influences must then be within the scope of internationally agreed-upon possibilities; otherwise countries may simply take unilateral actions to disengage.

A central problem is that, failing equivalent expansionist measures in other countries, an expansionist policy will result in balance-of-payments difficulties that can cut short any expansionist policy. The hope that the introduction of flexible exchange rates would contain this stop-go problem and create more scope for unilateral employment policies has only been fulfilled to a very limited extent. As things are, expansion creates increased demand for imports and results in devaluation, which can fuel inflation via the price-wage mechanism and thus cause serious problems – in addition to that of domestic inflation. Given the existence of free capital and currency markets, there are also likely to be strong speculative shifts in the value of the currency destabilizing both trade and economic policies. This then leads to dirty floating, or the reintroduction of fixed exchange rates, with which the balance-of-payments problem would again become acute.

It would therefore be desirable to provide for countries wishing to reflate in isolation the opportunities to take appropriate measures with regard to trade and capital flows without being too constrained by balance-of-payments and inflation considerations. This does not mean import controls but only the opportunity of preventing too big a gap from emerging between the expanding import growth and the stagnating export growth. In other words, the increase in imports resulting from increased economic activity should be acknowledged as an alternative to an increase in imports due to reductions in trade barriers. More consideration of such alternatives in international agreements could represent the first step towards a reduction in the asymmetry between the scope for employment and foreign economic policies mentioned earlier.

What possibilities are there if the transition towards more global concepts of employment policy should be seriously considered? First of all, it is important to take note of a fundamental difference between general policy goals and specific policy instruments and programmes. To some extent, it is not possible to consider the latter without agreement on the importance of the employment objective. It is, however, possible to agree on a common goal of high employment without agreeing on the details of common and co-ordinated policy instruments.

One can argue that, given the current state of the world economy and economic theory, a diffuse agreement on policy objectives not only makes sense but should indeed be given a high priority for economic reasons. First of all, history teaches us that such an approach promises not only the possibility of success, but success itself. There has never really been anything such as an internationally agreed-upon employment policy, apart from rhetorical fireworks. During the 1950s and 1960s, however, most developed industrialized countries gave employment objectives such a high priority that there was, in practice, an agreed-upon de facto policy objective for these countries. Every country could rely on the fact that others would strive for high levels of employment and demand, so that, in the medium term, domestic employment policies could be conducted in relative freedom and without fear of general disruption from foreign economic factors. The existence of common objectives therefore confirmed and endorsed national employment policy measures.

As is well known, the period after 1970 was characterized by a massive shift away from employment objectives as the top priority in economic policies moved towards the control of inflation, privatization and the restoration of private capital. This meant the end of de facto global agreement on employment policy objectives. When devising employment policies, countries wishing to expand had to take account now of the lack of parallel action by other countries, the ensuing dissipation of demand into deflating countries, and the resulting balance-of-payments problems. This change in policy objectives was not solely or even predominantly responsible for the change from the full employment of the 1960s to the long-term unemployment of later years. There were numerous other, largely real economic, reasons for this change. There is, however, a case to be made that the existence of full-employment objectives on a global scale did help and that their absence has made things worse.[2]

This historical point should illustrate the importance of global agreement on policy objectives even when these are not accompanied by agreement on specific methods and timing. There are a number of reasons why a broad agreement on the objective of employment has advantages over a detailed global employment policy, whatever form this takes. The first, obvious reason can be found in the continued heterogeneous nature of national employment policies. Differences between national policies are so great, especially between developing and industrialized countries, that a common policy is not feasible. Even among the advanced industrialized countries the differences are such that the creation of common methods and rules for policy instruments would reduce their efficacy. Distinct differences between countries – such as the scope for public sector involvement, income policies, the timing of political cycles, the structure of corporate organization and the like – suggest that different instruments need to be used depending on the particular national characteristics.

Independent of such differences there are also other reasons why different methods should be used. A single, global employment policy would have to be based on existing national thinking on – and knowledge of – employment policies. Given new developments in both economics and technology, as well as the inevitable clash of interests over policy objectives, there exists no broad consensus on what such national policies should be. There are a range of strategies, some more controversial than others, but all of which are subject to a constant process of testing and evaluation. There is indeed scope for gaining new experience from the experimentation with different approaches. In this way a global approach that allows for variations is better than one that does not, and all countries can benefit from the lessons learned by others. Furthermore, variation in approaches ensures that the errors that will inevitably be made do not have a cumulative effect and provides for a certain degree of inbuilt correction of such errors.

One can make similar arguments with regard to the timing of employment policy measures. Given the difficulties in producing exact diagnoses and projections and the unavoidable lags with which decisions are taken and policies become effective, it would not necessarily make sense for all countries to act at the same time. Asynchronous action also means that the inevitable fluctuations in employment due to cyclical effects and structural change will be unevenly spread. This means that the weakening of an economy in one country could be more rapidly eased by increased exports to countries undergoing expansion than would be the case if cyclical movements in the respective economies ran parallel. Analyses of the developments in the 1960s suggest that asynchronous economic cycles in the different countries significantly shortened the downward movements.

There are thus a number of grounds for arguing that the agreement on a global employment policy should be limited to a general agreement on the overall objective. The details of how this objective is to be attained should be left to national policies. This, however, leaves one major problem unanswered. How does one ensure that each country actually pursues and sticks to the agreed-upon objective? It is well known how easily the rhetoric of full employment slips from the tongues of politicians for whom the use of such rhetoric will always pay. It will take more than noncommittal declarations of intention to make a genuine global dedication to the goal of full employment.

One possibility would be to make the policy objectives credible by actually acting on them. This was in fact what happened during the 1950s and 1960s. The basis for a genuine global policy would be established without prescribing specific measures or results if governments were seen to be acting clearly and quickly to deal with employment problems and if they were to give employment problems an important place in all economic policy decisions.

Where the basis of mutual trust is not – or no longer – sufficient, more concrete indicators will be needed. The most obvious way to create these is to lay down specific targets. Just as specific targets are set for inflation, there could be concrete targets set for employment. If these targets were not met, there would then have to be an obligation to take additional employment policy measures. Such an approach was, for example, incorporated in the employment programs for Asia worked out by the International Labor Organization (ILO), which called for 'comprehensive employment programmes, indicating specific targets to be progressively achieved' for the Asian region.[3]

There are significant difficulties caused by such commitments to targets in market-orientated countries due to the dynamism of market-orientated economies, their susceptibility to disturbances and the limited effectiveness of economic policy instruments. Realistic objectives are difficult to set and are not independent of time. If they are set too low, so that they are easily achieved, they lose their effectiveness in tackling unemployment. If they are set too high, they will frequently not be reached, with the result that the approach would lose its credibility and effectiveness. But even realistic, flexible objectives will not be easy to achieve. What sanctions, for example, can one employ when a participating country does not hold to its commitments? As mentioned earlier, it is simply infeasible to take direct retaliatory action as one can in trade policy with retaliatory tariff increases. It is possible to devise other forms of penalty, but these are politically infeasible.

It is partly, but not exclusively, because of these difficulties in devising an operational set of policy objectives that concrete global measures and projects assume a complementary importance of their own, especially during times of persistent mass unemployment. There are three types of strategy deserving further consideration in this still underdeveloped but important area of policy.

One strategy would be to build on the very modest foundations of the existing multilateral instruments of employment policy. Its impact would be relatively limited because of the limited scope offered by these instruments. But as they already exist it would be relatively easy to pursue such an approach. In the first instance, one thinks here of the ILO, whose founding statute of 1919 included the objective of full employment. Although this objective has been regularly endorsed in ILO resolutions and programmes ever since, it has not been backed by sufficient resources or political support from national governments to enable the ILO to do very much.[4] In addition to the ILO, and in conjunction with it, the employment policy elements in other international organizations must be strengthened. Here one is concerned with all the UN organizations involved in work with the developing countries, the World Bank and, on a limited regional level, the European Social Fund and the European Regional Development Fund, which deal with the employment agenda in the European Community.[5]

All these existing approaches only play a minor role because their scale is limited and because there is often no additionality – that is, resources are used to finance existing national schemes. But they could become more important if they were expanded significantly. One should not, however, exaggerate the potential for expanding such instruments. The instruments themselves and the programmes associated with them are devised to assist in the implementation of national programmes and to improve the functioning of employment markets. The emphasis is therefore on research, the exchange of information, and the provision of finance for retraining and actions in special problem areas such as underdeveloped regions or youth unemployment. As important as these are, and as desirable as the easing of such special problems as youth and regional unemployment are, such action can at best be no more than a complement to a more substantial national or international effort. They are not a genuine alternative.

THE LOCOMOTIVE THEORY

To have the necessary impact on demand or cyclically induced mass unemployment, one must look to other strategies. In this context there are two possible approaches: the so-called locomotive theory and, in Bruno Kreisky's words, a 'Marshall Plan for the Third World' or the Brandt Plan. The basic concept of the locomotive theory, which was ventilated in the middle of the 1970s mainly in the OECD setting, is very simple and, with the exception of the name, not new. The concept was inherent in the saying 'when America sneezes Europe catches a cold', which was well known at the time of the 1930s' depression. It is based on the simple observation that, given differences in the size of economies, the same relative effort to expand economic activity in countries has very different absolute effects on other countries' trade flows. Economic weight is not the only factor, and trade dependence and the multiplier effects of various measures also play a role. But by and large it remains true that actions taken by large countries have a greater impact on others than those of small countries.[6]

The basic idea behind the locomotive theory is therefore that common and strong expansionary action by, in particular, the large economies can increase employment at a time of global recession. This would then provide a positive impulse in other countries the cumulative effect of which would be to add more steam to the locomotive and thus to the world economy. A stimulus cannot be created by small individual countries. Expansion by such countries is too small in relation to the world economy to have any significant effect, and all that would result would be balance-of-payments problems for the countries concerned because of increased imports with more or less static exports. The only real alternative to the locomotive approach would be a co-ordinated expansion by all or most of the countries affected by high unemployment, whether large or small. But this would clearly present much greater organizational and political problems than would the locomotive approach.

There is one important problem with the locomotive strategy. Even when the expansionary policy is successful, it can still cause a number of problems for the locomotive country or countries. These mainly take the form of budget deficits, the danger of inflation, and problems with distribution. Countries benefiting from a successful locomotive action experience only the expansion effect and avoid the problems, at least partially, or can more easily deal with them in the already expanding economy. With their export-led growth, these countries then become free riders of the expansionary policies, the costs of which are unevenly spread.

Such imbalances in the risks and benefits of locomotive policies can significantly reduce the necessary incentive for large economies to pursue them. In order to compensate for this it would be necessary to complement the global strategy based on a locomotive approach with commitments from the potential beneficiaries to contribute to global demand by taking respective national measures and thus taking some of the burden from the locomotive countries. The initial step cannot be taken by the smaller countries, because the tail cannot wag the dog. But these countries can play an active role once the process of growth has been started.

There is one further point to be made. The locomotive strategy is endangered if the locomotive countries seek to promote expansion mainly by means of export promotion, which is not an unusual occurrence. This is more likely to result in a relocation of employment or in the export of unemployment than in a general improvement in the global level of employment. This would in fact represent nothing more and nothing less than the misery of a 1930s type of beggar-thy-neighbour policy.[7]

The locomotive strategy is best suited to a global economic climate, like that of the mid-1970s or any recessionary phase of an international economic cycle, when there is persistent unemployment affecting most of the major trading countries. The locomotive countries should get the others moving again or moving faster, and the whole process should then be mothballed until it is needed again.

This contrasts with the permanent programmes first developed for the developing countries and then elaborated to meet employment policy objectives as called for in the so-called Brandt Plan,[8] but also repeatedly by Bruno Kreisky and others. If properly executed, a global plan, involving the co-operation of the developed industrialized countries and the international organizations, including especially the IMF, the World Bank and the United Nations, could provide the financial basis for permanent and significant transfers to developing countries that would provide the impulse for flows of supply and demand benefiting both sides.

It is not possible here to go into all the problems involved in the implementation of such a programme, such as the technical difficulties, the danger of inflation, the selection of suitable projects or the political resistance. These problems are by no means insignificant, but they are of the same order of magnitude as those already faced by the national and international economic systems. Nor can the development policy questions relating to such a programme, which are indeed important, be covered. Only the differences between such a programme and the locomotive strategy, which are in their essence twofold, can be discussed here.

First, as already pointed out, such a programme would be permanent. It would not compensate for cyclical events but would compensate for permanent trends in international purchasing power and demand weaknesses and thus in effect act as a floor for foreign trade and employment. On this base there would then be scope for other national or international employment measures whether expansionary or deflationary. The second important point is that, if the projects and structural policy measures are chosen in a more or less sensible manner, such a strategy could have an immediate impact on the extremely serious employment position in the developing countries. This would then help the developed countries cope with the difficult process of adjusting their employment markets to changes in trading patterns – the New International Economic Order – by facilitating a progressive change with a minimum of frictional losses.

Finally, it is important to stress that this article only meant to shed some light on the major aspects of the various employment strategies. No claim is made for comprehensiveness. It should be pointed out, in particular, that the various national and international approaches are not necessarily incompatible with each other and can be complementary. This is especially true when one distinguishes between employment policies and labour market policies more narrowly defined. There is certainly a need to look more fully at these problems. If any of these proposals are to be realized today, however, it will require a political change in the emphasis of economic policy as well as more knowledge about the mechanics of the strategies.

NOTES

1 On the question of the transfer mechanism, see Gerhard Graf, (1975)[6] 'Hypothesen zur internationalen Konjunkturtransmission', *Weltwirtschaftliches Archiv*, 111, 3, pp. 529–63.
2 In this context it is interesting to note the review of Sir William Beveridge's book *Full Employment in a Free Society* written by the English economist Austin Robinson in 1945. After discussing Beveridge's various proposals on employment policy, Robinson wrote, 'They [the proposals] are not so very different from, nor so very much greater than those with which we failed to defeat unemployment in the 'thirties that one can feel absolutely confident of success. But what, more than anything else was lacking in the 'thirties was an overwhelming national determination to defeat unemployment.' *Economic Journal* (1945) 55, p. 76.
3 International Labour Organization (1968) *Proposals for the Formulations and Implementation of an Asian Manpower Plan,* Report 4, Geneva: International Labour Organization.
4 See International Labour Organization (1969) *The World Employment*

Programme and (1977) *Employment, Growth and Basic Needs: A One-World Problem,* Geneva: International Labour Organization.

5 See François Vandamme (1984) 'The Revised European Social Fund and Action to Combat Unemployment in the European Community,' *International Labour Review*, 123, 2 (Mar.–Apr.), pp. 167–81.

6 The best example is the United States, which, because of its import propensity and size, has a profound impact on the activity of other countries. The theoretical discussion of the relationship between size, savings and import propensity can be found in Martin Bronfenbrenner (1979) 'On the Locomotive Theory in International Macroeconomics' *Weltwirtschaftliches Archiv*, 115, 1, pp. 38–50.

7 There is a similar problem today with the competition between countries in the provision of large subsidies and tax concessions to attract multinational companies. This results in the multinationals making big profits, in fiscal problems for the countries involved and in a shifting of employment from one country to another. It is doubtful that the net effect for the international economy is positive.

8 (1980) *North-South: A Programme for Survival,* London: Independent Commission on International Development Issues, see esp. chap. 3.

7 Some reflections on the growth of female labour supply and the tertiary sector

The economic literature on female participation in the labour market concentrates mainly on microeconomic supply decisions based on economic variables (wage rates, family income, human capital, etc.) and maximization under external constraints (marriage, children), and on structural (demand) influences stemming from a growing service sector. The influence of non-economic cultural factors ('feminist revolution') is frequently mentioned but is usually treated – if at all – as a time trend. In the present paper differences in religious denominations are taken as a proxy for different feminist attitudes and are used in a cross-section analysis of fifteen European countries. It is shown that a consideration of this factor has a significant effect on parameter values and on the perspective in which the growing share of women in total employment can be seen.

The famous German satirist of prewar days, Kurt Tucholsky, once wrote an ironic piece on economics in which he says: 'As far as the world economy is concerned, it is interlinked' ('Was die Weltwirtschaft angeht, so ist sie verflochten'). That economic processes – and not just world trade – are complex interdependent affairs has in the meantime become abundantly clear and is mirrored in the growing complexity of economic and econometric models. In this respect economics is probably well ahead of other social sciences. Yet dealing with interdependent systems and their ramifications has its special problems. The traditional thinking in terms of cause and effect can run into difficulties which are not easily overcome, in spite of the steady advances in sophisticated statistical and econometric methodology. Moreover, while a fairly high degree of success is achieved in allowing for interdependence in so far as economic factors are concerned, the situation is less satisfactory when it comes to mutual influences between economic and non-economic factors. In some cases this may not matter. But where such non-economic forces are important the tendency towards a narrow economic perspective can blur the vision. It can lead either to a sudden stop when the analysis reaches the borders of the economic scene, or to 'economic imperialism', to a tendency to treat the non-economic events according to the rules and viewpoints of economic theory. Both these strategies – though simplifying the procedure – may fail to indicate the full variety of possible and actual relations and crossconnections.

Table 7.1 The growth of female labour supply and the tertiary sector in Europe, 1971–86

	(1) Share of women as % in total employment (c. 1971) F'	(2) Share of women as % in total employment (c. 1986) F	(3) Employment in service sector as % of total employment (1971) S'	(4) Employment in service sector as % of total employment (c. 1986) S	(5) Real GNP per Capita (1980) OECD-Europe = 100 Y
Austria	37.0	38.9	47.2	56.0	114
Belgium	29.2	37.5	48.7	67.6	131
Denmark	37.6	47.4	55.0	67.8	144
Finland	43.4	48.6	52.2	61.1	121
France	34.2	42.2	49.8	63.7	136
Germany	34.2	39.1	45.0	55.6	148
Greece	25.1	31.8	48.2	57.0	46
Ireland	32.3	33.1	54.1	60.4	63
Italy	27.0	34.5	38.1	56.3	78
Netherlands	27.6	34.0	60.2	67.8	134
Norway	29.2	46.2	55.5	68.9	158
Spain	20.5	28.2	39.0	51.3	63
Sweden	37.8	48.6	52.7	66.9	167
Switzerland	35.0	38.6	45.8	54.9	178
United Kingdom	38.1	44.9	51.7	67.1	106
Unweighted average	32.5	39.6	49.5	61.5	

Sources: Columns 1–4, ILO, *Yearbook of Labour Statistics*; Column 5, IMF, *International Financial Statistics*.

As a fairly simple illustration of this problem I want to discuss some aspects of two dynamic processes in developed economies which have greatly accelerated in recent decades: the increase in female participation in the labour market on the one hand and the growth of the service sector (or, more specifically, of service sector employment) on the other. Both these well-known trends are quite general (in developed economies) as can be seen from Table 7.1, which provides the basis for all empirical observations and calculations in this paper. In each of the fifteen European countries covered in the table (Austria, Belgium, Denmark, Finland, France, the FRG, Greece, Ireland, Italy, the Netherlands, Norway, Spain, Sweden, Switzerland, the UK) the share of women (columns 1 and 2) and of service sector employment (columns 3 and 4) has risen quite distinctly between around 1971 and around 1986; on average (simple averages) from 32.5 per cent to 39.6 per cent for women and from 49.5 per cent to 61.5 per cent for tertiary employment.

Such developments ask for comment and theory to explain the trends and the reasons for differences in levels and growth between countries; and in fact the rise in female labour supply in particular has called forth a considerable and growing stream of empirical and theoretical economic literature.[1] There are many approaches to the question but two dominant tendencies can be observed: a microeconomic, supply-orientated 'neoclassical' approach and a more demand-orientated, macroeconomic and structural view-point. The microeconomic approach, which dominates the field, tries to 'explain' the determinants of female labour supply decisions in terms of the traditional elements of economic analysis: utility-maximization in response to market signals (prices) and given resources (material and human capital) under (special) constraints. Accordingly prices (wages of women and their husbands), human capital (educational levels) and various constraints (number and age of children, lack of nurseries, etc.) are the main components in an attempt to find the determinants of participation decisions.

Now, while there is no doubt that these efforts have produced interesting and impressive results in showing that at any moment of time and in given places some or all of these elements play a significant role in determining the probability of whether a woman will be in the labour force or not, they can hardly be described as an 'explanation' of the forces behind the trend nor can they account for the considerable inter-country differences. One of the difficulties is the interdependence between the constraints and the participation decision. Is the labour market entered because one has few children and a high level of education (as the theory suggests and as the calculations confirm) or does a decision to enter the labour market lead to a reduction in the number of children and the acquisition of more human capital? Cause and effect are easily interchangeable, but to see this one must be aware of other factors influencing the participation decision and these lie largely outside the 'normal' variables of economic analysis. Calling these factors for short the 'feminist revolution',[2] we find that these influences are either not sufficiently seen in economic 'explanations' or deliberately set aside.

Thus, to illustrate the first phenomenon, we might quote a passage from chapter IV of the US *1973 Report of the President's Council of Economic Advisers*, which is devoted to the economic role of women. There one can read (on p. 89): 'Women work outside the home for the same reason as men. The basic reason is to get the income that can be earned by working'. This suggests the adequacy and sufficiency of the traditional microeconomic analysis. But as Barbara Bergmann and Irma Adelman (women, so it happens!) rightly pointed out in their critical review of chapter IV, '[the above] passage, while clearly reflecting liberal intentions, misses some very important reasons why women (and men) work. They work not only to contribute to the family's funding for goods and services, but for greater autonomy in spending, for status inside and outside the family, to occupy themselves in an interesting way, to meet people, to have the excitement of being in a contest for advancement, to reduce the amount of housework they do, and to get away from spending all day with their children' (Bergmann and Adelman 1973: 512).[3] It is among these factors that we have to look to understand many of the changes that have taken place. The second 'stratagem' mentioned before is perhaps even more characteristic. The 'feminist revolution' is not overlooked, but it is not allowed to disturb the 'neatness' of the economic model. Thus, in a very detailed study of the factors affecting the labour supply of married women in Canada a single sentence does away with all the difficulties arising from 'non-economic' influences: 'Concepts like self-fulfillment, role models, the right of women to have control over their own bodies, equal pay for equal work, and so forth really lie outside the scope of this analysis' (Nakamura *et al.* 1979: 801). It is, of course, not maintained that a more or less complete neglect of non-economic factors is universal in the 'supply-side' literature. There are notable exceptions such as, for instance (to name just one example), Chris de Neubourg's attempt to explain the comparatively low level of female labour market participation rates in the Netherlands almost completely on the basis of historical and cultural influences (Neubourg, 1987: Chapter IV).[4] But the fact remains that the economic incentives – labour supply nexus is the typical pattern in the supply-side literature.[5]

Less dominant and of older vintage is the more loosely presented idea that the growth of female labour market participation is a consequence of structural changes. Based on the well-known 'empirical laws' by Clark and Fourastié one notes that with rising productivity and income there is a continuous shift in demand, production, and employment from the primary to the secondary and finally to the tertiary (service) sector. With female labour being traditionally biased towards service branches this trend had favoured the activation of a dormant supply of women whose share in employment has consequently risen.[6] In view of the parallel increase in importance of services and female employment in all countries it is obvious that this 'explanation' has a high degree of plausibility and its significance should not be denied. But are we not here too faced with the possibility of 'reverse causation'? Could it not be that an autonomous increase in women's propensity to enter the labour market has − by increasing the availability of suitable labour − helped to accelerate the expansion of the service sector? Not only that; an urge of women to leave the house is in itself a strong stimulus to expand the service sector as a substitute for work which was formerly done in households. Here we have (partly) a 'true Say's law' where the supply (of female labour) creates its own demand (for service employment).

In the remaining part of this paper I want to indicate the relevance of the reflections just made by presenting a very simple attempt to 'explain' differences in female and service employment shares in the fifteen European countries contained in Table 7.1. Both as regards levels and developments of shares I shall compare a purely economic sequence with an extended analysis which takes the non-economic factor into account.

The 'economic' sequence runs in the form indicated above: a higher economic standard (indicated by real per capita GNP) should be connected with a higher share of service employment and this in turn should lead to a higher share of female labour. The alternative hypothesis will be that while this chain from Y (per capita income) over S (service employment share) to F (share of female employment) may be valid to some extent, it needs enforcement and/or modification by a consideration of the non-economic elements ('feminist revolution') which may lead to different parameters and to reversed causation.

The great difficulty is, of course, how to quantify this non-economic element. I have adopted a very rough expedient to deal with this problem. Taking into account that Roman Catholicism has a strong bias for traditional female roles (housewife and mother), at any rate a much stronger one than Protestant religions, and further assuming that ruling religions either express or influence (or both) the attitudes of the population (even if they are not believers),[7] I simply introduce a dummy to distinguish between predominantly Roman Catholic and other countries in order to see whether this has a significant influence on the results. The allocation of the fifteen countries was quite straightforward in eleven cases. In six cases (Austria, Belgium, France, Ireland, Italy, Spain) Roman Catholics represent from 88 to 95 per cent of the population, while in five countries (Denmark, Finland, Norway, Sweden, the UK) their share remains well below 10 per cent. Greece is a special case with Greek Orthodoxy as the ruling religion. She has been added to the Roman Catholic group. This leaves three countries with a mixed fare of religions: the FRG (45 per cent Roman Catholics), the Netherlands (38 per cent) and Switzerland (48 per cent).[8] These three countries form a 'mixed group'.

After these preliminaries we can present the results of our calculations (linear regressions, all based on the data of Table 7.1). We start off with the simple economic sequence. At first we present the share of service sector employment in 1985–6 (S) as a function of real per capita GNP (Y). The latter (see column 5, Table 7.1) is expressed as an index number with the average per capita income of OECD-Europe taken as 100. The year chosen is 1980, because we shall look at both the *level* of service employment in the mid-1980s and its *development* between the 1970s and 1980s. The choice of another year for relative incomes would have a slight influence on parameters but would leave the basic picture unchanged. The relation we obtain is (figures in brackets are *t*-values):

$$S = 53.82 + 0.06 \quad Y; \ r = 0.44 \tag{1}$$
$$(11.61) \ (1.62)$$

A certain, but weak influence (significant at the 10 per cent level with a one-tail test)[9] is noticeable: a 1 per cent increase in real per capita income (compared to the European average) raises the tertiary employment share by 0.06 percentage points. Going on from the service sector to the percentage share of female employment in total employment in 1985/86 (F) we obtain:

$$F = -1.09 + 0.66 \quad S; \ r = 0.60 \tag{2}$$
$$(-0.07) \ (2.72)$$

Here we get a result with a much stronger affinity to the 'traditional' view: a high level of service employment does indeed show a high parallelism (on a 1 per cent significance level) with a high share of female employment, an additional percentage point in the service share being connected with an addition of two-thirds of a percentage point in the share of women.

Let us next take into account the 'cultural factor of feminism'. We start now at the other end. The share of women in total employment is 'explained' by the share of service employment as before and by the 'cultural' dummy D which takes the value of zero in the case of the seven predominantly Roman (and Greek) Catholic countries, the value of one in the case of the five Protestant countries and the value of 0.5 for the mixed group. This leads to:

$$F = 20.85 + 0.23 \quad S + 10.03 \quad D; \ R = 0.84 \tag{3}$$
$$(1.71) \ (1.11) \qquad (3.71)$$

The result, which is also shown in Figure 7.1, is interesting. Not only is the correlation coefficient much higher than in equation (2), differences in the size of the service sector (measured in terms of employment) cease to be a significant 'explanation' of female shares in employment. Instead the proxy for different feminist attitudes (D) becomes highly significant. A 'Protestant attitude' (with D = 1) can add 10 percentage points to the share of women as compared with a Roman Catholic background. Working our way backwards we next present the share of service sector employment as a

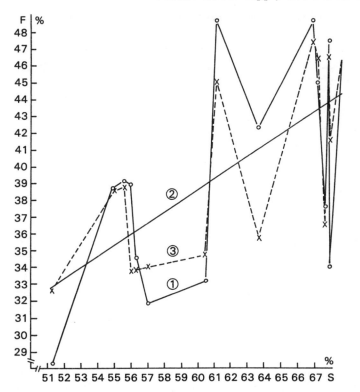

Figure 7.1 Share of women (F) and of service sector unemployment (S) in 15 European countries, 1985–6

Notes: (1) Actual data
       (2) F = −1.09 + 0.66 S
       (3) F = 20.85 + 0.23 S + 10.03 D

       F: Percentage of female employees in total employment.
       S: Share of employment in service sector
       D: Dummy variable (see text)

function of (relative) real income and 'feminist attitudes':

$$S = 55.93 + 0.03 \quad Y + 5.94 \quad D; \; R = 0.57 \qquad (4)$$
$$(12.12) \; (0.69) \qquad (1.55)$$

Comparing this with equation (1) we see again a sizeable increase in the correlation coefficient, with Y's influence falling far below the 10 per cent level of significance, while D's influence turns out to be significant at that level. Looking at the equations (3) and (4) and comparing them with (1) and (2) one obtains a strong hint that analyses of female participation in labour markets which concentrate on strictly economic variables may miss the decisive driving forces and may distort the chain of causation.

Since the fifteen nations analysed above contain rather different types of economic development, an alternative calculation was carried out by restricting the analysis to the 12 more developed countries, because of the possibility that the 'poorer' countries (Greece, Ireland, Spain) might belong to a different 'population'. It turns out that this rearrangement leaves the basic conclusions untouched, though there are, of course, some differences in the values of the parameters.[10]

The considerations up to this point have shown that present differences between countries as regards female labour market participation and service sector employment may be due to socio-cultural elements to a far greater extent than is normally indicated in predominantly economic studies. These noneconomic factors have been at work for a considerable time. In conclusion, we want to find out whether these forces also had an important influence on recent changes in female and tertiary employment shares. Following the same route as before, we now compare the *changes* in female and service sector employment shares in the fifteen countries between 1970–1 and 1985–6. The changes in female participation rates (*DF*) and of service sector employment shares (*DS*) are both measured in percentage points, i.e., they are obtained by subtracting column (1) from column (2) and column (3) from column (4) respectively in Table 7.1. The cross-section analysis over the fifteen countries without and with the socio-economic proxy (*D*) leads to the following results (with equations numbered in the same sequence as before):

$$DS = \quad 10.54 + 0.01 \quad Y; \; r = 0.12 \tag{1b}$$
$$(3.25) \; (0.39)$$
$$DF = \quad 0.52 + 0.55 \quad DS; \; r = 0.53 \tag{2b}$$
$$(0.17) \; (2.30)$$
$$DF = -0.97 + 0.53 \quad DS + 3.57 \quad D; \; R = 0.69 \tag{3b}$$
$$(-0.35) \; (2.49) \qquad (2.03)$$
$$DS = \quad 9.84 + 0.02 \quad Y - -0.79 \quad D; \; R = 0.18 \tag{4b}$$
$$(2.80) \;\; 0.60 \qquad (-0.27)$$

The impression one obtains is that in the more recent period there has obviously been a strong international drift towards the service sector (+ 12 percentage points on average in the 15 countries) which can probably be best explained on productivity and demand (Clark-Fourastié) lines with no significant influences stemming from either income differentials or 'feminism'. In contrast, the increased participation of women shows a significant relationship to both the economic factor (growing service sector) and the 'cultural' factor (inclusion of the latter raises the correlation coefficient from 0.53 to 0.69). It can be assumed that the upward effects of the two factors reinforced each other.

NOTES

1 For a representative choice of some recent work in this field see the papers contained in a special supplement on female labour supply in the *Journal of Labor Economics* (1985), 3, 1, 2.

2 The term 'revolution' is misplaced, because we deal here with a development which has its roots in the last century, but which has gained considerable momentum in recent decades. The parallel usage to industrial 'revolution' may be seen as an excuse. The remark that the 'feminist revolution' contains a multitude of non-economic elements is to be understood in terms of modern economics. It does not exclude the possibility that this revolution is itself 'caused' or influenced by economic elements in a wider sense. This would indeed be a main consideration in a Marxist approach which is characterized by the heroic attempt to combine economics and sociology in a single framework and thus to avoid the artificial separation and interruption of their interrelationships.

3 The passage from the *Report of the Council of Economic Advisers* quoted before is taken from this source.

4 Three historical periods which kept women more at home than in other countries are taken as a decisive influence on a lower propensity for participation in market work: the comparatively low share of agricultural employment in the Netherlands in the eighteenth century, a rather late and capital-intensive industrial development in the nineteenth century, and the absence of mobilization efforts to bring women into work during the Second World War.

5 'The growing literature on the history of women's work stresses the importance, extent and variety of women's contribution to both the market and non-market economy. Where participation is discussed, the role of women as wage earners is typically linked to household needs, labour market forces and institutional variables. These factors include the need to augment family income, the burden of domestic responsibilities, employers' willingness to use female labour, the degree of occupational segregation, industrial structure and organization and prevailing social attitudes' (Hatton and Bailey 1988: 695). That the sociopolitical factor comes last in the list is not due to chance: it is normally either neglected or just mentioned without entering the analysis.

6 See for instance Biffl (1988: 85).

7 Neubourg (1987: 161) stresses the differences in labour market attitudes and behaviour between Roman Catholic and other women in the Netherlands.

8 All the data concerning the share of Roman Catholics in the population are taken from *The Europe year book 1988* (London, 1988).

9 The critical values of t for the given sample (one-tail test) are 1.35 for 10 per cent significance, 1.77 for 5 per cent and 2.65 for 1 per cent. In subsequent regressions using the additional dummy variable, these critical values change to 1.36, 1.78 and 2.68 respectively.

10 In the twelve-country case the correlation coefficients for the formulae corresponding to equations (1) and (4) respectively are 0.16 and 0.45; for the formulas corresponding to equations (2) and (3) 0.41 and 0.78.

REFERENCES

Bergmann, B. R. and Adelman, I. (1973) 'The 1973 Report of the President's Council of Economic Advisers: The economic role of women; *American Economic Review* 63, pp. 509–14.

Biffl, G. (1988) *Arbeitsmarkt 2000*, Wien: Forschungsberichte aus Sozial- und Arbeitsmarktpolitik.

Hatton, T. J. and Bailey, R. E. (1988) 'Female labour force participation in interwar Britain', *Oxford Economic Papers* 40, pp. 695–718.

Nakamura, M., Nakamura, A. and Cullen, D. (1979) 'Job opportunities, the offered wage and the labor supply of married women', *American Economic Review* 69, pp. 787–805.

Neubourg, C. de (1987) *Unemployment, labour slack and labour market accounting. Theory, measurement and policy*, Groningen: University of Groningen.

Part II
Wages

8 Alternative dimensions in the theory of wages

(Translation of 'Unterschiedliche Dimensionen der Lohntheorie' in Arndt, H. (ed.) (1969) *Lohnpolitik und Einkommensverteilung*, Berlin: Duncker & Humblot, pp. 53–81)

There were times when the mentioning of a fourth dimension elicited creepy associations with mystical forces. I hope that no such effects will be caused by the title of my paper. What I have to say are more or less commonplace statements. Neither can I offer any sensational news nor do I have solutions for all the problems I am going to touch. The problems refer to a branch of economics which – so it seems to me – does not look very satisfactory at the present time: I refer to the theory of wages.

At a congress of the International Economic Association in 1954 which dealt with theoretical aspects of wage theory John Dunlop made the following remarks in his opening address:

> One of the consequences of improved and enlarged data is that we become less and less satisfied with existing theoretical systems. The ever-enlarging data challenge the theory at new points and impose new strains on theory. Part of the current dissatisfaction with wage theory arises from ever increasing factual knowledge of wage rates and the labour market.

And a little later he continues: 'It should also be reported as a fact that labour market or wage specialists have all been most uncomfortable with "received" theory. There have been no unabashed defenders in this group.'[1]

In the fourteen years that have passed since that conference information about wage formation and labour market processes has grown considerably. This has led to some interesting new theoretical hypotheses which will be mentioned later. These hypotheses, however, did not grow out of the traditional wage theory but were mainly developed in connection with new analyses of inflation, income distribution and labour market structures. As far as the basic models of wage theory are concerned, there seems little reason to be more satisfied with this theory today than was the case at the time of the above-mentioned congress.[2]

What are the weaknesses of neoclassical wage theory as it is presented in our textbooks? A look at this question will help us to get a better understanding for the recent attempts to find ways outside or parallel to the traditional theory which could throw more light on so far neglected dimensions of the wage problem.

If I had to answer a question about the inadequacy of neoclassical wage theory (based on marginal productivity theory) in brutal simplicity my answer would be that the basic weakness is that it was from the very beginning not a wage theory or a theory of the labour market but a price theory somewhat modified to meet labour market aspects. This was much less true – or not at all – for the wage theories of the classical period. They were genuine wage theories which tried to incorporate at least some of the specific aspects of wage formation into the main corpus of their analysis.

When dealing with these questions we should first of all note that the object of wage theory – the wage – itself displays very different 'dimensions'. One has to distinguish between money and real wages, between short-term and long-term wage developments, between micro- and macroaspects, and one has to analyse wage structures and wage dynamics. The wage-theoretical approaches of the physiocrats, of Smith and Ricardo, quite clearly tried to derive from an analysis of the specifities of the labour market an explanation of the long-term macroeconomic real wage level. The tendency of population to outgrow capital accumulation and agricultural production exerts a long-term pressure on wages and keeps them down to a subsistence level. Combined with a primitive quantity theory of money this approach also served as an explanation of long-run money wage levels.

A concrete labour market perspective also formed the base for Marx's views. He, too, derived a long-term real wage from forces which are typical for the labour market. In his theory biological (demographic) factors are replaced by (endogenous) economic factors – profit motive, technical labour-saving progress, competition – which lead to a continuous flow of job-seeking workers (reserve army of labour) which again has a tendency to shift wages towards a subsistence level. Marx admitted, however, that historically achieved standards can provide a counter-tendency and can become an element of long-term real wages ('historical subsistence wage'). It is characteristic for the formalistic bias of neoclassical theory that this last point is attacked as being a circular argument or as being too vague, instead of seeing it as an important attempt to come to grips with some specific sociological influences on labour markets. In some newer considerations of labour economists ideas of this sort are taken up.

With regard to wage movements in the short run the classical theory was less able to provide a specific labour market approach. Here we find already the reliance on market analogies taken over from price theory which later became so typical for wage theory in general and which led – as I shall try to show — to a severe limitation of the explanatory range of that theory. Short-term wages ('market wages') which can deviate from the 'normal' long-term real wage are in classical writings presented as the result of demand and supply without giving sufficient attention to the special circumstances which make an interpretation of demand and supply curves rather difficult in labour market conditions and reduce the meaning and importance of 'equilibrium solutions'.

When we turn to wage structures we have to acknowledge the remarkable contribution of Smith, which has retained its relevance till today. By pointing out that competition will tend to an equalization of 'net advantages' (rather than to an equalization of wages) he opened the door to a consideration of an important psychological dimension affecting the labour supply which goes beyond the purely pecuniary calculations of a narrowly defined *homo economicus*. With this approach he could, however, only cover part of the influences which determine existing wage differences and structural shifts. In this field there have been considerable theoretical advances in recent years. More will be said on this later.

The wage fund theory which came into vogue in mid-nineteenth century can also be said to have tried — at least in some of its formulations — to develop a specific and concrete wage theory. While the subsistence wage theories, with their biological and technological-sociological foundations, provided a long-term *supply* theory, the wage fund theory laid stress on *demand* elements in a short- or medium-period setting. In its real wage version this theory found a determinant of the average macroeconomic wage level: the available volume of wage goods which can not be augmented in the short period.

This is not the place for a critical evaluation of these early wage theories. They had a certain validity in the days when they were created and some of their ideas are still relevant for developing nations. In the context of this paper the only significant point is that these theories took their clues from the specific conditions ruling in labour markets. When they lost their influence in the second half of the nineteenth century their traditions survived only in the writings of some outsiders like Sydney and Beatrice Webb, Tugan-Baranowsky, Oppenheimer and among American institutionalists like Tannenbaum and Perlman. Part of this literature is theoretically not very satisfactory because of a predominance of vague and impressionistic formulations; but all these writers show a distinct tendency to enrich the economic analysis by sociological, political and psychological elements. The striking thing in the development of the 'official' academic wage theory over the past hundred years is how little notice was taken of the work and the endeavours of these outsiders.

The 'official' wage theory which after 1870 superseded the earlier classical theories was a child of the new and triumphant microeconomic price theory. The main ambition seemed to be to transfer the big X-diagram of demand and supply which performed so well in price theory lock, stock and barrel into the labour market setting. The marginal productivity theory provided a suitable tool in this process and could thus achieve a dominant position which it has maintained until today.[3] With demand and supply relations which exhibited more or less 'normal' forms it was then possible to apply the homely static and comparative-static methods of price theory in the analysis of wage formation. The probably most successful theoretical text-book of the interwar period, *The Theory of Wages* by John Hicks, opens quite characteristically with the following two sentences: 'The theory of the determination of wages in a free market is simply a special case of the general theory of value. Wages are the price of labour; and thus, in the absence of control, they are determined, like all prices, by supply and demand'.[4]

The parallels to prices which doubtlessly exist and which are important were thus made the centre of analysis while other elements became neglected or were not seen at all. The two-dimensional demand—supply relation held the stage. There were, of course, occasional remarks about the special role of the human element and at some stage or another one acknowledged the existence and possible consequences of labour market institutions (trade unions, employers' associations, public bodies).[5] But the human factor is often only mentioned because of a certain uneasiness that people and their services are treated like goods;[6] and the labour market organizations are usually treated as accidental exogenous factors instead as inherent phenomena of the labour market. If one had instead started primarily with an analysis of the *differences* between goods and labour markets then 'human' and institutional dimensions would have entered wage theory quite naturally and smoothly and the parallels between wages and prices would have been less conspicuous.[7] Let me elaborate this point a little further.

We start with a very trivial fact, the consequences of which are not always sufficiently considered. Wages as prices for labour and goods prices have, as we know, a twofold function: they are an instrument for a flexible regu-lation of demand and supply, and they present the income for workers and producers of goods. (Wages and prices are also important as cost elements, but this is irrelevant in the present context.) The neoclassical micro-economic price theory was mainly interested in the regulatory function of prices. The confrontation of demand and supply results in an 'equilibrium price' which obtains special weight because of its market-clearing qualities. As far as individual goods are concerned any equilibrium price level is in principle equally acceptable; the main point is that it secures the satisfaction of all demand and supply plans which are compatible with this price.

This model was transferred to the wage sphere, with some justification in the microeconomic case but with inexcusable carelessness in the macro-economic case. Let us begin with the less problematic microeconomic situa-tion, the determination of wages for a certain category of workers with prices and the wages of all other workers taken as given. This case could be particularly well approximated to the standard price analysis. Marginal productivity theory provided a (falling) demand curve and supply could be based on some simple plausible assumptions (e.g. fixed supply or mobility and slightly rising supply curves).

There are certain problems connected with the marginal productivity curve which will be treated later. For the present we can accept it as a realistic picture of the demand conditions for a given type of labour. Thus a falling demand curve and an inelastic or 'normal' supply curve – the usual X – was obtained and one could proceed to find an 'equilibrium wage' in full analogy to the 'equilibrium price'. If such an equilibrium wage could not be reached it could only be a consequence of disturbing interventions into labour market processes.

This analysis suffered from the very beginning from a neglect of the income aspects of wages and prices. When we consider these we find important differences which lead to significant differences in supply behaviour. The main difference is that the producer and/or seller of goods can arrange the amount and composition of his output normally much more flexibly than the seller of labour services. The producer can use more or fewer machines and workers, he can frequently use his equipment for a variety of goods, and after a certain time lag he can also move into quite different fields of production. Limiting factors are only the existing capital equipment and entrepreneurial capacities.

The situation looks quite different when we turn to the worker. When we neglect the happy Robinson Crusoe who picks his bananas when and for however long he chooses we have to face the normality of a regulated work period. There is no fine tuning of supply open to the individual worker: he or she must choose between forty hours per week or nothing at all. And the services she can and has to perform are – with her qualifications being given – fairly narrowly circumscribed and cannot be easily diversified. This is true quite independently of psychological resistances to regional or occupational change; it follows simply from a highly specialized division of labour, the difficulties of retraining, and the lack of time and money for affording bigger adjustment measures.

All this has obvious consequences for comparisons of the situation of a worker with that of an independent supplier of goods. The income of an entrepreneur is usually not completely dependent on the price of a single commodity. Partial demand reductions can be met by reducing the supply of the commodity in question (with possible reductions in cost) and a shift to other products. Considerable reductions in *individual* prices can therefore be borne fairly easily without endangering the income position of the producer. In the case of bigger firms there is the additional possibility of smoothing price and income fluctuations over longer periods. All these facts justify the use of a theoretical model which permits flexible adjustment towards equilibrium through relatively widely fluctuating prices.

Things look very different when we consider the normal case of wage receivers under this income aspect. The worker can only supply one rather narrowly defined 'commodity', his qualification, and he must sell it in narrowly circumscribed amounts of so many hours per week. To obtain a certain income the worker is left with only one action parameter: the wage rate. With the determination of the (hourly, weekly or monthly) wage rate his total income is already determined to a large extent. Changes in specific wages, and particularly reductions of specific wages, therefore acquire a much higher significance than changes of specific prices. With every specific wage change a certain group of people will experience a decisive and fairly uniform change in their income position. Price changes, on the other hand, will hit different producers very differently depending on their production programme and adjustment facilities. Only in cases of pure mono-production do we find a parallel to the wage case, although even there the producer has more room for output variation.

The differences in the price and wage situations just discussed make it understandable that wage reductions will be met with particularly strong resistance. To maintain a given special wage becomes a decisive question for a clearly defined group of people in their endeavour to uphold their habitual income and with it their economic and social status in society. This leads almost inevitably to solidaristic action and the emergence of defensive organizations.

Trade unions have often been viewed *exclusively* as organizations for protecting workers against the more powerful employers. This is certainly one and perhaps the most important aspect of unions. But a consideration of the strong income effects of wage changes for specific groups would have been enough to recognize that unions are not an accidental or 'disturbing' element but an endogenous phenomenon once the specifities of the labour market are taken into account. But instead of accepting this, one preferred – fascinated with the price model – to compare unions with price cartels and monopolies. We shall return later to the shakiness of these comparisons.

The close link between wage rate and total income thus provides a reason for particularly strong resistances against radical wage reductions. It is 'in the nature of things' that the ranges of variation for specific wages are normally much narrower than those for specific prices. This fact has been neglected for a long time. It is true that some economists – in recent times, for instance, Dobb and Kaldor – have pointed out that there exist lower limits for wage changes, viz the 'acceptable' subsistence minimum, below which revolutions would break out. But this limit is relevant only for big wage groups and presents the absolute minimum. Long before such limits are reached one can expect a considerable intensification of defensive action.

From this it follows that the theory of competitive prices, whose attraction lies in their capacity of fairly quick adjustments to equilibrium after demand or supply have changed, should not have been used as a model for the labour market or at least not without far-reaching modifications. It would then have been possible to elaborate more distinctly the comparatively narrow limits for wage changes, to point out the role of a 'recurrent linkage' in the wage setting process as Krelle has so aptly called it.

The greater rigidity of specific wages as compared with specific prices is fortified by still another factor when the income aspect is kept in mind. The income of all workers is the product of hourly wage rates times a fairly fixed multiplier (number of working hours). When the wages of a certain group of workers are under pressure their aspirations are not only influenced by their own existing wage but also by the wages paid to neighbouring occupational or regional groups. Every relative wage change automatically has repercussions on the relative economic and social status. Specific prices, on the other hand, have mainly their own past as the only standard of comparison; prices of other goods play a minor role. Even when entrepreneurs aspire to a 'conventional' income this will not be directly connected with the absolute or relative changes in the prices of specific goods.

The differences between prices and wages which have just been mentioned influence the adjustment process which takes place (under competition) when an 'equilibrium' has been upset. The wage level for a specific occupational group will not even approximately be the outcome of a flexible interaction between demand and supply forces but rather a hotly debated point within a range whose limits are determined by historical, sociological and political dimensions. Demand elements can then have an influence on the volume of employment in this occupation without necessarily ending up with a cleared market. Unemployment or labour shortages may exist for a considerable period without eliciting any tendencies towards an 'equilibrium wage'. Marginal productivity theory in its microeconomic setting therefore represents not a wage theory but rather an employment theory *after* the wage has been fixed. In the long run sectorial disequilibria have a better chance to be overcome through gradual changes in relative wages or through the migration of workers.[8]

In passing it should be noted that if wage theory had cut loose from competitive price equilibrium ideas right from the start in order to look at labour market conditions, it could have had a stimulating effect on price-theoretic developments. With the growing importance of big specialized investments many firms get tied to one or a few products for quite a time. This means that the price for these products obtains a decisive influence for the total income of the entrepreneur. Just as in the case of wages the price becomes a highly significant strategic instrument whose fluctuations have to be taken very seriously. A realistic wage theory could have been an important pointer to the problem of 'administered prices'. They, too, exist in an environment where the simple supply-demand cross has to be supplemented by additional dimensions and where the demand curve tells us more about sales at a given price than about the price formation itself. But the parallel between 'administered prices' and wages has its limitations. Firms have opportunities for monopolistic action which are not available to workers and they can try to increase sales at given prices through marketing strategies. Instead of the 'open bargaining', which takes place between employers and workers, we find 'hidden persuasion' in the consumer markets.

But let us return to wage theory as such. So far I have tried to show that the marginal productivity theory, by leaning heavily on competitive price theory and equilibrium concepts, has neglected a proper modelling of labour market specifities and has thus lost in relevance. But this is not the only weakness of marginal productivity theory. Other problems arise because the elements of marginal productivity theory do not correspond in a unique way to the different aspects of wage theory – micro–macro, short-term and long-term, real and nominal – so that it is difficult to come to a sensible unified combination.

A first difficulty of marginal productivity theory *as wage theory* is the tendency to neglect or simplify unduly the supply side which is required for finding the equilibrium wage.[9] When we look at the micro-aspect – a firm or a special sector – under a long-term perspective then the supply of labour can be almost perfectly elastic. At the wage which is normally paid for the required qualifications one can obtain any number of workers. The regulating mechanisms are migrations and the job choice of the younger generation. The wage level is given by conditions in comparable firms and sectors. Marginal productivity determines exclusively the number of workers employed. This constitutes a microeconomic employment theory.

In the short run, supply might prove to be fairly inelastic. Practical, financial and psychological obstacles restrict mobility. In this case we could obtain an equilibrium wage in the traditional fashion as the intersection between the short-run supply curve and the demand (marginal productivity) curve in the market concerned with ensuing sectorial full employment. Unfortunately this 'solution' suffers from the fact that under modern conditions of production marginal productivity analysis is not well suited to the short run period. The idea of a monotonously falling marginal productivity curve is based on the assumption of continuous and comparatively smooth opportunities for factor substitutions. This is certainly a plausible assumption for the long run. Depending on the cost relations between the various factors of production technologies and output mix can be planned and executed. But in the short run the possibilities for substitution are much smaller. The labour input of a firm or industry is determined to a large extent by the existing capital equipment. We have – in the terminology of Leif Johansen – an important difference between ex ante and ex post substitution. Ex ante substitution possibilities can be considerable, ex post they are much smaller. This means that at the level of the firm the physical marginal productivity of additional workers is fairly constant up to the point of full capacity (e.g. through employment at unused machines) and falls away rapidly after that point has been reached. Instead of finding a continuously falling marginal productivity curve we can be faced with a Z-curve with horizontal and vertical segments.[10]

If under these conditions the labour supply curve intersects the marginal productivity curve somewhere in the (almost) vertical segment the firm will find it profitable to produce at full capacity where marginal productivity and the corresponding potential wage lie above the point of intersection of demand and supply curves. Employment will be determined by the capacity level while the wage remains indeterminate between the minimum supply price of labour and the maximum demand price of the employer.

If we introduce collective bargaining and dismiss extreme wage pressure from unemployed workers as unrealistic we thus arrive at the conclusion that demand and supply do not deliver a unique short-term equilibrium 'solution' at the micro-level. There are certain limits within which there is room for bargaining. But traditional theory had little to say on this bargaining process.[11] When we move from firm to industry level these difficulties are less pronounced. For an industry the marginal productivity schedule approximates a 'normal' shape. Different firms enter the market at different limit wages and have different capacity outputs and − above all − with changes at the industry level the prices of the output are affected so that the value of the physical marginal product will fall as additional workers are employed.

Thus we see that at the micro-level marginal productivity theory fails as a wage theory in the long run and is only partly applicable in the short run. When we turn to the macro-level the situation is not much better. As an advantage it can be noted that here we get a genuine supply curve which is no longer dependent on given wage levels in other sectors. This supply curve is certainly not easy to ascertain and the question of its concrete form has been badly neglected by the marginal productivity school for a long time.[12] In many cases one chose an easy way out by simply assuming a fixed supply of labour. But this is a shortcoming which in principle can be overcome even though the practical difficulties are considerable. But now we find that under the macroeconomic perspective the demand side creates some special problems. The marginal productivity curve which in the micro-case could be at least of some service proves to be a blunt instrument in the macroeconomic analysis.

To show this we must distinguish between money and real wages. When we deal with money wages the marginal productivity curve ceases to be the determinant of the wage level. The demand for labour depends on both the real marginal productivity and the price of the good. But while in microstudies the price of the good can be taken as given and is independent of the wages paid by the firm, this is no longer the case when we deal with the macro-sphere. Here changes of the wage rate necessarily react on price. The demand curve, which is meant to explain money wages, itself depends on the level of money wages. A macroeconomic version of the marginal productivity approach modelled on the microeconomic example is therefore doomed to failure. A way out can only be found – as we know since Keynes – by looking at wages as the outcome of the macro-relations as a whole. This means that the traditional demand and supply categories must be supplemented by other dimensions such as monetary policy, expectations, foreign trade positions, etc. With these complications entering the picture one need not be surprised when a well-known macroeconomic theorist in his study of wages and income distribution suddenly comes to the conclusion: 'I am not sure where "marginal productivity" comes in in all this'.[13]

The situation looks more hopeful when we deal with macroeconomic aspects of real wages. The marginal productivity approach can indeed deliver an intellectually satisfactory frame when we look for equilibrium wages in a competitive (competition on labour and goods markets) one-product world. In this case we have a clearly defined real marginal product which can provide a basis for determining the equilibrium real wage.[14] The esoteric nature of such a model is obvious.[15]

As soon as we extend the model so as to include more than one commodity we run into some difficulties which are connected with the index problem. The real marginal product of labour is now a basket of goods whose contents can be changed by variations of the labour input. The wage goods which serve as payment for the workers have a composition which differs from that of the total output. Without a knowledge of relative prices it is not possible to compare the marginal product (of total output) with the wages paid to labour. But the price relations in turn are not independent of the wage level because this level affects the income distribution and with it the structure of demand and prices.

The remarks so far have been restricted to some problems which one has to face even when one uses the marginal productivity theory as a comprehensive wage theory only in the narrow confines of competitive equilibrium analysis. To this has to be added the neglect of those important special labour market aspects which have been mentioned earlier. The concentration on marginal productivity is also a step back compared with classical and Marxian economics in its failure to look into the social and power elements which lie *behind* demand and supply and which can influence factor scarcities and factor remunerations. Erich Preiser has strongly criticized this sin of omission.[16]

Summarizing we can say that the victorious marginal productivity theory can only provide a partial contribution for a solution of wage-theoretical problems and questions. It offers a useful basis for analysing labour demand at the firm and industry level, particularly in the longer run, and it contains useful hints for the analysis of wage levels and wage structures if and when wage formation follows the rules of competitive price models. Normally, marginal productivity elements will be involved, but they will only be able to explain some aspects of the wage formation process.

The dominant influence of the price and equilibrium perspective in the neoclassical wage theory meant that for a long time no proper access to the trade union problem could be found. While – as I tried to show before – the rise of unions can be expected almost as an inevitable development when the peculiarities of the labour market are heeded, it was seen as a monopoly enforced 'from outside' under the market-price perspective.[17]

The frequent equation of unions with monopolies is a particularly striking example of the dominance of price-theoretic thinking in traditional wage theories. Parallels between monopolies and unions do, of course, exist. In both cases we observe an endeavour to raise incomes above the level which would rule in the absence of intervention on the market. But with this the analogy ends and the differences become important.

The seller of goods has – according to monopoly theory – the unique and clear-cut aim of maximizing profits which he can tackle with a price or volume strategy. This is a maximization problem. We must also note that the monopolist can act unilaterally when he chooses his strategy (price or volume adjustments). He can experiment on the market without having to consult his 'opponents', the consumers.

Unions have to operate under very different circumstances. They cannot, like monopolies, simply aim at a maximum wage sum without any thoughts about volume effects. They cannot remain indifferent *vis-à-vis* the employment of their actual or potential members. Their main task consists of finding a compromise between two partly contradictory aims – the achievement of high wages and of high employment. It is not a problem of maximization but of optimization.[18] Also, most of the time the unions can use only price strategies and not volume strategies, and they can set their actions only at distinct times and by way of negotiation. Unilateral declarations are normally not feasible.

These differences, which are firmly rooted in the basic economic structure, should have been fully acknowledged from the very beginning (including historical circumstances influencing the concrete forms of different union organizations). If this had been the case unions would have been a 'natural' and essential component of labour market analysis. Such a realistic wage theory could have offered useful hints for some newer developments in price theory. Some oligopolostic behaviour patterns show a certain analogy to union strategies. Thus an oligopolistic firm is not only interested in short-term profit maximization, but aims also (for security reasons) at a continuous and long-term presence of its goods on the market. Just like unions it cannot be indifferent to quantity variations. Unlike the monopolistic firm its target is not maximum profits but a compromise between high profits and a big turnover.[19]

In other respects, too, parallels can be detected. The oligopolistic environment induces firms to keep prices fixed for certain periods at a time. Price setting thus becomes an important strategic element. But here the difference from unions is relevant: price setting does not require a direct agreement with the customers. Firms have more freedom of action than unions. In big firms where the fixing of the price is left to a committee on which the interests of different departments are represented (marketing, costs, finance, wage negotiations, etc.) price setting also becomes a bargaining process. But the fundamental conflict of interests typical for wage negotiations is absent.

After this short excursion into price theory I want to return to the subject of this paper. So far I have given a rough sketch of the wage-theoretic frame which has been handed down to us by our neoclassical fathers. The weakness of the basic approach, the neglect of important dimensions of the labour market problem, have led to that feeling of dissatisfaction to which I have referred earlier. But fortunately the dissatisfaction has been a productive one. The last twenty to thirty years have seen a considerable number of attempts to arrive at a more realistic analysis of the wage formation process. It is significant, however, that these new developments are not so much an expansion of the traditional theory (which proved rather sterile), but have been inspired by ideas from other branches of economic theory and of social sciences in general. Keynes's employment theory provided a strong impetus for a discussion of the determinants of the macroeconomic money-wage level and led to decisive debates about the relative roles of money and real wage changes;[20] the 'labour economists' (who had always stayed a bit outside mainstream economics), the institutionalists and some developments in organization theory have contributed interesting and realistic interpretations of interest divisions on the labour market;[21] economists with sociological and psychological leanings have seen to it that the bargaining process gets the attention it deserves;[22] other sociologically motivated economists have taken up the long-neglected questions of wage structures and their changes;[23] and more recently inflation theory has opened up new vistas on the theory of money wage changes.[24]

This is not the place for a detailed discussion of all the new developments which have proved relevant for the wage problem. Instead I shall try to give a short account of the new dimensions which have been added to the simple picture of demand, supply and equilibrium wage. In doing this I hope that the various aspects of the wage formation process will become visible.

We should begin with the rediscovery of macroeconomic thinking which has been so fruitful in almost all branches of economic theory. The greater consideration given to circular-flow relationships, which are highly relevant for the analysis of macroeconomic wage changes, have enabled us to obtain completely new insights into wage and distributional processes. The basis for this development has been laid by economists whose main concern was the study of employment, cycles and economic growth: Keynes, Föhl, Joan Robinson, Kalecki, Kaldor and some others. Wage theorists who had been used to partial analysis were at first rather reluctant to follow this line of reasoning. Today this has changed. Macroeconomic circular-flow analysis has 'made it' and today we are faced with an *embarras de richesse* rather than a lack of understanding when it comes to finding hypotheses about macroeconomic wage problems.

Another question – the sociological aspect as a dimension of labour markets – has perhaps been treated more continuously throughout the years (though at rather modest levels) but without achieving any startling results. In the writings of the classics – particularly in Adam Smith – societal aspects occupied an important place. Marx is, of course, an example *par excellence* for his attempt to cover economics and sociology and their inter-relationship in one single system. Neoclassical economics, however, pushed sociological considerations into the background: the age of 'pure economics' had begun. Only in Marxist literature and among a comparatively small circle of 'outsiders' in the historical and institutionalist 'schools' was an interest in the sociological and power elements of wage conflicts consistently maintained. In these works, however, the economic aspects did not always get the necessary weight.[25] But in more recent times we experience a richer stream of empirical data and new general considerations which permit a fuller treatment of all the relevant aspects.

Sociology is a wide country and when we speak of the sociological dimension of wage theory we must distinguish between different layers. First of all we are faced with the all-pervasive sociological occurrence of power and power hierarchies. That such a basic social phenomenon is hardly visible in a branch of social sciences is a serious shortcoming of modern economics in general as critical methodologists have frequently remarked.[26] But in the study of labour market problems, where unequal positions of the actors are far more decisive than on goods markets, such a neglect can have fatal consequences. The roles of unequal power and property positions and of the unequal bargaining positions derived from them are of such decisive significance for the wage system and for wage levels – particularly in the long run – that they have to be kept permanently in mind if one wants to avoid misinterpretations. Political power structures have also to be considered in view of their considerable legal and institutional influence on labour market processes. Quite a number of failures of policy recommendations for developing countries could have been avoided or at least mitigated if the economists had learned to develop a certain 'feeling' for sociological factors and power structures. Questions of power constellations, property and class relations, which form the background for the wage problem, took centre-stage in Marx's work. Before him Adam Smith had already shown a thorough awareness of these factors. In our century only a few economists outside the Marxist tradition have given power a proper place in their considerations. Oppenheimer, Preiser, Hans Peter and Galbraith can be mentioned as outstanding examples.

Another sociological aspect that is relevant in the context of wage theory lies in the cluster of problems which can be covered by the term group behaviour. Neoclassical wage theory is very distinctly a child of the competitive price model with its assumptions of atomistic competition and the individualistic *homo oeconomicus*. The special problems that arise when people act as a group and form organizations were neglected. With the growth of interest in organizations and corporate structures this neglect became increasingly apparent, and this not only in the field of labour economics, where this shortcoming was particularly prominent. In the past twenty years these problems have found growing attention, but no definite theoretical structures have emerged so far.

In this sphere we can distinguish two important approaches to the problems. On the one hand we have the French school of sociologically orientated economists like Marchal and Lecaillon, who analyse the different behaviour patterns of big interest groups (workers, salaried employees, entrepreneurs, peasants, etc.) in their struggle for income and income shares in the modern mixed economy. That in such a context wage adjustment processes follow other rules than those suggested by neoclassical models is hardly surprising.

The other type of approach follows a line which twenty years ago was argued with considerable force by the American economist Ross.[27] He stressed the special role of big organizations whose behaviour is motivated not only (or not even predominantly) by the interests of their members but also – and to an increasing extent – by their own organizational needs and interests. 'Mature' unions should be seen not only as economic interest bodies or monopolies, but also partly in the light of political theories and concepts. Representative organizations of employers, and to some extent big enterprises, could also be treated in this way.

The growing consideration of sociological and socio-psychological elements has stimulating effects on the theoretical treatment of wage structures. As mentioned earlier this is a branch where Adam Smith's elegant market theory of an equalization of net advantages dominated the field for a long time. It is true that ever since Cairnes it was known that the labour market is divided into almost watertight submarkets separated by individual, economic and social barriers, which prevent a tendency towards wage equalization. Over the years these barriers were studied in great detail but the basic concept of a long-term tendency towards equal wages (modified by non-monetary advantages and disadvantages) was maintained.

Up to a point such a tendency certainly exists. But even in the very long run it has not achieved that degree of levelling that one would have expected if it were a decisive force. It is also not easily compatible with the remarkable constancy of wage differences between various industries[28] which cannot be fully explained by skill differentials. In her book about the social foundations of wage policy, Barbara Wooton speaks – not without irony – of the unsatisfactory state of a theory which turns an exception – viz. strong levelling tendencies – into a rule and then tries to explain a contradictory reality with reference to special influences. This is, she continues, as if geographers – in view of the undoubted tendencies of rivers to exert pressure on the river banks – felt obliged to explain above all why river banks are not continuously flooded.[29]

Today few people would stick to the idea that a theory of wage structures can rely completely on demand and supply mechanisms in the various sector markets. Societal and institutional forces have direct effects on the structure of wages; these must to some extent conform to the conditions of the economic framework, but can also influence that framework on their part. In contemporary literature we find a rich menu of sociological and psychological elements, which have an influence on wage structures, but which are frequently neglected in the traditional theory of wages. Habit, wage leadership, maintenance of group relativities and bargaining rituals in collective negotiations are examples of the factors that can have a noticeable influence on wage structures (and thus on specific wages) at least in the short run, but which leave their mark on long-term developments too.

With group behaviour, organizations and interest lobbies becoming essential ingredients of labour market research (rather than mere disturbing elements), questions regarding bargaining and negotiation skills come to life. In a few cases economic theorists had already seen these questions as a decisive element for the wage formation problem. Early on the Webbs were aware of it and among later theorists we might name Pigou, Zeuthen, Dobb and a few economists who saw wage negotiations in the (false) light of a bilateral monopoly. But these 'outsider' approaches found only a faint echo in traditional wage theories. It was only after the Second World War that bargaining problems were attacked more seriously and on a wider basis. The original impulse however, came not so much from the wage-theoretical corner but mainly from other branches of economic theory (e.g. oligopoly theory) and other branches of social science (e.g. political science). The analysis of bargaining processes can follow different courses. It reaches from generalized game theory (Neumann-Morgenstern) via formalized wage-bargaining models à la Pen[30] to detailed studies about general principles of bargaining strategies and tactics.[31] What has been said about other sociological extensions is also valid here: the volume of relevant insights is growing at considerable speed but we are still missing firmly established theoretical constructions.

Another important dimension of the wage problem which partly intersects with sociological aspects is the time factor. As in the sociological case we can distinguish different aspects of the time dimension. In a recently published book[32] Shackle enumerates three different aspects of time which play a role in economic theory. There is, to begin with, 'mechanical' time, i.e. the normal lapse of time. It is the type of time which we use in dynamic and growth models where each economic variable has a date affixed to it. Then there is an aspect which Shackle calls 'biological' time. This is the span of time which a given adjustment process requires. A typical example is Marshall's distinction between the short and the long period in adjustments of capital equipment or in the entry and exit of firms on the path towards equilibrium. This meaning of time has always been important in comparative statics. Finally time has an economic significance in the form in which it enters the plans of economic agents. This 'imaginary' time reaches – as remembrance – into the past and – as expectations – into the future.[33]

'Biological' time made an early appearance in wage theory. Distinctions between short-term, long-term and very long-run equilibria in adjustment processes of population, occupational structures, production patterns, etc. were familiar to classical wage theorists and were taken over by neoclassical writers. The other aspects of time did not receive the same attention. It is only in our generation that their importance has become appreciated more fully.

In Keynes's employment theory the importance of time as a decisive factor in decision processes was duly stressed. This was particularly the case in relation to wages. His special emphasis on downward money wage rigidity involved an acknowledgement that memories of the past are a potent factor in the wage formation process. In our days of relatively full employment we see that this principle of 'linking on to the past' must be extended – in a slightly milder form – to real wages and even to wage increases, as can be seen in the presently much discussed 'wage rounds'.[34] This is certainly a very important factor in the wage formation process. Similar effects, of course, can also be found in the field of prices. But the direct income effect of wages, which we mentioned earlier, as well as the technique of wage agreements, make the past a far more significant element in the wage process than is the case for prices in general or for the model of competitive prices in particular.[35]

Expectations – the future-orientated aspect of 'imaginary' time – had also received increased attention before the war in Keynes's work and particularly in the writings of the Swedish school. But they played their main part in the analysis of investment and interest rates. Wage changes were important as *causes* for expectations which would then influence investment and employment. For wage theory as such it would be more important to obtain a clearer picture about the influence of expectations on the behaviour of the contracting partners and on the bargaining process. Here we have a fairly wide field for further research.

'Mechanical' time – time as date and time of the day – has slowly begun to take its share in dealing with the wage problem. But the problems are not specific to wage-theoretical questions. The dynamization of economic theory and growth processes had been neglected for a long time. Now that this neglect has been overcome the time dimension necessarily becomes explicit. Wage analysis is following this trend rather slowly. Price theory, for instance, can at least present the cobweb theorem as an early approach to a dynamic process. Growth theory has then occupied itself with the dynamic changes of the big aggregates– income, employment, consumption, investment. In the wage sector dynamization attempts are of more recent date with inflation theory and wage-price spirals as main impulses. Building on the Phillips curve – now in its tenth year – which made money wage increases a function of the unemployment rate (representing demand pressure on the labour market) further elements were added which could help to see the wage formation as a dynamic process. The rate of change of wages is in these models a 'dated' magnitude which is 'explained' by the dynamics of the model. As an example we can mention the model by Perry[36] in which the wage change is a function of the unemployment rate and of past changes of prices, profits and profit changes (this last item as a dummy for entrepreneurial expectations). Since the wage changes in turn have an influence (with a time lag) on prices and profits we obtain a dynamic model which gives us the course of wage rate changes (though not of wage levels) through time.

I hope that what has been said so far gives an impression of the many facets of the wage-theoretic problem. Many influences and dimensions which are relevant for the micro- and macro-aspects of wage formation have been neglected by the traditional wage theory or relegated to a minor position. This is the reason for the frequent dissatisfaction with the neoclassical model. As I have tried to show, things have begun to change and important new ideas have been introduced in recent years from various branches of economic theory.

This, then, is the position in which we find ourselves today. Wage theory certainly does not present itself as a nicely rounded theory. Indeed it would be difficult to give a convincing comprehensive account of the essential basics of wage theory. This state of affairs is responsible for the multitude of econometric models which aim at an 'explanation' of cyclical, inflationary and long-term developments. There are no clear and common ideas which relevant elements must be included in a wage function. Thus the experts are usually forced to construct their special wage function which will be more or less usable for the problems in hand.[37]

The 'solutions' – frequently makeshift solutions – can then range from exiling wage formation and wage rates into the exogenous framework (e.g. in the early models of the Central Planning Bureau of the Netherlands) via simple assumptions about growth rates of wages[38] to a variety of modifications of the Phillips demand model. In addition to the wage function of Perry, which was mentioned earlier, one can name as another typical specimen the wage functions used by Klein, Ball, Hazlewood and Vandome in their 'medium-sized' econometric model of the United Kingdom.[39] There the change in union (money) wage rates is made a function of unemployment and price changes (both lagged by two quarters) and of a dummy which covers the sociological fact of a switch in union strategies from a period of moderation to one of a more active wage policy. This equation – covering collective agreements – is supplemented by a further equation which 'explains' the wage drift (the deviation of actual earnings from contractual rates) on the basis of hours worked per week and labour productivity in industry. A similar model for Germany has been worked out by Harald Scherf.[40]

The econometric studies, with their realistic orientation, have contributed to a clearer insight into various relevant relationships. But they could not – and did not intend to – find a solution for the theoretical calamity. While the traditional theory too often proved to be 'theory without measurement', some of the econometric studies tend to be – in the phrase of Koopmans – 'measurement without theory' or at least with very loose theoretical ties. Let down by a theory which lacks a firm basis, econometricians feel their way towards statistically plausible explanations which are accepted when a satisfactory 'fit' is achieved.[41]

What about the future? Theories about theories are usually on still shiftier ground than these theories themselves, so no reliable forecasts can be expected. But a few concluding remarks might be in place.

One can expect that the numerous supplementary ideas and modifications which have come from other branches of economics and other social sciences will gradually find a more secure place in the main body of wage theory. Some problems will be consolidated, some neglected factors will be accepted as relevant. But with the acknowledgement of the multi-dimensional nature of the wage problem all hopes for relatively simple equilibrium solutions will have to be abandoned. The various dimensions which influence labour market processes – economic, sociological, historical, psychological – are interlinked in such a complex manner that one cannot expect the emergence of continuous and reversible functions.

Seen from this perspective some of the smooth and frequently linear relationships between wages and a few 'explanatory' variables which we find in present-day econometric studies[42] can only be regarded as a first and rough approximation. Gradually one will have to advance to more complicated models which can take care of the fact that some influences are only effective within or beyond certain limits, that some relations are non-linear and/or irreversible and so on. Thus – to take a simple example – wage changes may not depend in a continuously linear fashion on price and profit changes as assumed in various models. A more probable relationship might be that price changes lead to certain wage changes with a high probability and these might then be modified when profit changes surpass a certain threshold. Concretely: let us say a rise in prices of 5 per cent normally leads – within a certain range – to wage increases of 4.5 percent; with profits changing by (say) more than ±5 percent there will, however, be an additional reaction.[43] This simple 'threshold-example' should probably also include irreversibility. A reduction of prices by 5 per cent is likely to call forth other reactions than a rise of the same magnitude. Complications like these would have to be included to a much greater extent if the interdependence of the various dimensions of the wage problem are to get a proper hearing.[44]

A further group of questions which should be considered to a greater extent than so far in future wage studies are historical and institutional influences. They play – both in the short and long run – a far greater role in labour market research than in most other branches of economics.

In view of the multitude of influences, their mutual dependence and their varying cyclical, institutional and historical background it would obviously be Utopian to ask for a fully comprehensive realistic theoretical model.[45] An efficient wage theory will have to provide usable building elements — more usable than up till now — which can be combined in varying ways in order to find answers to concrete problems in concrete circumstances.[46] If we continue to progress on this path it should be possible to overcome the present stage of scepticism and to produce a comparatively well-developed wage and labour market theory. But even then its efficient application to reality will still require a considerable portion of experience, judgement and analytical skill.

NOTES

1 J. T. Dunlop, 'The task of contemporary wage theory' in Dunlop, J.T. (ed.) (1957) *The Theory of Wage Determination*, London: Macmillan. A much sharper formulation was chosen by P. Samuelson, in his paper 'Economic theory and wages' (in McCord Wright, D. (ed.) (1951) *The Impact of the Union*, New York: Harcourt Brace): 'I fear that when the economic theorist turns to the general problem of wage determination and labor economics, his voice becomes muted and his speech halting. If he is honest with himself, he must confess to a tremendous amount of uncertainty and self-doubt concerning even the most basic and elementary parts of the subject' (312).

2 More recently J. Lübbert has given a rather pessimistic opinion. After referring to the quotation from Samuelson given in the previous note he continues that he doubts 'that in the time which has passed since that statement was made our knowledge about the determinants of labour market processes has made any progress' (Lübbert, J. (1967) 'Lohnpolitik ohne Lohntheorie', *Hamburger Jahrbuch*, 12, p. 70).

3 Thus only fifteen years ago W. Fellner could still declare at the annual conference of the American Economic Association: 'By contemporary distribution theory we probably mean a qualified marginal productivity theory; that is to say, a combination of the marginal productivity theory with other analytical elements' (Fellner, W. (1953), 'Significance and limitations of contemporary distribution theory', *American Economic Review* 43, 2).

4 Hicks, J. R. (1932) *The Theory of Wages*, London: Macmillan.

5 L. Robbins speaks of the 'profound unease and uncertainty' among the later classical economists when they have to deal with trade unions. See Robbins, L. (1952) *The Theory of Economic Policy in English Classical Political Economy*, London: Macmillan.

6 As an example we can quote the following remark from a recently published monograph on wage changes and unemployment (Perry, G. L. (1966) *Unemployment, Money Wage Rates and Inflation*, Cambridge, MA: MIT Press). After stressing the price character of wages Perry adds: 'Requirements of human dignity surround the purchase and sale of labor services with special problems not associated with other commodities' (19). But it is not necessary to base the special problems on human dignity which does not always rank high in a profit economy. As we shall see a number of much more robust facts justify a special treatment of wages.

7 'The number of characteristics which are common to the labour markets of an economy and which are distinctly different from goods market characteristics is

in my opinion sufficiently big to justify a disengagement of the analysis of the determinants of wage formation from its strong dependence on the methods of price formation analysis' (Lübbert, *op. cit.*, p. 88).

8 These long-term adjustment and regrouping processes have been treated in several publications by J. Marchal.

9 This has been clearly criticized by Dunlop: 'Strictly, marginal productivity is not a theory of wages, but only a statement of the demand side. From the outset the supply schedule has been a weak tool.... In time, many writers came close to the position that the wage rate was determined outside the system, and marginal productivity indicated how much labour would be employed at that wage' (Dunlop, *op. cit.*, p. 9).

Also, E. Preiser has pointed out that marginal productivity theory suffers from a neglect of the supply side (Preiser, E. (1953) 'Erkenntniswert und Grenzen der Grenzproduktivitätstheorie', *Schweizerische Zeitschrift für Volkswirtschaft und Statistik* 89, 1, p. 32).

10 This case corresponds to empirical results where cost curves of a firm are not U-shaped but where average and marginal costs are constant up to capacity and these begin to rise sharply. See for instance Andrews, P. U. S. (1949) *Manufacturing Business*, New York: Macmillan, p. 102; Johnston, J. (1960) *Statistical Cost Analysis*, New York: McGraw Hill, p. 13 and ch. 5.

Conditions of this sort (among others) are given decisive influence on wage formation by E. Kuh (1967) in his paper 'A productivity theory of wage levels – An alternative to the Phillips curve' (*Review of Economic Studies*, 34, 100), where average labour productivity takes the place of marginal productivity as main determinant (338).

11 If production remains below capacity level, marginal productivity is even less suitable as a guide under these conditions. With a horizontal marginal productive curve we get (with constant prices) equality of average and marginal product per worker so that setting the wage equal to marginal product would mean that the entire revenue goes to the workers.

12 See W. Krelle's article (1961) on 'Löhne (Theorie)' in *Handwörterbuch der Sozialwissenschaften*, vol. 7, Göttingen: Vandenhoeck & Ruprecht, pp. 9–10.

13 Kaldor, N. (1955–6), 'Alternative theories of distribution', *Review of Economic Studies*, 23, 2, p. 100. See also the recent heated discussion about the relevance or irrelevance of marginal productivity in macroeconomic distribution models between Samuelson, Modigliani, Pasinetti, J. Robinson and Kaldor in the *Review of Economic Studies,* 33, 96 (1966), pp. 269–330.

14 We assume that a suitable supply function of labour can be constructed.

15 The relative usefulness of marginal productivity analysis in simple real macroeconomic models explains why the principle of marginal productivity can lead such an unmolested life in all studies which work with macroeconomic Cobb-Douglas functions. In these cases the condition of simple real macroanalysis is met.

16 E . Preiser, *op. cit.*

17 On this see Wooton, B. (1955), *The Social Foundations of Wage Policy*, London: Allen & Unwin, p. 17.

18 The economic problems of union strategy were excellently treated by J. Dunlop in his *Wage Determination under Trade Unions* (1944), New York: Macmillan. Elizabeth Liefmann-Keil has given a good characterization of the difference:

The strategy of the partners in collective bargaining is not a market strategy in the usual meaning of the word. The central question of price theory, the question of the equilibrium price, is therefore not relevant in this case. The assumption that one has only to look for the price which corresponds to the given demand and supply curves is here particularly artificial. The process is more directed towards influencing the assumptions of the other part in one's own favour and it can happen that for certain periods there exists no interest at all in finalizing a contract. All attempts to analyse these strategies with the instruments used in bilateral monopoly theory are inadequate because the assumptions under which this theory works (e.g. drive for maximum profits) are rarely applicable. In particular the strategy in wage negotiations is not a market strategy because the parties are neither for themselves nor for other buyers or sellers. The unions and employers' representatives are organizations of potential buyers and sellers.

(Liefmann-Keil, E. (1961) *Ökonomische Theorie der Sozialpolitik*, Berlin: Springer, p. 320)

19 See the oligopoly model in Baumol, W. (1959) *Business Behavior*, New York: Macmillan.
20 See several articles in the *Economic Journal*, 1938 and 1939.
21 See Ross, A. M. (1948) *Trade Union Wage Policy*, Berkeley: University of California Press; Lester, A.R. (1951) *Labor and Industrial Relations*, New York: Macmillan.
22 A good overview of bargaining approaches is given in Külp, B. (1965), *Lohnbildung in Wechselspiel zwischen politischen und wirtschaftlichen Kräften*, Berlin: Duncker & Humblot.
23 In this field German economic literature has produced a considerable output. Among others one can mention contributions by Hoffmann, Fürstenberg, Klaus, Lampert, Weissel, Mieth and Mayer. US authors have also given increased attention to these matters (e.g. Dunlop, Reynolds, Taft, Reder, Garbarino, Salkever).
24 An important impetus in this direction was given by Phillips, A.W. (1958) 'The relation between unemployment and the rate of change of money wages', *Economica* 25, 100, pp. 283–99.
25 Böhm-Bawerk's famous 1914 essay 'Macht oder ökonomisches Gesetz' ('Power or economic law' in *Zeitschrift für Volkswirtschaft, Sozialpolitik und Verwaltung*, 23, pp. 205–71) was a remarkable attempt to build a bridge between marginal productivity theory (which he accepted) and the 'power' theories proposed by 'outsiders' like Stolzmann, Lexis and Tugan-Baranowsky. His essay contained elements of many developments which gained importance in wage theory later on, such as monopsony, efficiency effects of higher wages, wage-price spirals (though these terms were not used by Böhm-Bawerk). Böhm-Bawerk's endeavour was to 'translate' various sociological phenomena into the language of productivity theory so as to 'save' the latter as the basic analytical instrument. (The same can be said, by the way, of Machlup's arguments in the famous controversy between the 'labour economist' Lester and the 'pure economists' Machlup and Stigler in the pages of the *American Economic Review* in the years 1946–7.) Böhm-Bawerk however, made no attempt to turn the sociological factors into an essential element in the basic structure of wage theory. But he showed at least an understanding for the importance of these factors which is more than can be said of many later wage theorists.
26 See Albert, H. (1960), 'Nationalökonomie als Soziologie', *Kyklos*, 13, 1, pp. 1–43.
27 A. M. Ross, *op. cit.*
28 See Hoffmann, W. G. (1961), *Die branchenmässige Lohnstruktur der Industrie*, Tübingen: JCB Mohr.
29 B. Wooton, *op. cit.*, p. 16.
30 Pen, J. (1959) *The Wage Rate under Collective Bargaining*, Cambridge, MA: Harvard University Press.

31 A good example of the latter group is Schelling, T. C. (1960) *The Strategy of Conflict*, Cambridge, MA: Harvard University Press.

32 Shackle, G. L. S. (1965) *A Scheme of Economic Theory*, London: Cambridge University Press. Similar ideas regarding the time problem had been touched forty years ago by Rosenstein-Rodan (see his article 'Grenznutzen' in *Handwörterbuch der Staatswissenschaften*, 4th ed., vol. 4, Jena 1927, pp. 1197–8). He distinguished between technological ('objective') and psychological ('subjective') components of the time problems, which he regarded – in line with Marshall and Edgeworth – as probably 'the most difficult of all economic problems'.

33 Expectations only play a role when the future cannot be fully foreseen. This assumption is made. Earlier models often accepted the hypothesis of perfect foresight so that expectations could be replaced by a known and discounted future as an element in present calculations and decisions.

34 Turner, H. A. (1952), 'Trade unions, differentials and the levelling of wages', *Manchester School* 20, 3.

35 If the aim were to find a 'construct' which guarantees a high precision of estimates of current money or real wages (single wages or general wage level) I think I would prefer to get information about the wages ruling the past two years rather than derive them from contemporary demand and supply information. Where (individual) prices are concerned such a practice would probably be less successful. Links with past levels provide, for instance, the basis for the wage function which Krelle, Beckerhoff and Lauger use in their macro-model of the German economy ('A medium term prognostication model for the German economy', paper prepared for the congress of the Econometric Society in Bonn, August 1967). The estimate for average hourly wage rates in the private sector is derived on the basis of average wage increases in preceding years with some modifications added to allow for changes in economic policies. In contrast to this, econometric wage functions which build on the Phillips curve are examples for a demand-determined approach (with special assumptions about downward rigidities).

36 G. L. Perry, *op.cit.*

37 The following sentence from a recently published study on inflation can be regarded as typical: 'The diversity of opinions among wage theorists, the lack of a general, accepted theory force us to make an attempt of our own to present the relevant problems' (Scherf, H. 1967, *Untersuchungen zur Theorie der Inflation*, Tübingen: JCB Mohr, p. 43).

38 See the previously mentioned model by Krelle and collaborators.

39 Klein, L. R., Ball, R. J., Hazlewood, A., Vandome, P. (1961) *An Econometric Model of the United Kingdom*, Oxford: Blackwell, pp. 17–18, 73–4.

40 Scherf, H. (1964), 'Zur Frage der Beziehungen zwischen Löhnen und Preisen in der Bundesrepublik Deutschland 1951 bis 1961', *Weltwirtschaftliches Archiv* 93, 1, pp. 44–78. The influence of prices and unemployment on German wage dynamics has recently been analysed in Enke, H. and Maneval, H. (1967) 'Die Einflüsse des Beschäftigungsgrades und der Preisentwicklung auf die Lohnentwicklung in der Bundesrepublik Deutschland', *Jahrbücher für Nationalökonomie* 180, 6, pp. 485–506.

41 The following quotation from Perry gives a good impression of these tactics (which, by the way, are not criticized under the circumstances as they are):

In examining the behavior of wages in this way, an essentially agnostic position is taken with regard to the different theories of inflation. The course of wages is described by the estimated relation, and wage changes can be traced to the explanatory variables. It is the relation between wage changes and these explanatory variables that is important.... The results may provide information that supports a particular explanation of inflation for some period; but the formulation of the problem in this way does not depend on any theory of inflation nor does it commit us to a sharp distinction between competing theories.

(Perry, *op. cit.*: 4–5)

What Perry says about inflation theory applies with equal – if not greater – force to wage theory. The econometric results are still waiting for a firm theoretical underpinning. 'A better theoretical foundation would make it easier to work out the causal relationships between the variables; disaggregation could show under what theoretical and empirical modifications the relationships are also relevant for individual sectors; finally the step from partial to total analysis should be attempted permitting the integration of the single equation into the total system'. (Enke and Maneval, *op. cit.*, p. 501).

42 In the Phillips curve the wage-change-unemployment relation is non-linear and is thus able to catch the effect of resistance against money-wage reductions. But some of the additional factors which are occasionally included are usually in linear form and without upper or lower limits.

43 The situation mentioned in the text can be illustrated by Figure 8.1, below, which shows the wage-change-profit relationship under the assumption that prices have risen by 5 per cent. Analogous functions can be drawn for every other price change. This family of curves can then also be subjected to non-linearities and limiting values.

44 The possibility of such complications is occasionally acknowledged but is then neglected in the interests of simplifying the analysis. Thus for instance Perry writes: 'Such arguments about the connection between wage changes and profits in the first period lend themselves to the use of a threshold effect in profits or a nonlinear relation between the variables. However, neither possibility was investigated here'. (Perry, *op. cit.*, p. 75).

45 'But the field of wage determination is, above all, one where not only the institutional framework, but also the general climate of opinion and individual decisions are of great importance. It is not surprising, therefore, that relations which hold for one period do not hold in the next' (Fellner, W., Gilbert, M., Hansen, B., Lutz, F., de Wolff, P. (1961) *The Problem of Rising Prices*, Paris: OECD, p. 49).

46 Already forty years ago J. W. F. Rowe – in a remarkable critical work – doubted whether it is possible to produce a complete and comprehensive wage theory (Rowe, J. W. F. (1928), *Wages in Practice and Theory*, London). In this context see also the paper by L. Reynolds 'State of wage theory' (Proceedings of Sixth Annual Meeting of Industrial Relations Research Associations, Madison, WI, 1954) where closer contact between the views of labour economists and general theorists is recommended. For the future Reynolds expects that instead of a unified wage theory we shall have a multitude of *accepted* theories which deal with various aspects of the wage problem. Similar ideas are stated by Tolles:

If one means by 'wage theory' a single simple generalization that will serve to answer any question about wages, then indeed twentieth-century experience has demolished any such theory. But a useful theory is one which is relevant to an issue or question. As the wage issues of the twentieth century have changed and multiplied, the need is seen for more and more specialised, limited, precise and complete theories to express the logic of the relationships involved in each new question. The twentieth century has yet to produce an

Alfred Marshall to knit all these specialised theories into a related and symmetric whole. However, the new and modified partial theories are increasingly representative of the facts and more closely responsive to the issues of doctrine than any single theory of wages yet devised could possibly be.

(Tolles, N. A. (1967) *Origins of Modern Wage Theories*, Englewood Cliffs: Prentice Hall, pp. 188–9)

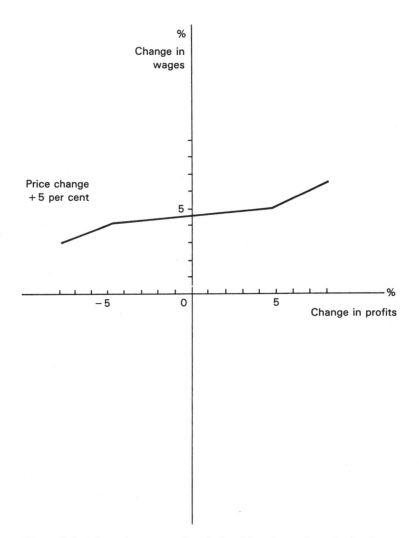

Figure 8.1   Wage-change–profit relationship when prices rise by 5 per cent

9 Wage levels and employment

(Translation of 'Lohnhöhe und Beschäftigung. Einige theoretische
Bemerkungen' in *Wirtschaftspolitische Blätter* 32, 6, pp. 540–6)

Is it possible to give a simple answer to a complicated question? This is
probably itself a complicated question but I shall have the courage to give
a simple answer: the answer is 'No'. Very complex relationships can lead
to various constellations which cannot be summarized in brief cause–effect
statements. But this is exactly what people frequently expect and demand
with regard to the wage–employment nexus which certainly is one of the
more complicated problems in the economic process. And unfortunately
this demand is frequently met with a supply of simple answers, some of
which are coming from economic 'experts'.

That statements about the effects of wages on employment are *desired* is
understandable in view of the enormous relevance of both items. It is also
understandable that 'strong' opinions are uttered in political debates where
the conflicting interests connected with wage questions are trying to score
points. But it is inexcusable when on the basis of very specific models
economists make very compact and apodictic statements 'from a scientific
point of view'. This must be misleading because in the complicated system
of our present-day world economy wage changes can have – depending on
the 'state of the world' – very different employment effects. Here – more
than in many other fields – the surrealistic view is justified: 'Anything can
happen, and it probably will.'

What can be *reasonably* said on this question from a scientific point of
view when it is not a *concrete* situation for which an answer is needed
(which then might very well be given in a unique and definite form)? What
one can offer – and what I am going to do – is to enumerate the most
important varieties of exogenous conditions and modifying circumstances
which make this or that effect of wages on employment probable. I shall
present my – far from complete – enumeration in several subgroups, but
it should be noted that these subgroups can be connected in various ways.
In concrete situations one has to diagnose which actual combination can be
applied – by no means an easy task.

Before presenting my 'catalogue' of important elements I want to point out that the wage–employment relation is not always (or necessarily) a symmetrical one. The widely held basic 'rules' that wage reductions will lead to more employment or that wage increases will lead to unemployment are not necessarily equivalent. Reactions to wage reductions and wage increases need not be symmetrical. I also want to mention that in an inflationary framework a reduction in wage rate *increases* (lagging behind price increases) corresponds, of course, to the case of wage reductions in a non-inflationary environment. To simplify matters this fact will not be specially mentioned in our further considerations.

MICRO–MACRO

Though labour markets differ in many respects from goods markets, traditional economics integrates them into a general market theory with wage rates (hourly, weekly or monthly) as prices and demand for and supply of labour services as the central and decisive market elements. In this perspective one arrives quickly at the usual market picture that with falling prices (= wages), the quantity demanded (= level of employment) will rise. As long as such a perspective is restricted to the micro level, i.e. to wages and employment in a single submarket (e.g. taxi drivers) under *ceteris paribus* conditions, this conventional wisdom can be justified, though cases exist where the structure of production does not permit employment changes in the short run (e.g. when a shortage of taxi cabs prevents the employment of more 'cheaper' drivers).

But one of the most important facts connected with greater systems is that relations which are true on the micro level need not apply for macro changes. This fact is of decisive importance for the wage–employment question. In analogy to the above-mentioned micro example that a reduction of their wages will lead to an increase in the employment of taxi drivers, the conclusion is frequently drawn that global unemployment (or at least unemployment over a fairly wide field) can also be reduced by lowering wage demands and wages. Since this is the decisive question when the wage–employment relation is discussed on a general level, I shall restrict myself in what follows to the macro problem where the intricacies of an interdependent system come into play.

WAGES: COST FACTOR AND PURCHASING POWER

In the micro example a wage reduction means lower costs for the firms in the sector concerned (taxi companies) while demand conditions remain unchanged. These firms can now lower their prices and increase their sales, leading to additional employment. But when many or all wages are reduced the *ceteris paribus* condition no longer holds; together with the costs demand is also reduced in so far as it is based on wage incomes. This double character of wages alone suffices to evoke contradictory conclusions. The argument that *lower* wages will stimulate employment (cost argument) is now confronted with the argument that *higher* wages will stimulate demand and with it employment (demand argument). The simple micro statement has been lost; further considerations are necessary in order to analyse the direction and strength of wage effects.

MONEY WAGES, REAL WAGES, UNIT LABOUR COSTS

When we talk of wage changes and their effect on employment we normally think of money wages as they are normally fixed in agreements between employers (employers' organizations) and workers (trade unions). These however, are, not the economically decisive magnitudes. Both employers and workers are above all interested in real wages. When prices and wages change at equal rates some inflationary or deflationary problems may arise, but the real situation on the labour market (relation between labour costs and sales revenues), including the employment situation, will hardly be touched. In the micro case, where only one specific wage rate is changed while the general price level remains unchanged, the situation is different: the change in money wage is at the same time a change of the real wage in the same direction. But when wages change on a broad front the demand effect has repercussions on prices which shift in the same direction as demand. The strength of these effects depends partly on monetary policy (whether it is accommodating or not), which together with wage policy, helps to determine the final outcome in terms of employment.

The important fact is that depending on the extent, capacity and divergence of mutually dependent wage and price changes, nominal wage increases or decreases can lead to different changes in real wages, which makes it impossible to make any generally valid statements about employment effects and their development. In order to analyse this question it is necessary to distinguish between 'fast' and 'slow' variables. Results depend on the speed with which wages, prices and employment decisions react in a changing environment. All these elements adjust only gradually to a new situation in the reality of modern industrial countries. If, for instance, in a period of unemployment wages are lowered while prices at first remain unchanged, then the immediate situation is one of lower real wages, which can set off an increase in employment. If this increase is sufficiently strong, total demand will be maintained or even increased and a positive employment effect will result. If, however, the wage reduction is not quickly followed by employment measures, the reduced purchasing power will depress prices and will so reduce or annihilate the fall in real wages and with it the impulse for additional employment. Since under normal conditions prices are probably a 'faster' variable than employment adjustments the latter sequence does not seem unlikely.

In a dynamic world with technical progress and human capital development, the real wage is not the only factor responsible for labour demand. Unit labour costs (labour costs per unit of output) become the strategic magnitude. Since these fall as labour productivity rises, wage increases are possible without requiring an increase in prices, so that real wages can rise without endangering sales or employment. This is generally recognized. Less obvious and less widely known is the fact that wage increases in turn can influence productivity. Higher wages can motivate workers to increase their efforts and they can put pressure on employers and managers to look for more efficient uses of their productive equipment (shock effect). As far as demands for higher wages have such effects they do not lead to higher unit labour costs and thus lose their negative impact on employment. It should, however, be noted that technical progress with a strong labour-saving bias can reduce labour demand to such an extent that wage depression tendencies set in and the possibilities for wage increases are narrowed down.

QUANTITY AND PRICE REACTIONS

In the previous section we showed that changes in money wages may leave employment unchanged because they may not affect real wages; and only these are considered relevant for labour demand. In this section we want to show that under certain circumstances even changes in real wages may have no or only little influence on employment levels.

The best way to show this is to start with the 'scenario' of an economy which had been in equilibrium with full employment and full capacity utilization and which is suddenly exposed to an exogenous demand shock, say a reduction in government expenditure, a deterioration of export conditions or something else of this sort. The economy is now in a stage of 'disequilibrium': demand is 'too low', the full employment output can no longer be sold at yesterday's prices. Under 'classical' assumptions prices and wages would in such a situation be the 'fast' variables while production and employment would move only slowly. The reduction in demand would therefore result in a quick fall in prices and (perhaps even more) in wages, which would call forth new demand at home and abroad which could make up for the original demand deficiency and achieve a return to full employment.

In real life, however, the sequence of events tends to be the other way round: quantity adjustments tend to take place more quickly than price decisions. And with this we get a completely different picture. A decline in demand is met at first with a reduction of output, with prices and wages remaining more or less unchanged. Production and employment are tailored to the new demand conditions. The unemployment thus created causes a further fall in demand, intensifying the decline in production and employment.

In such a situation a reduction in wages is no remedy against unemployment. The problem in this situation is not that real wages are too high. At the ruling prices and wages employers could profitably produce and sell their previous output. They abstain from doing it because they cannot find sufficient customers for their products. They are 'rationed' by an insufficient demand and it is this that restricts their demand for labour. A reduction of wages does nothing to revive the demand for goods and therefore does not lead to higher employment. This can only be achieved by a stimulation of final demand. This disequilibrium constellation occupies an important place in modern labour market theories in view of its obvious relevance. It has been named 'Keynesian unemployment', and cannot be overcome simply by cutting wages. As such it is contrasted to 'classical unemployment', which exists when demand would be in principle sufficient but workers are not employed because their real wages are too high. In this latter case wage reductions could achieve the desired aim of more employment.

UNCERTAINTY AND EXPECTATIONS

Decisions regarding employment levels have to some extent the character of investment decisions. The number of employees must be fixed for a certain period with a view on future production and sales conditions. This is the type of circumstances which is characteristic for investment decisions and which makes it so difficult to find a reliable explanatory and prognostic basis. The decisions have to take into account an uncertain future which may differ considerably from present conditions. They can therefore not rest exclusively on facts and existing information but must include 'mere' expectations about the future. This means that there cannot be a hard and fast relationship between present-day wage changes and future-orientated employment decisions. Uncertainty and the subjective nature of expectations about future wages, prices and demand conditions play an important role and can lead to a wide variety of 'scenarios'.

Expectations and uncertainty are particularly responsible for the fact that it is impossible to produce any 'hard' statements on the wage–employment question irrespective of the surrounding circumstances. In saying this it is important to see that expectations are not simply a single additional factor; they also modify and complicate many other factors which have an influence on the wage–employment relationship.

That expectations as such can affect employment has long been known to theorists and practicians of the business cycle. An 'optimistic' or 'pessimistic' climate can cause changes in production and employment even when wages and prices don't move at all. But here we are not concerned with such 'exogenous' fluctuations in expectations. From the theoretical point of view being discussed here, the more significant expectations are those which are *induced* by employment-orientated wage changes and which may then twist the effects of the wage policy in one direction or another. A few examples will illustrate this.

Let us take the case of a (general) wage reduction in times of unemployment. If the entrepreneurs have a rather favourable view of demand conditions in the near future (at ruling or slightly reduced prices), then they will probably react quickly with an increase in output and employment which will help to justify their optimistic sales expectations. If, on the other hand, there are various doubts about future sales possibilities – and such doubts are not unlikely in a period of widespread unemployment – then there might be no quick output reaction to the fall in wages and the main consequence can be a decline of wages and prices with little change in real wages and employment or even further reductions in employment. Negative effects will be particularly prominent when the decline in wages leads to expectations of further declines in the near future, which induces firms to postpone investments and stock-building until a future day.

The deflationary process which follows a decline in wages and prices has further employment effects whose nature greatly depends on expectations and reaction patterns. On the one hand it may stimulate consumption demand because with lower prices the real value of monetary wealth has grown; on the other hand depressive effects may follow on the investment front from the increase in the real burden of debt and the growing number of bankruptcies. It is obvious that in this jungle of possibilities, probabilities, improbabilities, 'ifs and whens', the relationship between wage changes and changes in employment tends to become rather loose and cannot be properly treated without consideration of a wider circle of factors.

THE OPEN ECONOMY

The considerations made so far were restricted to the wage–employment relationship in a single country without paying attention to its external relations. These are, however, important and will now be treated in outline. In doing this it is important to distinguish between fixed and flexible exchange rates. Let us begin with the case of fixed exchange rates.

Fixed exchange rates are a particularly favourable situation for positive employment effects in the wake of wage reductions. The price reductions which can follow the wage reductions strengthen the competitive position abroad so that exports and employment in the export industries can be increased. This positive result is possible even when the decline in wages and prices undermines employment effects at home. However, two restrictive remarks are necessary. The first is that this mechanism can only work if the other countries do not adopt a parallel policy of wage reduction. If this is the case the foreign trade position will remain unchanged. Second, there are limitations in time. It can become difficult to fight unemployment for a longer period with the aid of an export surplus. An export surplus implies import surpluses and balance-of-payments and employment difficulties in other countries, so that after some time these will retaliate by using protectionist weapons or by abandoning the fixed exchange rate.

This brings us to the case of flexible exchange rates. This theme became topical as a consequence of the breakdown of the Bretton Woods agreement. With flexible exchange rates the effectiveness of wage reductions via export stimulation is more or less lost. When exchange rates are *fully* flexible, i.e. when central banks never intervene on the foreign exchange markets, then the fall in domestic prices and the greater competitiveness will stimulate foreign demand as before, but this additional demand will above all force up the value of the domestic currency and with this appreciation the price of domestic goods to foreigners will return to the old 'equilibrium' level. The appreciation of the currency takes the place of the export surplus. In the real world of today we have no 'pure' system. Exchange rates are partly fixed, partly flexible and 'managed' so that a variety of combinations can occur with different partial effects of wage changes on employment and exchange rates. At the same time it is also true that irregularities in international financial relations and speculative influences on foreign exchange markets can have special and unsystematic repercussions on wages and employment.

This (incomplete) enumeration of factors which make it impossible to arrive at definite answers to the question about wage—employment relationships should not be interpreted in a nihilistic manner. The intention was to warn that in view of the extremely complex system of influences which act upon macroeconomic wage and employment processes, simple generalizing answers cannot be given, no matter how desirable such information would be. This is at least true as far as moderate wage movements within a traditional range are concerned. Extreme wage changes – up or down – would probably push employment in the expected (i.e. opposite) direction; but they would have such far-reaching social and political consequences that their treatment would require far more than a purely economic analysis.

10 Approaches to the theory of bargaining

For a long time wage bargaining, like unemployment, was relegated to a modest back seat in the main body of academic economic doctrine. While all great realistic writers from Adam Smith onwards did realize their importance and paid attention to them in special chapters and in appendices, it was mainly 'outsiders' like Marx, Hobson, the Webbs, and a few business cycle and duopoly specialists, who found room in the centre of their theories for a realization that unemployment may be more than merely a consequence of adjustment difficulties or outside interference, and that bargaining can play a major role in wage determination. The main stream of economic theory remained comparatively untouched by these important economic phenomena. While unemployed families were suffering severe hardships and trade unionists were risking their lives to secure collective bargaining rights, unemployment was regarded by many writers as practically non-existent and bargaining itself as an empty illusion.

It is not difficult to find the reasons for this astounding one-sidedness, if not to say blindness in many post-Ricardian economic treatises. Two strong motives (not necessarily conscious) combined to produce this result: the desire to preserve a neat theoretical structure, unblurred by such disequilibrating forces as unemployment and bargaining, and the wish to defend the capitalist system – at least in its pure, theoretical form – against criticisms from the growing socialist movement.[1]

It was comparatively easy to exclude bargaining from the leading nineteenth-century wage theories, or at least to show that it must be a futile undertaking. For all these theories relied on rigidly determined supply or demand conditions from which there was no escape. The Iron Law of Wages, by postulating a perfectly elastic supply of labour (in the long run) at the subsistence wage, could easily show that every wage advantage gained would soon be translated into more labourers competing for work and reducing wages to their old level. The wage fund theory in its various forms could dispose with equal ease all claims that bargaining could lead to an all-round improvement in labour's income: with a fixed stock of capital available for wage payments every improvement in one direction would be fully compensated by a deterioration in another direction. Finally, the marginal productivity theory, by taking perfect competition and the supply of the various factors of production as given, could construct an employers' demand curve and determine an 'equilibrium wage', any diversion from which would lead to unemployment or labour shortages, which in turn would press the wage back to its equilibrium level.

In all these theories, then, there was no room for bargaining. And this heritage was carried right into the twentieth century,[2] even though many theorists had expressed their qualms as to the correctness of this view,[3] and growing significance was accorded to bargaining as they descended from the level of pure theory.

It was not until the 1930s that bargaining broke in on a broader front into the framework of current economic theory itself. The realization that perfect competition was only one of many actual market-forms, and a very exceptional one at that, led to a reconsideration of the whole field of price economics and wage theory, considerably widening the scope for bargaining within the field of supply–demand analysis. About the same time the legislation and discussions stimulated by the New Deal favoured the growth of institutional studies and the blossoming of theories in which trade unions and collective bargaining do not enter by the back door but take a central place right from the beginning. The same is true for those theories which, though not taking specific institutional studies as their starting point, discard the traditional tools of analysis in order to approach the subject of duopoly (and related questions) from a new angle. There remains the wider question with regard to bargaining and the total and relative share of labour. This question, which was foremost in Ricardo's and Marx's mind, is still comparatively neglected in current economic literature.

It can no longer be maintained that the theory of bargaining is neglected. It will also be seen that bargaining theory has received its impulses from different sources so that we cannot speak today of a bargaining theory of wages or even of different, competing bargaining theories, but rather of various elements of a bargaining approach which in many cases supplement each other. I now propose to give a short appraisal of bargaining theory on the three different levels noted in the paragraph above. It should, however, be stressed that nothing like a complete catalogue is attempted, that the classification of a theory into one of the three categories will in some cases necessarily depend on a somewhat arbitrary decision, and that the authors named are given as examples of a certain type of approach and not necessarily as its only or principal representatives.

I. BARGAINING AND IMPERFECT COMPETITION THEORY

First, then, we have an approach which points out the scope for bargaining within the framework of marginal productivity theory. This is done by dropping some of the simplifying assumptions which had been part and parcel of the early stages of that theory. This approach has a long history, even though many of the contributors were not specifically concerned with the question of bargaining. With the development of imperfect competition and monopsony and oligopoly analysis, this approach was considerably broadened.

As an early example of a type of reformulation falling into this group we can name Edgeworth's distinction between the 'internal' and 'external' margin, once we drop the assumption of infinite divisibility of the labour factor. In many cases these two margins will lie so close together that they will leave little or no room for bargaining,[4] and for this reason the whole principle has been dismissed by some writers as a mathematical refinement with very little practical significance. But this principle may not be without significance for certain skilled jobs, particularly in the salaried range, and for personal services, where very often the employment of only one or a few persons will be considered. The range between the marginal productivity of an nth and an $(n + 1)^{st}$ man may then be wide enough to allow room for bargaining.

But whatever importance one may attach to this point, it remains on the whole a point of nicety. Of far greater significance were a number of objections which, like the slogan for an 'economy of high wages', were all directed against the static assumptions of marginal productivity theory. While the marginal productivity curve is accepted as the employers' demand curve, it is maintained that it is not so much the movements along this curve as the shifting of this curve (and of the labour supply curve, and possibly also the capital supply curve) that has to be watched when the effects of a wage bargain are considered. The imposition of a higher wage may lead initially to some unemployment, but may then produce such a change in the determinants of the wage–employment situation that the unemployment disappears and the higher wage becomes an 'equilibrium' wage.[5] There are different paths by which this new equilibrium may be reached: the higher wage may increase the productivity of the workers, it may force the capitalists to improve the efficiency of the production process (in these two cases the marginal productivity curve moves upward), or it may reduce the supply of labour, because women can now stay at home and children can be kept at school.

The technical refinement of the marginal analysis and the greater realism with regard to market forms brought about by imperfect and monopolistic competition theory opened up new vistas for the combination of marginal productivity analysis and bargaining opportunity. The most striking case was probably that of monopsony. For here it could be shown that where the supply of labour to a firm is not infinitely elastic – a not unrealistic assumption, under classical full employment conditions – the successful bargaining for a higher standard wage may actually lead to increased employment at the new, higher wage level.

But also the closer analysis of the commodity markets yielded results which had a bearing on the bargaining question. Particularly in the case of the kinked oligopoly demand curve it could be seen that the marginal revenue curve can be discontinuous (or vertical) over a considerable range and that within this range changes in costs will not affect the scale of output so that wage bargaining can be successful.[6] In other words, if the oligopolistic market situation imposes a certain output and price policy on the employer, he will be forced to swallow the whole increase in the wage bill consequent on a moderate advance of the wage level.

Finally, we may properly include in this section the related cases of oligopsonistic labour markets and of collusion among employers (open or tacit) not to raise wages. In the first case we have a kinked labour supply curve to the firm[7] and consequently a discontinuity in the marginal cost curve of labour which allows for a certain change in wage levels without affecting the demand for labour. In the second case, that of collusion, the employer, faced with a rising labour supply curve, does not push employment to the most profitable individual level (where marginal productivity equals marginal cost) because he realizes that his own action may induce others to do the same so that in the end wages have been raised throughout the industry and his higher bid remains without effect. In this case bargaining can raise the wage beyond the 'conventional' level without affecting the demand for labour. It is amazing that this rather simple case has received so little attention in wage theory, although it seems to correspond rather closely to the conditions observed in labour markets from Adam Smith's time till the present day.[8]

All the various facets of the bargaining problem advanced in this group do not add up to a bargaining theory. They do not show whether bargaining takes place or how it is done. They rather represent an attempt to rid the marginal productivity approach of some of its assumptions which made it incompatible with the idea of successful bargaining. This in itself has been an important step. But it remains to be seen whether a conclusive theory of modern wage determination and wage bargaining can be constructed along these in the last resort traditional lines, or whether a different approach would be more fruitful.

II. 'PSYCHOLOGICAL' AND 'INSTITUTIONAL' THEORIES

We turn now to several different approaches to the bargaining problem. There has been in recent years a remarkable growth of relevant literature. It would far surpass the limits of this chapter to give even a superficial account of these theories. All that can be done here is an attempt at a rough classification and appraisal, so as to set off this group against the theorems enumerated under the preceding section.

The diverse theories falling into this group have in common that they are all more or less dissatisfied with the assumptions of the classical perfect competition or wage theories, and they aim not so much at a reformulation

of the old structure as at a bold attempt to build on more realistic foundations. But here the similarity between the different theories ends and we can
distinguish two very different origins from which stem these new
approaches to bargaining. On the one hand we have the interest in the
theory of duopoly, bilateral monopoly, oligopoly, coupled with a recognition that questions of strategy, uncertainty, bluff, and so on, cannot be
regarded as exogenous forces, but must on the contrary be treated as decisive causal factors. While most of this literature does not deal explicitly with
wages (Neumann and Morgenstern, Brems, Shackle)[9] or deals with wages
only as a special aspect of a wider problem (Zeuthen, Fellner),[10] there can
be no doubt that its findings are highly pertinent to the bargaining processes
in the labour market. We may call this group of theories, which try to throw
light on the bargaining process as such in its most general form, 'psychological' theories.

From rather a different angle comes the other group of theories —
predominantly American — which also accord to bargaining a central place
in their theory, but are concerned specifically with the labour field and with
the institutions observed there. These theories, in all their variety (as
examples we may quote the work of Bronfenbrenner, Slichter, Shister,
Dunlop, Ross, Lester, Reynolds)[11] we may call 'institutional' theories, in
contrast to the 'psychological' theories mentioned before.

Now, both these groups of theories show in one respect definite progress
as compared with the theorems grouped under section I above. They take
bargaining as their starting-point, or at least introduce it at an early stage,
rather than 'explain it' into a theoretical structure hostile to bargaining.
From this it follows that these theories aim in principle at determinate solutions in bargaining situations, whereas the older theories were usually content (and had to be content, because of the nature of the determinant forces
in their basic structure) with pointing out indeterminate ranges within which
bargaining could take place. The theories in this group are, therefore, true
bargaining theories, and thus may be grouped together, in spite of their considerable differences.

But in spite of the ambitious endeavours incorporated in these theories,
it is too early to say that a completely satisfactory basis has been found for
the analysis and explanation of the process of wage determination under
bargaining conditions. The very number of different theoretical models suggests that one is still groping for a powerful and relevant model. The whole
subject is at present in a state of flux and it is obvious that it will take time
until shortcomings are eliminated and syntheses found. It seems that
progress must lie in finding some bridge between the 'psychological' and the
'institutional' theories, both of which are not completely satisfactory, but
could probably supplement each other.

The 'psychological' theories have developed impressive models on a high
level of abstraction, covering all processes of bargaining. To some extent
this result could, however, only be achieved by cutting out many important

elements and by concentrating the investigation on some very simple situations. More research will be needed in order to see how far the assumptions about human behaviour and 'rationality' underlying these theories are compatible with conditions in labour markets, and what additional assumptions and complications have to be introduced in order to make them serve more directly the needs of wage theory.

The 'institutional' theories have, of course, the advantage of dealing explicitly with the labour market and its peculiarities. They are more 'cut to measure', can take into account special factors and less 'rational' attitudes. But this greater vicinity to the fullness of real life carries its own dangers. The step from description to theory (although description involves, of course, some rudimentary theory) becomes difficult and there may be undue hesitation to march on to higher levels of abstraction. One cannot help feeling that some of the work done in this field is still unnecessarily complicated and hampered by the use of inadequate theoretical tools and concepts. It will also be necessary to find out how far the results of these 'institutional' theories are conditioned by the special structure of the American labour and commodity markets, and how far they are applicable to all industrialized capitalist countries. (For underdeveloped and colonial countries a special theory would in any case be indicated.)

As has been said before, it is not at all unlikely that in the search for a realistic theory of wage bargaining the 'psychological' and 'institutional' theories can aid each other. As they develop, a closer relation may also be established to the imperfect competition doctrines of section I which could then become mainly a theory of the immediate framework for bargaining situations. [12]

III. BARGAINING AND THE SHARE OF LABOUR

When the theories mentioned in sections I and II have done everything in their power to elucidate local and industry-wide bargaining processes, a big question remains, namely, the macro-economic question as to the scope and limits of bargaining in relation to labour income as a whole and its share in the national income. This important question which greatly occupied the minds of the classical economists has not benefited much from the recent upsurge of interest in bargaining. In most textbooks on wages and labour it receives only scant attention. [13]

Treatment of this question can be carried out at different levels. And since it touches the most fundamental class interests, it is not surprising that we shall find that we are quickly pushed into the sphere of sociology when we try to do justice to the problem.

One approach to this problem, the one which is already prominent in the writings of the classics and of Marx, starts from the 'real' side. How far can real wages *in toto* be expanded (or depressed)? The absolute upper and lower limits are easily enough established. For the continued existence of a stationary society they cannot permanently be pressed below the subsistence minimum (however defined) or above the net national product. But in a society which contains a capitalist class the upper limit will be lower. For a reduction in historically established capitalist incomes may lead to a reduction in their investment expenditure rather than in their consumption expenditure (assuming for the moment an uninterrupted circular flow). The lower the capitalists' marginal propensity to consume, the smaller will be the opportunity for pushing wages upward without causing a reduction in the stock of capital and thus undermining the basis for the higher wage bill. This case can be further developed by taking into account the possibility of a temporary reduction of investment expenditure by deliberate non-spending (causing unemployment), or the possibility of increasing the share of labour without making inroads into traditional capitalist consumption when we deal with an expanding rather than a stationary economy.[14] The upper limit for bargaining, minimum wage legislation, and the like, in a capitalist society will, therefore, be necessarily lower than the absolute limit, even if there is no unemployment. Unemployment will tend to reduce that limit still further.

With the widespread interest in full employment and in the stability conditions for full employment in an unplanned economy, more attention has been recently given to the macroscopic bargaining problem from a monetary angle. With the abolition of unemployment, a major check on the upward revision of the wage bill disappears. But if the monetary system is sufficiently elastic, does such a revision not simply lead to proportionate price rises so that all bargaining is necessarily self-defeating and leads to inflation? We cannot go here into the problems of costing, price and wage flexibilities, expectations and timing, which will determine when and to what extent bargaining can succeed under such circumstances. But a very important point arises here. Since higher wages are often passed on in higher prices under full employment conditions trade unions have begun to realize that it may not be sufficient to press for higher wages, but that it may be necessary to supplement this demand by asking for price control measures, workers' control, and so on. That is, in order to achieve success in bargaining, the parties will not necessarily restrict themselves to the wage bargain proper but will demand such institutional changes as to make a success possible.

Now, if it is granted, as I think it should be, that such demands for price control have also to be regarded as part of the bargaining process and must not be left out of account when the scope or limits of bargaining under full employment are discussed, then there is no reason why we should not go further and view all the institutions and finally the economic system itself as variables in the bargaining process. If we do so, we shall see that many events which are usually regarded as completely outside the field of wage theory or even economics are of vital importance for an understanding of the basic positions from which the adversaries start that finer process of adjustment which is the subject of the theories mentioned in sections I and II. [15] Arguments for and against the sacred nature of private property, racial ideologies ('the negro has to be kept in his place'), fascist endeavours to undermine trade unions and the fight against these tendencies, the position of women in society, all this and many other social, political, and cultural phenomena, no matter in what disguise they may be presented, will have to be evaluated in any historical situation as class attempts to secure or change their bargaining position. If such an extension of bargaining theory seems fantastic to some traditional wage theorists, let them be reminded that it is not by chance that, in Europe at least, the growth of trade unionism has been very closely interlinked with the growth of the political labour movement and of cultural and educational institutions, not least because workers and trade unionists realize that they have to advance on the political and ideological field (universal voting, women's rights, socialism) if they are to be more successful at the bargaining table. Similarly we see in many countries that employers' associations extend, for identical reasons, their activities into the political and ideological sphere. [16] Once we are prepared to proceed from the analysis of isolated workers and employers to trade unions and employers' associations, because these have proved to be of importance in the real world, then there is no reason why we should not go on and investigate the position and the actions of workers and employers, trade unions and employers' associations, outside the personnel office and the conference room, in so far as this has a bearing on the bargaining situation. This may make the theory still more complicated and less amenable to short-cut methods like geometry and algebra, but it will prevent us from looking merely for an explanation of the last five cents that were granted to some group without asking the very decisive question about the general starting-points.

This has been a very summary and incomplete review of bargaining theory, or rather of some of the theory relevant to the bargaining problem. The division of the theories into three groups has been somewhat arbitrary, and no doubt other more useful classifications can be devised. But it is hoped that the above remarks convey

1 that bargaining is at last receiving adequate attention in economic and wage theory;
2 that the concept and the process of wage bargaining are of a complex nature and can be fruitfully attacked from different angles; and
3 that it is now time for an advance on all fronts and a judicious combination of the results achieved.

NOTES

1 In many cases the treatment of these questions reminds one of the satiric lines

116   *Wages*

written by Christian Morgenstern:

Und er kommt zu dem Ergebnis:
Nur ein Traum war das Erlebnis.
Weil, so schliesst er messerscharf,
nicht sein *kann*, was nicht sein *darf*.

(From 'Die unmögliche Tatsache' in *Alle Galgenlieder*.)

2 Thus, in 1928, Mr Rowe could still claim that 'all existing wage theories appear to ignore the phenomenon which has completely changed the whole condition of the labour market ... namely, the rise to power of trade unionism', *Wages in Practice and Theory* (1928).

3 A famous case is John Stuart Mill's statement: 'The doctrine hitherto taught by most economists (including myself) which denied it to be possible that trade combinations can raise wages ... is deprived of its scientific foundation, and must be thrown aside.'

4 In this context, an opportunity for bargaining means that bargaining is possible without affecting employment. That bargaining can be effective via changes in the employment level has, of course, been recognized by all marginal productivity theorists.

5 For the sake of brevity the argument will always be restricted to the question of a wage increase enforced through bargaining. But the case of downward pressure is, of course, of equal importance and can be treated in an analogous manner.

6 Even with an unchanged output, unemployment can result, if capital can be easily substituted for labour.

7 This is assuming that a lowering of the wages would not be followed by the other firms for fear that workers would be quickly lost, while a rise in wages would be adopted by others in order to retain their workers. The increased wage offer would then only attract few new workers.

8 Adam Smith observed that 'masters are always and everywhere in a sort of tacit, but constant and uniform, combination not to raise the wages of labour above their actual rate. To violate this combination is everywhere a most unpopular action, and a sort of reproach to a master among his neighbours and equals.'

And as to present-day conditions we have the following results from a field study in an industrial New England town: 'Aggressive "pirating" of workers employed in another plant is definitely against the code of employers in the area. If the personnel manager of company A learns that someone from company B has approached an A worker and tried to hire him, he will immediately telephone the personnel manager of company B and ask him to let the worker alone. This request is usually sufficient; for each personnel manager knows that, if he steals a worker today, someone else will steal from him tomorrow, and all have an interest in playing by the rules.' 'Even if the worker takes the initiative and applies for work at another plant, he will usually not be considered for employment unless his present employer is willing to relinquish him.' – Lloyd G. Reynolds (1951) *The Structure of Labor Markets*, New York: Harper, pp. 51, 216.

9 John von Neumann and Oskar Morgenstern (1944) *Theory of Games and Economic Behaviour*, New York: Wiley; Hans Brems, *Product Equilibrium under Monopolistic Competition*, Cambridge, Mass.: Harvard University Press; G. L. S. Shackle, (1949) *Expectation in Economics*, Cambridge; Cambridge University Press.

10 F. Zeuthen, (1930), *Problems of Monopoly and Economic Warfare*, London: Routledge; William Fellner (1949), *Competition among the Few*, New York: A. Knopf.

11 M. Bronfenbrenner (1939) 'The Economics of Collective Bargaining', *Quarterly*

Journal of Economics (August); S. H. Slichter, (1941) *Union Policies and Industrial Management*, Washington: Brookings; R. Lester and J. Shister, (eds.) (1947) *Insights into Labor Issues*; John T. Dunlop (1944), *Wage Determination under Trade Unions*; Arthur M. Ross (1947), 'The Dynamics of Wage Determination under Collective Bargaining', *American Economic Review* (December); L. G. Reynolds, *op. cit.*

12 If, as has been suggested (Charles E. Lindblom (1948) 'Bargaining Power in Price and Wage Determination', *Quarterly Journal of Economics*, May), bargaining power should be defined as the outcome of three sources, viz. (a) tastes and motives, (b) skill in persuasion and coercion, and (c) competition from other buyers and sellers, then the necessity of combining the theories from sections I and II becomes quite obvious.

13 There are, of course, exceptions, as, for instance, Maurice Dobb (1946) *Wages*, Cambridge: Cambridge University Press.

14 This discussion of bargaining possibilities is not contradictory to Kalecki's theory of the share of wages in the national income, which is shown to depend on raw material prices and the degree of monopoly. Every successful wage bargain, by reducing the gap between price and marginal cost, will lower the degree of monopoly and thus increase labour's share. See Michael Kalecki (1939), *Essays in the Theory of Economic Fluctuations*, pp. 13–41.

15 For an excellent juxtaposition of the limited explanative value of marginal productivity theory and the wider, sociological background against which it must be viewed, see E. Preiser (1953) 'Erkenntniswert und Grenzen der Grenzproduktivitätslehre', *Schweizerische Zeitschrift für Volkswirtschaft and Statistik* (February).

16 See R. A. Brady (1943) *Business as a System of Power*, New York: Columbia University Press.

11 Wages and risk-bearing

I

Risk-bearing has for a long time taken an important place in the theory of distribution. In order to induce people to supply this productive service, a reward has to be paid to them, and this reward is regarded as part of the 'necessary' costs of production. It is this reward which partly explains differences in interest rates, while risk-bearing is made the basic explanation of profits in many current profit theories.

With regard to interest rates the existence of a relationship between them and risk is at once obvious from the evidence available. In the case of profits the position is far less clear, or at any rate, is not easily verifiable. First, detailed statistics about industrial profits (specified for each industry) in this country do not exist and can therefore not be correlated to an index of risk − assuming that such an index could be constructed. Second, risk-bearing is used as an explanation of differences in 'normal,' i.e. competitive, profits, but a large and increasing part of profits today is in the nature of monopoly profits. And in the case of monopoly profits the position is just opposite to that of normal profits: the higher the degree of monopoly the higher the profits tend to rise and the safety of the firms in the monopolistic industry tends also to be greater. Thus even if statistics of industrial profits were available the impossibility of separating normal from monopoly profits would still hamper any investigation.[1]

But it is not only the owners of capital who have to face risks; labour, too, is exposed to risks. Risks in this connection have been rather neglected in economic theory, but it has been realised that if there were free movement of labour, people would avoid occupations which are dangerous or where unemployment and wage fluctuations are frequent. Wages there would have to rise until the 'net advantages' in all occupations were equal.[2] In so far as free movement does not exist this tendency will not able to exert itself.

We shall now try to find out whether actually such a positive relationship between wages and risks exists or not. The main risks which workers have to face are occupational mortality, industrial diseases, fluctuations in wage rates and unemployment. We shall test the correlation between the wages of twenty-nine different occupations given in Table 11.1 and each of these risks with the exception of industrial diseases, the statistics for which could not be fitted into this study.

Let us then proceed to obtain first the coefficient of correlation between wages and occupational mortality (columns 1 and 2). The result is:

$$r_1 = -0.26$$

We see that there is no significant correlation between the two variables, but in so far a relationship exists at all it is negative, i.e. high wages are connected with a low occupational mortality and vice versa.

There is, therefore, here no sign of a reward for this risk. This result is not altogether unexpected. For occupational mortality and wages do not stand in a simple relationship of cause and effect but are interdependent. While we may assume that a higher occupational mortality will lead to a higher wage-level, we may also expect that a higher wage-level, and the higher standard of living and health that goes with it, will lead to a lower mortality.

To exclude this second factor as far as possible the following procedure was adopted. The Registrar-General's Report on Occupational Mortality divides the whole population into five social classes, starting with Class I, representing the professional and generally well-to-do section of the population, and ending with Class V, representing labourers and other unskilled callings. For each of these social classes the standardised death rate is calculated and thus the influence of social class and hence, in a general way, of income level on mortality is shown. In column (*a*) of Table 11.1 we have shown the social class to which each of the twenty-nine occupations belongs, and in column (3) we have the figures of column (2) (occupational mortality) divided by the class mortality of the corresponding social class. In this way the figures of column (3) show occupational mortality but exclude to some extent the effect which the wage-level as such exerts on mortality.[3] If we now correlate columns (1) and (3) we obtain:

$$r_2 = -0.16$$

As we should have expected, r_2 is (relatively) greater than r_1, but the result is still the same: the risk of occupational mortality has no discernible influence on the wage-level (unless we make the assumption that this influence is cancelled by other factors). In this case the absence of a relationship may be mainly due to the ignorance of workers as to the existence of these risks.

Let us see whether there exists any relationship between wages and fluctuations in wage-rates.[4] Correlating columns (1) and (4) we obtain:

$$r_3 = -0.33$$

Again the result is that no significant relationship exists, but that in so

Table 11.1 Wage levels and occupational risks in 29 occupations

(a) Social class	(b) Occupation	(1) Average weekly wage (1925–36) in London s.	(2) Occupational mortality	(3) Occupational mortality adjusted for social class mortality	(4) Index of wage fluctuations (1925–36)	(5) Percentage of unemployment (1925–36)	(6) Index of seasonal variations in employment (1924–32)
III	Fitters and turners	63.52	102	105	111	16.9	0.9
III	Ironmoulders (sand)	63.52	112	116	111	29.8	4.7
IV	Engine-shop labourers	45.89	134	133	116	16.9	0.9
III	Wiremen, etc.	85.32	104	107	109	19.3	0.6
III	Skilled men in vehicle-bldg.	71.32	81	84	106	11.3	1.2
III	Shipwrights	68.40	100	103	104	40.8	1.4
III	Shipjoiners	68.40	54	56	104	40.8	1.4
V	Shipbuilding labourers	53.40	166	148	105	40.8	1.4
III	Flourmilling: first rollermen	73.00	84	87	100	8.5	0.5
III	Baking fore hands	68.80	77	79	106	11.0	0.5
III	Cabinet makers	79.10	98	101	111	11.3	0.7
III	Upholsterers	79.10	90	93	111	11.3	0.7
III	Hand compositors	89.0	145	150	100	7.2	0.4
III	Linotype operators	96.00*	34	35	–	7.2	0.4
III	Bookbinders & machine rulers	80.00	112	116	100	7.2	0.4
V	Navvies (civil engineering)	56.90*	58	52	–	19.7	1.5
III	Building craftsmen	75.88	88	91	107	16.3	2.7
V	Building labourers	57.80	114	102	110	16.3	2.7
III	Tram drivers	69.90	85	88	110	4.4	0.4
III	Tram conductors	69.90	97	96	110	4.4	0.4
III	Boot and shoe workers	55.40	111	115	105	17.2	0.9

III	Paper machine men	68.80	102	105	113	7.7	0.9
V	Dock labourers	71.0	137	122	107	31.8	1.0
	Railway Service						
V	Porters	45.80	94	84	111	10.0	0.7
IV	Ticket collectors	56.00	88	87	100	10.0	0.7
III	Guards	65.00	77	79	100	10.0	0.7
III	Shunters	57.50	90	93	100	10.0	0.7
III	Engine drivers	90.00	84	87	100	10.0	0.7
IV	Firemen	66.00	77	76	100	10.0	0.7

Notes and sources:

* Wages on 31 December 1936.

Columns (*a*) and (2) are derived from Table 1 in the Registrar-General's Decennial Supplement for England and Wales, 1931, Part IIa, Occupational Mortality.

The figures in column (2) represent the number of registered deaths in 1930–32 of the corresponding occupation per 100 standard deaths (i.e. the effects of varying age incidence have been eliminated). An index of 100 means therefore that mortality in this group is the same as for the (male) population as a whole, while a higher figure indicates a supernormal, a lower figure a subnormal death-rate for that occupation.

Column (*a*) classifies each of the occupations, Class III representing Skilled Workers, Class V Unskilled Workers, and Class IV occupations intermediate between these two groups.

Column (3) is derived from column (2) by dividing each of the items there by the standardized mortality ratio of the class to which the corresponding occupation belongs. These ratios are derived from Table E on p. 20 and are: 97 for Class III, 101 for Class IV, 112 for Class V.

Columns (1) and (5) are derived from the Abstracts of Labour Statistics of the United Kingdom, Nos. 18–22. Column (1) is an average of the wages ruling at the end of 1925, 1927, 1930, 1933 and 1936 in the London area. Column (5) is the average of the quarterly percentage of insured persons recorded as unemployed, from 1925 to 1936.

Column (4), using the same data as column (1), expresses the highest wage of that period as a percentage of the lowest wage.

The index of seasonal variations in employment in column (6) is based on the book 'Seasonal Variations in Employment' by Christopher Saunders. Most of the index numbers in this column have been taken from Appendix I of this book, while the rest has been calculated on the same basis. These figures are the average of the monthly percentage deviation of the actual employment figures (insured persons minus unemployed) from the twelve-monthly moving averages of employment for the years 1924–32.

Since the descriptions of occupations in the various statistics are not exactly on the same basis, the figures in each row do not always cover exactly the same occupational field. But only those occupations were included in the table where these divergencies are probably not very considerable.

far any relationship can be found it is the opposite of what we should expect on a risk theory of wage differences, i.e. high wages tend to occur with small fluctuations and vice versa. A partial explanation of this phenomenon is, of course, the effect of trade unionism. A strong trade union will be able to obtain high wages as well as to resist frequent changes in the wage-rates. Trade unionism may also have an influence on the relationship between wages and unemployment, if wages are kept up by limiting entry to a trade.

Finally, we turn to the relation between wages and unemployment. From columns (1) and (5) we get:

$$r_4 = -0.27$$

thus arriving at the same conclusions as before. Against r_4 it might be objected that we have thrown together skilled and unskilled workers, and that the result is due to the fact that the latter group is notoriously a large pool of people from all sorts of sources and that in their case low wages and high unemployment are the rule. Though this fact is in itself significant and important for our considerations, its effects can be excluded by correlating wages and unemployment for the twenty occupations of Class III, i.e. of skilled workers, only. Doing this we obtain the strange result:

$$r_5 = -0.81$$

Inspecting the scatter diagram, however, it becomes obvious that this high negative correlation is almost entirely due to the influence of three occupations – ironmoulders, shipwrights and shipjoiners – where the continuous depressed condition of their trade led to low wages combined with abnormally high rates of unemployment. Excluding these three occupations, the correlation coefficient becomes:

$$r_6 = -0.13$$

and our result is not fundamentally different from the one we obtained for the whole group.

It may, however, be objected against the last point that in a period of depression, and with a low mobility of labour, one must expect higher percentages of unemployment to go with low wages for quite a considerable period. A further correlation has, therefore, been worked out, viz. that between wages and *seasonal* variations in employment. Even if people might not be able to escape quickly the impact of the considerable structural changes which followed the last war, we should expect labour to avoid those industries which show a strong tendency to discard part of their labour force at certain times of the year. Yet, again, when we correlate columns (1) and (6) we obtain a result which quite obviously differs from that we should expect. For we get:

$$r_7 = -0.22$$

II

The conclusion then, which we can draw from the preceding section is that 'risk-bearing' is not rewarded in the case of labour, i.e. it is not a 'necessary' cost of production. The bearing of these risks is a service provided freely by the workers. The reasons for this state of affairs are not far to seek. They consist partly of the ignorance of the workers as to the facts about risks, but the main factor is probably the impossibility for workers to move from one occupation to another or from one place to another, because they lack financial and other opportunities to do so and stand under continuous pressure to take up work quickly without waiting and weighing alternative possibilities.[5] Finally we must keep in mind that there are other factors reacting on wage differences, and that their influence may partly counteract the effects of risk on wages.

When we look at this list of explanations we see that the fact that labour does not get a reward for risk-bearing does not lie in the nature of the case but is predominantly an institutional factor. Take the case of ignorance first. Every modern newspaper carries its daily financial columns which provide ample information for every investor where and how to invest to avoid risks or what he might expect in order to be recompensed for them. Can we imagine similar daily labour columns where workers are advised as to the various risks in different industries and occupations and as to the wage differentials that may be expected to make good these disadvantages? Yet, there is nothing absurd in this idea and, under conditions of full employment, it may greatly help labour to get a reward for risks.

In the case of mobility, too, a change of institutions would greatly increase the mobility and variety of choice of labour. Availability and relative steadiness of jobs in conditions of high and stable employment will tend to eliminate many obstacles to spatial and inter-industrial mobility and to give, at least to the unskilled or semi-skilled workers, a wider choice of occupations and a chance of considering the risk factors in the various types of occupation open to them. The pressure of unemployment swamps all the other risk factors which, according to the classical view, would bring about differential rewards to workers.

Moreover, the anticipated (ex-ante) risks of say, fluctuations in wage rates and employment, may differ appreciably from the actual (ex-post) risks. Both workers and employers may misjudge the prospects of an industry or their expectations may be falsified by economic policies in this country or abroad. Unfortunately it is well-nigh impossible to measure anticipated risks and hence we were forced to evaluate the ex-post risks.

All these points lead to a final consideration which is of fundamental importance to the theory of distribution. Since Clark's 'Distribution of Wealth' was published, the usual approach was to explain the different types of income in terms of their productivity. Now this is certainly an important first step if we want to understand why people are prepared to pay certain sums to the factors of production. But it is not sufficient. For we do not only want to know, if we care to have a full understanding of the distribution of the national income, why people are prepared to pay for certain services, we also want to know how it is that certain services have their particular productivity (in terms of value, of course), i.e. what the reasons for their scarcity are. To explain certain aspects of normal long-run profits and margins between interest rates as a reward for the productive service of risk-bearing is an important first step. But the next step, which is at least equally important, is to find out why, for instance, in the case of labour risk-bearing is provided freely and is not charged for. That is, we have to find out how far certain services are as productive as they are simply because the providers of these services have a greater 'power to withhold.'[6] Only if this second step is taken shall we be better able to recognise the relative character of 'necessary' costs and what part institutional factors play in determining marginal productivity and the distribution of income. And this knowledge will be of great importance for a large number of questions arising from economic policy.

NOTES

1 It seems to the writer that if the relationship between 'normal' profits and risks could be tested the result would probably show a high correlation between profits and risks in the long run wherever large amounts of capital are involved, i.e. where the investors are usually well informed and under no particular pressure to invest their capital quickly in order to obtain a livelihood; this correlation may, however, be absent in the short run (and, owing to the longevity of modern capital equipment the short period may extend over a large number of years) because under-employment and imperfect mobility of capital resources hamper the necessary adjustments. On the other hand in the case of small businesses, like retailing of various kinds, small farms, and even small manufacturing establishments, where the investors do not enjoy the above-mentioned advantages, such a correlation will be non-existent or negligible. Indeed, the position of this second group may not be dissimilar to that of labour.

2 See, for instance, Dobb, M. (1946) *Wages*, pp. 110–11.

3 As the wage rates paid to workers in the three different social groups overlap to a considerable extent, even this method does not overcome the difficulty completely.

4 Here only 27 items are correlated, as in two cases – Linotype Operators and Navvies – wages are only given for 1936 and no fluctuations could therefore be calculated.

5 Even if mobility is possible, the new risks created by breaking up old connections, leaving low-rent houses, etc., are often greater than those one may try to escape.

6 This approach to the distribution of incomes in terms of monopoly and advantage is, of course, characteristic of Marx and some of the writers who were influenced by him. See, for instance, M. Dobb (1925) 'Capitalist Enterprise and Social Progress', London: Routledge.

12 The Phillips curve and all that

(Extended and revised version of a talk given to a Seminar at Glasgow University.)

INTRODUCTION

Oscar Morgenstern once concluded from an analysis of publications in scientific economic journals that probably only a small fraction of the articles is read by a wider circle and that only a tiny fraction finds an echo in subsequent writings. One article which very definitely belongs to this tiny fraction is that by Phillips (1958) on 'The relation between unemployment and the rate of change of money wage rates in the United Kingdom, 1861–1957'. In the thirteen years since his paper was published the stream of writings which in some way or other take their lead from his propositions or try to refute them has never stopped. There are now many dozens of books and articles in existence whose contents have some bearing on the problems posed by Phillips, and it would require a very specialized knowledge indeed (and lots of space) to give a full account of all the ramifications into which the debate has run.

The present article sets itself a more modest task. It wants to present the basic ideas of the Phillips curve and its possible implications, and to sketch the main trends which have become visible in the post-Phillips discussion. Neither a complete survey of the literature nor a complete coverage of all the problems is aimed at. The selection and interpretation of the problems will necessarily carry the imprint of the author's interests and knowledge; but it is hoped that the article will confer a general idea of the range of questions which are typical for the present-day literature in the Phillips tradition.

THE PHILLIPS CURVE

The original contribution by Phillips centred – as everybody knows – on the simple proposition that the rate of change of British money wages over the past hundred years had been largely determined by the rate of unemployment and to a minor extent also by the change in unemployment. A priori assumptions and inspection of the empirical data also suggested that the relationship between wage changes and unemployment rates is of a distinctly non-linear nature. Thus the basic Phillips relation took the form

$$\frac{dW/dt}{W} = a + bU^c + e\frac{dU}{dt}; \qquad \begin{array}{l} a, b > 0 \\ c, e < 0 \end{array}$$

where W stands for (money) wage rates, U for the rate of unemployment, and a, b, c and e are parameters. In addition Phillips noticed a certain influence of price changes on wage changes; but – again from a priori assumptions and data inspection – he regarded them as relevant only in years of big price increases, particularly in years of strong fluctuations in import prices. Thus, neglecting the minor deviations arising from *changes* in the unemployment rate and taking years of 'normal' price developments one obtains the simple[1] and classical Phillips curve (Figure 12.1).

The fact that money wages rise rather faster when unemployment is low and vice versa does not seem to be a sensational discovery; indeed, after a quarter-of-a-century of post-war experience many non-economists will regard this fact as more or less self-evident. Why, then, did Phillips's curve

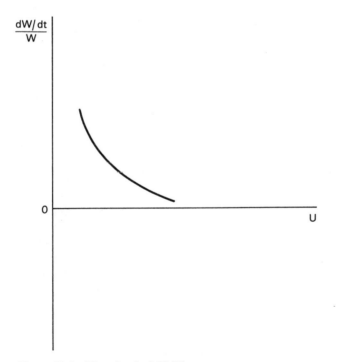

Figure 12.1 The classical Phillips curve

immediately become *the* Phillips curve? How is it that his interesting article achieved such quick and widespread fame?[2] I believe that an attempt to answer this question may be useful in order to see the Phillips curve in proper perspective.

A primary reason for the success of the Phillips article was that he had something substantial to offer in an important field where economic theory had failed to provide any guidance. For, strange as it may sound, traditional economic theory had practically nothing to say on the behaviour of money wage rates. Neoclassical marginal productivity theory adhered to the dichotomy between real and monetary phenomena. Wage theory was real wage theory and equilibrium theory at that.[3] Once the real wage was determined the money wage merely reflected monetary influences on nominal values.

The situation changed dramatically with the appearance of Keynes's *General Theory*. He was definitely aware of the peculiarities of money wage behaviour; downward rigidity of money wages plays an important part in his analysis. Also, he certainly did not stick to equilibrium economics. Yet, as far as our problem is concerned, another sharp dichotomy crept into his work: the division between states of underemployment and full employment. As long as less-than-full-employment prevails expansion of demand results in rising output with money wages remaining more or less constant,[4] while the situation immediately changes when full employment is reached: further increases in demand now lead to constant output and rising wages. This relationship is illustrated in Figure 12.2. The rise of wages at very low levels of unemployment is meant to show the influence of bottlenecks.

While the Keynesian approach was a definite improvement compared with the previous neglect of money wage dynamics, it did not provide much help when econometricians and inflation specialists tried to come to grips with the post-war situation. It became obvious that money wages were on the move most of the time and not only in periods of full employment. Finding themselves unaided by traditional theories the econometric model builders had to find pragmatic solutions of a 'do-it-yourself' type. While, for instance, the early Dutch models simply introduced money wage changes as an exogenous factor, others tried to 'endogenize' them. Klein (1950) introduced (absolute) changes of money wages as an endogenous variable into his model, making them linearly dependent on unemployment in the current and previous period,[5] the wage level in the previous period and a time trend. In the years that followed others, too, tried to get hold of the money wage movements by such *ad hoc* constructions (Garbarino 1950; Klein and Goldberger 1955; Valavanis-Vail 1955; Dunlop 1957). They used various 'explanatory' variables in addition to unemployment (prices, profits) and worked throughout with linear relationships. It is interesting to note that even these forerunners of Phillips had their forerunners, as far back as the 1920s. Bellerby (1923) made an attempt to relate price increases

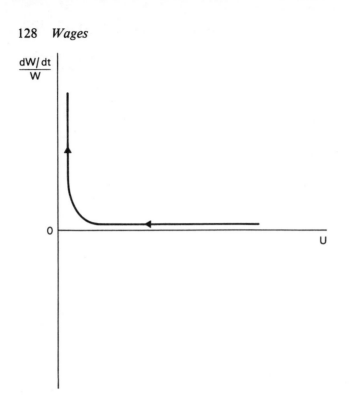

Figure 12.2   Keynesian money wage dynamics

to unemployment, and the wage change–unemployment nexus was used by Tinbergen (1936).

In view of these forebodings of the Phillips relation our question now becomes why his contribution to this open problem had such an outstanding impact. There are several reasons. First, there is no doubt that Phillips's work was distinguished by a more intensive study of this special problem and particularly by a grandiose attempt to see it in the very long perspective. Second, his conclusions seemed to indicate that he had hit on one of those grand constants in a changing world for which economists have always (and vainly?) been looking.[6] Third – and a very decisive point this is – taking the long-run reliability of the tested relationships for granted, Phillips's analysis provided a highly relevant instrument for policy decisions in a field where conflicting aims had become a major headache for the governments of most Western countries: in the dilemma between full employment and price stability.[7]

THE THEORETICAL IMPLICATIONS

While Phillips entered his investigation with some hypotheses in mind which he wanted to confront with reality, the actual outcome of his empirical analysis left the controversies between demand pull, cost push, and other 'explanations' of the wage-price-spiral as unsolved as before. The variables involved and their movements are so closely interrelated and so highly dependent on the ups and downs of the cycle that there is no shortage of interpretations that can be imposed on the original Phillips curve and its followers. The Phillips curve is 'measurement without theory'. The mechanism lying behind it (assuming that it depicts a 'real' relationship) has still to be discovered by more minute and detailed studies of labour market processes. They may, of course, vary between countries and periods.

While the Phillips curve failed to provide a definitive theory of money wage dynamics, it *did* act as a challenge to alternative theories to prove their compatibility with Phillips's empirical findings. Though this discussion did not lead to a final solution of all differences, it did at least help to sharpen the awareness for certain relationships in a hitherto neglected field.

Phillips himself tended to interpret his curve in a rather plausible and impressionistic manner which may very well be nearer the truth than some of the more 'purist' and formally more polished structures of later writers. In his view the curvi-linear relation between unemployment and wage changes results from a combination of demand pull and Keynesian wage rigidity. In times of high demand on the labour market (low unemployment) the market forces lead to rising (prices and) wages; when demand is low (unemployment high) a corresponding decline in wages is prevented by the resistance of trade unions. This asymmetry 'explains' the basic shape of the curve.

The two additional influences appearing in his analysis can also be fitted into this picture. When prices rise very strongly, in particular when they rise more than money wages,[8] then the threatening decline in real wages leads to additional wage demands which in turn may lead to further price increases and to a price-wage-price spiral.[9] The influence flowing from *changes* in the unemployment rate can be interpreted as the effect of expectations. In times of falling unemployment the business situation improves and firms are competing more heavily for labour – at a given *level* of unemployment – than when unemployment is rising and things seem to be heading for the worse. Such a behaviour would explain the systematic deviations of wage changes from the Phillips curve.

While this explanation given by Phillips – with its combination of market and institutional forces – had a firm basis in well-known theoretical and practical concepts, it was neither exclusive nor necessarily conclusive. In fact, it is not difficult at all to explain the Phillips curve entirely in terms of institutional and bargaining processes. This can be done on the basis of a simple trade union cost push assumption, or by regarding the wage changes as the outcome of a complex bargaining network, involving trade unions and employers' organizations, labour courts, government and public opinion. In both cases the Phillips curve would suggest that wage claims are more readily pressed and more readily accepted in times of high and/or improving employment conditions and when prices rise than when the opposite conditions prevail. The shape of the Phillips curve then summarizes the actual ways in which this bargaining process works.

In explanations of this type it is not essential to regard unemployment as an indicator of labour market conditions. It could also be a proxy for other cyclical factors which influence the bargaining process. Thus the Phillips curve as such was not incompatible with Kaldor's contemporaneous hypothesis that wage movements were decisively influenced by profits, high profits leading to stronger and more easily granted wage demands (see Kaldor 1959). Since profits and unemployment are (inversely) related such a view could be defended, though later and more detailed studies indicated that the impact of profits and their changes is normally less pronounced than the influence of unemployment.

While the link between the Phillips curve and a pure bargaining concept is easily established it was less clear whether the Phillips curve – with its peculiar shape and the persistence of wage increases in face of continuing unemployment – would also be fully compatible with a pure market model. That such a theoretical basis is indeed possible was established in a famous and ingenious article by Lipsey (1960) which appeared very shortly after Phillips' study had been published. More recently an argument on similar lines but using a different approach and resting on less specialized assumptions has been presented by Hansen (1970). The following very simplified sketch of a market-induced Phillips curve follows in the main the Hansen model. [10]

We start off with the simplest model of a competitive market, viz. one with linear demand and supply curves. We shall show that all that is required in order to derive a Phillips curve are two assumptions:

(a) adjustment towards equilibrium is not immediate (i.e. conditions of excess demand or excess supply can exist), and (b) the labour market is an imperfect market where a certain amount of frictional unemployment and frictional vacancies persist even in times of 'equilibrium' because some people are always on the move between jobs (or entering the labour market for the first time) and because the filling of vacancies requires time.

Let us now look at a simple labour market of the kind described. In Figure 12.3, where W stands for the wage rate and N for the number of workers, DD' depicts the demand for, and SS' the supply of labour at alternative wage rates. (Neglect for the moment the curved line EE'.) Obviously, the market would be in equilibrium when $W = W_0$; everybody who wants to work at this wage can find employment and all vacancies could be filled. There would be neither unemployment nor unfilled vacancies. With a wage rate of W_1, on the other hand, demand would be W_1C, while supply (and effective employment) would only be W_1B. There would be excess demand (and unfilled vacancies) to the extent of BC. Similarly, with a wage

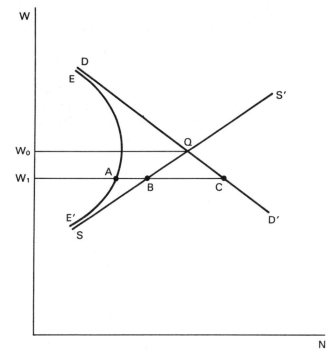

Figure 12.3 A competitive labour market with frictions

rate lying above W_0 effective employment would be limited by demand, and there would be a certain amount of excess supply (unemployment).

A simple assumption about the equilibrating process in a competitive market is that prices (wages) tend to rise or fall in proportion to the excess demand or supply existing at a certain point of time. No change occurs in equilibrium. If we write ΔW for the percentage change in the wage rate per period of time, and V_N and U_N for the number of unfilled vacancies and the number of unemployed at the beginning of the (short) period, the above assumption can be expressed as follows:

$$\Delta W = k(V_N - U_N),$$

where k is a positive parameter indicating the speed of the adjustment process. We can change this formula to vacancy and unemployment *rates* (V and U) by dividing V_N and U_N by N and changing k accordingly. Also, to make the approach more general, we can formally allow for possible institutional, bargaining and trend factors which provide a constant upward shift to the wage movement. Denoting this shift with r per cent per period we arrive at the following wage change equation:

$$\Delta W = k'(V - U) + r. \tag{1}$$

Disregarding the *r* for the moment (or setting it zero) and referring back to Figure 12.3 we have the following situation: for any given *level* of wages there is a certain amount of *effective* employment which will lie somewhere on the broken line *DQS*. When wages are below W_0 there exist only vacancies and wages rise at a rate of $k'V$; when they are above W_0 there is only unemployment and they fall at a rate of $k'U$; in equilibrium $V = U = 0$ and wages remain constant. The situation is summarized in Figure 12.4, where the slope of the line depends on the strength of the adjustment forces in 'disequilibrium' (k').

So far we have neglected the fact that there are frictional forces in the labour market which prevent the full matching of compatible demand and supply wishes. Thus unemployment and unfilled vacancies can exist side by side. But unemployment will, of course, be rather low and vacancies numerous when there is excess demand (i.e unemployed workers will quickly find new jobs) and vice versa in times of excess supply. Owing to these frictional factors effective employment at alternative wage rates is not located on the broken line *DQS* in Figure 12.3 but on the curved line *EE'*. Thus at wage W_1 there exist unfilled vacancies *AC*, but also unemployment *AB*. *AB* is the amount of frictional unemployment and vacancies, and *BC* is excess demand as before. In equilibrium we have still $V = U$, but they are

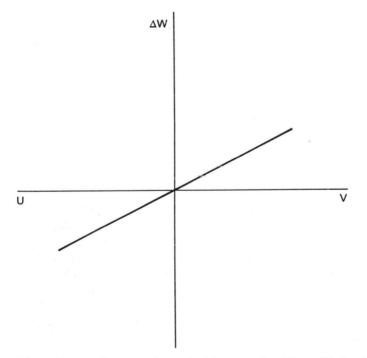

Figure 12.4   Adjustment forces in labour market 'disequilibrium'

no longer equal to zero. At extreme wage levels unemployment or unfilled vacancies will become very small indeed, but they will never quite disappear.

In the wage change equation (equation 1) V and U now exist side by side. But in equilibrium $V = U$ and we still have (apart from r) no tendency for wages to change. Movements still depend on the existence of an *excess* of demand or supply. By filling in the data for V and U in equation (1) the job of 'explaining' money wage changes would be completed. But Phillips curve analysis works only with unemployment figures. This is done for practical reasons. Statistics of unfilled vacancies are frequently non-existent, and even where they exist they are often of doubtful quality. Unemployment figures, on the other hand, are regarded as 'hard' statistics on which more reliance can be placed.

To obtain the transformation of equation (1) into a function where wage changes depend on unemployment only, we assume that − in addition to the demand and supply functions − the position of the EE' curve in Figure 12.3 is a more or less stable relationship determined by the strength of the frictional elements. We then obtain for each wage level a certain and definite combination of V and U (e.g. AC and AB at W_1). Depicting all possible combinations one derives the hyperbolic curve shown in Figure 12.5, i.e. a relationship of the type

$$VU = h \qquad (2)$$

The parameter h indicates the strength of the frictional elements. With no friction at all $h = 0$ and we have *either V or U* = 0 as before (along the line DQS in Figure 12.3).

From equation (2) we can derive V as a function of U

$$V = h \frac{1}{U}$$

Substituting this value in equation (1) we obtain

$$\Delta W = k'h \frac{1}{U} - k'U + r$$

showing the wage change as a non-linear function of unemployment. The first term depicts the typical curved Phillips relationship particularly in the regions of low unemployment. With unemployment becoming very large the relationship tends to become more linear, but the decline into negative values may be slowed down due to trade union resistance or other institutional elements (r). Only when there are no frictional forces ($h = 0$) does a linear relationship between wage changes and unemployment (typical for the pre-Phillips approaches but used in some later studies too; e.g. United Nations, 1967) depict the situation in a competitive labour market with linear demand and supply schedules.

If we allow for the co-existence of several labour markets with structural

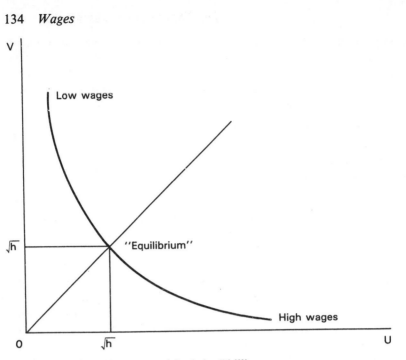

Figure 12.5   The Hansen model of the Phillips curve

barriers between them the possibilities for the simultaneous appearance of unemployment and excess demand are enhanced and there is additional scope for Phillips-type relationships. Also the influences coming from *changes* in unemployment can be fitted into the picture. One explanation rests on the observation that at the beginning of an upswing (falling unemployment) vacancies rise relatively fast while the unemployed can only be gradually absorbed. The 'normal' *V-U* relationship is disturbed and excess demand (which 'determines' the wage rise) is underestimated by the isolated use of unemployment figures. Conversely, when the recession sets in (rising unemployment) vacancies fall off rapidly while workers are not dismissed at the same speed. Again. the 'normal' relationship is distorted, and unemployment underestimates the existing excess supply (leading to an upward bias in wage change estimates).[11]

Both bargaining and market approaches can thus be shown to be compatible with the Phillips curve. While resting on alternative assumptions they have one thing in common: they both derive the Phillips curve from direct macroeconomic pressures on the money wage rate. They show no connection with traditional wage theory in which productivity and the firms' labour demand springing from it play a decisive part in explaining wage levels and wage changes. An interesting attempt to criticize and reinterpret the basic Phillips results from this point of view was presented by Kuh (1967).

Kuh starts from a theoretical basis in which value productivity is the decisive influence on wage levels and their changes, and he wants to show why other influences – in particular unemployment, price changes and profits – seem to be decisive in the Phillips curve and its later extensions.[12] The following variables play the main part in Kuh's model:

X: real production (in constant values)
P: price index of production (not consumer prices)
W: hourly wage rate
M: man hours in production
U: unemployment rate.

The average value productivity per man hour is given by the observable relationship PX/M. Kuh assumes that the *movements* of this magnitude, which plays an important part in his model, are closely related to *movements* in the (not observable) marginal productivity of labour. This would have an obvious appeal to neoclassical theorists. But even if this assumption is dismissed, Kuh would maintain that the stress has to lie on productivity, with average productivity (and not market variables!) being decisive for the labour demand of entrepreneurs and the claims of unions.

A further assumption in Kuh's argument is that the mark-up on wage costs is a useful indicator of the profit situation. Writing Z for this mark-up and noting that total wage costs are equal to WM, profits, therefore, move in sympathy with

$$Z \equiv \frac{PX}{WM}.$$

We can now proceed to confront Kuh's model with the ideas put forward in Phillips-type studies. In the centre of his model Kuh places an equation which he regards (on the basis of theoretical and empirical considerations) as a good 'explanation' of the equilibrium level of the money wage rate:

$$W = B\left(\frac{PX}{M}\right)^{\alpha} \cdot U^{-\beta}$$

In this equation, in which B, α and β, are parameters, the (equilibrium) wage *level* is decisively influenced by the value productivity of labour. In addition there are some bargaining elements which are caught by the unemployment variable: in times of low unemployment the equilibrium level will be somewhat higher, and it will be lower when there is a lot of unemployment.

How do the empirical facts about wage *changes* revealed in Phillips-type studies look when viewed from this angle? Let us deal with profits and price changes first, and then turn to Phillips's V.I.P., the unemployment rate.

The main agent in wage dynamics for Kuh is the (value) productivity of labour; it 'determines' the wage level, and when it changes the wage level will also change. Now assume that productivity (PX/M) increases, be it that P or X rises relatively faster than M. This will be the 'real cause' for a greater demand for labour and a rise in the equilibrium wage rate. But the shift to the new equilibrium will take time. At first, with PX/M rising, wages (W) will lag behind so that in the adjustment period Z ($= PX/WM$) and profits will show a distinct increase. This 'disequilibrium' relationship between high profits and rising wages is statistically caught in various wage change equations. It is then interpreted as a *direct* causal relationship: with high profits prevailing, unions put forward higher claims and entrepreneurs are more capable and more willing to give in to these claims.

A similar divergence in interpretation arises with regard to prices. Rising *industrial* prices lead to an increase in the value productivity of labour and this, in Kuh's view, is the 'real' cause for an increase in the (productivity-determined) wage level. This hypothesis is set against the usual interpretation that rising *consumer* prices lead to higher wage demands ('real bargaining') which are again more readily conceded because of the rising prices. Kuh's interpretation thus shifts the weight from consumer prices to industrial prices; but since the two usually move together their relative importance cannot easily be derived from empirical data.

The fundamental difference between the Kuh and the Phillips approach becomes apparent in the different interpretations of the unemployment variable. In the Phillips 'theory' unemployment is a measure of market pressure which in turn 'determines' wage *changes*. Low unemployment results – be it through demand pull or strengthened bargaining power – in *persistently higher wage increases* than can be observed in a state of greater unemployment.

In Kuh's view the *change* of wage is determined through changes in productivity. High or low unemployment may lead to a once-and-for-all shift in the wage level but will not cause a constant deceleration or acceleration in the wage movement. In Kuh's view the employed and the unemployed are largely non-competing groups. Even if unemployment is high wages can, therefore, rise in step with productivity: the continuing wage increases in times of recession are derived from 'profit'.[13] If, nevertheless, an apparent relationship exists between unemployment and the *rate of change* of money wages this is again due to indirect effects. In times of business expansion and boom, when unemployment is low, we usually have rising prices and above-average increases in production due to rationalization and better capacity utilization. Labour productivity (PX/M) thus rises more sharply in these periods leading to a corresponding acceleration of wage increases: hence the observed relationship between unemployment and wage changes.

In recent years still another sort of theoretical interpretation of the Phillips facts has made its appearance. It consists of a variety of models which more or less supplement each other. They all lay stress on specific labour market adjustments at the micro-level of firms and employees, and they attribute special weight to the problems of incomplete transparence, uncertainty and expectations. Phelps has been pioneering in this direction, but several others have followed suit (see for instance, Phelps 1968, 1969, and 1970; Holt 1969; Mortensen 1970). The following few paragraphs do not attempt to give a full and detailed picture of these various (and partly highly sophisticated) models, but simply aim at a general idea of the type of reasoning involved.

A characteristic difference in these studies is that their argument does not stress a one-way causal chain from macroeconomic market pressures *reflected* in unemployment rates to corresponding pressures on wage rates. Rather, there are typical behaviour patterns at the micro-level leading to interdependent relationships between wage changes and unemployment which in turn give rise to Phillips-type observations, though not necessarily to stable ones.

Take, for instance, some aspects of the wage-paying considerations of firms.[14] Firms will want to pay wages that can secure them the desired labour force at minimum costs. In particular, wages have to be set sufficiently high, in order to attract new labour when firms try to expand; and they have to be set high enough to keep the old labour force and to reduce labour turnover which is costly because of the expenses involved in recruiting and training new workers.

The first influence is, of course, the one which comes closest to the Phillips-type demand pull approach. When most firms try to expand they will bid up wages and unemployment will be low: the Phillips relationship will be clearly visible. But the rate of increase in wages will not depend directly on the rate of unemployment but on the urge of firms to expand employment and to lure away workers from other firms. The rate of unemployment may be a poor indicator for variations in this urge and this may account for the poor fit of some of the Phillips curve calculations. Wage changes at any given level of unemployment may still vary in response to other indicators of expansionary intentions, such as changes in the number of vacancies or in employment.

The second influence mentioned above may also be important and it may contribute further to loosen the relationship between wage changes and unemployment rates. When firms have to decide what wages and wage advances they have to grant in order to keep their labour force they will be decisively influenced by their expectations of wage changes in general. In this way general changes in expectations at the firm level can become a factor influencing the course of wages making them less tied to the present market or unemployment situation. But a certain relationship will continue in so far as expectations will normally be closely geared to certain stages of the cycle with its different rates of unemployment.

Or take a look at micro-adjustments on the employee side. A typical characteristic of labour markets is – as we saw – that even in 'full equilibrium' frictional unemployment persists. This is due not only to the time it takes to move from one (lost or quit) job to another, but also to incomplete information with regard to market conditions, Thus, a certain part of unemployment arises from the fact that some people are moving around in the search for good or better jobs. This 'search unemployment' (a term made widespread by Stigler, 1962) is an information process in the course of which people find what they hoped for or learn to adjust their targets downwards until the wage offered becomes the 'acceptance wage'. The size of this (frictional) search unemployment will depend on such labour market characteristics as amount of information available, search periods, probability of contract in case of negotiations, flow of new hires (depending on layoffs, retirements, labour turnover).

Search unemployment can exist even if the market is in equilibrium and if there is no 'involuntary' unemployment. Now assume that in such a situation the economy expands with production and prices rising. Firms will want to hire new labour (or to prevent their workers from quitting) and wages will be rising more rapidly. This will have its effects on search unemployment. First, the higher number of vacancies will reduce the search period per worker and increase the probability that concrete talks will come to a successful conclusion. Second, with rising wages the obtainable wage will more frequently be regarded as the acceptance wage. Fewer workers will leave their firms in order to search for better wages. For both reasons – shorter search periods and fewer quits – unemployment will be reduced. Thus, higher wage increases and lower unemployment will go together. This is a Phillips relation, but it will be noted that the argument here runs rather in the reverse direction: from wage increases to unemployment. This difference in viewpoint can – as we shall see later – lead to discrepancies in the interpretation of Phillips curves and in policy matters (see pp. 143 and 148–9).

THE POST-PHILLIPS DEVELOPMENTS

In the previous section we have seen that there is no shortage of theoretical interpretations that can be imposed on the Phillips curve and some of its extensions. A similar *embarrass de richesse* developed in the empirical sphere. The attempts to catch the wage change influences in more detail and more 'accurately' than Phillips could have done in his pioneer study stretching back far into the last century, have been growing continuously. They cover different countries, regions, sectors, periods, etc. In this section some of the main trends in this literature will be pointed out.

(a) Extensions of the Phillips curve

The attraction and the beauty of the 'simple' Phillips curve was its strong and highly relevant one-way connection between unemployment rates and wage changes. True, changes in unemployment and heavy price increases also played a part in Phillips' considerations. But it was a minor part and it could be neglected at no great cost.

One of the characteristics of the post-Phillips literature is that in most cases the number of explanatory variables has been increased; a 'modified Phillips curve' has become the rule. The Phillips aspect of these investigations – as contrasted to alternative constructions mentioned in section (d) below – is that unemployment, mostly in a non-linear form,[15] still makes a strong appearance, though it may no longer be the principal agent.

Among the additional variables price changes have probably become the most regular visitors. Further factors considered include change and dispersion of unemployment, profits and change of profits, vacancies and employment variables, productivity, trade union strength, etc. One important element in many studies is the use of dummy variables to set off certain periods of institutional change and policy adjustment. Since most studies – and particularly the American ones – showed that the Phillips relation, even if duly modified, is by no means close and stable, the dummy variables were introduced in an attempt to discover factors making for systematic shifts in the Phillips curve, such as changes in trade union militancy, the introduction of an incomes policy and other influences of this sort.

(b) Methodological advances

Phillips obtained his results on the basis of rather crude methods which were justifiable considering the crudity of his data, but also in view of the very long period he considered. The later studies, dealing mostly with post-war periods, had the advantage of a much greater supply of relevant and more reliable statistics, but suffered from the relatively short time span for which these were available. The latter fact was partly overcome by the increased use of quarterly data which multiplied the number of 'observations'. Quarterly data also opened the way for greater experimentation with all sorts of lags and distributed lags which would have been out of place with annual data.

The advances in statistical techniques and the availability of computers have greatly increased the choice of equations which can be and are drawn up for comparisons. Added to this variety of equational structures there is a multitude of 'respectable' variables (see section (a)) so that the range of choice is very great indeed. One of the problems of empirical research in this field is that because of the lack of an accepted theory and the incomplete insight into the mechanics of wage formation there are no clear criteria on which to rest the decision for a particular equation. The exclusive reliance on purely statistical considerations ('goodness of fit', etc.) cannot be regarded as satisfactory in view of the wide dispersion of the data, the incomplete coverage of 'explanatory' variables, and the high degree of multicollinearity existing between some of them.[16] The obvious intertemporal instability of some of the parameters also means that the choice of period may be crucial for the size and relevance of the values obtained.

(c) Specification of data

In addition to the choice of the variables to be included in the wage change equation there arises also the question which type of statistics should be used to represent a given variable. Compared with the amount of work invested in equational and methodological innovations surprisingly little attention has been given to this point.

It comes up quite clearly and unavoidably when we turn to the dependent variable: the wage change. What sort of wage statistics is to be used? Does one restrict the investigation to manufacturing, to production workers, or does one extend it to wider areas and bigger groups? Should money wages alone be considered or should changes in fringe benefits also be taken into account? And, most important of all, is it wage rates (determined in collective agreements) or (actual) hourly earnings that are to be explained?

It is obvious that the choice between these alternatives already involves some conception about existing connections and interdependences. Yet, one cannot help feeling that in many cases those statistics are chosen which are readily available or seem more reliable without too much thought being given whether the conclusions aimed at are permitted on the basis of these special choices. Thus it is probably availability that explains the fact that in British studies wage rates are prominent while in US studies earnings are the rule, though a good case for this difference can be made in view of the importance of plant bargains in the States.

At any rate, it seems likely that something could be gained by more speculation about the type of series to be chosen and the type of hypothesis that should go with it. Speculation alone will, of course, not solve the problems; but it may indicate where further investigations into the functioning of the labour market would be fruitful. Take, for instance, this difference between rates and earnings. Rates would obviously be the proper series if we want to test the influence of unemployment (the labour market situation) on bargaining; earnings, on the other hand, would be more appropriate if the demand pull is regarded as decisive.

Unfortunately, acceptable results in one direction or the other need not be decisive in answering competing hypotheses. The picture is complicated by the many possible interrelationships. Thus, the original 'cause' of wage changes may come from the pushfulness of unions but the setting of rates may immediately be translated into corresponding adjustments in earnings. Conversely, the 'true cause' may be the market forces pulling up earnings, but trade unions may follow swiftly in order to keep rates in contact with actual payments. Thus, closer regard for the specification of the basic variable reveals new problems and suggests the collection of additional factual information and possibly the construction of more disaggregate models which show the related developments of wage rates, wage drift, wage earnings.[17]

What has been said about wages[18] applies with equal force to the other variables involved. It has already been mentioned in connection with Kuh's theory that opinions are divided whether consumer or producer prices are the 'proper' series for price changes (see above, p. 135). When a profit variable is used the problem usually is not only how they are to be delineated, but also how reliable the data are.

But even the unemployment figures, the 'hardest' statistics in the whole relationship, may deserve closer scrutiny. At least for the United States the work of Simler and Tella (1968) seems to show that in some periods the consideration of labour reserves (potential teenage and female workers, etc.) and participation rates will give a better indication of the labour market situation and better-fitting Phillips curves than the use of official unemployment figures.[19] Since European countries, too, know some 'hidden unemployment', there seems to be room for experiments in this direction.

(d) Alternative routes

More disquieting than the watering down of the simple Phillips relation through additional variables and methodological variations must be – to the addict of the Phillips curve – the fact that investigations using a rather different frame-work also led to statistically acceptable and economically meaningful results. There is no sharp dividing line between studies falling into this group and those which were treated in section (a). It is not easy to say where a strongly 'modified Phillips relation' shades into a 'non-Phillips relation'.

A good example for such a border-line case is the famous study by Eckstein and Wilson (1962). In common with Phillips unemployment still plays a part in the wage change dynamics, but it is a more restricted part. Its macroeconomic influence on demand pressure or bargaining strength is to some extent of an indirect nature. Sectoral unemployment has a decisive role (in addition to profits) in the determination of certain key bargains in key industries (steel, motor cars, etc.). From there the wage advances move on to the other industries (spillover effects). In this secondary adjustment the current labour market (unemployment) situation is still of some influence, but it is a very reduced one, with prices and profits as further agents. This chain process covers one wage round and then repeats itself.

Eckstein and Wilson's results thus suggest that historical and institutional factors, such as the evolution of key industries and the duration of wage rounds, may have a decisive effect on wage change mechanisms. This would lessen the general validity of the Phillips curve and more attention would have to be paid to national peculiarities. One thing, however, remains certain. The Eckstein-Wilson approach has not come nearer to a stable relationship (for US data) than the more traditional Phillips studies. In a later investigation Eckstein (1968) found that the relations obtained for the 1950s and early 1960s were less applicable in subsequent years. Not only did they lead to 'wrong' estimates; the governing elements – key industries and wage rounds – became less clearly visible.

A complete break-away from the Phillips curve was presented by Hines (1964), though in a later and more disaggregated study (1969) he slightly mitigated his extreme counter-position. Hines showed that he could satisfactorily 'explain' British wage changes over a long period from changes in the degree of trade union organization. The rate of change of the percentage of the labour force unionized and to a minor extent the level of unionization itself proved to be significant influences, with prices acting as a further important element. Unemployment did not show up in a significant manner when added to these variables.

Hines's interpretation of his results is that trade union pushfulness is a decisive influence, and that this pushfulness – in contrast to a Phillips-type bargaining hypothesis – is not a function of the labour market situation (unemployment). Pushfulness cannot be directly measured. But Hines suggests that a more militant attitude of trade unions will normally be accompanied by a drive for additional members. Changes in the degree of unionization can thus be regarded as an index of changes in pushfulness. Hines also guards against certain obvious objections to his conclusions. Through additional calculations he firstly shows that there is no correlation between his union variable and unemployment which would leave the (indirect) influence of the latter intact. Second, lagged correlations indicate that the wage increases follow the change in unionization and not the other way round. The rise in membership can thus not be a *consequence* of successes in the bargaining process.

IS THE PHILLIPS CURVE A STABLE LONG-RUN PHENOMENON?

While the basic Phillips curve obviously lost its simplicity and uniqueness in the subsequent discussions it proved sufficiently strong as an empirical phenomenon and a theoretical concept to survive in most discussions about wage dynamics, employment and inflation. True, the multitude of results and interpretations sharpened the sense for the relativity of many Phillips-type models. It was realized that shifts in the parameters may occur and that attention must be paid to institutional and policy elements, etc. But all this could be taken as a warning to use Phillips curves more cautiously, and not as a complete dismissal of the entire concept.

A much more fundamental onslaught on the Phillips-type argument and its policy implications has recently come from a basic theoretical standpoint. Connoisseurs of economic disputes will guess that a fundamental onslaught is likely to come from Milton Friedman. The guess is correct. It was above all Friedman (1968) and Phelps (1967) who advanced the idea that while a Phillips curve 'offering' various combinations of wage rises and unemployment rates may exist in the short run, it could not present a permanent long-run relationship.

The argument runs roughly as follows. To begin with a framework is adopted which rests heavily on neoclassical equilibrium thinking. It is assumed that all individuals enter the markets with certain *real* aspirations. The diverging aspirations of different individuals are then brought into line by market forces, in particular, by the pricing process. The process tends towards a (static or dynamic) 'equilibrium' in which everybody accepts the current situation in real terms. Disequilibria may exist for some time because of insufficient information, adjustment lags or short-period money illusion. But ultimately people will react until the market ensures the compatibility of their different demand and supply schedules.

Translated into terms of the labour market the following picture arises. [20] Employers want to employ different amounts of labour depending on conditions in the product market and the real wage rate. Workers offer employment in response to the real wage they can get. At any particular real wage rate there will be some unemployment, because some people do not want to work at this rate and because some people are on the move looking around for a suitable and well-paid job (search unemployment). This 'voluntary' unemployment also exists in full equilibrium and may be called 'natural' unemployment.

Let us now assume that we are in a state of equilibrium with stable wages and prices and, therefore, stable real wages. The situation is characterized by a certain rate of 'natural' unemployment. Next let us assume that the government wants to reduce the unemployment rate by introducing expansionary policies. The increased demand in the product market will lead to a rise in demand for labour and money wages will rise. The increase in wages will reduce unemployment; people who regarded work as unrewarding at the old rate will now be prepared to enter employment, and search unemployment will be reduced for two reasons. First, some people will not quit when wages rise at their old place of work, and second persons between jobs will find acceptable wages more quickly when the wage level is rising.

But this happy state of reduced unemployment coupled with rising wages would not – so the argument runs – last long. For along with rising wages prices would rise too (because of higher demand in the product market, unchanged real productivity and rising labour costs). The workers would soon learn that the rising wages they can earn in the tighter market do not improve their real position. The money illusion would vanish and the – expected – rise in money wages would return the real situation to its old level. Firms would raise wages at the 'customary' rate knowing that prices rise at this rate too and that this adjustment of wages is necessary to maintain their labour force. Workers would take up as much time in looking for employment as before, because they would now look for jobs with *above-average* wage increases which alone would promise an improved real wage. Search unemployment would return to its old level, people who were dissatisfied with the real wage in the initial position would be just as unwilling to accept the rising wage which could do no more than maintain the previous level of real wages. 'Natural' unemployment would be at the same rate as before in an unchanged *real* situation. Only prices and wages would now rise from period to period in line with the expectations carried over from the past.

In order to keep unemployment at the below-normal rate the previous process would have to be repeated at a higher level. Additional demand pressure would have to drive up wages faster and these increases above the expected rate would again induce some people to stay at work or to accept a new offer more quickly. Voluntary unemployment would be reduced until the learning process had caught up with the new rate of inflation and expectations were fully adjusted to it. Then the 'natural' unemployment and the real situation would once again be the same as before, only with wages and prices rising at a faster rate.

Unemployment could not be kept below its natural level through a constant rate of wage increases. The traditional Phillips curve would be a transitory phenomenon. To keep unemployment at the lower rate one would have to resort to ever faster wage and price increases, constantly surpassing past expectations and creating new money illusions. Once this process of evergrowing inflating is stopped unemployment reverts to its 'natural' rate which is tied to the real wage rate and compatible with any amount of (expected) wage-price uplift. The 'true' long-run Phillips curve emerges as a vertical line running through the point of 'natural' unemployment.

The whole argument is summarized in Figure 12.6. Assume that we start off with an 'equilibrium' position characterized by point E. Wages are stable ($\Delta W = 0$) and everybody who wants to work at the current real wage is employed. 'Natural' (voluntary) unemployment equals U_n. Now, suppose one wants to reduce unemployment to U_1. Demand pressure drives wages up and we move along a normal Phillips curve (R_1) until we reach the point A. Wages rise now at a rate of W_1, and the growing wages induce people to cut down search unemployment etc. Unemployment falls to U_1. As soon, however, as people have learned that the wage rises of W_1, are necessary to match the corresponding and expected price rises they will adjust to the real situation and move to point B. Wages and prices now rise in line with expectations and behaviour is fully adapted to the inflationary environment. Unemployment is again at U_n.

To get it back to U_1 one would have to climb up a new Phillips curve (R_2) appropriate to the expectations ruling at B. This would lead to point C with higher wage and price increases from where a further move to D would follow as soon as the new rate of inflation is fully discounted. Then a still higher short-run Phillips curve would become operative. To stay at U_1 would require climbing up along AC to increasingly higher short-run

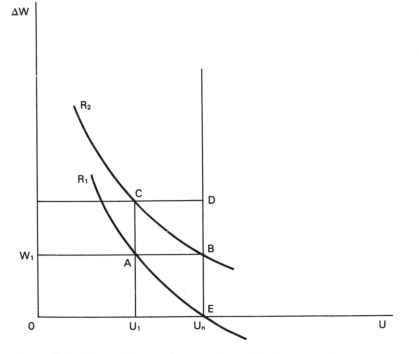

Figure 12.6 'Natural' unemployment in an inflationary environment

Phillips curves, while the only stable long-run 'Phillips curve' is the line *ED* where unemployment is U_n. It remains invariant to any *expected* rate of wage and price increases.

The answer to this argument can be given on general lines or with specific reference to the results of Phillips curve research. On general lines one has to point out the weakness of neoclassical equilibrium thinking which does not show up here for the first time. After all, the above reasoning resembles very closely the repeated warnings that the creeping post-war inflation would soon be discounted and would inevitably lead to galloping inflation.

The main weakness lies in the belief that strong tendencies towards a clearly definable real equilibrium are at work and that this equilibrium can be easily achieved in a flexible market environment. But as we know, reality is rather different. Things are moving all the time in a world full of uncertainties and rigidities. Tendencies towards equilibrium may exist, but adjustment is slow and costly, and while it takes place the equilibrium point may have shifted. Expectations play a part, but the irregularities (e.g. of inflationary rises) and uncertainties of changes make it unlikely that very firm, general expectations can be formed from short-run experiences. In a world like this a certain amount of inflation can help to overcome rigidities in the money-price and money-wage structure and thus ease adjustment processes. This will lead to a permanent reduction of structural and frictional unemployment, because – contrary to the assumptions of the Friedman-Phelps model – a certain amount of this unemployment is involuntary. People might be prepared to take jobs at the current real wage, firms might be prepared to hire people; but the downward rigidity of some costs and prices slows down the required adjustment to a constantly changing demand *structure* when total demand is to be kept at all costs at a non-inflationary level (see Rees, 1970).

Perhaps more important than these general considerations are the specific experiences gained from Phillips curve research. In two ways they point against the assumption that the observed 'normal' Phillips curves would only exist for a short time and then resolve into a vertical line running through a point of 'natural' unemployment. The first counter-argument is simply the fact that some of the observed Phillips relations have survived the inflationary periods which we have experienced so far without showing any tendency to disappear (see, for example, Reuber, 1968).

The second point is more general. In almost all modified Phillips relations containing a price-change variable we find that the coefficient of this variable is less than unity, often considerably less.[21] When prices rise by a certain percentage, wages do not normally follow immediately and to the full extent.[22] There is no mechanism pressing towards a constantly accelerating inflation, and nothing so far points to a full 'real wage' adjustment behaviour as stipulated in the Friedman-Phelps hypothesis.

It may be worth while to establish this last point more exactly.[23] Let us introduce a simple Phillips curve in a growing economy where the money wage increase depends on unemployment and the *expected* price change:

$$w_t = f(u) + a p_t^e. \tag{1}$$

In the above equation w_t is the percentage change in wage rates in period t, u is the unemployment rate ($f'(u) < 0$), and p_t^e is the *expected* price change in period t. The higher p_t^e the greater the wage demands, and the greater the readiness of employers to accept the demands. a is a positive parameter showing the degree by which price expectations influence the wage change.

Let us now assume that an inflation has continued for a sufficiently long time to be fully anticipated. Prices in period t will be expected to rise at the same rate as they rose in the previous period (periods):

$$p_t^e = p_{t-1} \tag{2}$$

Substituting (2) in (1) we obtain

$$w_t = f(u) + a p_{t-1} \tag{3}$$

We now add the assumption that labour productivity rises by q per cent per year and that prices are fixed by adding a constant percentage margin to labour costs (constant mark-up pricing). Prices rise when and to the extent that wages rise faster than productivity (i.e. in proportion to labour costs):

$$p_t = w_t - q \tag{4}$$

Substituting (3) in (4) gives

$$p_t = f(u) + ap_{t-1} - q. \tag{5}$$

An equilibrium solution for constant, non-accelerating inflation is obtained by setting $p_t = p_{t-1} = \bar{p}$ in equation (5):

$$\bar{p} = \frac{1}{1-a} \left\{ f(u) - q \right\}. \tag{6}$$

We see that the size of a is of decisive importance. When $a = 1$, i.e. when wages are fully adjusted to the expected (long-run) price increase, then equation (6) does not yield a solution: there is no equilibrium. In this case equation (1) becomes

$$w_t = f(u) + p_t^e$$

or

$$w_t - p_t^e = f(u). \tag{7}$$

i.e. we have *real* wage bargaining. There is a relationship between unemployment and the (expected) rise in real wages. Equation (5) then becomes

$$p_t - p_{t-1} = f(u) - q. \tag{8}$$

This is the Friedman model. There is a 'natural' unemployment rate u_n, for which the desired and expected increase in real wages is exactly equal to the rise in labour productivity.[24] At this level of unemployment the right-hand side of equation (8) is equal to zero and we have

$$p_t = p_{t-1},$$

i.e. 'natural' unemployment is compatible with any (constant) inflation rate whatsoever. If, however, u is to be pressed below this level, we have

$$p_t - p_{t-1} > 0, \text{ since } f'(u) < 0.$$

The demand for a faster rise in real wages connected with lower unemployment implies an accelerating inflation.

Now let a be smaller than 1 (and this is the empirically relevant case). Equation (6) has a solution and the situation is no longer 'explosive'. Expected price increases have only a damped effect on wage increases. These, in turn, lead to price increases and to further (but again damped) wage increases and so on. We obtain a converging process which finally settles down at the 'equilibrium' rate of inflation indicated by equation (6), the size of which depends on the rate of unemployment. We have arrived at a permanent and stable Phillips curve of the traditional type.

General and specific considerations thus show that the principal onslaught on the *possibility* of a long-run Phillips curve cannot be maintained. This does not, however, imply that the views put forward in this debate should be completely dismissed. They have drawn attention to the neglected aspects of expectations and 'learning by experience'. The consequences are not as far-reaching as the pure and flexible neoclassical model suggests. But it may well be that *some* effects may follow. Thus it could be that prolonged demand pressure coupled with high rates of inflation may gradually increase the steepness of the Phillips curve in its left-hand, upper branch.[25] But even this effect cannot be deduced from a priori principles. Whether it occurs in the real world of shifting inflation rates, uncertainties, rigidities, lagged adjustments etc. will have to be established empirically.[26]

THE 'TRADE-OFF' QUESTION

One of the main attractions of the original Phillips curve was that it seemed to offer an extremely useful instrument for policy decisions of highest priority. At the end of the fifties the dilemma between full employment and price stability had begun to worry governments in most developed industrial market economies.[27] Since price movements are related to wage movements, a reliable Phillips equation offers the policy maker a chance to see more clearly how much price stability he has to sacrifice in order to obtain more employment and vice versa. The Phillips curve revealed the 'trade-off' between employment and price stability.

This aspect of the Phillips curve was already presented in the original Phillips article itself where it was pointed out that maintenance of a stable price level would probably require an unemployment rate approximating 2.5 per cent. The argument rested – in this case and in most of the literature that followed – on a simple hypothesis of mark-up pricing with unit labour costs serving as a basis. Prices would accordingly remain stable when money wages rose in line with labour productivity, and would increase to the same extent as wage increases surpassed the rate of productivity change.[28] Shortly after the publication of Phillips's article Samuelson and Solow (1960) carried his analysis fully into the sphere of inflation policy. They shifted the Phillips curve to a price change–unemployment diagram with prices behaving in accordance with the 'rules' mentioned above,[29] and named this construct a 'menu of choice' for policy decisions. Since then the 'trade-off' question has been continuously discussed in general and quantitative terms. To some aspects of this discussion we now turn.

To begin with an obvious point must be stressed. The whole discussion is only meaningful if a somewhat stable and inverse relationship between the basic Phillips variables (wage change and unemployment) *does* exist, and if the price fixing assumption is not too far removed from reality. The idea that price stability and employment can be 'traded' against each other must, therefore, be dismissed – at least for long-term policy – by all proponents of the Friedman-Phelps hypothesis. Their long-term 'Phillips curve' is vertical and no inflation rate whatsoever can permanently 'buy' a lower rate of unemployment. Their view gives a free hand to price stabilization policy; (permanent) employment has nothing to fear from it. At the other end of the scale we find the view – to some extent expressed by Harrod (1967), for example – that money wage increases have largely become an institutional phenomenon depending on bargaining processes which are not much influenced by current economic conditions and unemployment. Here the 'Phillips curve' becomes horizontal; the creation of unemployment does not help to dampen the wage and price increase; and employment policy need not bother about repercussions on the price front.[30]

The following considerations refer to the field in between these two extreme positions. It is assumed that there is *some* relationship between unemployment and wage and price changes, and that the discussion around the 'trade-off' problem is not entirely meaningless.

Policy discussions frequently involve value judgements. It is desirable that these value judgements should be made explicit. (This, too, is a value judgement!) This has not always been the case in the problem under review. Sometimes a preference is already implied in the way the policy dilemma is presented. This is the case when a special 'critical' value is read off from the Phillips curve (or the price–unemployment diagram), viz. that unemployment rate which yields price stability.[31] Putting the problem this way means that price stability is in some way regarded as a special priority. That may be so; but then this should be stressed and the reasons for this decision should be given. Otherwise attention is distracted from the fact that any other point on the curve (e.g. unemployment equal to 1 per cent) has the same 'right' to be pointed out specially.

If a special point on the curve is to be chosen, i.e. if we do not just want a 'menu for policy choice' but a 'solution', we must know what value judgements are to be met. Formally. it is not difficult to find an elegant solution for this case. If we can define a social preference field for the various combinations of price change and unemployment, then an 'optimum' solution can be determined.

This approach. which was suggested by Lipsey (1965) and which appears in several later discussions is illustrated in Figure 12.7. There ΔP represents the increase in prices and U the unemployment rate. AB is a Phillips curve transposed into a price change diagram. R_1 and R_2 are two sample indifference curves depicting the social preferences with regard to price stability and employment. The assumption is that people are prepared to sacrifice some price stability in order to reduce unemployment, but that they become less willing to do so the higher the price rise and the lower the level of unemployment. Hence the concavity of the indifference curves towards the origin; R_1 represents, of course, a locus of preferred points as compared with R_2 where price increases and unemployment rates are higher.

Where preferences are so clearly defined, a stable and simple Phillips curve can indeed deliver an optimum solution. It is given by the point M

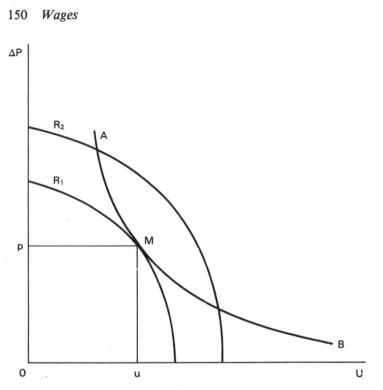

Figure 12.7   Unemployment, inflation and social preferences

in Figure 12.7 yielding the inflation rate p and the unemployment rate u. The irrelevance of this solution in practical affairs is obvious. Not only do we have no methods of measuring social preferences over the whole field of potential solutions, the idea of a unique ordering of social interests is itself highly artificial. Employment and price stability are targets which involve the interests of various classes and groups in such different ways that conflicting views are unavoidable (see note 27). Thus, there can be no 'objective' solution for our policy dilemma to be read off from a Phillips curve. It is the *whole* curve that has to remain under discussion (provided it is reliable) when a compromise between conflicting interests is looked for.

An implicit value element is also contained in the uncritical acceptance of a special price formation hypothesis. The following identity will help us to illustrate the point in question. Writing P for the price index of national income in a certain year, Y for the nominal, and Y_r for the real national income (measured in base year prices) in that year, then − by definition − $P = Y/Y_r$. This latter expression can be split up in the following way:

$$P = \frac{Y}{Y_r} = \frac{\overline{W}}{L} \cdot \frac{1}{Y_r/L} \cdot \frac{1}{\overline{W}/Y}$$

where $\overline{W}$ stands for the total wage bill and L for the total employed labour force (dependent employees). $\overline{W}/L$ thus represents the wage per worker, Y_r/L labour productivity, and $\overline{W}/Y$ the wage share in national income.

The equation shows clearly that the usual pricing assumption in trade-off discussions where prices remain stable, if and only if wages do not move out of step with labour productivity, *involves* the assumption of a constant wage share. Now, if a constant wage share were an irrefutable theoretical and empirical phenomenon, this would be alright. But this is not so. And the price hypothesis in the trade-off debate has thus created the one-sided impression that inflation can only be cured by concessions on the employment front. The possibilities of attacking the problem from the distributional angle are frequently disguised by the very way the problem is presented.

Turning now to a more concrete discussion of the possible uses of Phillips curves in the inflation-unemployment dilemma we can distinguish two alternative approaches: (a) using a given Phillips relation in order to choose some acceptable and practicable combination from it; and (b) attempts to shift the Phillips relation so that better combinations can be obtained than heretofore and/or that the trade-off in the decisive region can be improved. A few remarks on each of these approaches should help to show in what directions the efforts go and with what sort of problems they have to contend.

Table 12.1 Wage changes and unemployment in different Phillips curve calculations

	Rate of unemployment associated with a percentage change in wages equal to	
	Own productivity growth rate	$2\frac{1}{2}\%$
UK		
Phillips (1861–1913)	2.3	2.1
Lipsey (1923–39, 1948–57)	1.8	1.7
Klein and Ball (1948–58)[*]	2.1	2.0
Dicks-Mireaux and Dow (1950–56)	–	2.0
USA		
Samuelson and Solow (post-war)	–	5.5
Bhatia (1948–1958)	7.5	8.0
Bowen and Berry (1948–58)	7.8	8.2
Klein and Bodkin (1948–57)[*]	5.4	5.6
Perry (1947–60)	6.0	6.6
Canada		
Klein and Bodkin[*]	5.2	5.6
Kaliski (1946–58)	6.5	10.0
Reuber (1949–61)	4.4	5.2

Note
[*] Linear relationship between wage change and unemployment.

Moving along a given Phillips curve, i.e. using it as a 'menu of choice' in policy decisions, was of course the method that offered itself as an immediate after-thought in view of Phillips's stress on the stability of his simple relationship. To the extent that the trust in this stability has gone and the number of additional variables has grown this hope for a forceful and clear-cut policy instrument had to be reduced.

Table 12.1 which is based on calculations by Reuber (1968:751) shows that rather different results are obtained for 'critical' unemployment levels depending on the period chosen, the structure of the model, and the additional variables included.[32] The variation is particularly wide in American calculations where wage changes of 2.5 per cent are related – according to the study chosen – to unemployment rates ranging from 5.5 to 8.2 per cent. The British results are far more uniform, with unemployment ranging from 1.7 to 2.1 per cent.[33] With the inclusion of recent years the variation in results would increase. In any case, there remains the problem of choice between the 'menus of choice'. The problem becomes more involved when alternative price mechanisms are introduced and estimates about the probable productivity development have to be added.

Similarly, the simple beauty of the Phillips curve as an aid in decision-making disappears when the multi-variable 'explanation' in all the later Phillips-type studies is considered. Instead of choosing one point on a more or less reliable curve one is faced with a multitude of different combinations which all yield the same rate of wage or price increase. Thus Perry (1966: 59) concludes from his model that to keep the wage rise at the price stabilizing level of 3 per cent (assuming productivity to increase at that rate) 'requires' 5.4 per cent unemployment with profit rates standing at 10.8 per cent, the average of the years 1953–60; but that the same wage increase could be obtained for 4.8 per cent unemployment, if profits were reduced to 10 per cent. It is obvious that these differing combinations quickly multiply when several equations are offered, each with its own special choice of variables, structures and lags.

The interlocking dependence among several variables also means that even where the impact on unemployment and price changes can be foreseen with some accuracy, there remains the probability that the measures and the resulting employment and price developments have important side effects in other spheres of economic and social interest. This indicates that Phillips curves – even at their best – should be used with care in view of their limited range of observation. This aspect has been clearly stressed by Brechling (1968):

'The major objection to the notion of a trade-off between unemployment and inflation is that, as a rule, unemployment and inflation cannot and should not be treated independently of other objectives of economic policy. The balance of payments, economic growth, structural change, and income distribution are all likely to be arguments in the collective utility function and to be affected by unemployment and inflation. In a consistent over-all optimization procedure, all arguments in the collective utility function and their interrelations ought to be considered. An optimization procedure which has singled out unemployment and inflation and neglected the other objectives is highly likely to yield a suboptimal solution.'

Finally, we may mention that conclusions from empirical Phillips curves may run into difficulties when they reach into ranges which lie beyond recently observed unemployment rates and wage/price changes. In view of the wide dispersion of observations and the lack of an adequate theory 'explaining' the 'proper' shape of the curve, any extrapolation outside the cluster of current and recent data is bound to be capricious.

To escape the dismal choice between more inflation or more unemployment one can try to go behind the Phillips curve. By attacking some of its underlying causes one could shift it to a lower level and thus be able to have more of both, employment and price stability. Most anti-inflationary programmes have something of this sort in mind. Owing to the many and competing theoretical ideas involved there are several prescriptions available.

Since the imperfections of the labour market loom large in the market interpretations of the Phillips curve, it is obvious that some theoreticians and policy experts hope to achieve improvements by adjustments in this field. Everything that reduces frictional unemployment and lowers the barriers to structural adjustment will lead to less unemployment in equilibrium and to fewer price-raising bottlenecks in less-than-full-employment situations. Better information would, for instance, reduce search unemployment, better labour exchanges would create quicker contacts, and training facilities on the job would reduce labour turnover. Sweden's 'active manpower policy' is a forceful attempt to shift the Phillips curve in an economy that does not want to buy price stability at the cost of unemployment.

A somewhat different procedure would have to be adopted if the forces behind the Phillips curve are not regarded as over-all pressures on the labour market but rather as specific mechanisms in labour market procedure. When, for instance, key bargains, spillovers and wage structures are decisive magnitudes, then successful adjustment may require selective interference in certain branches and areas, and at specific times (when wage rounds start).

The most comprehensive efforts to escape the constraints of the Phillips curve can be found in the various attempts towards a prices and incomes policy. While the methods applied may differ considerably from country to country and from period to period they have one thing in common: they try to break traditional mechanisms of wage and price formation as they become visible in the Phillips curve and its transposed form in a price-employment field.

The various techniques used in the field of incomes policies ranging, as they do, from strict interference through price and income boards to the sweet sounds of moral suasion need not detain us here. Nor do we have to pass judgement whether the rather limited effects of such policies have been due to a wrong kind of approach or to some inherent tendencies in contemporary capitalist economies. Perhaps the time for experimenting has been too short to draw any definitive conclusions. But what seems to be important in our context is a point recently raised by Lipsey and Parkin (1970). They argue that even where an incomes policy *does* affect the Phillips curve the result may not be an unmixed blessing for the policy maker faced with the dilemma between unemployment and inflation.

Put very simply the argument boils down to the following consideration. Normally one hopes – by means of an incomes policy – to shift the whole Phillips curve downwards so that each rate of unemployment becomes connected with a lower rate of wage pressure and vice versa.[34] In view of the several factors influencing the Phillips relation and the various ways they may respond to incomes policy measures it is, however, not certain that all points on the Phillips curve will be affected in the same way or even in the same direction. In fact, instead of causing a general downward shift of the Phillips curve, the incomes policy may result in a *rotation* of the curve, lowering it in some parts, raising it in others.

Suppose that the original Phillips curve has the shape AA' in Figure 12.8. An incomes policy is now introduced recommending (among other measures) the limitation of annual wage increases to W^*. We assume that

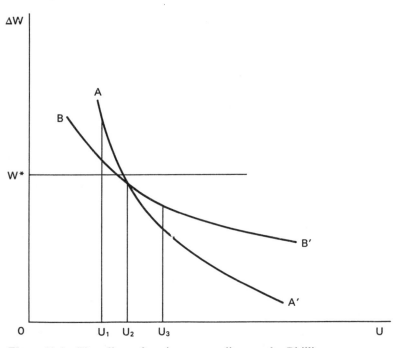

Figure 12.8   The effect of an incomes policy on the Phillips curve

this is offered as a guide-post which is not strictly enforced and where exceptions are permitted. In times of strong demand and low unemployment wages will now rise less. Employers and the government in particular will be reluctant to offer wage increases beyond W^* (i.e. the wage drift will be smaller), and trade unions will have difficulties in pressing for higher wages. It may not be possible − in the face of high demand pressure − to stick exactly to the target of W^*, but wages would increase less than if there had been no incomes policy.

On the other hand, when demand slackens and unemployment rises the wage target W^* may not completely lose its force. While intended as a maximum it may acquire the character of an 'aspiration level'. Trade unions would continue to press for this amount of wage advance, and while employers would try to resist these demands in recessions, they would be − profits and budgets permitting − in a weaker position to do so than if there had been no target level.

Under these conditions the incomes policy would result in a rotation of the Phillips curve from AA' to BB'. Whether the policy is a 'success' or not would largely depend on the criterions used and on the cyclical developments after its introduction. If in the subsequent periods the economy is kept at a high level of activity with unemployment in the range between U_1 and U_2 (Figure 12.8), the policy will be 'unsuccessful' in so far as the recommended target of W^* is somewhat surpassed, but it will be 'successful' in keeping the upward trend of wages below what it would have been without the policy. If, on the other hand, the economy is allowed to run into recessions with unemployment in the region of U_2-U_3, then W^* will normally not be surpassed but wages may on the average rise faster than they would have done in the absence of the incomes policy.

CONCLUDING REMARKS

Thirteen years of intensive discussion of the Phillips curve have shown that the original hope for a clear-cut and reliable relationship in an important sphere of economic activity has not been fulfilled.[35] The relevant empirical relationships are more numerous, more complicated, and less stable than the Phillips article suggested, there are competing alternatives, and the observations lack a secure theoretical framework.

Yet there can be no doubt that these years of research have not been wasted. For the first time we have a broad supply of empirical and theoretical material to cover the formerly neglected problem of money wage dynamics. While the concrete results of specific investigations may be too dependent on the methods and periods chosen to be absolutely reliable, comparison of different studies does produce a certain 'feel' for the orders of magnitude involved in the wage-employment-price-and-what-not-mix. We stand on somewhat firmer ground than before; some of the earlier beliefs about labour market mechanisms can no longer be maintained, others have found support in the results of the Phillips curve developments. But a lot remains to be done. We need more insight into the working of labour markets and wage-price mechanisms, and plenty of more reliable and more detailed data, if we want to pick the really relevant candidates out of the present multitude of eligible models and calculations.

From what has just been said it will be clear that the Phillips curve – in all its different forms – can only be of limited use in policy decisions. The idea of the trade-off and/or shifts of the curve can act as a useful element in the inflation–employment discussion. But for actual quantitative intervention it would be inadvisable to rely too heavily on some special Phillips curve.[36] More help can probably be obtained from a judicious use of competing Phillips models and a careful juxtaposition of their results. Even then, however, the ramifications of the Phillips variables extending to many other matters of economic and social significance will have to be kept in mind. Thus even at their best Phillips curves could only serve as one element among many in economic decision-making.

NOTES

1 By 'simple' I mean that wage changes are related exclusively to the rate of unemployment. I shall speak of 'modified' Phillips curves whenever additional variables are introduced to explain the course of wages.
2 Similarly remarkable is the resilience of the Phillips curve in face of the numerous restrictions it had to accept in later studies. Leijonhufvud's remarks are worth quoting in this context:

> Phillips' original article was of course an impressive piece of work. Still, it is curious to note that the dejà vu reaction was so strong that the Phillips curve immediately achieved a life of its own in professional discussion and teaching even while the numerous attempts to reproduce the experiment with American data, which quickly followed, failed entirely to isolate a comparably 'neat' and reliable relationship. Neither the failure to find a similar simple and stable relationship for the United States nor the fact that the simplicity of the Phillips relation soon began to dissolve in the further work of British economists seems to have affected the widespread conviction that the Phillips curve 'makes sense' and points out an important issue.
>
> (Leijonhufvud 1968: 738–9)

3 The use of the past tense means that the theory has been formed long ago, not that it no longer exists.
4 Real wages may fall as prices rise with rising output.
5 Introducing lagged unemployment as an additional variable permits the recognition of lags or of the effects emanating from *changes* in unemployment (which are represented in Phillips's analysis).
6 The path of this search is littered with such things as the Pareto curve, wage shares, capital-output ratios, saving propensities, Engel curves etc.
7 If a malicious remark is permitted: a further reason for the Phillips success was perhaps the non-linearity of his solution which looked slightly frivolous in the linear world of the econometricians.
8 Which have a rising trend because of rising productivity.
9 As later investigations showed, Phillips's analysis was too hesitant about the

price influence. It seems to be at work all the time, not only when price changes are above-average.

10 One simplification in particular is that I shall speak most of the time of a single labour market. The argument is easily extended to a multitude of sectional labour markets. The extension actually reinforces – through the appearance of structural unemployment – the tendencies lying behind the Phillips curve.

11 A different, but empirically doubtful 'explanation' was given by Lipsey (1960). He assumed that a Phillips-type relationship applies to each partial labour market with sectional unemployment as the decisive influence. He then goes on to say that in the upswing labour markets will at first be affected very unevenly. Unemployment will become more widely dispersed and this will – owing to the curvi-linear relationship – yield higher wage increases for the corresponding *average* unemployment rate than if all labour markets were at this average or showed less dispersion of unemployment. The recession, on the other hand, is assumed to hit all labour markets with more or less equal force so that their individual unemployment rates become less dispersed and the resulting wage increase less removed from the average relationship.

12 In the following section some of these later developments are summarized.

13 Needless to say that they can also be 'explained' in different terms: institutional forces, continuation of price advances, etc.

14 The following remarks refer to actual wage payments rather than to wage settlements in collective bargaining. On this point see below, p. 140.

15 One of the *formal* changes that have come to stay is that in the post-Phillips literature the non-linear influence is represented by U^{-1}, while Phillips allowed the exponent of U to vary (by using the form $U^{-\alpha}$). Occasionally stronger types of curvature are allowed for, e.g. by adding a term U^{-2} or higher powers. At the same time, in some studies the pre-Phillips linear dependence on unemployment has been maintained, partly because a first approximation was considered sufficient, partly because – alongside with other variables – a linear relation gave a sufficiently satisfactory fit over the observable range.

16 'The "hypotheses" tested seem all too often to be of the type: "It seems reasonable to suppose that, by using variable x as an additional or substitute independent variable, a better regression result should be obtained". When the theoretical underpinnings are no more ambitious than that, there is almost no basis on which to compare results, and new studies seldom knock old ones out of consideration' (Leijonhufvud 1968: 739).

17 For an analysis taking account of wage drift see, for instance, Klein and Ball (1959).

18 One further variation with regard to the wage series has lost most of its importance. In the earlier studies we find occasionally wage changes expressed in absolute terms rather than – the usual practice – in percentage terms. It seems that absolute changes could be justified when wage demands are in fact made in absolute amounts rather than in percentage terms. But when the calculations refer to the post-war period with its constant inflation the use of absolute changes introduces a bias. Wage changes in absolute terms are a trend magnitude increasing with time while the 'explanatory' variable, the unemployment rate, is free from trend.

19 See also the article by Vroman (1970) about the variation of results following from the use of alternative wage and unemployment indices.

20 The presentation is at first given in static terms with no technical progress and no rise in productivity. An inclusion of these, which does not alter the basic argument, follows later.

21 For instance, in the extensive study by Perry (1966), this coefficient has a value of 0.367 in the basic wage-change relation (equation 3.8).

22 This does not mean that in times of rising prices real wages actually fall. In a growing economy with growing productivity, money and real wages have a continuous upward trend. A lag of money wages behind price rises then just means that real wages grow somewhat more slowly in times of quickly rising prices than in times of moderate price advances.

   The fact of a growing trend in real wages quite generally weakens the Friedman argument. With irregular rates of real wage growth it is likely that people's behaviour becomes adjusted to expectations of further *increases* in real wages. But it is unlikely that very exact ideas are formed about the extent of 'necessary' advances. As long as money wages rise faster than prices (because of growing productivity) it is unlikely that people withdraw from employment. On the other hand, rising prices may ease the expansion and regrouping of production and employment.

23 The following analysis is based on Smith (1970).

24 This is the adaptation of the previous static formulation to a growing economy.

25 This possibility is suggested by Rees (1970).

26 Thus Reuber (1968) could not discover any tendencies towards a steepening of the Phillips curve in Canadian data. He suggests that adjustments to changed expectations are very slow and long-term processes (30 years?), and that even in hyper-inflation adjustment lags occur.

27 This is a statement of fact. Whether full employment and price stability are really problems of the same order of urgency is, of course, a matter of personal judgement. People who have experienced the misery of the 1930s will probably regard full employment as the important target with price stability playing only a subsidiary role. (Too much inflation might endanger full employment in an open economy.) Financial circles may take a completely different view.

28 Let P be the price per unit of output, W the wage per worker, and Y the real output per worker. Then the assumption about price determination is

$$P = k \cdot \frac{W}{Y}$$

where k is a fixed mark-up factor. We can also write

$$\log P = \log k + \log W - \log Y$$

Differentiating by t we obtain

$$\frac{d \log P}{dt} = \frac{d \log k}{dt} + \frac{d \log W}{dt} - \frac{d \log Y}{dt}$$

or

$$\frac{d \log P}{dP} \cdot \frac{dP}{dt} = \frac{d \log W}{dW} \cdot \frac{dW}{dt} - \frac{d \log Y}{dY} \cdot \frac{dY}{dt}$$

since $\dfrac{d \log k}{dt} = 0.$

But $\dfrac{d \log P}{dP} \cdot \dfrac{dP}{dt} = \dfrac{dP/dt}{P}$

and similarly for the expressions involving W and Y. Thus we obtain

$$P' = W' - Y'$$

where P', W', and Y' are the relative changes in prices, wages, and productivity per unit of time.

29 A shifted Phillips curve is illustrated in Figure 12.9 below. The lower axis together with the right-hand scale on the ordinate depicts the values of the original Phillips curve. Assuming that labour productivity rises by 3 per cent per annum the price-employment relationship is obtained by an upward shift of the axis by 3 points and applying the left-hand scale of the ordinate. Where the Phillips curve cuts the new axis we have the point of price stability (U_1).

30 'I prefer the Swedish target, which they cannot, of course, achieve fully, of having unemployment at 0 per cent.' (Harrod, 1967, p. 17).

31 U_1 in Figure 12.9.

32 The additional variables are not contained in the table. They have been held at their average level.

33 The percentages of unemployment are not comparable *between* countries. The wider variation in the USA may be due to the fact that calculations there refer to earnings which are affected by agreements and adjustments on an enterprise level. These may be more sensitive to cyclical influences and, therefore, to the period chosen than the general wage *rates* whose changes are investigated in the British studies.

34 Separating periods without incomes policy from those having one with the aid of a dummy variable denoting the latter ones, the parameter of the dummy should have a negative sign (the wage increase being the dependent variable).

35 A recent test of the predictive performance of Phillips-type models and a comparison of these predictions with other models and reasonable 'naive' forecasts

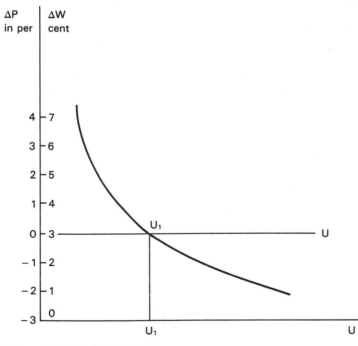

Figure 12.9   A shifted Phillips curve

clearly shows that no superiority can yet be claimed for the Phillips approach from this point of view. See Pencavel (1971).

36 'Our final caution is that we have been astounded by how many very different Phillips curves can be constructed on reasonable assumptions from the same body of data. The nature of the relationship between wage changes and unemployment is highly sensitive to the exact choice of the other variables and to the form of all the variables. For this reason, the authors of Phillips curves would do well to label them conspicuously, "*Unstable. Apply with extreme care*"' (Rees and Hamilton 1967; italics in the original).

REFERENCES

Bellerby, J. R. (1923) 'The Controlling Factor in Trade Cycles', *Economic Journal*, 33.

Brechling, F. (1968) 'The Trade-off Between Inflation and Unemployment', *Journal of Political Economy*, 76.

Dunlop, J. (1957) 'The Task of Contemporary Wage Theory', in Dunlop, J. (ed.), *The Theory of Wage Determination*, London.

Eckstein, O. and Wilson, T. A. (1962) 'The Determination of Money Wages in American Industry', *Quarterly Journal of Economics*, 72.

Eckstein, O. (1968) 'Money Wage Determination Revisited', *Review of Economic Studies*, 35.

Friedman, M. (1968) 'The Role of Monetary Policy', *American Economic Review*, 58.

Garbarino, J. W. (1950) 'Unionism and the General Wage Level', *American Economic Review*, 40.

Hansen, B. (1970) 'Excess Demand, Unemployment, Vacancies and Wages', *Quarterly Journal of Economics*, 84.

Harrod, R. F. (1967) *Towards a New Economic Policy*, Manchester.

Hines, A. G. (1964) 'Trade Unions and Wage Inflation in the United Kingdom 1893–1961', *Review of Economic Studies*, 31.

—— (1969) 'Wage Inflation in the United Kingdom 1948–1962: A Disaggregated Study', *Economic Journal*, 79.

Holt, C. C. (1969) 'Improving the Labor Market Trade-off Between Inflation and Unemployment', *American Economic Review*, Papers and Proceedings, 59.

Kaldor, N. (1959) 'Economic Growth and the Problem of Inflation', *Economica*, 26.

Klein, L. R. (1950) *Economic Fluctuations in the United States 1921–1941*, New York.

Klein, L. R. and Goldberger, A. (1955) *An Econometric Model of the United States 1929–1952*, Amsterdam.

Klein, L. R. and Ball, R. J. (1959) 'Some Econometrics of the Determination of Absolute Prices and Wages', *Economic Journal*, 69.

Kuh, E. (1967) 'A Productivity Theory of Wage Levels – An Alternative to the Phillips Curve', *Review of Economic Studies*, 34.

Leijonhufvud, A. (1968) 'Is there a Meaningful Trade-off Between Inflation and Unemployment?' *Journal of Political Economy*, 76.

Lipsey, R. G. (1960) 'The Relation Between Unemployment and the Rate of Change of Money Wage Rates in the United Kingdom, 1862–1957; A Further Analysis', *Economica*, 27.

—— (1965) 'Structural and Deficient Demand Unemployment Reconsidered', in Ross, A. M. (ed). *Employment and the Labor Market*, Berkeley.

Lipsey, R. G. and Parkin, M. (1970) 'Incomes Policy: A Re-appraisal', *Economica*, 37.

Mortensen, D. T. (1970) 'Job Search, the Duration of Unemployment, and the Phillips Curve', *American Economic Review*, 60.

Pencavel, J. H. (1971) 'A Note on the Comparative Predictive Performance of Wage Inflation Models of the British Economy', *Economic Journal*, 81.

Perry, G. (1966) *Unemployment, Money Wage Rates and Inflation*. Cambridge, MA.

Phelps, E. S. (1967) 'Phillips Curves, Expectations of Inflation and Optimal Unemployment Over Time', *Economica*, 34.

—— (1968) 'Money Wage Dynamics and Labor Market Equilibrium', *Journal of Political Economy*, 76.

—— (1969) 'The New Micro-Economics in Inflation and Employment Theory', *American Economic Review*, Papers and Proceedings, 59.

—— (1970) *Microeconomic Foundations of Employment and Inflation Theory*, New York.

Phillips, A. W. (1958) 'The Relation Between Unemployment and the Rate of Change of Money Wage Rates in the United Kingdom, 1861–1957', *Economica*, 25.

Rees, A. and Hamilton, M. T. (1967) 'The Wage-Price-Productivity Perplex', *Journal of Political Economy*, 75.

Rees, A. (1970) 'The Phillips Curve as a Menu for Policy Choice', *Economica*, 37.

Reuber, G. L. (1968) 'The Specification and Stability of Estimated Price-Wage-Unemployment Adjustment Relationships', *Journal of Political Economy*, 76.

Samuelson, P. A. and Solow, R. M. (1960) 'Analytical Aspects of Anti-Inflation Policy', *American Economic Review*, 50, Supplement.

Simler, N. J. and Tella, A. (1968) 'Labor Reserves and the Phillips Curve', *Review of Economies and Statistics*, 49.

Smith, W. L. (1970) 'On Some Current Issues in Monetary Economics: An Interpretation', *The Journal of Economic Literature*, 8.

Stigler, G. (1962) 'Information in the Labor Market', *Journal of Political Economy*, 70.

Tinbergen, J. (1936) 'An Economic Policy for 1936', reprinted in *Selected Papers*, Amsterdam, 1959.

United Nations (1967) *Incomes in Post-War Europe*, Geneva: Economic Commission for Europe.

Valavanis-Vail, S. (1955) 'An Econometric Model of Growth, U.S.A. 1869–1953', *American Economic Review*, 45, Supplement.

Vroman, W. (1970) 'Manufacturing Wage Behavior with Special Reference to the Period 1962–1966', *Review of Economics and Statistics*, 52.

13 Stagflation: how much of the Phillips curve survives?

(Translation of (1982) 'Stagflation: Was bleibt von der Phillipskurve?',
Wirtschaft und Gesellschaft 2 : 3, pp. 183–94)

I

It is now almost a quarter of a century since (in 1958) that famous article by Phillips was published, [1] introducing the Phillips curve. Ever since it has populated countless numbers of theoretical and policy debates and books. Yet the contents of that article were anything but sensational. With the aid of very long-term, though not absolutely reliable data, it showed that an inverse relationship exists between wage inflation and unemployment: the higher the inflation rate the lower is normally the rate of unemployment and vice versa. This was not a new discovery – it had already been observed in earlier studies without making a great noise about it [2] – and it is moreover a fact which is easily understood even for a person with no special economic training. This is so because experience has proved that in the ups and downs of the business cycle prices, wages and employment have a tendency to move together. This suffices to make the stipulated relation between wage inflation and unemployment a plausible phenomenon.

But what Phillips said was a little more than this. Using comparatively simple methods he could show on the basis of English price and employment data that over the previous hundred years the relationship between wage changes and unemployment had a certain form which had remained more or less stable over the whole period. The prototype of the Phillips curve was born: a *given* size of wage change could be linked with a *corresponding* rate of unemployment.

Though Phillips intended no more than to present and interpret the historical data without drawing far-reaching conclusions regarding a general validity of the concrete results, [3] the ensuing discussion very quickly moved towards such generalizing statements. Hopes were generated that here one could find one of those hotly desired 'constants' in the economic process which would offer a chance of getting a better understanding of and hold over the 'chaotic' course of economic events.

Theorists and politicians were equally fascinated by this aspect. This is probably the reason for the rapid proliferation of the Phillips curve in theory and practice after 1958. An enormous number of empirical and theoretical studies have been carried out and policy concepts have been deeply influenced. The question whether a Phillips curve exists, whether it is constant and 'reliable', what its causes are, which form it takes, etc. has provided material for endless discussions.

The massive appearance of stagflationary tendencies in the 1970s has acted like a shock on this ongoing discussion. Suddenly it was seen that high rates of inflation[4] and of unemployment can exist side by side. Both economists and politicians were faced with new and open questions. Was the Phillips curve a thing of the past or had it been an illusion from the very beginning? Have we to reckon with interdependencies between price stability and employment policies or not?

Stagflation forces us to see the theoretical, empirical and practical aspects of the Phillips curve in a new light and to reconsider previous arguments. This is particularly important because the Phillips curve is one of the rare examples where a close contact between theory and practice has been established so that the subject has to be attacked on this broader front. The following remarks are intended as a modest contribution to this topical reinterpretation.

II

As has been mentioned, the Phillips curve started a very broad empirical, theoretical and political discussion which is still under way. In this discussion different strands can be distinguished which partly overlapped, partly followed each other in time.

Seen from the point of view of theoretical progress the period immediately after the publication of the Phillips article was particularly fruitful. On the one hand – as behoves an empirical science – Phillips's 'experiment' was critically examined and repeated in various forms under different circumstances. It triggered a multitude of empirical studies which analysed the relevant data of different countries under a Phillips perspective.[5] They showed a sensitivity of results depending on the chosen period, on historical and institutional influences; they introduced additional and alternative determinants (price movements, profits, unions); and they fostered a more critical concern regarding measurement (*what sort* of unemployment, wage and price statistics) and methods (*which sort* of estimating procedures, functional forms, etc.). The investigations resulted in a Phillips curve that was less sharply defined than before. Whether a Phillips curve exists and how reliable the relationships are had now to be considered in a more differentiated way depending on time, place and other factors.

On the other hand, alongside the empirical studies theoretically orientated studies began to look for plausible theoretical reasons for the Phillips curve *on the assumption* that such a curve exists and is a long-term phenomenon.[6] Factors like excess demand, union strength and bargaining power, wage and price strategies, etc. and their influence on simultaneous movements of unemployment and inflation were analysed in more detail. Not surprisingly, several plausible hypotheses proved to be possible explanations for the existence of a Phillips curve.

Both these developments − the empirical and the theoretical investigations − had and have an enormously stimulating effect which proves that the Phillips article has kept its significance and relevance through all the years. An intelligent and pointed paper, even when it is based on only a few new data and theoretical ideas, can indicate questions and relationships which provide an important impulse for further and broadened research. In this sense the Phillips curve in its various forms has remained an important factor whose significance is not diminished through the appearance of stagflation. It only means that Phillips curve research *today* must try to muster, modify and supplement the broad material that has been accumulated in the 1960s and early 1970s so that the question of *when and under what circumstances* inflation and unemployment are negatively or positively linked can take centre stage. The Phillips curve as a historical and theoretical phenomenon can still act as an orientation for a useful array of relevant questions.[7]

A more questionable development following on the heels of the Phillips article was the attempt to jump directly from a heuristically valuable, but still uncertain Phillips curve to practical policy applications. An outstanding example was a paper by Samuelson and Solow, published in 1960,[8] which took the policy aspect of the Phillips curve as its central theme. The relationship between inflation and unemployment offers the politician − so it was argued − a 'menu of choice' in his search for an acceptable compromise between the conflicting targets of full employment and price stability. Depending on social and political preferences a certain combination between unemployment and inflation could be chosen, unemployment could be 'changed' against inflation and vice versa. The idea of a 'trade-off' was born and quickly invaded both theory and practice.

This approach was based − like parts of the theoretical discussion − on the assumption of a comparatively constant Phillips curve, but with a decisive difference. In the theoretical considerations the assumption of constancy was a provisional hypothesis in order to find out what the *possible* causes of such a phenomenon could be if it really existed (an open question!). In the policy debate, however, the constancy had to be an (approximate) fact to make the argument relevant. If it turns out to be a wrong assumption the adherence to a Phillips approach can have disastrous consequences. Moreover, for policy requirements it is not only important to make sure that a reliable Phillips curve does in fact exist, one has also to find out whether there is a direct relationship between inflation and unemployment or whether this relationship is caused by some third factors like demand or price setting processes. Such knowledge can be decisive for a correct choice of policy instruments.

The enthusiastic reception of the Phillips curve led at first to a neglect of these problems. Application-orientated economists abstained – as 'terrible simplifyers' – from warning the practitioners that the Phillips curve is at best only a primitive picture of one sector of a complex whole, and the politicians – under the pressure of conflicting aims – were only too ready to accept such a simple and easily understandable message. Thus, the naive idea could arise that one could 'play about' with a simple trade-off; that one could obtain more price stability by permitting more unemployment, or obtain more employment by giving in on the inflation front. In addition this was often regarded as a symmetrical, reversible affair. Although comments of such ideas can still be found,[9] stagflation has given a clear signal that the conflict between inflation and unemployment cannot always be treated or overcome within the framework of such a primitive scheme.

The trade-off debate suffered under the uncritical acceptance of the existence of a reliable and fairly constant Phillips curve. Ten years after this early effect a new development set in which went to the other extreme by denying the existence of a durable Phillips curve altogether, mainly for dogmatic theoretical reasons. I am referring to the discussions, which were started by Friedman and Phelps, about the concept of 'natural unemployment'.[10]

The allegation of dogmatism rests on the impression that the main motive for these studies was not a desire to study in more detail the historically existing Phillips curve phenomena, but rather an irritation about their existence. Phillips curves do not fit into the picture of neoclassical theory, with its tendencies towards price-determined full employment and market clearing.

In such a world one can only expect 'voluntary' and some frictional unemployment. Workers have – in this perspective – clear ideas about the real wage they must (at least) obtain in order to sell their labour services. If they cannot get that wage they either search (as temporarily unemployed persons) for a suitable job or they decide after some time to exit from the labour market altogether. Search and (voluntary) exit present 'natural' unemployment, which is the only type of unemployment which 'fits' the model. That general inflation, which leaves relative prices and wages more or less unchanged so that real relationships (including the real wage) are not touched, should have an influence on employment or unemployment cannot be reconciled with this view.

If one wants to stick to one's paradigm one has to reinterpret reality so that it fits into the model. With noteworthy effort sophisticated models have been constructed to 'explain' the *temporary* existence of Phillips curves as the consequence of such factors as imperfect information, mistaken expectations, money illusion. These modifications permit the maintenance of 'natural unemployment' as the guiding concept. It will become effective in the longer run as soon as the errors of the short period are recognized so that the real situation can be fully taken into account. Then unemployment is again at its 'natural' level, which is exclusively determined by real factors irrespective of the inflation rate which only affects nominal magnitudes. According to this analysis, a long-term Phillips curve does not — cannot! — exist.

It may seem that this approach has found a certain empirical justification by recent events. With the spread of stagflation many Phillips curves have become steeper or have disappeared altogether. In this respect neoclassical theorists have been in a better position to digest the new situation than orthodox 'Phillips curvers'. But there are two facts which still fail to find satisfactory explanation when one remains within the neoclassical natural unemployment perspective: first one has to ask why in some countries Phillips curves did prove to be long-living, and second one has to explain why 'natural' unemployment was so much higher in the 1970s than in the 1960s. What is obviously needed is a theory which could explain why, when and where Phillips curves exist or do not exist for considerable periods of time. To advance in this direction it is necessary, however, to free oneself from the axioms of an equilibrium model and the concept of 'natural unemployment'; they make it difficult to consider some factors which are of decisive importance.

Without attempting to discuss potential alternatives, a few hints are in place. They are meant to indicate some of the relevant factors. From the very start it is a strange idea to assume that workers whose wage income is the mainstay of their livelihood will react sensitively to every change in real wages. In our world of steadily growing productivity, workers expect and fight for increases in real wages without having any exact ideas about the extent the rise should take. Employment and unemployment are far more influenced by fluctuations in demand than by fluctuations in labour supply. This is one of the reasons why we observe different levels of hard unemployment cores in different periods. These basic facts are further modified by wage and price rigidities and by collective and monopolistic processes of wage and price formation so that the labour market (and quite a number of goods markets) cannot be properly treated from a predominantly equilibrium point of view.

This leads to the conclusion that the negation of the existence of long-term Phillips curves derived from equilibrium and natural unemployment theories is — as such — just as shaky as the former firm beliefs in the eternal character of the curve. The stagflation experience demands new non-dogmatic empirical and theoretical efforts in analysing the questions of inflation—unemployment relationships which had been raised so sharply by the Phillips article. In these efforts the history of the Phillips curve and its treatment can provide important impulses and orientations without, however, being able to regain that dominant role which it played in the 1960s. More probably the appearance of semi-constant Phillips curves will be a special aspect in a far more extensive theoretical structure in which historical and institutional factors will have to find a place.

III

So far I have tried to show that the stagflation experience makes it necessary to see the previous Phillips curve research in a new light. Primitive affirmative or negative answers will not do because it is obvious that there are longer periods with and without Phillips curves and it is this state of affairs that requires explanation. So much seems to be clear: there is no permanent and *necessary* close relationship between inflation and unemployment. All sorts of variations are possible and it will be necessary to return to a greater extent to the old practice of keeping inflation theories and employment theories in separate compartments in order to see where there are common causes and points of contact. This could then give us a better understanding when and under what circumstances we can expect a certain direct relationship between the two phenomena.[11]

Before this research delivers more reliable results it will be advisable to handle the heuristics of the Phillips curve with care. Most of all one should beware of loading it with non-existing *causal* relationships as happens, for instance, in the frequently expressed opinion that the Phillips curve implies that the creation of inflation as such could be a cure for unemployment.[12] The inadequacy of such arguments can be shown in a simple 'model' which is here presented as a small contribution to the Phillips curve discussion.

When we want to look beyond primitive Phillips curve hypotheses and weak empirical conclusions we should make use of the fact that there exist well-developed inflation theories, on the one hand, and employment theories on the other. Though most of these are partial and not undisputed theories, they nevertheless can serve as a good starting point. This means that one first looks *separately* at inflation and its determinants (quantity of money, distributional conflict, liquidity preference, structural shifts, balance of payments, etc.), then at employment and its determinants (effective demand, profit expectations, export opportunities, credit situation, labour participation rates, etc.) and ultimately tries to see if and under what circumstances Phillips curves of one sort or another might be expected.

In some combinations which were offered as an explanation of the Phillips curve after 1958 we find hypotheses which already indicate such a dual perspective from which an inverse relation between inflation and unemployment is derived. Examples are: demand as an inflationary and employment-creating factor; bargaining power as a consequence of high employment and as a cause of inflation; profits as a consequence of boom conditions and as a stimulus for wage demands. But in view of the multitude of causes affecting inflation and employment, these special combinations do not guarantee the general existence of a Phillips curve and still less its permanence. Other possible combinations imply *parallel* movements of inflation and unemployment, e.g. distributive fights in an environment of permissive monetary policy and low profit expectations or worsening export chances. With such alternatives stagflation can find an explanation just as well as the Phillips curve in different conditions.

Instead of following this path of showing if and when a Phillips situation (linking high inflation with low unemployment and vice versa) is likely to exist, I want to take the opposite road; I want to show that it is extremely *unlikely* to obtain long-term combinations of high price stability and high employment. When we go beyond the very short period it is typical for a modern growing economy with high employment that we are – for demand and technological reasons – constantly confronted with structural change. This requires shifts and adjustments of capital and labour if structural unemployment is to be avoided. In times of widespread unemployment such adjustments can be affected simply through the availability or non-availability of jobs in expanding or shrinking industries. But under conditions of full employment the adjustment process requires a shift in relative prices and wages.

To this we add the realistic assumption that many prices and wages are characterized by downward rigidity in the short and medium period. Relative changes in price and wage patterns are then not possible if the general price- and/or wage-level is to be held constant, because this would require prices and wages to rise in expanding sectors and to fall in those that are shrinking. If price (wage) reductions are not easily obtainable, the 'correct' pattern of relative prices (wages) can only be achieved via absolute and relative price (wage increases) in the growing sectors. We get the type of inflation which Schultze has called 'demand shift inflation'.[13] If one attempts to fight this inflation through a restrictive monetary or fiscal policy in order to obtain *absolute* price stability, the adjustment process will be choked and structural unemployment will appear.[14]

This constellation is summarized in a very simple generalized way in Figure 13.1, with the unemployment rate on the abscissa and the rate of inflation on the ordinate. Let OA be the highest unemployment rate which can possibly occur in the period under observation and OC the highest possible inflation rate. All possible combinations of inflation and unemployment must lie below CB and to the left of AB. But if we take into consideration what has been said in the previous paragraphs about economic dynamics and price-wage rigidities, the area of possible combinations is reduced to the hatched part of the diagram. Low unemployment rates (below $\bar{u}$) are not achievable without a certain degree of inflation which eases the adjustment process.[15]

Two things follow from this constellation. First we see that as far as there is a trade-off between inflation and unemployment it will not be a *symmetrical* relationship. Though it is not possible to obtain high employment without inflation, it is not the case that one can 'buy' more employment by just permitting more inflation. If one is, for instance, in situation A and now permits (or produces) inflation, the ensuing path may go in a north-

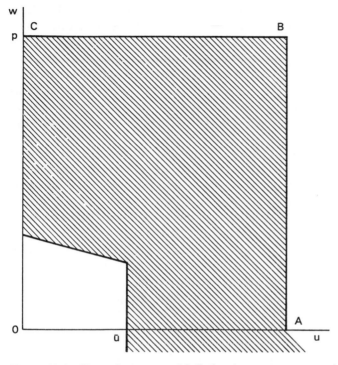

Figure 13.1 Unemployment and inflation (as percentage rates) in fifteen industrial countries

westerly direction, leading to the desired employment effects, but it can also go straight north, which would mean stagflation. The actual course will depend on the initial situation and the dynamics of the process.

The second remark is of direct significance for the Phillips curve discussion. If we accept Figure 13.1 as a picture of the real situation and if we further assume that the actual combinations of inflation and unemployment over time are distributed *completely randomly* within the (hatched) possibility area then we obtain a relationship which conforms (weakly) to a Phillips curve. *On average* small unemployment rates will be linked to higher inflation rates more often than large ones.[16] If we add to this the theoretical models which support the likelihood of Phillips-type relationships for other reasons it is perhaps permissible to conclude that *in normal times* the appearance of vaguely defined Phillips curves can be expected to be a frequent phenomenon.

As an illustration of this hypothesis I present in Table 13.1 a comparison of inflation and unemployment rates of fifteen developed industrial countries (Austria, Belgium, Canada, Denmark, Finland, France, Germany, Italy, Japan, Netherlands, Norway, Sweden, Switzerland, UK, USA). The comparison suffers, of course, from differences in the definition and calculation of unemployment rates and price indices. But for a rough comparison these data are sufficient. Five years within the range 1938 to 1980 were chosen and for each of these years the fifteen countries were ordered by rates of unemployment and then divided into three equal groups (of five countries each). For each group the average of the unemployment rates and the average inflation rate (based on the consumer price index) were calculated. For the post-war years an additional calculation was made, excluding Switzerland whose labour market developments are untypical because of the big and changing role of foreign workers. These alternative calculations are shown in brackets.

Table 13.1 shows that *in this rough grouping* a Phillips relation becomes visible in all years with the exception of 1980. (In 1950 Switzerland has to be excluded.) Though it would be wrong to read too much into this vague cross-section it nevertheless strengthens the idea that − for the reasons mentioned before − some sort of Phillips relation has a better chance to make an appearance than non-Phillips relations. The deviating results in 1980 can be seen as an expression of the special stagflation tendencies of the 1970s due to extraordinary factors (breakdown of the Bretton-Woods-system, decline in productivity growth, restrictive policies, etc.). In any case it seems too early to dismiss the Phillips hypothesis altogether just because stagflation has 'disturbed' this picture in recent years. In the longer run it may still turn out to be true that though inflation does not lead to high employment, high employment cannot be obtained when very ambitious price stability targets are set. This would suffice to lead to Phillips curves and trade-off considerations. But the idea that there exist *constant* Phillips curves which can serve as a base for reliable trade-offs will have to be buried for good.

Table 13.1 Unemployment and inflation (as percentage rates) in fifteen industrial countries

	1938		1950		1960		1970		1980	
	U	*P*	*U*	*P*	*U*	*P*	*U*	*P*	*U*	*P*
1st third	2.5	7.1	1.1	4.4	0.9	2.3	0.7	5.7	1.5	8.5
			(1.3)	(5.9)	(1.6)	(2.5)	(0.9)	(6.2)	(1.8)	(9.7)
2nd third	6.2	3.2	3.2	4.7	1.9	2.1	1.9	5.4	5.6	10.1
3rd third	15.6	0.2	9.1	1.4	5.3	1.3	3.9	4.9	8.4	12.9

Sources: International Labour Office, Yearbooks of Labor Statistics; Statistische Jahrbücher für die BR Deutschland; Statistische Taschenbücher der Arbeiterkammer Wien; and own calculations.
Notes: The fifteen countries are ordered in three equal groups with rising unemployment rates. *U* is the group average of the unemployment rate, *P* is the average inflation rate. Figures in brackets are excluding Switzerland.
    The fifteen countries are Austria, Belgium, Canada, Denmark, Finland, France, Germany, Italy, Japan, Netherlands, Norway, Sweden, Switzerland, UK, USA

NOTES

1 Phillips, A. W. (1958) 'The relation between unemployment and the rate of change of money wage rates in the United Kingdom, 1861–1957', *Economica*, 25, 100, pp. 283–99.

2 See Santomero, A. M. and Seater, J. J. (1978) 'The inflation–unemployment trade-off: a critique of the literature', *Journal of Economic Literature* 16, 2, pp. 499–544 (here p. 500).

3 'These conclusions are of course tentative. There is need for much more detailed research into the relations between unemployment, wage rates, prices and productivity' (Phillips, *op. cit.*, p. 299).

4 Phillips dealt with the relationship between wage changes and unemployment rates. Since, however, price changes are closely connected with wage changes (after allowance has been made for productivity changes) it is possible to transpose the wage inflation–unemployment relationship into a price inflation–unemployment relationship. See, for instance, Samuelson, P. A. and Solow, R. M. (1960) 'Analytical aspects of anti-inflation policy', *American Economic Review*, 50, 2, pp. 185–94. In this paper I shall normally just speak of inflation.

5 Detailed information on this and later aspects can be found in Santomero and Seater, *op. cit.*

6 The first important step in this direction appeared already two years after the publication of the Phillips article: Lipsey, R. G. (1960) 'The relation between unemployment and the rate of change of money wage rates in the United Kingdom, 1862–1957: a further analysis', *Economica*, 27, 105, pp. 456–87.

7 As an example (with interesting results for Austria) see Breuss, F. (1980) 'Gibt es eine stabile Phillips-Kurve für Österreich?', *Monatsberichte des Österreichischen Instituts für Wirtschaftsforschung*, 53, pp. 210–22.

8 Samuelson and Solow, *op. cit.* See also Frisch, H. (1980) *Die neue Inflationstheorie*, Göttingen: Vandenhoeck & Ruprecht.

9 As an example among many I want to quote an article in the *Frankfurter Allgemeine Zeitung* of 30 July 1981, which gave a report about a monetary symposium in Herrsching. Among the participants were Kurt Nemitz, president of the Landeszentralbank Bremen and member of the council of the Deutsche Bundesbank and Heinrich Irmler, former member of the directorate of the Deutsche Bundesbank. In this article we read: 'An essential point in the argumentation of Nemitz is that it is still an open question whether there exists a positive relationship between the inflation rate and the level of employment (Phillips curve). According to Irmler such a relationship does not exist; an acceleration of inflation will not bring about the end of unemployment.' Here we see a perfect example of a union between primitive ideas about the Phillips curve and a misunderstanding about the trade-off mechanism.

10 Friedman, M. (1968) 'The role of monetary policy', *American Economic Review* 58, 1, pp. 1–17; Phelps, E. S. (1967) 'Phillips curves, expectations of inflation and optimal unemployment over time', *Economica*, 34, 135, pp. 254–81.

11 As an example of such an analysis see Falkinger, J. (1979), 'Stagflation and ökonomische Theorien', *Wirtschaft und Gesellschaft*, 5, 3, pp. 283–302.

12 See note 9.

13 Schultze, C. (1959) *Recent Inflation in the United States*, Washington: Government Printing Office.

14 With downwardly rigid prices production and employment in the shrinking sector, would decline. A policy of price stability would have to concentrate on keeping in check the inflationary tendencies emanating from the price rises in the expansionary sector. This would have a dampening effect on demand in both

sectors and would make adjustment through wage and employment shifts more difficult.

15 This hypothesis can find support in the data of Phillips's initial paper. When one examines the data for the period 1913–48, in which unemployment rates and wage changes fluctuated within a considerable range (including declines in money wages) it strikes one that in the years of wage deflation unemployment was never less than 8 per cent. Lower unemployment was obviously only possible under conditions of positive wage changes. See Phillips, *op. cit.* p. 294.

16 Here is a simple 'experiment' which corresponds to the assumptions underlying Figure 13.1. Twenty two-digit random numbers were drawn within the range 00 to 99 and in each case the first figure was interpreted as unemployment rate u (in per cent) and the second as inflation rate p (in per cent). Combinations of $u < 3$ and $p < 3$, i.e. low unemployment in combination with low inflation, were not admitted. Otherwise every possible combination within the given range (0 to 9 per cent, round figures only) had an equal chance of acceptance. Three samples with twenty cases each were drawn. They resulted in the following linear relationships (with considerable deviations):

1 $p = 8.24 - 0.46\,u$
2 $p = 6.81 - 0.12\,u$
3 $p = 5.85 - 0.21\,u$

14 Is there a Weitzman miracle?

I

When an author presents an analysis of which he thinks that it can 'offer some foundation for a permanent solution to the problem of stagflation' (Weitzman 1985: 952) and when a book in which he expands his ideas (Weitzman 1984) is praised – on the dust cover – as 'marvellous' by Robert Solow, as 'important, stimulating, readable and persuasive' by James Meade, one tends to be torn between hope and scepticism. While I can easily agree with Meade that Weitzman's ideas are important, stimulating, readable and persuasive, I find it more difficult to accept Weitzman's high hopes that he has found a comparatively simple method to escape from a world of Keynesian unemployment into a non-inflationary full employment world. While this problem is not the only subject of his book, it is the predominant and most important theme which occupies the centre of his book and of the two articles in which he has given the gist of his ideas (Weitzman 1983; 1985).

My remarks will be restricted to the unemployment problem; and since Weitzman is obviously not just playing with an economic model but is trying to solve real world problems, my (tentative) remarks and doubts will refer both to the analytical and to the practical aspects of his papers. In section 2, I shall give a highly condensed version of Weitzman's basic ideas. This section can be read by itself for quick information: 'Weitzman in One Lesson'. Section 3 then contains some critical observations on the analysis and practicability of Weitzman's model.

II

Weitzman's central proposition is that a change from a system of fixed wages to some system of profit-sharing would fundamentally alter the output, employment and price behaviour of contemporary capitalist economies. In his articles and in his book he presents models of a wage and of a share economy where the output, employment and price effects are all considered. Everybody who is interested in the details of these models will have to turn to the original. Since I only want to comment on some labour market features I shall restrict myself to an extreme simplification of Weitzman's ideas which will be partly presented in diagrammatic form. As far as I can see these simplifications do not limit the significance (or otherwise) of my remarks; they only cut out all details, additions and modifications which are not absolutely essential for the present discussion.

Weitzman's basic macroeconomy is a mixture of neoclassic and Keynesian-Kaleckian elements. One important modification to 'normal' neoclassicism is the adoption of monopolistic competition as the standard case for all firms in the production sector. As long as additional labour can be obtained the firms can use their excess capacity to expand output at constant marginal labour costs. (There is no falling physical marginal productivity of labour within the range of unused capacity and unemployment.) Output will be influenced by demand which in turn depends on autonomous (private and public) expenditure which translates – via a consumption function with its multiplier effects – into total demand. But consumption is also affected by real cash balances. Thus – with the quantity of money given – each *and all firms* can expand sales by lowering prices, thereby increasing the real money stock and consumption. With monopolistic competition being the rule (*n* firms producing *n* 'commodities') there is no atomistic market clearing price; prices are set by the firms through a markup system on wage costs aiming at maximum profits. Consumers are never rationed: production and/or prices adjust to the given demand.

In contrast to the imperfectly competitive goods market the labour market is characterized by a homogeneous labour supply which – for reasons of convenience (and without loss of generality) – is assumed to be completely inelastic. In long-run equilibrium, competition among firms and workers will drive the wage towards the traditional profit-maximizing level where the unique money wage equals the marginal revenue productivity of the fully employed labour force. But for the short run money wage rigidity is assumed so that shocks and disturbances can lead to temporary (but long-lasting) unemployment or inflation.

In Figure 14.1, I summarize this framework with special reference to the labour market for the traditional wage economy, that is, an economy where the money wage is the only parameter determining the labour contract. On the abscissa we measure labour input (L) and real output (Y), which is proportional to labour over the relevant range (constant returns to labour). Let L^* be the given (inelastic) supply of labour with Y^* as full employment output. If the firms want to expand their sales at given external conditions (autonomous expenditures, spending propensities, quantity of money) they must lower their price. The R-curves (net-revenue curves) show the conditions facing each firm and all firms. The R-curve depicts the revenue obtainable by the firm per unit of sales (setting $Y = L$) after the deduction of all non-wage variable costs. By neglecting these other variable costs we can denote this net-revenue per unit as 'price per unit' (P). The MR-curves

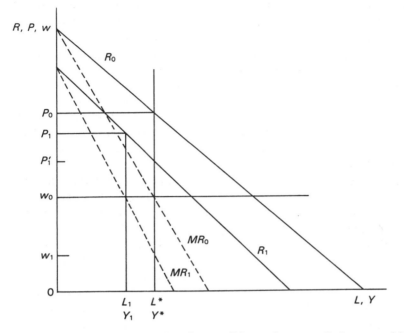

Figure 14.1 Labour demand under conditions of monopolistic competition

are the marginal revenue curves corresponding to the respective net-revenue curves. Finally, w denotes the money wage which is fixed in the short period.

Let us now consider long-run equilibrium. We assume that the demand conditions are given by the R_0-curve. Then competition in the labour market will lead to an equilibrium wage w_0 ($= MR_0$) where full employment is secured and the wage equals the marginal revenue product. The firms will set prices at P_0, which is the optimal price when the wage level is w_0. Labour and goods markets are in full equilibrium.

But this is a 'razor-edge equilibrium'.[1] When equilibrium is disturbed by a change in demand, cost structures, economic policy and so on, short-period problems arise. If, for instance, demand increases, R_0 will move to the right and upwards. Since Y cannot be expanded beyond Y^* because of labour shortage, inflationary price rises will occur up to the point where real demand is brought back to Y^* (because w_0 remains fixed and the real money stock is reduced).

For our considerations – unemployment, demand reduction, which is the opposite case, is the relevant situation. Suppose that because of a decline in investment or in spending propensities or because of deflation R_0 and MR_0 shift to R_1 and MR_1. Wage rigidity will keep wages fixed and labour demand will be cut back to L_1 where marginal revenue productivity is once again equal to the money wage. The optimal markup price will move to P_1. Thus the possibly lengthy short-period disequilibrium is characterized by persistent unemployment of $L_1 - L^*$. This will only disappear as (a) either the pressure of unemployment gradually lowers money wages and prices (with full employment being reestablished at w_1' and P_1') or (b) as government policy intervenes to shift R_1 back into the R_0 position. It will be seen that this Weitzman scenario of unemployment represents the usual neoclassic acceptance of *one* of Keynes's arguments, namely, the case of wage rigidity as *the* cause of unemployment. This limited perspective lies behind Weitzman's reference to the 'short-run Keynesian underemployment characteristics of a wage economy' (1985: 949).

Let us now turn to the 'share economy', the alternative advocated by Weitzman. In the share economy labour does not get a fixed wage; its pay is at least partly linked − directly or indirectly − to the profits achieved by the firm. If we take direct profit-sharing as the simplest case we have now *two* parameters determining the wage contract: a fixed money payment v and a fraction λ ($0 \le \lambda < 1$) determining the share of net profits π accruing to the individual worker. With $\lambda = 0$ we have the pure wage system; with $v = 0$ we have a pure share system. In what follows I shall illustrate the share system for the more general mixed case. The results apply even more strongly for the pure share system (which Weitzman uses in some of his simplified models). As in the case of the wage economy the assumption is that in the long run the labour contract parameters (v, λ) are flexible and influenced by competitive forces, but that they are rigid in the short and medium period. (At some stage in his book Weitzman thinks of three-year periods for recontracting.)

The main ideas of the share economy in relation to employment are summarized in Figure 14.2. The symbols L, Y, L^*, Y^*, R, MR and P have the same meaning as in Figure 14.1. And v is the fixed money pay per worker. The dashed curve $\bar{R}$ shows the total pay per worker including his share λ in the net profits which remain after the fixed wages have been paid. In our diagram the R_0-curve shows that at the ruling demand conditions the firm can sell the output Y^* at a net revenue (after deduction of non-wage costs) of P_0. After paying the fixed amount of v_0 per worker, the sum of $\overline{v_0 P_0}$ remains as gross profit per worker (π_0), of which he gets $\lambda \pi_0$, which can be read off the pay-curve $\bar{R}_0$. (The steeper the $\bar{R}$-curve compared to the R-curve the bigger is λ.) The net profit of the firm per worker is $\overline{w_0 P_0} = (1 - \lambda)\pi_0$.

As before we take as our starting point a long-run full employment equilibrium. Let this be characterized by the demand conditions R_0 and the given v_0 and λ (as mirrored in the position of the $\bar{R}_0$-curve). Since we start with a neoclassical equilibrium we can postulate that the pay per worker should correspond to his marginal revenue product, which is indicated by w_0 in the diagram. So we assume that v and λ are so fixed that the pay obtained by the workers is exactly what they would get in a wage economy;

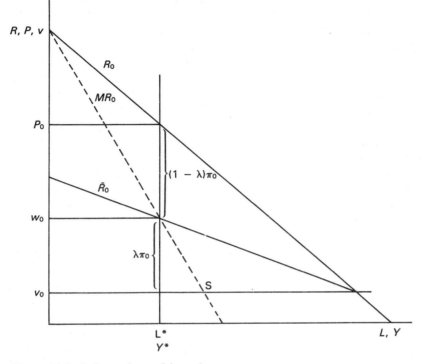

Figure 14.2 Labour demand in a share economy

that is, $v_0 + \lambda\pi_0 = w_0$.[2] So at first sight the long-run equilibrium positions of the wage and the share economy appear to be completely identical: output, employment, price and labour income are all the same.

But there is a fundamental difference with regard to the *nature* of the equilibrium. As we saw, the wage economy equilibrium is a delicate 'razor-edge' situation where any negative diversion in connection with the rigid wage contract causes 'temporary' unemployment. The equilibrium in the share market, on the contrary, is a robust one. This is so because the marginal labour cost to the firm is not what the additional worker gets (w_0 in the wage economy) but only the much lower fixed element v_0 in the share-paying agreement. Since price and output in the relevant range of the profit-maximizing firm is necessarily in the elastic range of the demand curve, there is always an incentive for the firm to increase its revenue and profits by lowering prices and increase employment, production and sales. This would pay as long as the additional revenue (net of non-wage costs) accruing to the firm is greater than the marginal labour costs, that is, as long as marginal revenue is greater than v_0.

Thus the firms pictured in the economy of Figure 14.2 would have an interest to expand employment and output *beyond* $L^*(Y^*)$ (along $\bar{R}_0$) up to the point *S* but are prevented from doing so because the labour supply sets a limit to further expansion. The share economy's full employment equilibrium is, therefore, characterized not by a precariously balanced demand for the existing labour force but by the unsatisfied (and unsatisfiable) demand for more labour at the given parameters.

Suppose now that demand declines from R_0 to R_1 (see Figure 14.3, where the dashed lines refer to the changed situation). At the old price (represented by the net revenue P_0) sales, production, and employment would be drastically reduced to Y_1. But at this point unused supplies of labour would be available and the firms would expand — with *unchanged* v and λ! — along their $\bar{R}_1$ path by reducing their prices until (at P_1) all available labour is used up and the expansion comes to an end. The mechanism of low marginal labour costs and the profit-wage link leads to permanent demand pressure and full employment in the labour market. All that has changed is that the *potential* demand for labour has fallen from *S* to S_1, (in Figure 14.3) where the respective marginal revenue curves (not drawn in the diagram) cut the v_0-line. Of course, in the new position characterized by R_1 the distribution between wages and profits will have changed so that the parameters of the labour contract (v, λ) will come up for renegotiation at the next renewal to bring v and/or λ into line with the long-run

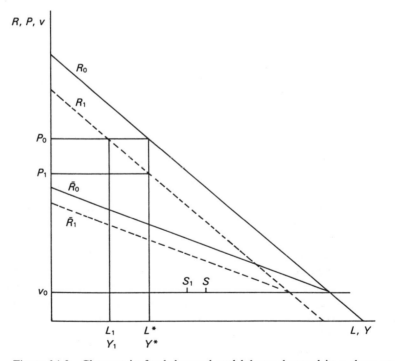

Figure 14.3   Changes in final demand and labour demand in a share economy.

equilibrium wage. But during the period of adjustment and rigidity unemployment would be – in contrast to the situation in the wage economy – avoided.

But not only would unemployment be avoided; the employed workers may also be better off during the adjustment process. But here we must sharply differentiate between the share solution in a single firm and in the whole economy. Let us first assume there is a negative disturbance (demand decline) and let us compare *for a single firm* the position of the workers who *remain employed* under the wage system on the one hand and under the share system on the other. Under the wage system the rigid wages and prices protect the full real income of those who stay employed. But some workers will become unemployed. Under the share system the firm will keep the full labour force but with unchanged labour productivity and falling prices profit payments *per worker* will decline so that those who would have remained in employment are now worse off than under the wage system: they earn less.[3] On the other hand the workers and employers in the rest of the economy benefit from the lower prices (and higher output) in the 'share' firm. It is this externality which induces Weitzman to plead for tax incentives to introduce the share system in single enterprises if and so long as a general adaptation is not possible.

With a general adaptation the picture looks quite different. If *all firms* work under the share system then – as we have seen – a negative demand shock will lead to a *general* reduction in prices while employment and real output will remain at the full employment level. Total real income will, therefore, remain unchanged and in the *pure* share economy this will also be true for real profits and wages. But in the mixed system the workers will benefit from the increased real value of their *nominally* fixed payment v so that during the adjustment period there will be a shift from profits to wages[4] which cannot be avoided by dismissing workers and reducing the profits going to both sides. A correction can be achieved only when the wage contract comes up for renewal.

III

The previous section has shown that Weitzman's share economy does indeed seem to be full of promise. On the basis of his analysis he concludes that 'a profit-sharing economy can avoid dreaded Keynesian unemployment, even when conducting anti-inflationist monetarist policy. The wage variant of capitalism, on the other hand, does not have built-in stability and so must rely more heavily on skillful discretionary adjustments of financial aggregates in reacting to each unforeseen event as it occurs' (1985: 952). But if such a cure is available, why has it not been adopted before or why does one not jump at it right now? Or are there perhaps more difficulties involved than are immediately obvious? These are the questions raised in this section.

Let me first deal with some theoretical problems; later I shall turn to some more practical aspects. On the analytical plane my principal objections to Weitzman's strong claims quoted in the previous paragraph are all connected with the preponderance of the neoclassic assumptions in his models. This preponderance is quite marked in spite of his important departure in the direction of monopolistic competition. Weitzman's resounding victory over 'dreaded Keynesian unemployment' is achieved easily because – in full accordance with neoclassical and IS/LM tradition – he equates Keynesian unemployment exclusively with the rigid-wage case. If wages (and the prices set on wage costs) were fully flexible there would be no unemployment in his model. With falling prices and a smoothly working real balance effect, long-run full employment equilibrium would always and immediately be established. Only wage rigidity prevents a quick adaptation and thus causes unemployment

If this were the only cause of unemployment then Weitzman's proposal would indeed offer one way out of the difficulties. What he in fact does is to introduce the required wage flexibility by the back door. If there *has* to be rigidity in the labour market let it be a rigidity of shares instead of wages. Then negative shocks (e.g., a reduction in government expenditures, investment, money supply, etc.) will lead *automatically* to reductions in prices and nominal wages and this will help to keep up employment. But the same result could be achieved (in such a situation) if trade unions and workers would agree to some reduction of wage rates in Weitzman's wage system (see Figure 14.1). So the question arises why a society or group which resists downward flexibility of nominal wages should be persuaded to accept a share system with flexible pay. This problem will be taken up when we turn to the practical aspects of a share economy.

Here it is important to stress that Keynesian (and also structural) unemployment is not restricted to the wage-rigidity variety. Indeed, it is amazing how persistently Keynes's remarks about the futility of wage adjustments in certain situations are ignored.[5] When we turn to other such situations – not necessarily embedded in the general equilibrium assumptions – the automaticism of the share solution disappears. Let me take just two familiar cases.

First there is the typical Keynesian problem of an *absolute* shortfall of effective demand. Indeed, all the speculations about possible saturation and liquidity phenomena in mature societies would be baseless if this problem did not exist. If it does, the share economy could run into unemployment problems just as much (though not to the same extent) as a wage economy. All that is necessary is that demand falls off so much that marginal revenue equals the fixed labour payment (v) before full employment is reached. Even when $v = 0$ – in the pure share economy – demand could be too small to deliver a profit above non-wage costs at full employment output so that unemployment would occur. The availability of additional labour would not attract additional demand for labour because prices would already correspond to the profit-maximizing point. An exogenous demand-creating shock would be required. Even when there is room for positive profits and expansion, total profits of the firm may be too small for some entrepreneurs to keep them in business. Just as too high a wage (w) may cause unemployment, too high a share (λ) may also lead to reductions in global labour demand. In *both* cases more flexibility is needed.

The second and more important neglect in Weitzman's world is the problem of uncertainty, also a question dear to Keynes and Keynesians. A negative shock in Weitzman's share world is immediately absorbed because firms are facing a smooth demand curve *and* know it. So when demand declines a movement along the demand curve by lowering prices (ever so little!) will bring increased profits when labour becomes available. But there are two flaws in this story. The first refers to the existence of Weitzman's demand assumptions. His macroeconomic demand function is $Y = \alpha A + \beta M/P$ where Y is total demand, A is autonomous expenditure, M/P is the real money stock, and α and β are the consumption multipliers for income and real cash balances, respectively. By attributing to real cash balances a strong and independent influence Weitzman – like most neoclassical disequilibrium theorists – has found the *deus ex machina* for smoothing the adjustment process. As soon as difficulties arise firms will lower their prices and the rising (real) cash balances will bring the additional demand. But not only have empirical studies shown that real cash balance effects may be small and uncertain; even more damaging is the assumption that A, the autonomous expenditure in Weitzman's equation, remains unaffected by the general fall in prices. That a deflationary environment can have restrictive effects on government expenditure and on investment is a possibility which should at least be acknowledged.

But even if we accept the existence of a Weitzman demand function we are still faced with the difficulty that the firms may not know the course of this function and the time lags involved in the adjustment process. After all, disequilibrium theory and Clower's dual decision hypothesis have shown quite clearly that after an equilibrium has been disturbed the *potential* demand conditions which would obtain once full employment is restored lose their force for decision making. It becomes optimal to adopt quantity adjustments if the path to a new general equilibrium is uncertain. Also, disequilibrium theory since Patinkin has shown that once equilibrium has been disturbed there is no easy and automatic return to full employment *even when marginal revenue lies above the wage rate*. For all these reasons, which are reinforced if we include structural maladjustments, it should be clear that the share economy could not be a *general* solution to the unemployment problem and could not – as Weitzman seems to hope – free fiscal and monetary policy from the need to take employment effects into consideration.

But even when we turn to a state of the world where the Weitzman scenario can be applied – and situations of 'pure' wage rigidity do exist and are important – even then his proposals come up against some practical difficulties. One problem has been touched before. Since the secret of the share economy lies in introducing flexibility into workers' (nominal) earnings under *given* contract parameters, why should it be easier to introduce a share economy rather than persuade employers and employees to adopt flexible wage contracts? The important fact, obviously, is that a certain amount of wage rigidity is not just an outcome of tradition, inadaptability, or sheer obnoxiousness of trade unions but meets various 'legitimate' desires on both sides of the wage bargain. Indeed, the literature of the past two decades has shown that there is no dearth of 'good' reasons for nominal wage rigidity even if one sticks to relatively narrow interpretations of 'rational decision making'. This is not the place to review this literature, but just as a hint here are a few catchwords: workers' interests in *relative* positions in a dynamic and nontransparent world; need for reliable money payments for small incomes with relatively high proportions of fixed outlays (rent) and debt; divergent risk attitudes of (risk-averse) employees and (risk- and profit-orientated) employers; wages as elements in hierarchically organized wage structures of internal labour markets; 'efficiency' wages as a screening device; and various other contract features.

A certain stability in labour income – at least nominally and for a limited period – is, therefore, not only an occasional brake on additional employment; it also corresponds to some real needs and requirements, and this explains the viability and the resilience of the wage system. This is not by itself an argument against Weitzman's proposals. But it means that a share economy – even if it has positive employment effects – cannot be regarded as an unequivocal and problem-free improvement. The fickleness of a capitalist market economy demands sacrifices: they can be shifted to unemployment, affecting *some* people heavily *for limited periods*, or to *all* employees in the form of pay uncertainty *all* the time.

The problem would be particularly pressing during the changeover to a share economy. As we have seen, as long as only some firms adopt the system before it has become a general principle, the employees in the share firms may suffer considerable income losses when the firm expands by lowering prices and profits *per worker* (while increasing company profits). The problem can be clearly seen in the case of commercial agents who work on a commission basis, a case which Weitzman presents as a (positive?!) example of a share arrangement with expansive employment effects. But what is the position really in this case? Of course, firms are ready to take on additional salesmen if they have to pay them only by results. But it is also a fact that it is not always easy to find efficient recruits for such posts (who can hope to earn fixed incomes elsewhere), and – even more to the point – those already in the field usually object to the inroads on their income which such a practice involves. Thus we find that a firm which adopts such a system *and* wants to secure the services of efficient salesmen has to offer them protected areas with exclusive sales rights, which, of course, means limitations on employment expansion.

Weitzman realizes that the disadvantages suffered by existing employees may militate against the adoption of share plans in individual firms. He, therefore, advocates that the government should 'encourage firms to choose a high share component by offering to tax share income at a more favourable rate than wage income' (1983: 780). But if one is prepared to accept such government action Weitzman's basic idea could be realized in a much simpler and less 'revolutionary' way by adopting marginal wage subsidies as suggested by the Swedish economist Gösta Rehn and others. The government would offer wage subsidies for *additional* workers taken on over and above existing (or base period) levels. This would have the same effect of reducing marginal labour cost below current wages as the Weitzman scheme without the need to abolish fixed wage rates. Also the subsidy would be restricted to additional workers while Weitzman's tax benefits would have to cover all workers in the share firm.

But even if we neglect this question of income certainty and changeover problems there remains a further question of a more practical nature which would probably require some deep organizational changes, deeper than Weitzman seems to realize.[6] Business, as we know, is hierarchically controlled and not democratically. Workers have neither a say in nor full information of the firm's affairs. The wage is the only thing they determine in their contracts with certainty so that they can prove at any time whether the firm has fulfilled its obligation (in this respect) or not.[7] If pay were linked to profits, not only certainty of income would be foregone, but also certainty with regard to the proper fulfilment of the contract. The popular games of tax avoidance and tax evasion could be supplemented by wage avoidance and wage evasion. It is difficult to see how a general shift to a share economy could be accepted by employees and trade unions without fundamental shifts in the organizational and control structure at the managerial level.[8] If this view is accepted it is obvious that – for this reason alone – Weitzman's repeated hints to have offered a more or less 'simple' economic key to 'eliminate the worst features of stagflation by, in effect, restoring the direct link between prices and wages characteristic of atomistic self-employed enterprises' (1983: 782) are not only economically questionable but also suffer from political naiveté.

NOTES

1 'Wage capitalism is fundamentally a precariously balanced system. The slightest change ... can move it away from the razor-thin region where there is just full employment and pay is exactly competitive' (Weitzman 1985: 951).
2 Since the mixed system has *two* parameters there are obviously different combinations of v and λ which yield the equivalent of w_0. This means that there is room for wage *structure* bargaining.

3 The pay per worker (W/L) with given v and λ is

$$W/L = v + \lambda \frac{R - vL}{L}$$

where R is total revenue net of non-labour costs. When L (and Y) are increased, vL rises proportionately, but R rises less than proportionately because prices have to be reduced.
4 The real (deflated) pay per worker is obtained by dividing the nominal pay given in note 3 by the price index P. Writing $X(= R/P)$ for the unchanged *real* total revenue we get

$$(W/L)_{\text{real}} = \frac{v}{P} + \lambda \frac{X}{L} - \lambda \frac{v}{P}$$

$$= \lambda \frac{X}{L} + (1 - \lambda) \frac{v}{P}$$

With X unchanged and P falling the real wage rises.
5 On this see also some of the critical contributions in a discussion of an earlier paper of Weitzman on the foundations of unemployment theory (1982) which took place in the *Journal of Post Keynesian Economics*, (1985), volume 7, number 3, pages 350–409, and particularly pages 368–369 in the paper by Darity (1985).
6 On the following point and some additional difficulties see also the thoughtful remarks by Matthews (1985).
7 This does not apply to the other side of the contract, the kind and intensity of the services to be supplied by the employee. Here some vagueness is the normal thing and is probably in the nature of the case. But it is also *in this field* (and not on the wage side) that conflicts about control are endemic and demands for codetermination arise.
8 It might be objected that we can see already today functioning examples of profit bonus and profit-sharing agreements. But in all these cases we have either some very exceptional circumstances (special products or groups of persons) or the profit bonus represents only a comparatively small supplement to the normal wage and salary earnings so that exact information is not important. It is a sort of incentive premium.

REFERENCES

Darity, W. (1985) 'On Involuntary Unemployment and Increasing Returns', *Journal of Post Keynesian Economics*, 7, 3, pp. 363–72.
Mathews, R. C. O. (1985) 'Review of Weitzman, *The Share Economy*, *Journal of Economic Literature*, 23, pp. 658–60.
Weitzman, M. L., (1982), 'Increasing Returns and the Foundations of Unemployment Theory', *Economic Journal*, 92, pp. 787–804;
—— (1983) 'Some Macroeconomic Implications of Alternative Compensation Systems', *Economic Journal*, 93, pp. 763–83.
—— *The Share Economy* (1984) Cambridge, MA: Harvard University Press.
—— (1985) 'The Simple Macroeconomics of Profit Sharing', *American Economic Review*, 75, pp. 937–53.

Part III
Income distribution

15 The share of wages in total income
Some remarks on a disputed problem

(Translation of 'Der Lohnanteil am Gesamteinkommen. Einige Bemerkungen zu einem umstrittenen Problem', (1957) *Weltwirtschaftliches Archiv* 78, 2, pp. 157–202)

AN OLD QUESTION REVIVED

In 1938 Michael Kalecki published an article on income distribution in *Econometrica*[1] which evoked surprise, interest and contradiction. But there are times which are favourable for an extended scientific discussion and there are times which are not so favourable. 1938, the year before the outbreak of war, belonged to the second category. Thus a proper discussion of Kalecki's paper could not develop right away. Only gradually, after the war, was the subject taken up again by several economists, so that the discussion has become rather intermittent and involved. In this paper I shall not attempt to offer a comprehensive survey of this literature or to pass a final verdict on its results. All I want to do is to present the essential aspects of the discussion with the addition of some sceptical and modifying remarks.

Two reasons were responsible for the surprise effect of Kalecki's article: the statistical picture, on the one hand, and the theoretical treatment, on the other. On the basis of various statistical calculations Kalecki pointed out that the share of wages (excluding salaries) in total income[2] had remained almost constant − both in the long and in the short run (over the cycle) − in the United States as well as in Great Britain. That such a constancy may exist had been observed before by empirically orientated economists. Bowley,[3] Bellerby,[4] and Knöpp[5] are examples of economists who had already remarked in the 1920s that the share of wages or of total labour income in national income tends to be constant or to change very slowly. That the repetition of that statement by Kalecki could agitate the minds of economists was probably due to two circumstances. The first − trivial − one is that quite generally some questions have a tendency to disappear for a while only to emerge again later on when they have regained the attractiveness of a 'novelty'. More decisive, however, is the second reason, viz. that

Kalecki was able – in contrast to the earlier writers – to include the Great Depression in his observations and could show that even this shattering event left the wage share more or less untouched.

This statistical surprise was supplemented by a theoretical one. The model with which Kalecki tried to explain the share constancy deviated from the traditional path of competitive marginal productivity theory and turned to a world of imperfect competition with price-setting assumptions which were more in line with contemporaneous empirical studies than classical price theories. The new approach found particular interest because in those years doubts about the usefulness of the Cobb-Douglas function began to be uttered.[6]

THE STABILITY OF THE WAGE SHARE

As mentioned already Kalecki's calculations resulted in fairly stable wage shares for the United States and Great Britain. For Great Britain he found a share of 41.4 per cent in 1880 and of 39.4 per cent in 1913. In the period 1924 to 1935 the share fluctuated (on the basis of a slightly changed method of calculation) between 40.8 per cent (1925) and 43.7 per cent (1931). For the United States he obtained 37.9 per cent in 1909 and 40.2 per cent in 1925; between 1919 and 1934 – again calculated in a different way – the share fluctuated between 34.9 per cent (1919 and 1931) and 39.3 per cent (1923).[7] In neither country was there any recognizable trend, in either the long run or in the course of the business cycle.

Since Kalecki's publication several studies have appeared which have analysed the same or similar data. Apart from studies which accept Kalecki's and related investigations as sufficient proof,[8] they do not arrive at unique and clear-cut conclusions. All studies agree that changes in the share of wages remain within a fairly narrow corridor; but while some see the share (like Kalecki) as a stable magnitude with small random variations, others find some notable influences acting on the share fluctuations. One member of the first group who merits particular mention is Barna, who in 1945 derived – in a small interesting volume[9] – a remarkably stable British wage share. According to his calculations it remained between 39 and 41 per cent for the entire period 1880 to 1944. Dudley Seers, who also 'believes' in the basic stability of the wage share, has shown that a share of about 40 per cent has also been maintained in the first post-war decade.[10] The exact value of the share depends however – as Seers shows – on the question whether changes in the value of stocks are taken into account in Gross National Product calculations or not. In the study of Phelps Brown and Hart,[11] which analyses British data for the years 1870 to 1950 (without the First World War), the stability phenomenon is also acknowledged – their share estimates range from 36.6 per cent (1913) to 42.7 per cent (1893) – but in their theoretical considerations sudden jumps of this share (within the given range) play an important role.

In the United States all attempts to estimate wage shares had to suffer from the fact that for considerable sections of the economy separate data for wages and salaries do not exist. This had already forced Kalecki to adopt some 'heroic' assumptions in his calculations of the US wage share. Most American investigations have decided to content themselves with treating wages and salaries together. Dunlop, [12] who analysed cyclical variations of the wage share in the US economy, stresses the weakness of the statistical basis, but shows that – as far as the data can be used – the comparative stability of the wage share during the cycle in the 1930s was the result of shifts in the industrial structure which led to an averaging out of considerable wage share changes within individual sectors. The cyclical stability of the total wage share was not a summation of sectorial stabilities, but the (accidental) result of diverging movements in wage shares and industrial structure. [13] For wages *and* salaries taken together Dunlop finds an anti-cyclical pattern (higher share in the depression, lower share in prosperity). This is a familiar pattern which is also acknowledged by Kalecki. [14] The same anti-cyclical movement shows up in German data used by J. Müller [15] who studies the period 1925 to 1952 (excluding war years). For the long run he detects a 'constant' wage share, which in his case includes salaries. This share fluctuated between 57.2 per cent (1938) and 66.1 per cent (1931).

These few examples, which track only a small section of the relevant literature, give an indication of the conclusions reached in the statistical investigations which had been stimulated by the renewed interest in the stability hypothesis. We end this section with a look at Kalecki's own views as he expressed them in 1954. In 1954 he published a new edition of his *Essays* [16] in which he not only changed the form of his theoretical model but also renewed and modified his statistical estimates. In view of the absence of long-term data for the US he restricts his American part to the share of wages in the industrial net output in the period 1879–1937. For this share he obtains a falling tendency (from 47.8 per cent to 36.2 per cent) for the years 1879 till 1929 and a rising tendency thereafter with 38.6 per cent in 1937. For Great Britain the wage share in national income (1881 to 1924) is estimated and it is shown that it stands round about 40 per cent both at the beginning and at the end of the period. A decline can be detected for the years before the First World War but the share never falls below 37 per cent. Calculations for the depression years of the 1930s give fairly stable wage shares in the US and in Britain.

In contrast to his paper of 1938, Kalecki refrains from laying stress on the existence of a constant wage share in his later publication. But he also refrains from repudiating his earlier statements. This question, whether *in fact* there is such a thing as a stable wage share, will come up again in a later part of this paper. But before we turn to it I want to give a short description of the theoretical discussion which developed around the stability hypothesis. Here again no comprehensive survey is intended. A few important and characteristic approaches will be discussed in order to give an impression of the present state of the debate.

THE THEORETICAL DISCUSSION

It has already been said that Kalecki's pre-war 'rediscovery' of wage share stability made a particular impression because he tried to provide a theoretical basis for the empirical phenomena. It therefore seems justified to start this 'survey' with Kalecki's contribution. I shall not, however, present it in its original form, but rather in the radically changed (and simplified) form which he used in the post-war edition. In spite of the considerable change in form the content of the theory remained practically unaltered. Like the other theories which follow later it will be summarized rather briefly.

Kalecki develops his theory on the basis of his cost and price theory. He assumes that in the industrial sector the existence of free capacities is a normal state of affairs and that – as long as direct costs (wages and materials) remain unchanged – changes in demand are answered not so much with changes in prices as with changes in output. Prices are set by the firms on the basis of direct costs with a margin added which should at least suffice to cover fixed costs (including salaries and depreciation) but must not be so high that the competitiveness of the firm is endangered. Since Kalecki assumes that in the normal situation (with below-capacity production) direct costs per unit of output are constant he obtains for the relevant ranges of output equality between direct unit costs and marginal costs. This implies that his margin on direct costs has a definite relationship to Lerner's 'degree of monopoly.'[17]

Building on these assumptions Kalecki first takes a look at the determinants of the wage share in the income of a single firm or industrial branch. Using W for total wage expenditure and M for total costs of materials the gross revenue of the firm will be $k(W + M)$, k being the factor with which direct costs are multiplied in order to fix the price for the commodity.[18] A higher k implies a higher degree of monopoly.

Since the total revenue of the industry is $k(W + M)$ and W and M must be paid to workers and producers of materials respectively the firm or industry is left with an amount of $(k - 1)(W + M)$ to cover fixed costs and profits. When we deduct the expenditure for materials we obtain the gross value of the industry's output: $W + (k - 1)(W + M)$. This is the sum of wages, salaries, other fixed costs, depreciation and profit. Consequently we obtain for w, the share of wages in gross output value,

$$w = \frac{W}{W + (k - 1)(W + M)}$$

Dividing numerator and denominator by W and writing j for (M/W) the relation of costs of materials to wage costs, the wage share becomes

$$\overset{.}{w} = \frac{1}{1 + (k - 1)\,(j + 1)}$$

With some additional considerations Kalecki then extends this formula to the industrial sector as a whole and finally to the entire private part of GNP (gross national product excluding income of public employees). Since k and j are not the same in all industries the weights of the various sectors play also a role in the aggregate result. We have thus derived the three elements on which Kalecki rests his theory and explanation of the wage share in private GNP: degree of monopoly, relation of costs of materials to wage costs and industrial structure of the economy. The higher the degree of monopoly, the higher the relative prices of materials, the greater the weight of industries with high degrees of monopoly, the lower the wage share will be and vice versa.

This is the formal structure of Kalecki's model. Two supplementary remarks are necessary for a proper evaluation. First, an objection against this approach can be raised because it makes the degree of monopoly a decisive explanatory factor and must, therefore, break down when we deal with perfect competition which after all has been the ruling assumption in most of the traditional work. Formally this objection is certainly true. In case of perfect competition the factor k is equal to 1 (this meets the condition that price equals marginal cost) and this leads to a wage share equal to 1 which would leave nothing for fixed costs and profits. But this objection is not applicable to a theory which looks at a world of non-perfect competition. As we saw, Kalecki takes unused capacities and comparatively constant direct costs as the normal case. Under such circumstances the condition that prices should equal marginal costs (the optimal solution of the competitive model) becomes impossible if permanent losses are to be avoided. The competitive solution demands a rising marginal cost curve. When marginal costs do not rise or are very flat a certain degree of monopoly is a precondition for a permanent solution. That Kalecki's theory cannot be applied to the competitive case is therefore not a decisive objection. The decisive question is rather whether the real world is better approximated by a competitive model or in Kalecki's approach. Several empirical cost and price studies of the past twenty years give the impression that unused capacities, comparatively constant unit costs, and cost-determined price setting are fairly widespread phenomena.

A second objection is methodologically of greater weight. Since the degree of monopoly is *defined* as the difference between price and marginal cost and since this difference (in toto) *must* also be equal to the sum of salaries, fixed costs, depreciation and profits when (as assumed) direct unit costs and marginal costs are equal, it follows from the assumptions and definitions that the sum of wages and costs of materials must be *directly* linked to this definition of the degree of monopoly so that the monopoly index must determine the wage share after the development of the costs of materials has been taken into account. The accusation that Kalecki's formulation is tautological[19] is thus not completely unjustified. But is it a decisive objection? I do not think so. After all the degree of monopoly – as defined by Kalecki – does have a real significance in economic life quite independent of questions relating to the wage share. It has something to do with the structure of firms and their power of price setting. The tautological formulation is therefore not useless; it draws attention to certain phenomena which one should observe and consider when one wants to explain the size and the changes of the wage share. Of course, a tautological formulation cannot by itself provide an explanatory theory; but it can provide a useful starting point for such a theory.[20] This is exactly the case in Kalecki's approach who uses his *formulation* of elements of the wage share as a starting point for a *theory* of the wage share.[21]

This theory says that the degree of monopoly has a long-run tendency to increase because of a growing concentration of production and an increasing role of fixed costs and marketing expenditures, but with a certain counter-tendency coming from growing trade union influence. With regard to prices of materials and industrial structure, Kalecki hesitates to develop any long-term hypotheses[22] so that he also refrains from laying down any long-term 'law' for the wage share and its development. All he does is to use his formulation to interpret past movements of the British and US share in the light of his 'basic' factors. As far as the *cyclical* stability of the wage share is concerned he regards it as the result of two diverging tendencies. In a depression the degree of monopoly rises as firms try to cover fixed costs and to uphold profits while prices of materials decline faster than wages; in times of prosperity a reverse movement sets in.[23]

Thus it can be seen that the degree of monopoly (in combination with the other elements) is not used in a tautological manner but is brought into contact with structural changes in production and with price and cartelization policies of the firms. This shows that it has a useful function in the theory.

But it should not be forgotten that the degree of monopoly as here defined is a very complex construction which cannot be the 'last' cause of a full explanation. The degree of monopoly is itself the result of several economic and sociological elements which require consideration. It is therefore a misunderstanding when Müller writes that in Kalecki's opinion 'neither inventions nor elasticities of substitution of labour and capital have an influence on income distribution'.[24] This is not correct. Technological change, for instance, can have an influence on income distribution. If it reduces direct and marginal costs while prices are not reduced proportionally the share of wages will decline. But it declines only because the new invention was used as an opportunity to increase the degree of monopoly, i.e. to widen the span between price and direct costs. This connection is explicitly stressed by Kalecki in the first presentation of his theory. There he states: 'The change of basic data may of course influence the degree of monopoly. For instance, technical progress by affecting the size of enterprises influences the degree of monopoly in an industry. In this case such changes influence the distribution of income, but this is not in contradiction with our results, because it is via the degree of monopoly that the influence operates.'[25]

Like technological change other economic and sociological factors can be pictured as working 'via the degree of monopoly'. Whether it is expedient to bundle all these influences into a single degree of monopoly depends on the question how far one considers the degree of monopoly as a central strategic element in price formation which is also influenced by other factors but not dominated by them. The widespread practice of setting prices on the basis of costs and the existence of habitual views regarding 'normal' profits are empirical props for such a view.[26]

The Kaleckian theory was treated somewhat extensively because it introduced new aspects into the stagnating discussion about the determinants of the wage share. A few later theoretical contributions will now be presented in a far more concentrated form.

As a first example one should mention the book by Mitra,[27] not because it is a particularly outstanding contribution but because Mitra more than other economists bases his study on Kalecki's theory and tries to give it a new twist. After a full and useful critical survey of earlier attempts to explain the wage share Mitra sets himself the task to attack the problem in a new way, both statistically and theoretically. As far as the statistical side is concerned it suffices to say that Mitra – in his attempt to 'measure' the degree of monopoly – manipulates, aggregates and correlates all sorts of complex and dubious data from Britain's past without ever coming near a critical awareness of the problems and complications involved.[28]

But let us look at the theoretical part. There Mitra develops a formula which is far more complicated than Kalecki's and which – in Mitra's opinion – shows in an 'elegant' way the wage share as the result of a variety of basic data. These include labour and import shares, the wage–price ratio, the price at 'zero-demand', and the number of competitors in the market. With the aid of his formula Mitra arrives at the 'really startling discovery'[29] that a rise of the import share leads to a higher wage share while Kalecki concluded that a rise in the price of raw materials[30] will cause a fall of the wage share.

This is not the place to discuss in detail the abstruse formula at which Mitra arrives. But in as few words as possible I shall try to show how Mitra arrives at his strange conclusion and why his model as a whole is not suited to give the required answers. The main weakness of Mitra's model must be ascribed to his untenable simplifying assumptions. The error of treating imports and raw materials as equals has already been mentioned. Among the other 'heroic' assumptions of Mitra we find:

1 inclusion of depreciation in direct costs;

2 the assumption of a comparatively rigid price–wage relationship in the short run which becomes variable in the longer run; and particularly daring,
3 the use of a Cournot model (duopoly–imperfect competition–perfect competition) plus a linear demand function for the entire economy.[31]

With these assumptions the range within which the wage share can move becomes so narrow that in view of the arbitrariness and unrealistic nature of the hypotheses the birth of 'truly startling discoveries' is not surprising. Thus Mitra obtains, for instance, from his demand function and the number of competitors a rigid price limit whose distance from costs must fall when the import share rises. Since the wages remain unchanged the increased import share necessarily 'creates' a higher wage share. In Kalecki's theory by contrast no such built-in counter-tendency of raw material (import) prices and degree of monopoly exists (though he believes that empirically such a relationship occurs during the cycle). Kalecki's model has room – as Mitra's has not – for the possibility of rising raw material prices with the degree of monopoly remaining unchanged; and this must lead to a fall in the share of wages.

Mitra's attempt to explain the constancy of the British wage share (as he sees it) is, of course, based on his theoretical model. A decisive role is played by diverging movements of raw material prices on the one hand and the wage–price ratio on the other (with raw material prices playing an opposite role to Kalecki's assumptions). The wage–price ratio is determined by the reaction of the workers vis-à-vis price movements. Towards the end of his book Mitra shifts to a more sociological interpretation by speculating that the stability of the wage share may be the result of a power equilibrium between the main social groups and classes. This explanation comes near to the ideas of a number of other, mainly French economists to whose contributions we shall return later.

While Mitra starts off with Kalecki's framework and then – after various additions and modifications – arrives at different results, other writers regarded Kalecki's theory with scepticism but ultimately arrived at similar results which can be easily 'translated' into Kalecki's terminology. Kalecki's resolute departure from the cost curve of the traditional competition theory – his assumption of a horizontal marginal cost curve in particular – had an irritating effect on some economists. Thus Rostow[32] doubts whether this assumption is 'admissible' and prefers to explain the British wage share in the second part of the nineteenth century (the period he analyses) in a 'conventional' manner by looking at relative shifts between labour and capital and their effects on marginal productivities and elasticities of substitution.[33]

For Keynes, too, a horizontal marginal cost curve seemed an unlikely phenomenon, at least in times of boom.[34] He stuck to this opinion even after Tarshis[35] had shown (on the basis of US data) that on average rising marginal costs seem to be untypical. Accepting the cyclical stability of the wage share as a fact Keynes proposed a picture of events which differs from Kalecki's. In contrast to him he expected in times of recovery and boom not only rising raw material costs (in line with Kalecki) but also rising marginal wage costs (traditional cost curve). Both these developments would reduce the wage share. But this effect would be counteracted by a predominance of long-term price strategies which would keep prices comparatively rigid in this period of rising costs. As a consequence the degree of monopoly would fall sharply, leaving the wage share comparatively stable. In times of recession an opposite development would take place. The question of the long-term trend of the wage share was not treated by Keynes. But Kalecki's work convinced him that the theory of income distribution required serious new efforts.

As closely connected with Kalecki's ideas but with other questions in the foreground (particularly the development of profits in the US) Steindl's important book has to be mentioned.[36] His theory works out in greater detail the mechanisms of output adjustment via capacity variations which set certain limits to fluctuations in profit and wage shares.

Stimulated by Kalecki's theory but choosing ways of his own Dunlop has shown considerable interest in the question of the cyclical behaviour of wage shares.[37] He is particularly concerned with the difficulties of establishing the facts which – depending on definitions and statistical estimates – can take on rather different faces. Instead of trying to arrive at a 'general theory' of cyclical wage share developments Dunlop prefers to enumerate factors which influence the wage share in an individual firm in the short run. He arrives at a list of six factors of which he says: 'These conditions are not inconsistent with Kalecki's stimulating model.'[38] These six factors are:

1 extent of output fluctuations;
2 shape of labour cost function;
3 relative factor prices and possibilities of short-run factor substitution;
4 effects of fluctuations in the prices of variable factors on output prices (e.g. the wage share will rise when falling raw material prices have a marked effect on output prices);
5 technological change; and
6 elasticity of demand for the final output.

As one can see this is not a theory of the wage share but rather a box of tools for dealing with questions of this sort. When it comes to the economy as a whole Dunlop stresses the importance of shifts between firms and industries in the course of the cycle.[39] Structural change together with changes in import prices are also the main factors in Seers's interpretation of the stability of the wage share in war and post-war Britain.[40]

Several interesting statistical and methodological ideas have been contributed by Phelps Brown and Hart in their analysis of the long-term development of the British wage share.[41] They include in their analysis the movement of shares of different income groups and arrive at the conclusion that the comparatively stable wage share alongside a falling proportion of wage earners is at least partly due to shifts between 'mobile' income groups (wages *and* profits) and 'stable' groups (rents and other contractual payments, salaries). In the long run wages *and* profits were able to gain as compared with the 'stable' group and this has supported the share of wages in total income. For the business cycle the authors detect a rise (fall) of the wage share *within* the wage–profit sector in the depression (prosperity) but an *opposite* movement of the wage–profit sector *as a whole*. These opposite movements contribute to the comparative stability of the wage share in total income over the cycle.

This explanation based on shifts between various income groups is then supplemented by a theory about wage–profit ratios. Here also a certain stability is ascertained but with certain 'sharp' changes occurring from time to time which can shift the wage share to a new level.[42] The main elements of this theory are cost structures, the degree of monopoly and profit policies of the entrepreneurs. Ideas about 'normal' profits secure for longer periods a rather rigid relationship between costs and prices[43] and thus contribute to a stability of income shares. In critical periods, however, these relations can be disturbed and a new wage share and new ideas about 'normal' profits may develop.

In the view of the authors such changes are likely to occur when certain trade union policies coincide with a certain market environment. When trade unions grow more militant (for whatever reasons) and firms are at the same time faced with a 'hard' market environment, which makes it difficult to charge higher prices, then it is possible that gross profit margins can be somewhat reduced. The wage share increases. If, however, the market environment is 'soft' so that costs increases can be shifted on to prices, then the wage share will be unaffected. In an analogous way one can deal with trade union weakness. If unions are weak and the market environment is 'soft' then entrepreneurs will be able to raise prices more than wages (or lower wages at constant prices) and the wage share will fall; but if the market environment is 'hard' prices will be held in check so that even with weak unions the wage share will not be much affected.

This second part of the Phelps Brown-Hart theory shows an obvious similarity to Kalecki's theory: trade union activities and various elements which make up the 'market environment'[44] including prices of raw materials are at the basis of the degree of monopoly. But quite apart from the vagueness of the term 'market environment' the theory suffers from the fact that it may be quite useful for explaining the past but does not offer any help for forecasting future developments. No 'laws' regarding movements of trade union strength and market environments are indicated.[45] This, by the way, is also a weakness in Kalecki's theory where some things are said about probable tendencies in the development of the degree of monopoly but nothing about raw material prices and industrial structure. Most of the other hypotheses which have been advanced in this field have also suffered from this weakness.

Just like Phelps Brown and Hart, Wilhelm Krelle[46] is not so much concerned with explaining a certain *constancy* the long-run wage share (which in his view follows from a close relationship between wage and price levels) but with reasons for the *fluctuations* of this share (or the share of wages and salaries). He feels a need for such an explanation because he does not believe that these fluctuations can be easily derived from changes in economic base data (demand patterns, market forms, technological conditions). He looks for an explanation which extends far beyond distribution theory and comes near to a new perspective on general equilibrium. Like Kalecki, Krelle bases his ideas on an oligopolistic market environment. But in contrast to Kalecki he does not attack directly the question of the wage share in an oligopolistic firm and its dependence on the degree of monopoly, but starts with the wider question what effect such an oligopolistic environment has on the entire process of price and wage formation. Dealing with this question – using to some extent game theoretical approaches – he comes to a rejection of the deterministic Walras-Pareto equilibrium system (which would be applicable in a world of perfect competition or perfect monopoly). In its place he puts an extended equilibrium area within which every point can be an equilibrium. Which of these points will actually be realized depends on history, chance, policy measures, etc.

The important idea is that each of these points is compatible with a whole group of surrounding data within which they can continue to exist. This means that some variables (like prices or wages) can change without setting into motion the entire economic system. Some variables which 'fitted' into the old combination and continue to fit into a new combination will not change. This leads to a new constellation which can be just as stable as the previous one until a new shock changes the situation. In this perspective a relative constancy of the wage share may be assumed as a consequence of basic structural characteristics of the economy (not particularly treated by Krelle), but oligopolistic indeterminacy will permit considerable fluctuations and deviations around this constant value which can be triggered off by all sorts of influences (union or government action, monopolistic strategies, chance events) and which cannot be foreseen or subsumed to a systematic or cyclical pattern.

All the theories described so far have one thing in common: they base their explanation of the wage share predominantly on economic factors (price movements, degree of monopoly, elasticities of substitution). Sociological factors (trade unions, employers' associations, government action) are sometimes taken into account, but mostly they become visible only via their appearance within one of the economic elements or as exogenous influences.

In contrast to this we find a group of economists for whom sociological factors are the main element in their attempt to provide new impulses for income distribution theory. This trend had found particular support in France where Jean Marchal and other economists have entered into intensive discussions about the influence of group behaviour and group policies on income distribution in modern times.[47] In the opinion of these authors the processes of income distribution have taken on new forms with the growing influence of big organizations and interest lobbies. Distribution can no longer be studied at the level of single individuals or even whole income groups (wage earners, salaried personnel, entrepreneurs, peasants, apprentices), but must be seen within a wider relationship where each of these groups struggles to maintain its share in total income. The social tensions produced by these struggles and the mobility between the different groups are the forces which have a decisive influence on the income distribution.

Here we cannot go into a discussion of the mechanisms of this process which have so far only been developed in outline and await further research. But it is easily understandable that such a theory of groups, suspiciously watching the maintenance of their own shares, is miles apart from the traditional competition theories. It is able to explain why the share of each income group – including the wage share – has a tendency to remain fairly constant in the short run. In the longer run, however, changes can take place in various ways (e.g. through entry and exit, changes in the social standing of a group). The French economists who developed this perspective never regarded a *secular* stability of wages as something to be proved or explained. Their theory tries to model distribution processes under contemporary conditions. It cannot be applied to the nineteenth century.

The 'French' theory[48] can thus be seen to have some relevance for an analysis of the wage share, but it does not provide any definitive clues for its probable development (except a certain stability in the short run). But there exist also attempts to use sociological arguments in the context of long-term stability. Here we can mention the final part of Mitra's book[49] where he adopts the hypothesis – not connected with his earlier theory – that a certain power equilibrium between the main social classes will tend to preserve the stability of the wage share. But no reasons are given why such a power equilibrium should be stable.

In a similar vein are ideas presented by Solterer[50] though his argumentation has a somewhat metaphysical bias. He sees the working of a 'law' of power and countervailing power forming a union between 'power and purpose' which leads to a stable wage share not only in the economy as a whole but also in its various sectors. The rather confused arguments of the author make it impossible to enter into a critical evaluation. The hypothesis of stable wage shares in the different sectors of the economy[51] seems to be clearly contradicted by the empirical studies of Dunlop and others.

With this we conclude our survey of recent theoretical attempts to find an explanation for wage share developments. The survey is by no means complete and a number of relevant papers were not mentioned. This applies particularly to articles which touch only some special aspects of the problem.[52] But the theories discussed should suffice to indicate the nature and contents of the current debate. It has introduced several interesting ideas but has not been able to provide a firm theoretical basis for the empirical discussion. Was the wage share stable or not? What should we expect on theoretical grounds and how far is this in accordance with the facts? What about the future? Questions like these have hardly been treated. Most of the work has been an attempt to find a theoretical description for actual events as they could be inferred from a scant statistical material. To this real picture and its statistical mirror we now return.

IS THE STABILITY OF THE WAGE SHARE A MIRACLE?

When Keynes was confronted with data indicating a stability of the wage share he wrote: 'This is one of the most surprising, yet best-established facts in the whole range of economic statistics, both for Great Britain and the United States'. And a little later: 'the result remains a bit of a miracle'.[53]

Keynes was not the only person who regarded the relative stability of the wage share as a miracle. Other economists made similar remarks.[54] Yet the question whether one sees a miracle or not will depend largely on the temperament and philosophy of life of the observer. Dunlop has quite rightly remarked that the fact that some authors regard the wage share as surprisingly constant while others see it as rather volatile has something to do with differences in the 'propensity to be surprised'.[55] Looking at Keynes's big surprise one is reminded of the poet Syme in G. K. Chesterton's 'The Man Who Was Thursday'[56] who regards regularity as the greatest miracle and thus is opposed to the anarchist Gregory.

Like Syme, Keynes seems to regard a regular and constant development as a very rare event. But it would be far more surprising if the share of wages in total income were characterized by wild fluctuations. In fact it is a 'built-in' characteristic of the wage share that its changes — if there are any — will be slow and confined within comparatively narrow limits. This tendency to relative stability can be seen when we look at the wage share formula and the relationships between its elements.

In the definition of Kalecki the wage share is given by the simple formula

$$\frac{W}{W + P}$$

where W stands for wages and P for gross profits, including salaries. In this fraction W constitutes a comparatively big sum so that its presence in the numerator and denominator secures already a considerable degree of constancy. Assuming, for instance, that $W/(W + P)$ equals 50 per cent to begin with, a rise in profits by 20 per cent with wages remaining unchanged (a strong proposition!) would involve a fall in the wage share to 45.5 per cent. This is not a terribly heavy decline and may even lie within possible margins of error. Added to this we must remember that P includes salaries, which on economic and sociological grounds (mobility, union tactics) will move parallel to wages. This will be a further brake on the movements of $W/(W + P)$.

When we add in our previous example the assumption that 50 per cent of P are salaries which follow the same course as wages, then profits (without salaries) can even rise by 40 per cent until the Kaleckian wage share comes down to 45.5 per cent. Furthermore, the strategies of unions and employers' organizations can cause a certain parallelism between wages and profits, adding still another element to a stable or at least slowly changing development of wage shares.[57]

This tendency towards stability which follows from the very definition of the wage share is embedded in a framework which sets limits to radical deviations in one direction or the other. On the one hand a certain minimum income must be guaranteed to workers, and this rises with the higher skill requirements; on the other hand a certain profit level is a condition for the functioning of a capitalist economy. Taking all these influences together we can see that a tendency towards considerable stability (though not constancy) is not quite so miraculous and indeed far less surprising than would be a state of strong fluctuations.

...OR A MYTH?

So far we saw that stability need not cause exceptional surprise. We now turn to the question whether the 'surprising' stability as such should not be viewed with more scepticism. Once we recognize that very wide and sudden fluctuations of the wage share are hardly possible we have to interpret 'stability' in a stricter and narrower way than if it could vary between say 0 and 100 per cent. And this poses the question whether the data, reaching back several decades, are sufficiently 'hard' to permit reliable statements about stability for lengthy periods and perhaps even for the entire capitalist world. The answer to this question can only be a sceptical one.

The main support for the stability thesis came from British estimates. Similar statements were then made for some other countries, but since these had to use fewer and less reliable data it will be sufficient if we restrict our remarks on data problems on the comparatively well developed British and US estimates.

Of the two components which enter the general wage share formula (wages and national income) wages display greater accuracy than the national income. But even the wage sum is afflicted with a considerable degree of uncertainty.

Britain has been lucky to find in Bowley a theoretically informed statistician who spent time and effort for as exact a calculation of the British wage sum as possible. This provided a more solid basis for calculations of the wage share – already introduced by Bowley himself[58] – than was possible in most other countries. But even the very thorough Bowley estimates leave room for critical modifications. This is shown by a study of Agatha Chapman (carried out under the auspices of the National Institute of Economic and Social Research and the Cambridge Department of Applied Economics) which deals with wages and salaries in Britain in the interwar period.[59] Chapman arrives at estimates of the wage sum which lie in most years above the estimates of Bowley and Colin Clark. This in itself would not matter so very much for *changes* in the wage share if the upward bias were more or less constant over the years. But this is not the case. Thus the deviations of the Chapman estimates from Bowley's figures range from – 1.1 per cent (1926) to + 9.7 per cent (1938), and compared with Colin Clark from + 4.9 per cent (1935) to + 11.7 per cent (1924).[60] If such differences can occur in a period which had at least a modestly satisfactory data basis one can imagine what uncertainties must exist regarding earlier years.[61] Yet one cannot neglect these earlier years if the thesis of long-term stability is to be tested.

Conditions are even more serious when we come to the denominator of the fraction – national income. Simon Kuznets and two of his collaborators have used their long experience to derive estimates for the probable margins of error in US national income estimates for the inter-war period.[62] Aggregating error margins of several components the authors arrive at a margin of about 20 per cent for total income,[63] with 10 per cent as a more likely estimate if the possibilities of compensating errors is taken into account.[64]

The uncertainties connected with earlier decades are even weightier in national income estimates than in the case of wages. One has only to look at the heroic assumptions and manipulations which Phelps Brown and Hart[65] or Prest[66] have to adopt in their skilful and thorough attempts to derive estimates of the British national income for the second half of the nineteenth century. The problems are further intensified by the fact that difficulties arise not only from the lack of data but also from systematic biases in those data which are available. Thus the understatement of profits is not a recent invention and it provides an upward bias to the wage share.

But the decisive question for us is: how does this bias (and others) *change* in the course of years? This can influence the picture we get about the course of the wage share. Prest refers to an investigation on profit statements for 1864 which were separately given for tax purposes on the one hand and for subsidy arrangements in a reconstruction programme on the other. The declarations in the second case were higher by 52 per cent than in the first case, mainly (in the opinion of the tax authorities) as a consequence of understatements in the tax case. These are sources of error about whose importance we have little information. Prest, who tries to include tax evasion in his national income calculations, assumes – on the basis of a few statistics for selected years – that tax evasion declined in the course of years. But is this valid for all countries and all periods? Have not the extentions of state activities and the rising tax burden led to increased endeavours to conceal one's true income position?[67]

Even weaker than in Britain and the US are the available data in most other countries. Germany is one of the few nations whose statistical material does approach the standard of the United Kingdom and the United States. But even there J. Heinz Müller[68] calls his time series of labour incomes since 1925 only a 'well founded estimate'. National income is even less well founded. For most other countries historical data are either completely missing or full of uncertainties.

Combining the previously discussed inherent restrictions for wage share fluctuations with all these possible margins of error it becomes obvious that it is very difficult to decide whether one should regard the existing wage share data as an example of 'surprising stability' or should deny the existence of a stable share. And in fact both these interpretations can be found. As we already mentioned Phelps Brown and Hart[69] were inclined to see 'sharp changes' occurring from time to time in an otherwise stable wage share.[70] These 'sharp changes' consist, for instance, in a rise of the share from 38.6 to 42.6 per cent in the years 1870 to 1873 or from 42 to 39.8 per cent in the years 1926 to 1928.

When dealing with these changes, which take a prominent place in their theoretical considerations, the authors write: 'It is probable that these shifts mark a change in the economy, and not merely a jump in the estimates of wages and national income, for their size, though it may lie within the margin of error of these estimates in any one year, seems greater than could arise from discontinuities in them between one year and another.'[71] Now while one can agree that it is very unlikely that the *entire* shifts (of 3 to 4 percentage points) are caused by *changes* in the margins of error within two to three years, it is not absurd to consider the possibility that *some part* of the shift may be so caused. But if this is the case are we still justified to talk with assurance of 'sharp' changes? Conversely, there might have been significant changes in other years which have gone unnoticed because they were partly compensated by statistical errors.

It does not require a large portion of scepticism to come to the conclusion that the theoretical discussion concerning constant wage shares rests on a very thin empirical basis. This is one of the reasons why this discussion has remained so vague and lacking substance. Whether wage share stability is a 'miracle' or a 'mythos' seems to be an open question and one has to agree with Rostow when he says: 'The distribution of shares in the national income remains still to be investigated.'[72]

ADDITIONAL REMARKS CONCERNING THE SHARE OF WAGES IN NATIONAL INCOME

What has been said so far provides – so I hope – a rough outline of the main aspects of the theoretical and empirical discussions which have recently taken place around the question of wage share tendencies. The sceptical note of my remarks is not meant to belittle the efforts and achievements in this field. It should only help to prevent a belief in a stable wage share to harden – like Pareto's 'law' of income distribution – into a dogma before a more secure statistical basis and firmer theoretical insights have enabled us to come to a clearer decision. Nevertheless we can probably admit today that a certain stability of the wage share does exist at least for some periods in some countries which justified discussions about the reasons for this phenomenon (and deviations from it) without necessarily touching the question of a 'law' of wage share constancy. As a contribution to such an ongoing discussion I now want to add a few further observations which were left out before because they would have disrupted the main line of the argument.

Wage and gross profit shares, wage and gross profit incomes

Discussions concerning the wage share (or share of total employee income) are sometimes connected with the question of a 'just' return to labour. We shall later have to say something in this connection.[73] Here it should only be noted that – if ethical criteria are to be discussed – no a priori reasons exist to regard a stable wage share as more 'justified' than a rising or falling one. The 'ethical' attraction which a stable wage share seems to exert on many people can only be interpreted as the expression of a feeling that the capitalistic status quo at a certain point in time represented an 'ideal' distributional relation. Stability of the wage share would then guarantee a continuation of that ideal state of affairs.

Whatever the views held in this matter, two very simple points must be mentioned which are quite obvious but are often overlooked. They are not unimportant for distributional questions. The first point is so simple that it can be put in to one sentence. Stability of shares in a growing national income implies that the *absolute* distance between gross profits and wages continually grows. But absolute differences can play the same or even bigger roles in distributional disputes than relative ones. This can occasionally be seen when in wage negotiations equal relative or absolute wage increases are confronted.

The second point concerns the well-known, but not always sufficiently considered fact that for the individual income receiver – be he worker or capitalist – the size of income shares is far less interesting (if at all) than his personal income. Constant shares in total income will result in equal percentage increases in personal incomes only if the relative numbers of wage and profit earners remain unchanged. This is, however, not the historical tendency. The blurred and sometimes changing definitions of 'wage earners' (particularly if separated from salaried employees!) and of 'self-employed' persons make it difficult to arrive at exact figures about the changing proportions of the various groups of income receivers. One tendency, however, can be quite clearly seen in all industrial states: both wage earners and self-employed persons lose relatively in comparison to the quickly rising number of salaried employees. Thus for Germany (within the frontiers of 1934) we find that the proportion of self-employed persons decreased from 29 to 17 per cent between 1882 and 1939, the proportion of wage earners from 65 to 61 per cent while the proportion of salaried employees rose in the same period from 6 to 22 per cent. In France the proportions of self-employed persons (including helping family members) and of wage earners fell from 40 to 39 per cent and from 55 to 47 per cent respectively between 1876 and 1936. Long-term data are not available for all countries, but as a more recent example I add data from Austria, where between 1934 and 1951 the proportions of self-employed persons and of wage earners declined from 19.2 to 17.6 per cent and from 45.4 to 44.9 per cent respectively. Only rarely and then for short periods only can we see exceptions to this trend (particularly after some shock event). Thus the proportion of wage earners changed from 56 to 57 per cent in Italy between 1936 and 1954 (salaried employees: 10 to 12 per cent, self-employed 34 to 31 per cent); it remained unchanged (at 59.5 per cent) in Germany (post-war era) between 1939 and 1950 (with a falling proportion of self-employed). For longer periods, however, the tendency of a falling relative role of wage earners and self-employed persons is discernible in all industrial countries.[74]

Assuming a stable wage share the long-term development can thus be summarized by stating that a constant share of total income went to a relatively shrinking group while the remaining share of gross revenue went to another shrinking group (the entrepreneurs) who spent growing amounts of it to the absolutely and relatively growing group of salary earners. Taking wages and salaries together their share in national income has therefore in general risen while the share of net profits has declined. But we leave the question of salaries to the next section, and continue for the moment with the division between wages and gross revenue. When the division of total income between *wage* earners and employers is under discussion only this distinction is relevant and it is of interest which of these two groups has grown more quickly, i.e. which group has won or lost in relative size.

As an example of relevant considerations I refer to the statistical division which Mills has used in his book on the American middle class.[75] He distinguishes between an 'old middle class', a 'new middle class' and the wage workers. The old middle class comprises the self-employed persons, the new middle class the salaried employees. There are, of course, difficulties in drawing exact lines and Mills's figures have the additional disadvantage (in our context) that they refer to the combined private and public sectors. However, the picture shown by his data is clear enough. Between 1870 and 1940 the share of the new middle class in the total labour force rose from 6 to 25 per cent, while the shares of the wage workers and the old middle class declined from 61 to 55 per cent and from 33 to 20 per cent respectively. In absolute terms all three groups have grown, but the new middle class by 1600 per cent, wage earners by 255 per cent and the old middle class by only 135 per cent. [76]

What does this figure mean for the interpretation of an − assumedly − constant wage share? (In reality the wage share in US *industry* declined from 48 to 39 per cent in the above mentioned period. [77] No data are available to calculate the wage share in national income over this long period.) The relatively faster growth in the number of workers compared with employers implies a concentration of production: the average size of firms has grown. Constant shares then means that the revenue which goes to the *single* employer after deduction of direct costs (wages and raw materials) has grown faster − absolutely and relatively − than the wage income of the *single* worker. These (higher) gross revenues are then the source for investments, salaries, profits, etc.

From a sociological point of view this means that the 'new middle class' has been formed partly by small and medium independent entrepreneurs (or their offspring) who were eliminated from their traditional basis, and partly by people (and their offspring) who have 'risen' from blue-collar to white-collar work. The concentration of entrepreneurial activities has led to a relatively fast growth of the sums passing through individual firms as gross revenue of which a growing part is turned into salaries which to some extent can be seen as payments to former self-employed persons who now obtain their income indirectly rather than directly. So much should be clear that when questions of distributional developments and 'distributional justice' come up, the relative shifts between workers and employers and the rise of the 'new middle class' require at least the same attention as wage or labour shares in national income.

Why wage share and not wage plus salaries share?

In the previous section salaries and salaried employees made their explicit appearance after having been neglected in earlier sections, where the wage share was confronted with a gross revenue share of entrepreneurs in which salaries are included. The time has come to look into the reasons and justifications for this isolated treatment of the wage share. This is the more necessary as from many points of view the comparison of employee incomes (wages and salaries), on the one hand, and profits on the other hand can be considered as more relevant. And in fact the US literature on distribution concentrates almost exclusively on such a division (employee compensation and property income). Was it perhaps only the empirical accident of a fairly stable wage share — contrasting with a far more fluctuating wages-plus-salaries share — which attracted the attention and the theoretical interest of economists? Reading some of the relevant contributions one can, in fact, get the impression that this is the case. Some authors make no attempt to explain why they restrict their investigation to this particular category of employee compensation. One can almost say that a neglect of the question 'Why wages only?' is typical for the whole discussion.

I would, however, maintain that there are better reasons for the isolation of the wage share than a mere historical accident of stability. In his original contributions Kalecki already indicates the reasons for his juxtaposition of direct costs (wages and raw material prices), on the one hand, and gross revenue of entrepreneurs on the other. But his hints are not properly elaborated. As we saw earlier, his ideas about distribution are closely connected with his theory of price formation. Wages and raw material costs — the variable costs — form the basis for price setting. Added to them is a gross margin whose size is influenced by competitive conditions and traditional views about 'normal' profits. Out of this additional revenue all fixed costs have to be covered. In this perspective the separation of wages and salaries makes sense. We start off with a primary distribution process between wages and gross profits (characterized by the degree of monopoly and influenced by raw material prices) which is then followed by a secondary distribution between salaries, rents, depreciation and profits.

This approach can be directly linked to Marx's distinction between material and non-material production or — as he also called it — productive and unproductive labour.[78] And I would suggest that this Marxian perspective provides a main *raison d'être* for a separate treatment of the wage share.

At any given moment wages and salaries are more or less a homogeneous category in the eyes of the entrepreneur. Both represent costs which he has to incur if he wants to continue in production. Even when he fixes his price by a margin on wages (and other direct costs) alone this does not make any difference. He would quite rightly stress that this is just a method of calculation, but salaries and depreciation are nevertheless necessary costs in the same way as wages.

However, when we look at the structure of incomes not at a certain moment in time but in their historical development since the early days of modern capitalism, a different story can be told. We can begin with an early stage where we meet almost exclusively entrepreneurs on the one side and (manual) wage labour on the other. Most of the managerial and white-collar activities, frequently including technical supervision, were in the hands of the capitalist himself. The produce was, therefore, distributed mainly between wages and gross profits (after deduction of raw material costs). *In step with the growth of gross profits* entrepreneurs could then gradually acquire more machinery and delegate more and more entrepreneurial functions to salaried employees. In this way 'fixed' costs grew and had to be covered out of the gross profit receipts. To a considerable degree it was not the case that 'necessary' fixed costs pressed on a wage share, but rather that a low wage share enabled entrepreneurs to expand their capital equipment and human capital, leading to higher expenditure for depreciation and salaries. The primary division between wages and gross revenues is thus not irrelevant. It helps to determine the extent to which entrepreneurs are capable to pay salaries, i.e. to draw a new type of employee into the productive process.

In this historical context it is irrelevant whether the salaried class which comes into existence later becomes an essential element in the productive process or whether it remains 'unproductive' in more than in a purely Marxian terminology. [79] In other words (and somewhat simplified) the gross margin of entrepreneurial price setting, which is a determinant of the wage share, is not high because salaries require a high amount but salaries are extensive because it was possible to widen the gross margin. [80] This can be seen as a reason why the question of the wage share and its development can be more than just an accidental diversion. [81]

Nominal and real shares

For some strange reason the wage share discussion has dealt almost exclusively with the share of *money* wages in national income. But an unchanged nominal share can deviate from real shares when productivities and degrees of monopoly among wage goods and other goods develop differently, i.e. when relative prices between these two sectors change. Such developments are not unlikely when we consider the considerable differences in the composition of goods bought out of wage incomes compared with those which are acquired with profits and salaries. A parallel development of prices is anything but self-evident. In national income calculations such factors have occasionally been considered, but hardly ever in discussions about the wage share. Among the authors mentioned in the previous sections Dudley Seers is the only one who – in a discussion of the distribution of personal incomes in the post-war era – takes up the question of relative price shifts reaching among other things the conclusion that the 'nominal' rise of the share of wages and salaries between 1950 and 1954 turns into a 'real' decline when the relevant price indices are taken into account. [82]

It is, however, easier to acknowledge that relative price movements can influence the distribution problem than to find a satisfactory description of such changes. In addition to the general difficulty of obtaining reliable data for earlier periods one is faced with a lack of information about expenditure patterns for profit and salary earners (consumption and investment goods) and about long-term changes in qualities. To make useful statements on these matters would require considerable research efforts. But just in order to indicate the problem I want to refer to the long-term movements of grouped price indices in a form which has been provided for the US by the National Bureau of Economic Research.

William H. Shaw worked out price indices for four groups of manufactured goods for the period 1879 to 1939.[83] The groups are: 'short-term' consumption goods (food, heating, writing paper, etc.), 'medium-term' consumption goods (clothing, shoes, household articles, etc.), durable consumption goods (furniture, cars, etc.), and durable investment goods (machinery, office equipment, etc.). In Table 15.1 we present Shaw's data for every tenth year.

Perhaps the most remarkable characteristic of these price indices is their comparatively parallel movement over all these years. There occurred, of course, some relative shifts, but a more detailed analysis would probably not *completely* destroy the impression one gets from a purely nominal analysis. The shift to a 'real' analysis would not lead to *extreme* deviations from the nominal results. If one tries to say a bit more than this one can perhaps add that it seems that durable goods (consumption and investment) tended towards a slower price rise than short-term consumption goods. The difference is not big enough to make this a statistically well founded conclusion. But such a development does not sound implausible when one considers the enormous technical progress in the period considered, a progress which on average benefited durable goods more than short-term consumption goods.[84]

Since one can assume that short-term and medium-term consumption goods dominate working-class budgets while investment goods are bought by entrepreneurs and durable consumption goods play a larger part in the expenditure patterns of higher-income groups, it is probably safe to conclude – notwithstanding the earlier statement that the 'real' calculation will not result in fundamental changes – that the real share of wage earners developed less favourably than the nominal share.[85]

Relative price shifts are of interest not only in relation to long-term

Table 15.1 Price indices of four groups of manufactured goods in the United States, 1889–1939 (1879 = 100)

Year	Short-term consumption goods	Medium-term consumption goods	Durable consumption goods	Durable investment goods
1889	102	94	98	92
1899	87	79	84	92
1909	112	97	109	99
1919	227	214	162	193
1929	170	128	128	137
1939	125	123	117	122

Source: Shaw, W. H. (1941) *Finished Commodities Since 1879*, New York: National Bureau of Economic Research.

changes but also with regard to the cyclical pattern. This, too, has been neglected. Returning once more to the US calculations the data show that the prices of short- and medium-term goods display wider fluctuations in the course of the cycle than durable goods (see Table 15.2). This is very pronounced for the time after the First World War, less so before that time. The difference in variance, which can find its explanation in a higher degree of monopolization (and 'oligopolization') in the durable goods industries, implies that behind a constant nominal wage share during the cycle there is a 'real' wage share which falls slightly in the recovery period and rises in the depression.[86]

Constancy of the wage share and Marx's theory of the 'impoverishment of the working class'

The 'theory' of wage share stability could create more interest than other (true or imagined) 'constants' in economic life because it has a bearing on the time-honoured conflict between wages and profits. An obvious conclusion which would follow from a stable wage share would be a refutation of Marx's so-called (he actually never used this expression) 'law of the impoverishment of the working class'.[87] Now there can be little doubt that Marx underestimated the power of trade unions to improve the lot of workers in a capitalist society (a power, by the way, which his ideas helped to establish). But the mere fact of a stable wage share in Britain and the United States is in itself not necessarily a refutation of those ideas of Marx which are covered by the term 'impoverishment theory'.

Table 15.2 Cyclical price movements for four groups of manufacturing goods in the United States, 1891–1938 (average annual change in %[a])

	13 cycles[b] 1891–1938		7 cycles[b] 1891–1914		6 cycles[b] 1914–38	
Group	Recov	Recess	Recov	Recess	Recov	Recess
Consumption goods						
Short-term	+2.7	−4.1	+0.4	+0.3	+5.4	−9.2
Medium-term	+3.5	−6.5	+1.0	−2.2	+6.5	−11.5
Durable	+0.3	+0.4	0.0	0.0	+0.6	+1.3
Investment goods						
Durable	+0.3	−1.0	+0.5	−0.7	+0.1	−1.4

Source: Shaw, W. H. (1941) *Finished Commodities Since 1879*, New York: National Bureau of Economic Research, pp. 27, 32.
Notes:
[a] The percentage changes are measured from the average of the corresponding cycle.
[b] The cycles correspond to the 'reference cycles' of the National Bureau of Economic Research. See Burns, A. F. and Mitchell, W. C. (1947) *Measuring Business Cycles, Studies in Business Cycles*, New York: National Bureau of Economic Research.

First of all it must be stressed that Marx's wage theory does not imply that wages cannot rise in the long run. Marx acknowledged that higher wages would be paid for skilled work. Such wage increases are seen as a necessary condition for the reproduction of these higher qualifications and do not represent an autonomous improvement in the worker's position even if he perceives them as such. If, for instance, a worker in a modern factory needs more protein-containing food and more holidays to cope with the additional stress, he or she will register the improved diet and the increase in leisure time as an advantage. But in Marx's perspective it is not permissible to talk of an improvement if the wage was just sufficient to maintain the long-term working capacity both before and after the job change. A large part of the long-term wage increases in the industrialized countries was a consequence of an enormous increase in workers' qualifications to an extent which Marx did not even dream of.[88] Anyway, in his terminology this part of the wage increase cannot be adduced without further analysis as a proof for an improvement in working class standards.[89] According to Bowley, about half of the rise in British average wages between 1880 and 1910 was due to shifts to better-paid jobs (which in most cases meant from lower to higher skills).[90]

A further aspect to be considered is the limited significance of a stable wage share for Marx's argument if it only applies to some countries like Britain, the US and a few others. Already Marx noted the existence of a 'labour aristocracy', a section of the working class which is able to secure for itself comparatively high levels of wages.[91] (It should be mentioned that Marx refers to this section in the context of economic crises in order to show that even these privileged workers are not protected in times of crisis.) When Marx wrote his books he was thinking of a small group of better-off workers *within* a given country. But with the expansion of colonialism and trade between developed and underdeveloped countries considerable parts of the working class in the dominant industrial countries could obtain 'aristocratic' conditions as compared with the workers in the food and raw material producing less developed countries. This difference in conditions is reflected in high profits and unfavourable terms of trade in the underdeveloped world. The emergence of national labour aristocracies was one of the developments which Lenin stressed when he tried to adjust Marx's theory to the imperialistic and monopolistic stage of capitalism.[92]

If these ideas are taken into account one comes to the conclusion that it would be useful to analyse the development of wages and profits not only in the mother country, say Britain, but in the entire British empire and all countries which are politically and economically dependent on Britain. We have no proper information on which to base any statements about wage share developments in this wider context which would also require information about the relative growth of self-employed and wage workers. In the case of the United States (where the statistical material does not convincingly show wage share stability even in the mother country[93]) one would have to include the Philippines and those Latin American countries in which US capital plays a dominant role and which are closely tied up with the US market.

It can be assumed that Marx was thinking of a falling share of wages in national income when he spoke of the impoverishment of the proletariat. But this is not the decisive element in his economic and sociological approach to the impoverishment question. It seems that two aspects were uppermost in his mind. The first is that capitalism is bound to give birth to recurrent crises and periods of unemployment[94] which cause misery for the working class. The second aspect is that the growing accumulation of means of production in the hands of capitalists leads to a growing dependence of the workers on capitalists and the capitalist system with all its critical developments. That these two aspects were more important for Marx than the ups and downs of wages comes out very clearly in the following passage taken from the first volume of *Das Kapital*: 'It thus follows that as capital accumulates the position of the worker must deteriorate *irrespective of the payment he receives*, be it high or low. The law which secures an equilibrium between a relative over population or industrial reserve army with the extent and energy of accumulation forges the worker more firmly to capital than Prometheus was fastened to the rock by Hephaestos'.[95] If this view, which sees impoverishment mainly in crises, wars and increasing dependency, is adopted, the share of wages in national income fades into the background. Even when this share remains unchanged workers will suffer in crisis periods if they have no reserves, and in the long run a stable share will not prevent – in view of unequal initial positions – a constantly growing one-sided accumulation of the expensive means of production.

Ideological aspects of the stability thesis

As we have seen the hypothesis of a constant wage share is by no means firmly established, neither statistically nor theoretically. Many economists would not subscribe to such an assertion or would at least formulate it in a very cautious way. But it is also true that the ideological and practical aspects of this thesis have induced some authors to introduce it more or less uncritically into the time-honoured confrontation between profits and wages.

Ever since economic theories have existed there have been attempts to use some aspects of them to 'prove' that attempts towards obtaining higher wages are 'useless' or even 'harmful' for the workers. Thus the wage fund theory could be used to show that the wage sum is a fixed amount and that sectional wage increases must be at the cost of other workers. After the demise of the wage fund theory, marginal productivity theory took its place to prove the 'justice' of competitive wage levels and the unavoidable unemployment that must follow if they are surpassed. The ethical underpinning of marginal productivity theory could not be maintained and the relationship between wages and unemployment is nowadays seen in a more macroeconomic setting than was the case in traditional marginal productivity theory, with its microeconomic and static background. These developments have reduced the usefulness of marginal productivity theory as an ideological weapon in the fight against wage demands.

It seems that for some authors the thesis of a stable wage share can replace the former arguments which have gone out of fashion. Already in 1928 Knöpp wrote – after having found a statistical tendency pointing to a constant wage share – that 'The distribution of income is determined by objective forces and that changes by political means in spite of trade union policy and the efforts of owners and workers have poor chances of being successful.'[96] Knöpp failed to say which objective forces are meant to establish a natural law of income distribution, but he hoped to have proved the futility of trade union activities.

With the revived interest in the wage share and its stability this kind of argument reappeared leading to two different interpretations which contradict each other. On the one hand we find a repetition of the view which we just mentioned. The fixed share is seen as a 'law' which undermines all union endeavours to obtain higher wages. Their effects can only lead to inflationary wage–price movements. A good example for this type of argument is given in an article by Horst Knapp, in which he accepts the evidence of a stable wage share and comes to the following conclusion: 'This empirically based experience is of considerable practical relevance. It shows that any attempt to raise wages and salaries faster than national productivity is bound to fail. Even the strongest trade union movement cannot increase labour's share in national income; equally incomes of the entrepreneurs cannot grow faster than productivity.'[97]

In this view an 'invisible hand' sees to it that the wage share is constant so that the efforts of trade unions and employers' organizations are sheer folly. Against this we find an alternative interpretation of the (accepted!) stability – e.g. in the article of Solterer and also partly in Mitra – which regard this phenomenon as the result of constant trade union pressure (Mitra) or of an equilibrium between the pressures from unions and employers' organizations (Solterer) which in some (mystical) manner achieve a permanently stable wage share.

In view of what has been said in earlier sections one must regard these attempts to use the stability theses in actual confrontations as illegitimate. It has no reliable foundation – neither empirically nor theoretically. The role of unions and employers' organizations for the level and development of wages, what opportunities they have in a growing economy and during a cycle, these and related questions are still requiring considerable economic and sociological research. The same is true with regard to the wage share. One would like to have more reliable data for various regions and longer periods to provide a firmer basis for a 'deeper' theoretical analysis. Only when both statistics and theory can deliver more material may it be possible to say a bit more about the relationship between the activities of the labour market organizations and the level of the wage share.

NOTES

1 Kalecki, M. (1938) 'The determinants of distribution of the national income', *Econometrica*, 6, 1, pp. 97–112. This paper was later included with some alterations in Kalecki, M. (1939) *Essays in the Theory of Economic Fluctuations*, London: Allen & Unwin.
2 The rather vague expression 'total income' is chosen deliberately. Kalecki's theory deals with the share of wages in *private domestic gross product* (i.e. excluding income from capital abroad and excluding the public sector). But neither was Kalecki able to stick strictly to this delineation in his statistical calculations nor was it always adhered to in ensuing contributions. It seems, therefore, justified to speak of 'total income' with the understanding that total income and total wages are not always calculated in exactly the same way.
3 Bowley, A. L. (1920) *The Change in the Distribution of the National Income 1880–1913*, Oxford: Clarendon.
4 Bellerby, J. R. (1927) 'L'établissement d'un systeme de détermination des salaires', *Revue international du travail*, 16, 1–3, pp. 1–26, 204–24, 345–78.
5 Knöpp, H. (1928) *Das Verhältnis zwischen Arbeits- und Besitzeinkommen*, Halberstadt: H. Meyer.
6 The Cobb-Douglas function was developed at the turn of the 1920s and found a detailed presentation in Douglas, P. H. (1934) *The Theory of Wages*, New York: Macmillan. A critical survey of the literature is contained in Mitra, A. (1954) *The Share of Wages in National Income*, University of Rotterdam dissertation.
7 These figures are taken from Kalecki's *Essays in the Theory of Economic Fluctuations*, *op. cit.* They are slightly different from those in the *Econometrica* paper.
8 See, for instance, Scitovsky, T. (1951) *The Economics of a Fully Employed Economy*, Chicago: Irwin.
9 Barna, T. (1945) *Profits During and After the War*, London: Gollancz.
10 Seers, D. (1956) 'Has the distribution of income become more unequal?' *Bulletin of the Oxford Institute of Statistics*, 18, 1, pp. 73–86.
11 Phelps Brown, E. H. and Hart, P. E. (1952) 'The share of wages in national income', *Economic Journal*, 62, 2, pp. 253–77.
12 Dunlop, J. T. (1944) *Wage Determination Under Trade Unions*, New York: Macmillan.
13 The different developments in various industrial sectors, which Phelps Brown and Hart point out in their treatment of the British economy, assumes an important role in Steindl's study (1952) of American capitalism (Steindl, J., *Maturity and Stagnation in American Capitalism*, Oxford: Blackwell). Steindl calculates the share of wages in industrial net value added and finds that this share declined after 1921 (followed by some increase in the 1930s) with a sharper fall in the 'oligopolistic' industries than in the 'competitive' ones.
14 The investigation (1956) by Creamer (Creamer, D., *Personal Income During Business Cycles*, Princeton: Princeton University Press) indicates – on the basis of data covering several cycles of the US economy – that the influence of salaries on the cyclical pattern of labour incomes originates mainly in the non-industrial sector (finance, transport, services, public sector). Within the manufacturing sector the share of wages usually increased in boom periods and declined (with falling employment) in the depression while salaries contributed little to these

fluctuations (see the tables on pp. XVI and XVII of the above volume). When using Creamer's data one has to be aware that he refers to shares in *personal* income, not in national income. This means that his total income includes transfer and public-sector incomes and excludes retained profits.

15 Müller, J. H. (1954) *Nivellierung und Differenzierung der Arbeitseinkommen in Deutschland seit 1925*, Berlin: Duncker & Humblot.

16 Kalecki, M. (1954) *Theory of Economic Dynamics: An Essay on Cycles and Long-Run Changes in Capitalist Economy*, London: Allen & Unwin.

17 Lerner, A. P. (1933–4) 'The concept of monopoly and the measurement of monopoly power', *The Review of Economic Studies*, 1, 3: pp. 15–75. In this article Lerner defined the degree of monopoly as $(p - m)/p$, with p for price and m for marginal cost of a good.

18 Expressed as a percentage addition to direct costs the margin is $100 (k - 1)$ per cent.

19 See for instance, Mitra, *op. cit.*, p. 29; Bauer, P. T. (1941) 'A note on monopoly', *Economica*, 8, 2: p. 201; Kaldor, N. (1955–6) 'Alternative theories of distribution', *The Review of Economic Studies*, 23, 2, p. 92. Kaldor, however, acknowledged that Kalecki's theory contains a realistic aspect in spite of the tautological formulation. Kaldor develops in this article a distributional model of his own which combines Keynesian elements with elements coming from modern growth theory. In this model comparatively constant shares of profits, on the one hand, and wages and salaries, on the other, can arise from group resistance against relative deterioration and from a long-term constancy of the rate of investment as a percentage of national income (which in turn is derived from the growth of productive capacity and the development of capital intensity). But since for Kaldor the constancy of the wage share (or rather the wage and salary share) is only a side issue which would need further analysis, it will not be taken up in this paper.

20 As an example of a distinction between tautological and theoretical statements and their relationship see the remarks on the quantity theory of money in Brunner, K. (1955) 'Ein Ausblick auf die ökonometrische Forschungsarbeit', *Schweizerische Zeitschrift für Volkswirtschaft und Statistik*, 91, 2, pp. 171–97.

21 This is completely overlooked by Mitra, with the consequence that his argument is beside the point when his objection to the *formula* is that it does not constitute a theory (*op. cit.* p. 30).

22 It would seem that the faster growth of the tertiary sector (Clark, C. 1951, *The Conditions of Economic Progress* (2nd edn), London: Macmillan) would exert a negative influence on the wage share (wages *without* salaries). Against this one has to see the relative decline of agriculture.

23 Kalecki (*Theory of Economic Dynamics, op. cit.*, p. 38) speaks of cyclical shifts in industry which exert a negative influence on the wage share in depression insofar a shift from industry to services is concerned this is a plausible argument. But it is odd that Kalecki rests his statement on shifts *within* the manufacturing sector pointing to the relatively stronger decline in the investment goods sector. But there is no evidence that the wage share in the investment goods industries is higher than in consumption goods industries.

24 Müller, *op. cit.*, p. 32. The same misunderstanding occurs in Rostow, W. W. (1948) *British Economy of the Nineteenth Century*, Oxford: Clarendon. See the Appendix 'Mr. Kalecki on the distribution of income 1880–1913'.

25 Kalecki, *Essays in the Theory of Economic Fluctuations, op. cit.*, p. 28. On p. 24, however, Kalecki has a rather unhelpful and contradictory passage: 'According to our formula, the distribution of the product of industry is at every moment determined by the degree of monopoly....And contrary to the usual

view neither inventions nor the elasticity of substitution between capital and labour have any influence on the distribution of income.' It is obvious that this badly formulated passage caused the statement by Müller which is criticised in the text.

26 See, however, the remarks about the 'shaky' character of cost-determined prices in Kuhl, K. Ch. (1955) 'Eine Analyse des Vollkostenprinzips', *Weltwirtschaftliches Archiv*, 75, 2, pp. 137–95.

27 Mitra, *op. cit.*

28 There is also Mitra's strange attempt to 'test' Kalecki's formula on the basis of his data although he had denounced this formula as being tautological. If this is true and Mitra could measure the different elements properly the 'test' would necessarily produce positive results.

29 Mitra, *op. cit.*, p. 67.

30 Mitra makes the mistake to equate Kalecki's 'raw materials' with imports. But the relevant element for Kalecki was not the origin of the goods but the process of price formation.

31 In addition to these heroic assumptions Mitra's formula also suffers from some questionable simplifications. He neglects some important functional relations whose inclusion would make the formula even more unwieldy. But this does not concern us here.

32 Rostow, *op. cit.*

33 See Chapter IV and the Appendix. Some of Rostow's arguments are dealt with in other parts of this paper, some have to be neglected. I just want to point out one error of Rostow which – as far as I can see – has remained unnoticed. On p. 226 he writes: '"The degree of monopoly", for a firm, over the whole relevant range of output, may be said to be constant, then, when average variable costs are constant and equal to short-period marginal costs; when prices are assumed to be determined uniquely with reference to short-period marginal costs; and when the demand curve it faces is of constant elasticity.'

But the last point is not a necessary condition. It is true that in a situation of *equilibrium*, where marginal costs equal marginal revenue, the degree of monopoly is equal to the reciprocal value of demand elasticity (see Lerner, *op. cit.*). But that does not mean that we have to stipulate an iso-elastic demand curve in order to arrive at a constant degree of monopoly. Kalecki does not restrict himself to 'equilibrium' conditions. He assumes a cost-determined price formation and all that is necessary for a constant degree of monopoly is that the price thus fixed is maintained while demand and revenue vary. The actual situations need not represent an equilibrium (which is unknown to the firm anyway). Under these conditions the necessity of constant demand elasticity for a constant degree of monopoly disappears.

But even in an equilibrium perspective the iso-elasticity of demand need not be an absolutely necessary condition. It suffices that whenever it comes to a shift in demand the different demand curves have the same elasticity *in the point of equilibrium* (where marginal revenue equals the constant marginal costs). Constant elasticity of demand is an essential condition for a constant degree of monopoly *under equilibrium conditions* only when this constancy is expected to prevail after there has been a change in variable costs.

34 Keynes, J. M. (1939) 'Relative movements of real wages and output', *Economic Journal*, 49, 1, pp. 34–51.

35 Tarshis, L. (1939) 'Changes in real and money wages', *Economic Journal*, 49; 1, pp. 150–4.

36 Steindl, *op. cit.*

37 Dunlop, *op. cit.*

38 Dunlop, *op. cit.*, p. 187.
39 See above, p. 189.
40 Seers, *op. cit.*
41 Phelps Brown and Hart, *op. cit.*
42 See above, p. 188.
43 This means that the degree of monopoly will remain fairly constant.
44 Important ingredients of the market environment are, according to Phelps Brown and Hart: technical change, development of raw material sources, monetary policy, cartelization.
45 In a later paper ('The long-term movement of real wages' in Dunlop, J. T. (ed.), 1957, *The Theory of Wage Determination*, London: Macmillan, pp. 48–65) Phelps Brown suggests that prices of raw materials are of decisive influence for the market environment. An ample supply of raw materials with falling raw material prices leads to a hard market environment, rising raw material prices foster a soft environment.
46 Krelle, W. (1956) 'Unbestimmtheitsbereiche in der Preisbildung als ein Erklärungsgrund für Änderungen in der Einkommensverteilung', in Schneider, E. (ed.), *Beiträge zur Theorie der Einkommensuerteilung*, Berlin: Duncker & Humblot.
47 A short overview of these tendencies in French theoretical thinking is contained in Marchal, A. (1955) 'Die neuen Tendenzen im französischen Wirtschaftsdenken', *Jahrbücher für Nationalökonomie und Statistik*, 167, pp. 321–58. See in particular the sections on 'Anglo-Saxon "macrocism" and French "sociologism"' and on 'Structures and economic theory'.
48 I am talking about a 'French school' because this approach has been rather intensively discussed in France in recent years. But similar ideas can, of course, also be found in other countries.
49 See above, p. 194.
50 Solterer, J. (1953–4) 'Zur Frage der Wirtschaftsmacht. Die Machttheorien von Wieser, Russel, Galbraith und die Stabilität des Arbeitanteils am gemeinsamen Produkt', *Zeitschrift für Nationalöknomie*, 14, 2–4, pp. 467–86.
51 For this assertion Solterer quotes one solitary example: experiences in the Nunn-Bush Company in Milwaukee.
52 In this group one can mention Archibald, G. C. (1955) 'Inventory investment and the share of wages in manufacturing income', *Economic Journal*, 65, 2, pp. 257–70. He shows that the practice of valuing stocks at prices below selling prices must – in times of involuntary accumulations of stocks – lead to an increase in the wage share even when the gross margin (degree of monopoly) on sales remains unchanged. At the beginning of a depression one should, therefore, expect a slight rise in the wage share, and at the beginning of recovery (when stocks are reduced) a slight decline. Should the wage share in fact be cyclically stable, the Kaleckian hypothesis that the degree of monopoly rises in the depression and falls during recovery would obtain additional support. (In Kalecki's model the counterweight to the swings in the degree of monopoly consists only in changes in raw material prices.)
53 Keynes, *op. cit.* p. 48.
54 See, for instance, Seers, *op. cit.*, p. 74.
55 Dunlop, *op. cit.*, p. 151.
56 Chesterton, G. K. (1918) *The Man Who Was Thursday*, Bristol: Arrowsmith.
57 These considerations are less applicable when one is faced with greater short-term changes in the number of wage earners. Such changes are important elements in the business cycle. If we assume horizontal marginal costs curves and constant gross profit margins W and P will increase together when new workers

are hired in the recovery period. The wage share will remain unchanged but the share of net profits will rise at the cost of salary earners whose numbers will increase less and whose payments fluctuate less than wage rates. In recession we have the opposite development: falling share of net profits, rising share of salaries and a fairly stable wage share. This 'stylized' scenario about shares during the cycle is simpler than Kalecki's hypothesis which expects falling gross profit margins during recovery whose effect on the wage share is compensated by rising raw material prices.

58 See Bowley *op. cit.*

59 Chapman, A. L. (1953) *Wages and Salaries in the United Kingdom 1920–1938*, Cambridge: Cambridge University Press.

60 Chapman, *op. cit.*, pp. 41, 43. In her own estimates Agatha Chapman thinks it unlikely that the margins of error are higher than 10 per cent for 1920 and higher than 5 per cent for 1938. No estimates about error margins are given for other years and the material is also not sufficient for an analysis of possible changes in statistical bias between the years (see p. 234).

61 In *Wages and Income in the United Kingdom since 1860* (Cambridge: Cambridge University Press, 1937) A. P. Bowley wrote: 'I do not think that the statistics are sufficient for any fine measurements of income, earnings or wages prior to 1880; there is indeed sufficient uncertainty after that date.'

62 Kuznets, S. (1941) *National Income and Its Composition, 1919–1938*, New York: National Bureau of Economic Research, ch. 12. See also: Morgenstern, O. (1949) *The Accuracy of Economic Observations*, Princeton: Princeton University Press, p. 116.

63 Kuznets's estimates show possible errors of up to 10 per cent for wages, though Kuznets believes that the actual errors were smaller.

64 When we compare year-to-year changes of a relation between two amounts (wages and national income) the probability of errors is reduced when the errors of the two quantities involved lie in the same direction and are of comparatively similar size. Since in our case we are frequently faced with systematic biases, this condition will be partly met. On the other hand, errors in year-to-year changes of relations can become worse when the changes in the two elements are small and independent. This will also apply in the case of wages and national income. We can say little about the probable compensation between these two diverging effects. See on this Kuznets, *op. cit.*, p. 529, and Anderson, O. (1954) *Probleme der statistischen Methodenlehre in den Sozialwissenschaften*, Würzburg: Physica-Verlag, ch. IV.

65 Phelps Brown and Hart, *op. cit.*, Appendix.

66 Prest, A. R. (1948) 'National income of the United Kingdom 1870–1946', *Economic Journal*, 58, 1, pp. 31–62.

67 This is even true for a country like Great Britain, which has a comparatively high tax morale. Reviewing a book by Kaldor (*Expenditure Tax*, London, 1955) I.M.D. Little wrote: 'There is the very height of income tax itself, which now makes many property owners... exploit legal loopholes in the tax structure in a manner which they would not have dreamed of twenty years ago' (*Economic Journal*, 1956, 66, 1, p. 118).

68 Müller, *op. cit.*, p. 16.

69 Phelps Brown and Hart, *op. cit.*

70 Some doubts about the solidity of this stability did arise: 'Does it (the stability of the wage share) arise out of the working of the distributive process, or does it only show the inertia of statistical aggregates?' (Phelps Brown and Hart, *op. cit.*, p. 264).

71 Ibid., p. 268.

72 Rostow, *op. cit.*, p. 103.

73 See below, pp. 211.

74 See (1956) 'The World's working population: Its distribution by status and occupation', *International Labour Review*, 74, pp. 174 ff, in particular the diagrams on pp. 180 and 188. This article is the source for the figures in the text (with additional data from Austria's population census). See also the data about the development of the proportion of wage workers in Phelps Brown and Hart, *op. cit.*, and the US data further below.

75 Mills, C. W. (1951) *White Collar*, New York: Oxford University Press.

76 Ibid., p. 63.

77 Kalecki, *Theory of Economic Dynamics*, *op. cit.*, p. 32.

78 It should be noted that in the terminology of Marx (and before him Smith) 'unproductive' labour did not mean 'worthless' or 'unnecessary' labour.

79 Jostock, P. (1955) 'The long-term growth of national income in Germany' (in Kuznets, S., *Income and Wealth*, Series V, London: Bowes and Bowes) refers to the growth of 'unproductive' activities among salaried employees. 'It is impossible to express quantitatively the amount of nominal increase in income not backed up by a real increase in wealth (no increment in goods and actually useful and productive services)' (p. 88).

80 This is particularly obvious in the hypertrophy of modern advertising and marketing expenditures. A vivid description is contained in Sweezy, P. (1942) (*The Theory of Capitalist Development*, New York: Oxford University Press): 'In the efforts of monopolists to enlarge their sales without jeopardizing the existence of extra profits we find the fundamental explanation of the enormous development of the arts of salesmanship and advertising which is such a striking characteristic of monopoly capitalism.... The entire trend is predicated upon a substantial and continuing rise in the productiveness of labor. Only if this condition is satisfied is it possible for the proportion of the labor force engaged in unproductive pursuits to increase without serious adverse consequences for the general standard of living. Conversely, given a steady increase in the productiveness of labor the stage is set for an expansion of surplus value and the social classes which are maintained out of surplus value.'

In this context it may be of interest to point out that Marx did see this 'middle-class' question though he is often accused to have neglected it. In his *Theorien über den Mehrwert* (edited by Karl Kautsky, vol. 2, 1905, Stuttgart: Internationale Bibliothek) he writes 'What he [David Ricardo] forgets to note is the constant increase of a middle class which stands between workers on the one side and capitalists and land owners on the other which is largely paid out of revenue and represents a burden on the working basis contributing to the social security and power of the upper ten' (p. 368).

81 As a recent example see Dobb, M. H. (1956) 'A note on income distribution and the measurement of national income at market prices', *Economic Journal*, 66, 2, pp. 357–360.

82 Seers, *op. cit.*, p. 79.

83 Shaw, W. H. (1941) *Finished Commodities Since 1879*, New York: National Bureau of Economic Research.

84 The influence of differing rates of technical progress was partly underminded by different growth rates in monopolization. These were probably more pronounced in the technically advanced sectors than in the traditional consumption goods industries. But these differences were not big enough to annihilate altogether the effect of technical progress on relative prices. German data show a similar picture as the US data (with the exception of crisis years) but have the disadvantage of an even less detailed breakdown of price developments. A

Table 15.3 Price indices for consumption goods and means of production in Germany, 1913–37 (1913 = 100)

	1925	1929	1933	1937
Consumption goods	172	172	112	133
Means of production	136	139	114	113

Source: Statistische Jahrbücher für das Deutsche Reich

distinction exists only for consumption goods (non-durable and durable) and means of production (mainly durable). For these two groups the development between 1913 and 1937 is shown in Table 15.3.

85 The following numerical example, which approximates the previously mentioned US data, can give an impression of orders of magnitude involved. Let us assume that over the period 1880 to 1940 the prices of wage goods had risen by 24 per cent and the prices for a basket of goods representative for other income receivers by 20 per cent. This can be regarded as a rather modest change in relative prices. If the nominal wage share turns out to be 40 per cent in the beginning and end-year this implies (when calculating wage earners' and other expenditure at 1880 prices) a decline in the real wage share from 40 to 39.2 per cent.

86 This question of the development of the wage *share* during the cycle must not be mixed up with the widely discussed question about the course of *real wages* during the cycle. In the latter case we are comparing the relative movements of nominal wages and of prices for wage goods, in the wage share case the comparison comprises movements of wages and other incomes as well as prices of wage goods and of 'other people's' goods.

87 See, for instance, Zimmerman, L. J. (1954) *Geschichte der theoretischen Volkswirtschaftslehre*, Köln: Bund-Verlag. On p. 103 he writes: 'As has been said there is hardly anybody today who would defend the theory of impoverishment. Statistical studies by Bowley, Douglas, Edelberg, and Kalecki have proved that the distribution of national income has remained almost constant in the last 30 years.' See also Solterer, *op. cit.*, p. 483.

88 Speaking of 'complicated work' in *Das Kapital* (vol. 1, 4th edn, Berlin 1951, p. 206, note 18) Marx remarks 'that the so-called "skilled labour" is quantitatively not very important in the national labour volume'. There is no indication that Marx foresaw the enormous changes which technical progress would bring to the occupational structure.

89 The reason is that the increase in wages following greater skills, intensity and responsibility does not change the relation between wages and the value of labour (i.e. the means necessary to maintain these labour services). The worker does not get 'wealthier' and does not gain more independence *vis-à-vis* the capitalist, two elements which were decisive for Marx. That the worker may regard the additional consumption as a welcome experience has already been mentioned. This explains the demand for industrialization (irrespective of the economic system) by workers in underdeveloped countries. They recognize that a relationship exists between industrial skills and a *necessary* increase in wage levels.

90 Bowley, *Wages and Income in the United Kingdom*, *op. cit.*, Appendix C.

91 Marx, *Das Kapital*, *op. cit.*, p. 704.

92 Lenin, W. I. (1946) 'Der Imperialismus als höchstes Stadium des Kapitalismus', *Collected Works*, vol. 1, Moscow, p. 854.

93 See above, p. 189.

94 Later Marxists would add wars to the list.
95 Marx, *Das Kapital*, *op. cit.*, p. 680.
96 Knöpp, *op. cit.*, p. 86.
97 Knapp, H. 'Lohnpolitick – bis wohin?', *Die Industrie* 56, 15, p. 3.

16 The arithmetic and the interpretation of the wage share

(Translation of 'zur Arithmetik und Interpretation von Lohnquoten' (1968), *Hamburger Jarhbuch für Wirtschafts- und Gesellschaftspolitik*, 13, pp. 143–58)

INTRODUCTION

The regular calculation and increasing reliability of national income data since the end of the war have created new possibilities for the analysis of economic relationships. Time series and ratios between important sub-categories – which were not available before – can now be constructed. But difficulties remain because the standardized OECD scheme of national accounts does not always contain those disaggregations which are required for some problems and the additional statistics needed are not easily obtained. This leads frequently to discussions which use a few significant key data without giving sufficient consideration to the consequences this may have for the interpretation of the results. Some of these problems arising in connection with the income account and particularly with the share of wages and salaries in national income are the subject of this paper.

WAGE SHARE AND LABOUR SHARE

The ratio between a more or less modified wage sum[1] and total national income (net social product at factor cost) is a datum which commands interest for two very different reasons: it plays a role when questions of the production function and the productive contribution of different factors are discussed, and it is a widely used information in considerations regarding income distribution. On the whole the problems of measurement and interpretation have received more attention in the production context than in the distribution context, particularly as far as economic theorists are concerned. These production-orientated aspects will, therefore, be treated rather briefly in this section. The following section will then deal with distribution aspects where the interpretation problems are often neglected.

In the theory of production the two-factor model with capital and labour occupies a dominant place. Land is subsumed under capital. We can neglect the difficulties which arise when one tries to separate land rent from other property incomes.[2] Our interest is directed towards the distribution of national income between the factors labour and capital (including land), between labour and property incomes. We also neglect the question how far it is justifiable to aggregate such heterogeneous units as workers and investment goods into the two categories 'labour' and 'capital'. Without further discussion we simply adopt the traditional theoretical practice. Similarly we will pay no attention to the numerous possible statistical errors which can occur in national income accounting, particularly in the sphere of profits and depreciation. In short, we shall accept the national income statistics as the best available basis for the needed informations.

The basic difficulty faced by a production-orientated analysis using national income data is the lack of a clear-cut separation between labour and property incomes.[3] Instead we get a tripartite division based on institutional elements and the statistics derived from them. The (OECD) standardized national income account[4] contains at the one end pure labour incomes of dependent employees (wages and salaries, item 1) and at the other end pure property incomes of corporate firms, households and public bodies (items 3–7). In between there is a mixed category: the income of self-employed persons (item 2). In this category we find a great variety of economic agents: farmers, small business, professional services, etc. What they have in common from our point of view is that their income is a mixture of compensations for labour services and for the supply of capital. If total income is to be divided into labour and capital income, the income of this mixed group has to be partitioned. This is the central problem of a factor-orientated national income analysis.

This partition of the income of the self-employed into labour and capital components can only be accomplished with the aid of hypotheses and analogies which have to make use of such statistics as there are. A certain amount of arbitrariness is unavoidable. Four different methods have been mainly used to deal with this problem.[5]

a) All self-employed persons are credited with a labour income which corresponds to the average wage of the dependent employees. Their (different) remaining incomes are treated as capital income. The advantage of this method is the easy availability of the necessary data, though the number of self-employed persons cannot always be exactly determined outside census years.[6]

The easy access to the needed data was the main reason for using this method in a recent investigation of the development of incomes in post-war Europe by the European Commission of the United Nations.[7] In the case of states which could provide the necessary statistics the method was modified by differentiating the attributed labour income according to sectors (agriculture, industry, building, others).

The weakness of this method lies in the extreme heterogeneity of the activities of self-employed persons which makes the use of a single wage figure a questionable affair. A particular problem arises – as Kuznets has pointed out[8] – in the case of less efficient peasants and small artisans who may earn subnormal labour *and* capital incomes but stay in their occupation because they prefer an independent status.[9] If they are 'given' an average wage in the labour income calculation it can happen that the capital income comes out as a negative amount. A further disadvantage is that in time series all special fluctuations in the incomes of the self-employed will be attributed completely to the capital component.

b) In analogy to (a) one can take the opposite road; each person is 'provided' with the average return on capital for his/her total capital input and the remainder is counted as labour income. This method is normally not applicable because in most countries the required statistics about capital inputs and capital returns are lacking. Apart from this the same weaknesses as in (a) are present. All special fluctuations are now fully attributed to labour income.

c) In order to avoid the effect that irregular and special fluctuations are always ascribed fully to one component only, one can adopt (in time series) a fixed ratio for dividing the self-employed persons' income into labour and capital components. When using this method one does not require special statistical informations and calculations for every year and some of the weaknesses of methods (a) and (b) disappear.[10] On the other hand an element of arbitrariness is introduced through the choice of the ratio to be applied. In fixing this ratio the very question one wants to analyse – viz. the division of income between labour and capital – is already answered in advance. The fixed key fails to catch changing trends and cyclical fluctuations in labour and capital incomes. They will show a different pattern in this sector than in the rest of the economy.

d) In order to overcome this disadvantage of a rigid ratio one can divide the income of the self-employed year by year in the same ratio as is shown in the corporate sector (or some other relevant sector) of the economy. This method requires additional statistics which go beyond the standard national income programme. This by itself will frequently prevent the adoption of such a calculation.[11] This method avoids the basic weakness of (c) but suffers from the fact that conditions in the self-employed and in the corporate sector are rather different so that the transfer of the ratio and its fluctuations from one to the other is a questionable procedure.

All these basic methods can, of course, be improved, modified, and combined. Thus we have a recent suggestion by Kravis[12] to use methods (a) and (b) to obtain separate estimates for the labour and capital incomes of self-employed persons broken down by industry as far as data permit, and then to combine the two estimates by changing them proportionally until they correspond to the actual self-employment income in each industry. But this and other modifications cannot really overcome the difficulties we have met before. They rest ultimately on the impossibility to find a 'correct' key for separating labour and capital elements in the amorphous mass of self-employed incomes. A recognition of this problem can at least help to be aware of the care that is needed when the results of such calculations are interpreted.

WAGE SHARE AND INCOME DISTRIBUTION

National income calculations are often used in political and socio-economic discussions in order to compare the development of the income of wage and salary earners with that of all other income receivers. While the production-orientated approach is mainly concerned with the division of income between labour and capital revenues, irrespective of the status of the persons to whom these revenues accrue, the distributional discussion looks at the question how far dependent employees have been able to be in step with the general development of income, how far they have participated in the fruits of a growing productive capacity. As an index answering this question the share of wages and salaries in national income – the wage share for short – is frequently chosen.[13] In most Western European countries this share shows a long-run tendency of growth. This is also true for the development since 1950.[14]

In what follows we shall neglect the question how far the big and heterogeneous aggregates of the national income accounts and the wage share considerations based on them are a satisfactory foundation for a discussion of social problems and relations. But it should be noted that the sum of wages and salaries includes the incomes of managers and other top earners who both politically and sociologically represent quite a different category than 'ordinary' employees. Another 'irregularity' is that the incomes of service men (in the army) are also included. On the other hand the incomes of small peasants and artisans are not counted although their social position and problems are not so different from those of dependent employees. But these 'irregularities' are not very disturbing, first because their absolute and relative size is not very important[15] and second because they play a minor role when we deal with *changes* in the wage share. The picture of changes will only be falsified when the share of these 'disturbing' elements (within wages and salaries) changes.

A far more important problem is that the wage share is not only influenced by shifts in the development of relative per capita incomes of employees and other income receivers but also by changes in the social structure of the labour force. The rest of this section will deal with this problem.

When one is interested in the social status of employees and their share in national income one is mainly concerned with the income of an *individual* employee and its relation to the general development of per capita incomes.

But the wage share calculated from the aggregated wage sum is influenced by the development of individual incomes *and* by changes in the social status of labour force participants. Critical socio-economic studies have, therefore, always tried to isolate and eliminate the influence of changes in the labour force structure when calculating the wage share and its development.[16]

The usual way to meet this problem is the calculation of a 'modified' wage share series which would have been the result merely on the basis of structural changes, and then to compare this modified share with the values of the actual wage share. Only when the latter lies above the 'modified' (structure-determined) wage share can one speak of a genuine improvement of the relative position of employees.

The modified wage share is easily calculated. Writing E for dependent employees, L for the total labour force, W for the sum of wages and salaries, Y for national income and using suffixes 0 and 1 for two different periods, the modified wage share for period 1 as compared with period 0 is

$$\frac{W_0}{Y_0} \cdot \frac{\dfrac{E_1}{L_1}}{\dfrac{E_0}{L_0}} \tag{1}$$

The formula shows how the wage share would have changed between periods 0 and 1 merely because of changed proportions in the labour force. If the actual wage share in period 1 corresponds to this value, then the per capita incomes of workers (short for dependent employees) have risen in proportion to the per capita incomes of the total labour force from all primary income sources.

This can be immediately seen when we set the per capita wage of a worker equal to w and write y for per capita income of the total labour force. This gives us $W = E \cdot w$ and $Y = L \cdot y$. Equality between the actual and the modified wage share in period 1 is assumed:

$$\frac{W_1}{Y_1} = \frac{W_0}{Y_0} \cdot \frac{\dfrac{E_1}{L_1}}{\dfrac{E_0}{L_0}} \tag{2}$$

This can be written as

$$\frac{E_1 w_1}{L_1 y_1} = \frac{E_0 w_0}{L_0 y_0} \cdot \frac{\dfrac{E_1}{L_1}}{\dfrac{E_0}{L_0}} \tag{3a}$$

or

$$\frac{w_1}{y_1} = \frac{w_0}{y_0} \quad \text{or} \quad \frac{w_1}{w_0} = \frac{y_1}{y_0} \tag{3b}$$

i.e. the equality of actual and modified shares implies proportional changes in the respective per capita incomes.

Modified wage shares are introduced in many studies to obtain a more telling measure for judging the development of wage shares. While 'progress' or 'retrogression' of the labour position (between two periods) depends on

$$\frac{W_1}{Y_1} \gtreqless \frac{W_0}{Y_0} \tag{4}$$

in the case of simple wage shares the condition becomes

$$\frac{W_1}{Y_1} \gtreqless \frac{W_0}{Y_0} \cdot \frac{\dfrac{E_1}{L_1}}{\dfrac{E_0}{L_0}} \tag{5}$$

when modified shares are introduced.[17]

The use of the modified share as a standard of comparison is certainly an advance. It prevents quick and superficial conclusions regarding income developments and the relative experiences of important socio-economic groups.[18] The use of this method is, therefore, rightly recommended and frequently enacted. But it is not always sufficiently stressed that equalities or differences between actual and modified wage shares can come about in different ways representing different social constellations. This problem, which should be taken into account in wage share comparisons, will now be illustrated with some simple examples.

The changes in the employment structure which enter the modified share can occur in different ways. Normally one thinks of shifts within the labour force with a secular trend from self-employment to employee status.[19] But shifts can also occur through differentiated rates of migration or differentiated birth rates affecting the various occupations and sections of the population. In the real world all these influences will be at work side by side. Here we shall deal with each one separately.

Let us start with the classical case of a 'pure' shift from self-employment to wage-earning status with the size of the total labour force remaining unchanged.[20] As we saw before, under the modified approach the wage share should be interpreted as unchanged when we have

$$\frac{W_1}{Y_1} = \frac{W_0}{Y_0} \cdot \frac{\dfrac{E_1}{L_1}}{\dfrac{E_0}{L_0}} \tag{2}$$

or

$$\frac{w_1}{w_0} = \frac{y_1}{y_0} \qquad\qquad (3b)$$

i.e. the average wage has increased in proportion with the per capita income of the total labour force. Since, however, the per capita incomes of workers (wage and salary earners) and of self-employed persons differ,[21] *proportional* growth of the average wage and of the average income of the *total* labour force (employees *and* self-employed) necessarily implies *different* growth rates for workers and for self-employed people. And normally it is the latter comparison which is of interest in a socio-economic context.

Since in most countries the average income of the self-employed is higher than the average wage, a shift from self-employment to wage-earning should lead to a decline in the average income for the total labour force. If it moves, on the contrary, *in step* with the wage development, as stipulated by a 'neutral' distributional change according to equation (2), the per capita income of the (reduced number of) self-employed persons *must* have increased relatively to the average wage of the (now more numerous) wage earners.[22]

This relative shift from wage to non-wage incomes under 'neutral' wage share conditions,[23] which can be socially significant, can arise in different ways. Two typical possibilities may serve as an illustration. In the first case we assume that chance, fate or institutions see to it that every self-employed person faces the same risk to be pushed into the group of wage earners. In this 'model' the outgoing self-employed earned an average self-employment income and suffered an income reduction after the change. A neutral wage share then implies rising per capita incomes for the remaining self-employed with wages remaining unchanged (or self-employment per capita incomes rising faster than wages). The formerly self-employed receive a 'normal' wage so that average wages do not change. The shift has, however, reduced the average labour force income (wages are lower than self-employed income). The per capita income of the self-employed must, therefore, rise if the wage share is to stay 'neutral' (equal rise of wage and average labour force income).

This case may have been typical in early capitalism when peasants and artisans were forced out of their livelihood and had to join the proletariat. Disqualification and impoverishment of the migrants and rising incomes among the property-owning population can in this case form the background for a 'neutral' wage share.

In the second example we assume that the displacement in the self-employment sector is not the work of chance but that a marginal group of less successful persons with below-average incomes is the source for migration. Let us assume that the persons leaving had an income which was not higher than the average wage income. When they enter the employee sector their personal income does not change. Also the average wage and the average labour force income remain unchanged. Consequently the wage share stays 'neutral'. The average income of the self-employed rises also in this case, [24] not through an effective rise in the income of the remaining self-employed but through the arithmetic effect on the average which follows from the elimination of the low-paid members.

These two examples, to which others could be added, should suffice to illustrate the argument of this section. Even in the classical case of a simple shift of some people from self-employment to employee status the modified wage share can tell more than one story. 'Neutral' developments within the frame of this method can cover different changes of average wage and non-wage incomes [25] and these changes can be accompanied by unchanged or changing per capita incomes in the two groups.

Additional combinations and interpretations arise when we go beyond merely 'static' shifts within a given population. As a not unrealistic example we look at the case of immigration under the assumption that − at least to begin with − all immigrants work as dependent employees. As before we shall only consider the case of a continually 'neutral' wage share, i.e. we assume that after the immigration the actual wage share corresponds to the modified wage share.

As in the previous example of a simple shift the expansion of the working population, in combination with a proportional development of wages and per capita labour force income, implies an increase of self-employed income (per capita) relative to wages. The immigrants earn only wages, which reduces the average income for the total labour force so that parallelism between the two magnitudes demands (arithmetically) the relative increase of non-wage incomes. But the 'arithmetic' of the necessary change differs from the static case. [26]

The important point is that in this case, too, a 'neutral' wage share development can be caused by different socio-economic sequences. As before this can be illustrated by simplified 'typical' cases. Three examples will be given.

In the first 'model' we assume that the immigrants get the same average wage as the inhabitants. The numbers of workers grow at an unchanged average wage. The wage share stays 'neutral' when at the same time there is an actual increase in the income of the self-employed persons whose number remains unchanged. Such a development could be typical in times of labour scarcity when the immigration of foreign workers permits a better utilization of capacities leading to higher profits. The distance between the per capita incomes of employers and workers widens.

The situation is different when immigrant workers are mainly hired for less pleasant and ill-paid activities. With their entry the average wage declines. The conditions for a 'neutral' wage share can in this case be met without any actual increase in per capita earnings of the self-employed. The necessary *relative* increase is achieved through the fall of the average wage. The per capita incomes *of the country's citizens* remain unchanged. [27] A social, sociological and economic problem is created in the form of foreign workers who are concentrated in jobs of a 'lower' quality.

In the third example we start off as in the first example with equal opportunities for the immigrant workers. But the increase in numbers now depresses wages in general.[28] This absolute and relative (to the unchanged self-employment income) reduction of wages can again secure a 'neutral' share development. In this case, which lies behind trade union opposition against the admission of foreign labour, the economic position of the workers deteriorates as compared with the self-employed sector even though the modified analysis shows an unchanged wage share.

These examples represent a few 'stylized' developments. In reality we must reckon with combinations between and within these 'scenarios'.[29] Modified, 'structure-free' wage share analysis is an important aid for a better interpretation of distributional issues. It can eliminate errors and misunderstandings connected with an uncritical use of actual wage share data. But modified wage shares are still not able to disclose fully the various social and economic facts which lie behind them and influence their course. To obtain a fuller understanding one has to go beyond a pure share analysis and has to consult data and information which lie outside the national income framework.

APPENDIX 1

(a) Using our previous notation we can construct a relative (modified) wage share index which takes account of the labour force structure. At time t the index is

$$\frac{\dfrac{W_t}{E_t}}{\dfrac{Y_t}{L_t}} \tag{1}$$

Comparing years 0 and 1 the wage share has 'improved', 'remained equal' or 'deteriorated' depending on

$$\frac{\dfrac{W_1}{E_1}}{\dfrac{Y_1}{L_1}} \gtreqless \frac{\dfrac{W_0}{E_0}}{\dfrac{Y_0}{L_0}} \tag{2}$$

This can be reformulated as

$$\frac{\dfrac{W_1}{Y_1}}{\dfrac{E_1}{L_1}} \gtreqless \frac{\dfrac{W_0}{Y_0}}{\dfrac{E_0}{L_0}} \tag{3a}$$

or

$$\frac{W_1}{Y_1} \gtreqless \frac{W_0}{Y_0} \cdot \frac{\dfrac{E_1}{L_1}}{\dfrac{E_0}{L_0}} \tag{3b}$$

Formula (3b) shows the equivalence of this derivation with the relevant passages in the main text (Formula 2 on p. 225).

(b) We now add two further variables: S for the number of self-employed and n (non-wage income) for their average per capita income.

The total labour force consists of employees and self-employed persons:

$$L = E + S \tag{4}$$

Total income is the sum of the group incomes:

$$Ly = Ew + Sn \tag{5}$$

In the cases treated in the text a constant modified wage share was adopted as standard, implying a parallel movement of wages and average labour force income, i.e. a constant value of w_t / y_t for all t. At any moment of time we have therefore

$$y = kw \tag{6}$$

where k is a constant and greater than 1, since according to our (realistic) assumption $n > w$ and y is the weighted average of w and n.

Using (6) the income equation (5) becomes

$$Lkw = Ew + Sn \tag{7}$$

From this one obtains

$$n = w \cdot \frac{Lk - E}{S} \tag{8a}$$

or

$$\frac{n}{w} = \frac{Lk - E}{S} \tag{8b}$$

Let us now assume that between periods 0 and 1 the size of the labour force remains unchanged, but that r self-employed persons become wage-earners. Taking the case of a proportional rise in the per capita incomes of employees (w) and of the total labour force (y), i.e. k constant, the relation of average employee incomes to per capita self-employed incomes in the two periods is:

$$\frac{n_0}{w_0} = \frac{Lk - E_0}{S_0} \tag{9}$$

$$\frac{n_1}{w_1} = \frac{Lk - (E_0 + r)}{S_0 - r} = \frac{Lk - E_0 - r}{S_0 - r} \tag{10}$$

Since $S_0 = L - E_0$ and $k > 1$, we have $Lk - E_0 > S_0$ so that $n_1/w_1 > n_0/w_0$.

The proportional development of employee and *labour force earnings* (per capita) imply in this case a growing margin between wages and other incomes.

(c) We now look at the changed condition that 'neutral' development should mean a proportional development of the per capita incomes of employees and *self-employed* persons. We start with our previous income equation (5):

$$Ly = Ew + Sn$$

and introduce now the condition that the relation w_t/n_t should remain constant:

$$n = qw \tag{11}$$

with $q > 1$ and constant.

Substituting (11) in (5) we obtain

$$Ly = Ew + Sqw \tag{12a}$$

$$y = w \cdot \frac{E + Sq}{L} \tag{12b}$$

and

$$\frac{w}{y} = \frac{L}{E + Sq} \tag{12c}$$

We now assume again an unchanged labour force between periods 0 and 1 and a shift of r persons from self-employment to employee status, stipulating that the relation between the per capita group incomes should remain unchanged (q constant). This gives us:

$$\frac{w_0}{y_0} = \frac{L}{E_0 + qS_0} \tag{13}$$

$$\frac{w_1}{y_1} = \frac{L}{E_0 + r + q(S_0 - r)} = \frac{L}{E_0 + qS_0 + r(1 - q)} \tag{14}$$

and

$$\frac{w_1}{y_1} > \frac{w_0}{y_0} \tag{15}$$

since $(1 - q) < 0$. Proportional development of per capita incomes of the two groups requires (in the described circumstances) an increase in the traditional 'modified' wage share.

(d) Returning to a 'neutral' wage share development in the traditional sense we now look at the case of immigration, assuming that all the r immigrants become dependent employees. Equation (8b) gives as the relation of wage to self-employment income and 'neutrality' conditions (k = constant):

$$\frac{n}{w} = \frac{Lk - E}{S}, k > 1$$

This gives us for the time before and after immigration:

$$\frac{n_0}{w_0} = \frac{L_0 k - E_0}{S_0} \tag{16}$$

$$\frac{n_1}{w_1} = \frac{(L_0 + r)k - (E_0 + r)}{S_0} = \frac{(L_0 k - E_0) + r(k - 1)}{S_0} = \frac{n_0}{w_0} + \frac{r}{S_0}(k - 1) \tag{17}$$

Thus

$$\frac{n_1}{w_1} > \frac{n_0}{w_0} \tag{18}$$

since $k > 1$. This result can be compared with the similar case under (b).

(e) Figure 16.1 illustrates for case (d) (Immigration of workers with subsequent relative wage depression) the different results one can obtain maintaining the condition of an unchanged (modified) wage share.

The line e_0 is the locus of all combinations between the average wage (w) and the per capita income of the self-employed (n) which correspond to a given ratio in period 0 (before immigration). The equation of this line (for k = constant) has been derived in equation 8a under (b):

$$n = \frac{L_0 k - E_0}{S_0} \cdot w$$

Let us assume that before the immigration the average wage is w_0, the average self-employed income n_0. After r persons have immigrated the condition of an *unchanged* modified wage share is given by line e_1 whose equation is (see section d)

$$n = \frac{(L_0 + r)k - (E_0 + r)}{S_0} \cdot w \tag{17}$$

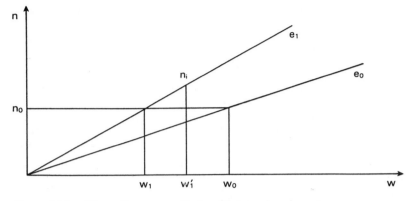

Figure 16.1 Alternative wage effects of labour immigrants

In the text we have assumed the case where the increased labour supply depresses wages while the income of the self-employed remains unchanged. This 'solution' is illustrated by the $w_1 - n_0$ combination in the diagram. But other outcomes are also compatible with the same 'neutral' wage share as, for instance, the combination $w_1' - n_1'$, with wages falling less, but with the incomes of the other group rising (e.g. because of a better capacity utilization).

APPENDIX 2

The national income account (OECD standard)

1 Compensation of employees.
  a) Wages and salaries.
  b) Pay and allowances of armed forces.
  c) Employers' contributions to social security.
2 Income of independent traders.
3 Interest, rent and dividends to households, etc.
  a) Interest
  b) Net rent
  c) Dividends
4 Corporate grants to households.
5 Saving of corporations.
6 Direct taxes on corporations.
7 Government income from property and entrepreneurship.

NOTES

1 'Wages' will be used throughout as meaning 'wages and salaries'.
2 Difficulties arise because the disaggregated national income accounts show only the rent incomes of households separately but not the rent elements in corporate

profits. There is also an element of arbitrariness in the calculation of imputed rents of house owners.

3 A further difficulty is connected with the combined presentation of market and public activities. When questions concerning the theory of production are under discussion it would often be preferable to obtain wages and salaries excluding those earned in public administration and public services. To overcome this difficulty one tries occasionally – with the aid of additional information – to find income data restricted to the private or the manufacturing sector. This practice, however, frequently neglects the fact that the size and the activities of the public sector influence the results in the rest of the economy. This is a subject which deserves further research. It could be an important corrective factor in intertemporal and international comparisons. In this paper, however, we shall deal exclusively with total income, without distinguishing between private and public activities.

4 See Appendix 2 and Bombach, G. (1961) 'Volkswirtschafftiche Gesamtrechnung', *Hamburger Jahrbuch für Wirtschafts- und Gesellschaftspolitik*, 6, pp. 45–67.

5 All four methods are used – for US data – by Kravis, I. (1962) *The Structure of Income*, Philadelphia: University of Pennsylvania Press.

6 A further complication arises in connection with the treatment of incomes of helping family members.

7 United Nations, Economic Commission for Europe (1967) *Incomes in Postwar Europe: A Study of Policies, Growth and Distribution*, Geneva: United Nations.

8 Kuznets, S. (1959) 'Quantitative aspects of the economic growth of nations: IV. Distribution of national income by factor shares', *Economic Development and Cultural Change* 7, 3, Part II.

9 In developing countries and in the case of older people there may also be a lack of opportunities for a switch to wage-earning activities.

10 These are the reasons given for adopting this method in Gunthardt, W. (1965) *Das Problem der Konstanz der Einkommensverteilung*, Winterthur: Keller.

11 For some European countries estimates of this sort were attempted in addition to estimates following methods (a) and (c) in a (so far) unpublished OECD study on income distribution in Western Europe since 1950.

12 In the *International Encyclopedia of the Social Sciences* (1968, New York: Macmillan and Free Press), vol. 7, pp. 132–43.

13 See, for instance, Stobbe, A. (1966) *Volkswirtschaftliches Rechnungswesen*, Berlin: Springer. He writes 'The wage share's development can command interest because the trade unions sometimes declare an increase of the wage share as one of their targets' (p. 178).

14 If we, however, distinguish between labour and capital income in line with our previous considerations the development is less uniform. The labour share has risen in some countries and fallen in others. This is shown in the previously mentioned studies of the ECE and the OECD.

15 The share of managerial income in national income has been estimated to be 2.8 per cent in the US at the beginning of the 1950s and around 1 per cent in France. See Kravis, *op.cit.*, p. 124 and Tavitian, R. (1959) *La part des salaires dans le revenue nationale*, Paris: Genin, p. 212. The pay of the armed forces amounted to an average of 2.5 per cent of total wages and salaries in seven Western European countries at the beginning of the 1960s (OECD, *National Accounts Statistics*).

16 See the previously quoted ECE and OECD studies. Also Kausel, A. and Seidel, H. (1964) 'Zur Verteilung des Volkseinkommens', *Monatsberichte des Österreichischen Instituts fur Wirtschaftsforschung*, 37, 1, pp. 17–22.

17 An equivalent method in a slightly different form is used in the ECE study, *op. cit.*, Ch. 2, pp. 29–31. It calculates an index of relative wage income (average wage relative to average total income) whose movements yield directly the information about movements of the wage share *after elimination of structural shifts*. See also Appendix 1, (a).

18 Thus the previously quoted ECE and OECD studies show that the general rise of the wage share in post-war Europe is mainly a consequence of the change in occupational structure with small deviations up or down.

19 Rising wage shares 'have their main explanation in the fact that the number of self-employed persons declines at the same rate as industry and tertiary activities gain importance at the cost of agriculture' (Kausel and Seidel, *op.cit.*, p. 17).

20 The following considerations can be easily extended to the case of a rising population.

21 Our simplifying (but not necessarily unrealistic) assumption is that the income of wage earners consists almost exclusively of wages and that all other incomes go to a section of the population which we call 'self-employed persons'. Pure rentiers are included in this group and also the non-distributed profits of corporations. Government income from property and entrepreneurship should be excluded.

22 This relationship can be easily derived. See Appendix 1, (b).

23 For reasons of simplicity all statements will be restricted to the case of a 'neutral' development of the share, i.e. a change where the actual wage share coincides with the change in the modified wage share. All the considerations can be applied *mutatis mutandis* to 'improvements' and 'deteriorations' of the wage share.

24 This follows necessarily from the wage share arithmetic. See p. 225 above and Appendix 1, (b).

25 Instead of taking the relation between the average wage and the per capita labour force income as a standard for wage share interpretations, one could choose the relation between average wages and the average income of the self-employed persons. Using this standard a 'neutral' development of the wage share (after a shift from self-employment to wage earning) would demand a relatively faster rise in wages than in per capita labour force income. See Appendix 1, (c).

26 See Appendix 1, (d).

27 The native workers now earn an above-average wage.

28 To make matters simple only the case of a static economy is discussed. In a growing economy we can have in place of a declining wage a relatively slower growth of wages (relative to self-employed incomes).

29 See Appendix 1, (e).

17 Some recent contributions to a macroeconomic theory of income distribution [1]

(Reprinted from *Scottish Journal of Political Economy*, Vol. VIII, pp. 173–99.)

I

In the days before Keynes, distribution theory had its recognized place side by side with price theory. The marginal productivity theory provided an explanation of (unit) factor incomes and also, so it was believed, of factor demand and factor employment. This should also have provided the basis for total factor incomes – nothing but unit incomes times units employed – and factor shares.

The Keynesian employment theory shattered the belief that total employment could be deduced from an addition of all sectional marginal productivity schedules. In *aggregate* analysis these schedules are no longer independent of the prices paid to factors and can, therefore, not be treated as independent variables. Aggregate effective demand was introduced as the main determinant for the volume of employment. By concentrating on *aggregate* demand the question of income *distribution* had faded into the background. To be sure, distribution problems loomed large in the economic policy debates that were stimulated by Keynes and his school. The influence of distribution on consumption and total demand was duly noted. But what really causes the main income shares to be what they are was a question which Keynes did not attack. On the whole he seems to have accepted the traditional marginal productivity approach without realizing that with his new theory about the determinants of employment he had undermined the foundations of the old microeconomic distribution theory. For aggregate demand determines factor employment and incomes and the distribution of these incomes in turn influences the level and structure of aggregate demand.

The Keynesian theory thus provided a challenge for a reconsideration of the distribution problem. In this respect the situation was not unlike the one in the field of economic growth. Here, too, Keynes with his stress on the need for net investment had laid the foundation for a problem which he himself did not follow up but which awaited treatment.

It took less than three years after the publication of the *General Theory* for important contributions to appear in both these fields: Kalecki's article on the share of wages in the national income[2] and Harrod's essay in dynamic theory.[3] Both these contributions suffered from the date of their appearance; the ensuing war left little time for basic discussions on economic theory. A flicker of interest was shown here and there, but it was not until after the war that these post-Keynesian developments could expand more organically.

Growth theory quickly took centre-stage. In distribution theory the search for a new approach has been less forceful and less systematic. But here, too, the literature has grown in recent years. Its place in the body of 'recognized' theory is, however, far less established than that of growth theory. At the American Economic Association meeting of 1952, where Boulding made a heroic attempt to 'sell' his new macroeconomic distribution theory, Fellner had the participants in the discussion pretty much on his side when he said:

> By contemporary distribution theory we presumably mean a qualified marginal productivity theory; that is to say, a combination of the marginal productivity theory with other analytical elements.[4]

Since then quite a number of new macroeconomic distribution models have been put forward. Although – as we shall see later – they all still suffer from serious shortcomings, they can no longer be overlooked, and they tend to become part of contemporary distribution theory. In the following pages the characteristics of some of these models will be exhibited. There is no attempt at completeness and the choice of theories is rather random. It is hoped that the chosen models will give a fair indication in what directions the winds are blowing at present. Also, in order to keep the length of the paper within reasonable limits it was necessary to strip the theories that were included to their bare essentials in order to make the basic argument visible. This is rather unfair on the authors who often have significant things to say when it comes to modifying and elaborating their basic results. But in a broad survey this is unavoidable and the concentration on essentials may help to bring out more clearly the points of contact and the differences between the various theories.

II

Let us start with Kalecki's theory, it being chronologically the first in the field among the contributions dealt with in this paper. Kalecki's theory of the share of wages in the national income was actually a by-product of his special approach to the theory of the firm. Basing his approach on empirical observations of the cost function and the pricing process in manufacturing in the 1930s, Kalecki abandoned the traditional U-shaped average cost curve of the firm. Instead he assumed that normally firms operate at a level below full capacity, and that at this level average and marginal prime costs per unit of output are more or less constant. Additional units of output can be produced with the existing plant by applying additional workers and raw materials more or less in the same proportions as before.

With conditions like this the marginal productivity of production workers within a firm becomes constant. Instead of a falling marginal productivity curve representing the demand for labour and determining the level of employment (by being equated to the wage level) we obtain a horizontal marginal productivity curve. The number of workers employed will depend on the level of output and this in turn will depend – since we deal with a world of imperfect competition – on the firm's pricing policy. Since the number of workers and therefore the wage bill for the production workers (roughly the manual labour force) is taken as approximately proportional to output, the *share* of wages in a firm's output will be given by the share of wage costs in the value of (each unit of) the product.

This, then, is the industrial setting for Kalecki's distribution theory.

Let us now see which elements he isolates for special consideration in order to explain the main determinants of distribution. Before doing this let me just say a few words about two different stages in model building between which we should draw a clear line of distinction. In many theories – and this is true for most of the macroeconomic income distribution models I shall discuss – one first splits up some economic aggregate into certain parts. This splitting up is usually based on the definitions used and does not give us any new knowledge of the outside world. It just yields certain identities, as, for instance, Keynes's subdivision of income into consumption and investment: $Y \equiv C + I$. Here C and I are so defined that they are necessarily equal to Y. Such identities, since they do not tell us anything about real events, cannot be judged by the terms 'true' or 'false'. Rather we can regard them as 'useful' or 'not useful'. They are useful if we can find some valid rules for the sub-parts so created. If we can, for instance, find certain 'laws' for consumption and investment behaviour, then the splitting up of income into these two components (rather than into some other of a host of possible subdivisions) will have been 'useful' and will have opened the way towards an empirically valid theory.

These remarks do not contain anything that has not been known in the field of methodology. If I repeat it here it is only because the distinction between these two stages in model building seems to me to be particularly important in connection with the theories we are discussing at present. The attempts in this field are still at a very early stage and most of the writers are still experimenting with different ways of grouping and regrouping a few economic aggregates. The laying down of a few fundamental identities is, therefore, still the main content of these theories while the empirical part is usually only sketched in outline and rather underdeveloped. This has sometimes led to an accusation that these theories are purely tautological.[5] This attack is, however, in most cases unjustified. It is usually a consequence of failing to recognize the positive part played by identities in the formulation of a theory, or of overlooking the empirical elements which most of these theories contain. In order to reduce the occurrence of this kind of misunderstanding I shall occasionally try to draw a rather sharp line between the formal apparatus and the empirical 'laws' in some of the theories, even though the authors did not always regard it necessary to keep the two kinds of argument separate.

After this interlude let us return to Kalecki's model.[6] Let us call the wages spent by a firm on production workers W, and the amount spent on raw materials M. The prime costs of the firm are, therefore, $(W + M)$. The price-setting process is assumed to take the form of adding a margin to unit (prime) costs. Prime costs per unit are multiplied by a factor, say k ($k > 1$), to give the price of the commodity. Since we have assumed that prime costs are constant, the multiplication of total prime costs by k will give us the gross value of the firm's output: $k(W + M)$. The margin over $(W + M)$ so created is called 'gross profits' out of which the salaries of non-production workers, interest, depreciation and net profits have to be covered. Gross profits will be higher, the higher the value of k, and k in its turn will be higher, the higher the 'degree of monopoly'. The 'degree of monopoly' is a catch-all phrase for a number of influences making for a higher k (a higher margin), but this special terminological choice has some justification in previous monopoly literature.[7]

With a gross value production equal to $k(W + M)$, and W paid out to the workers and M to the raw material producers, gross profits (as defined above) are equal to $(k - 1)(W + M)$. If we leave out of account the expenditure for raw materials, which goes to previous stages of production, we obtain the gross value added (wages plus gross profits) for the firm: $W + (k - 1) \cdot (W + M)$. We can now write down the share of wages (for production workers) in the gross value added. Let us call this share w. We have

$$w = \frac{W}{W + (k - 1) \cdot (W + M)}$$

Dividing numerator and denominator by W, and writing j for M/W we obtain

$$w = \frac{1}{1 + (k - 1)(j + 1)}$$

From this it can be seen that the share of gross income going to (manual) wage-earners will depend on the 'degree of monopoly' (k) and the relative changes in raw material prices to wage expenditure (j). The higher the degree of monopoly or the worse the 'terms of trade' between raw materials and wage-earning labour the lower the share of wages and vice versa. When one adapts this model for the economy as a whole (excluding the public sector) a further factor is added, which plays a role in determining the wage share: the industrial structure. According to the size of different industries, their k's and j's will have different weights and this will influence the global picture.

So far we have not moved beyond the elements which were already contained in our initial position. Granted Kalecki's model of the firm, the determinants of the wage share as given above follow directly from the definitions of gross profits and the degree of monopoly. This can be seen immediately with the help of a simple diagram. In Figure 17.1 the price of a product is split up into the parts discussed before. W and M are defined as before and GP stands for gross profits. It can be seen without difficulty that with this subdivision the share of wages in the gross value of the product ($W + GP$) will depend on GP (degree of monopoly) and the relation between M and W within the prime cost sector. Since these cost relationships are assumed to hold independently of the level of output the same relationship holds for the total production of the firm.

To this formal, 'tautological' framework Kalecki adds fragments of an 'explanatory' theory. With regard to long-run tendencies it is maintained that the degree of monopoly will tend to rise owing to the growth of concentration, and the increase in fixed costs, selling and distribution costs. This tendency will, however, be slowed down or checked by the increase in trade union power. Nothing is contained in Kalecki's theory on long-run trends in raw material prices (relative to wages) and in industrial structure. This is

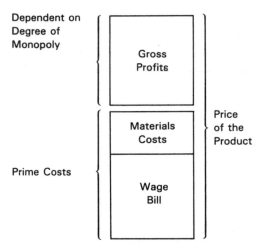

Figure 17.1   Costs and price in the Kalecki model

somewhat surprising, since at least with regard to the development of industrial structure several hypotheses have been suggested by empirical data which could have been tentatively incorporated into Kalecki's theory of the wage share. As the theory stands it is what we might call an 'open' theory, trying to explain some of the components but leaving others unexplained so that no rounded picture of past events or prospective future developments can be obtained.

Kalecki is a bit more explicit when he turns to the cyclical picture. The apparent stability of the wage share during the cycle he regards as the outcome of opposite movements in the degree of monopoly and raw material prices. In the depression the degree of monopoly (i.e. the gross margin over prime costs) is raised in the attempt of firms to recover as much as possible of their fixed costs over the smaller volume of output. A higher degree of cartelisation may be attempted to achieve this end. On the other hand raw material prices tend to fall more rapidly than wages in the depression, thus counterbalancing the depressive effect which the rising degree of monopoly exercises on the wage share. There is also a hint in Kalecki's treatise that structural changes during the cycle will tend to lower the wage share during the depression.[8] But this passage is not very convincing.

Kalecki's theory has not created a 'school', but the interpretation of the empirical material in some other works has been stimulated by it. Thus Dunlop[9] investigating the stability of the wage share in the American cycle of the 1930s, refers his results to Kalecki's framework and points out that structural changes between industries played a major part in maintaining stability, covering up considerable changes in the wage share within some industries.

Phelps Brown and Hart,[10] who start with an empirical investigation of the same type of income distribution as Kalecki's (wages without salaries as share of total income), add some theoretical remarks to their results which seem to me to be akin to the Kaleckian framework (though the authors would probably not share this opinion).

They distinguish between two major long-run developments influencing the share of wages in national income. First, there has been a movement from the 'stable' income groups (rent, contractual interest, salaries) to wages and profit. Second, there are occasional shifts in the wage–profit relationship itself. Usually this relationship is stable because price policy is governed by prevailing ideas about 'normal' profits. But at certain times changes in the 'normal' relationship occur. Whether such changes take place and in which direction they go will depend on the state of the market environment and of trade union activity. The market environment can be 'hard', when it is difficult or impossible to pass on cost increases, or it can be 'soft', when cost increases can be passed on fairly easily. An active trade union policy combined with a hard market environment will produce a certain squeeze on profits and increase the share of income going to wages. Conversely, weak trade unions and a soft market environment will lead to a lower wage share, while the remaining combinations (strong unions and soft environment or weak unions and hard environment) will have little effect on relative shares.

It will be seen that this is more in the nature of a classification which helps to explain the course of past events rather than a guide for forecasting the future. For nothing is said about the economic or sociological ' laws' which make for militant or timid trade union action, for hard or soft market environments.[11] If one tried to tighten these elements up into a more formal model the relationship to Kalecki's model would become apparent. The first factor – changes in rent and interest payments – is of direct significance for the degree of monopoly. Trade union action appears explicitly in both models. And Phelps Brown's and Hart's catch-all category, the rather vaguely defined 'market environment', refers in addition to one of Kalecki's strategic variables (raw material prices) to a number of economic phenomena which are equally important in the shaping of Kalecki's 'degree of monopoly' (technical changes, cartel agreements, monetary policy etc.).

III

Kalecki aimed at a macroeconomic theory of distribution. But like the marginal productivity school he starts at the microeconomic level: the single firm. The categories he uses do not, however, land him in the sort of adding-up problems which make the extension of marginal productivity reasoning to the entire economy such a doubtful procedure. Raw material prices and pricing policy do not become so irritatingly shiftable as marginal productivity schedules when we drop the 'ceteris paribus' clause of sector analysis.

Kalecki's departure from the neoclassical distribution theory was then not so much the result of a deliberate search for a macroeconomic distribution theory, but rather a macroeconomic theory developing out of his changed assumptions about the theory of the firm. In this respect it differs from the distribution theories to be discussed in the following pages, which all aimed *directly* at a macroeconomic theory. What Kalecki has in common with these theories (apart from the macroeconomic end-stage) is the disappearance of marginal productivity as a basic and explicit explanatory variable. Kaldor's puzzled remark in connection with his 'Keynesian' distribution theory (to be discussed presently): 'I am not sure where "marginal productivity" comes in in all this'[12] could just as well have been uttered by Kalecki.

IV

I turn now to some of the immediately macroeconomic distribution models, which owe their inspiration direct to the aggregates and the mode of macroeconomic thinking introduced and revived by Keynes. With Kaldor we might therefore call them Keynesian distribution models.

As far as I am aware the first attempts in this direction originated some ten years ago with Boulding and Hahn.[13] Both these theories remained – in spite of their new approach – without much echo. This was mainly due, I believe, because they were presented in a context which made them *unnecessarily* clumsy and complicated looking. Both these authors did not just present a new distribution model, but did so in connection with some major reform they wanted to see in the basic assumptions of economic theory. Boulding felt that the role of assets requires far greater stress, while Hahn wanted to switch from a profit-maximizing entrepreneur to one who maximizes an index of utility. These 'innovations' were not essential to the distribution theories of the two authors. But these were cast in the terminology necessitated by the new approach. And since the need for such a new approach did not become convincing in either case, the distribution theories suffered from the unhappy circumstances under which they were born.

A few years later other writers, like Joan Robinson, Kaldor and Schneider, dealt with the distribution problem in the more familiar setting of Keynesian and economic growth theory. Their models were simpler in form and easier to assimilate on the basis of 'accepted' doctrine. On closer inspection they show, however, a definite family resemblance to the earlier pioneer work.

I do not intend here to follow the chronological order. Rather I am going to start with a simple exposition of the (already simple) Kaldor[14] model in order to show the essentials of the 'Keynesian' approach, and will then refer to some other models – irrespective of the time of publication – in order to indicate the variety of assumptions and conclusions that are at present connected with this approach. In order to facilitate the argument I shall use, as far as possible, the same symbols in all the models I am going to discuss. The connoisseur of economic literature will not be surprised to hear that in the original articles the choice of symbols is indeed wide.

V

A common characteristic of the current 'Keynesian' distribution theories (and Kalecki's) is that they restrict themselves to a split-up of total income into two categories. This restriction is not an essential attribute of these theories, but it greatly simplifies the construction of the basic model. The subdivision is not the same in all cases. Kalecki, as we saw, distinguishes between wages of manual labour and gross profits, which embrace all other incomes (including salaries). Kaldor starts with the familiar division between wages (including salaries) and profits. The two together make up total income so that we obtain the obvious identity

$$Y \equiv W + P \tag{1}$$

where Y represents income, W wages and P profits. We further have the familiar Keynesian identity between ex-post savings (S) and investment (I):

$$I \equiv S \tag{2}$$

In contrast to Keynes's concentration on the savings and saving propensities of the total community, we distinguish now between savings of wage-earners (S_w) and profit earners (S_p). This yields us still another identity:

$$S \equiv S_w + S_p \tag{3}$$

The savings of the two population groups will depend on their respective incomes and saving propensities. If we denote the (average and marginal) saving propensity of the workers by s_w and the propensity of the capitalists by s_p we obtain:

$$S_w = s_w W \qquad S_p = s_p P \tag{4}$$

These basic relationships are the building bricks of Kaldor's distribution model.

Substituting (3) and (4) in (2) and removing W with the aid of (1) we obtain:

$$I = S = s_p P + s_w W = s_p P + s_w (Y - P) = (s_p - s_w)P + s_w Y \tag{5}$$

Next we divide (5) by Y:

$$\frac{I}{Y} = (s_p - s_w)\frac{P}{Y} + s_w \tag{6}$$

or

$$\frac{P}{Y} = \frac{1}{s_p - s_w} \cdot \frac{I}{Y} - \frac{s_w}{s_p - s_w} \tag{7}$$

i.e. the share of profits (and similarly of wages) in total income depends on the sectoral savings propensities and on the volume of investment (*total income being given*).

This much is obtained from the definitions and the way the aggregates were split up. What, then, are Kaldor's ideas about the behaviour of these elements? From equation (7) it will be obvious that the whole system depends on the condition that $s_p \neq s_w$. This condition is implicit in Kaldor's theory since he assumes that the adaptation of savings to a given volume of investment is achieved *at a given total income level* by income shifts from low savers to high savers and vice versa. [15] This is in contrast to the Keynesian adjustment process which takes place (on the basis of a single savings propensity) via expansions and contractions of total income. The assumption that $s_p \neq s_w$ is not difficult to swallow. In fact, by assuming that

$s_p > s_w$ one refers to the empirically acceptable proposition that profit-earners save a higher proportion of income than wage earners. Kaldor, however, does not only stipulate that the saving propensities of wage and profit earners differ; he also assumes – and this is far less self-evident – that these propensities are fairly stable in the long run.[16]

If we can take the saving propensities as data given from 'outside' the system, then – as can be seen from equation (7) – the income distribution is solely dependent on investment as a proportion of income. In his first essay Kaldor still considered the possibility that the profit–wage relationship may influence the capital–output ratio.[17] I/Y would then not be independent of P/Y, and there would be no unique one-way causal relationship between investment (I/Y) and income distribution (P/Y). But Kaldor dismissed this problem by *assuming* a constant capital–output ratio (independent of the profit–wage relationship). In his later article on economic growth this assumption is made an integral part of his theory with the help of a technical progress function which independently determines a stable long-run capital–output ratio. Granted Kaldor's 'behaviour' assumptions – full employment in the long run, 'psychological' determination of the saving propensities, 'technological' determination of the capital–output ratio[18] – we obtain a complete theory of income shares. How far these assumptions *should* be granted is another matter.[19]

To this basic model Kaldor adds two minimum constraints. Real wages cannot fall below the 'subsistence minimum', the profit rate must not fall below the 'risk premium rate'. I must confess that I find a bare statement of this sort rather unsatisfactory. If the (rather vague) terms 'subsistence minimum' and 'risk premium rate' are defined near their absolute feasible minimum, the statement about the constraints is probably beyond reproach but it also becomes rather uninteresting. For these limits will normally not come into play in a developed capitalist economy. If, on the other hand, subsistence and risk premium are so defined as to include historically acquired standards, then they may very well play an active role in the distribution process. But if this is so it is not sufficient for a realistic distribution theory to state that they act as constraints. It is necessary to show how these constraining standards are formed in the struggle for wages and profits.

VI

Now that we are familiar with the basic structure of a 'Keynesian' distribution model we can deal rather briefly with some other specimens of this category. Let us first return to the previously mentioned pioneer effort by Boulding.

Boulding divides total income into wages and non-wages, the latter comprising profits, rent, interest. For simplicity's sake we shall use again P to denote non-wages. Thus we have, as before,

$$Y \equiv W + P \tag{7}$$

But Y must be either consumed or invested, so we have also

$$Y \equiv C + I \tag{8}$$

Now, both consumption and investment will depend on income. Not just on total income (Y) as in the pure Keynesian model, but also on the distribution of the total. Thus we get the level of consumption and investment as functions of the level of wages and non-wages:

$$C = F_c(W, P) \tag{9}$$

$$I = F_i(W, P) \tag{10}$$

In the search for a 'prime mover' for this basic set-up Boulding presents a further division of non-wages into business *distributions* (dividends and interest) and business *savings* (internally financed investment,[20] increased money holdings, loans to consumers). Introducing these elements into our system we obtain two further relationships (writing D for business distributions, dM_b for the additions to business' money holdings and dK_b for increased credit to consumers, and I_n and I_e for internally and externally financed investment):

$$P = I_n + D + dM_b + dK_b \tag{11}$$

$$W = Y - P = C + I - I_n - (D + dM_b + dK_b) \tag{12}$$

or (since $I - I_n = I_e$)

$$W = C + I_e - (D + dM_b + dK_b) \tag{12a}$$

Here we are still in the realm of identities as can be easily seen when we simplify equations (11) and (12a) by setting dM_b and dK_b equal to zero (i.e. assuming there is no increase in the money stock and consumer credits of business firms). We obtain then

$$P = I_n + D \tag{13}$$
$$W = I_e + (C - D) \tag{14}$$

Equation (13) says that non-wages are equal to capitalists' savings and consumption, and equation (14) that wages are equal to workers' savings and consumption.[21]

The specific contribution of Boulding is that he regards the (exogenously given) business behaviour with regard to self-finance, dividend payments, liquidity, and consumer credit as strategically decisive. The higher, for instance, the payment of dividends and interest[22] (i.e. the lower the propensity to save out of non-wage incomes), the higher will be the level of profits, *the volume of investment being given*.

This follows from the same logic which we encountered in Kaldor's model. Since the adjustment of savings to (a given amount) of investment does not take place via changes in the volume of employment (the Keynesian case), it has to be achieved by shifts from low-saving wage earners to more-saving profit-earners. If business saves *comparatively little* (though still more than workers) the shift to profits will have to be *greater* in order to reach a given level of savings. This is the basic cause for the 'widow's cruse' character of these theories.[23] In fact the *formal* similarity between Boulding's and Kaldor's models is quite easily shown. Taking Boulding's formulas in the simplified form to which we have reduced them[24] we have

$$Y = W + P$$
$$P = I_n + D$$
$$W = I_e + (C - D)$$

Now, I_n and I_e will depend on the savings propensities of the two income sectors:

$$I_n = s_p P; \qquad I_e = s_w W \qquad (s_p > s_w)$$

For a *given* level of investment we have

$$S = I = I_n + I_e = s_p P + s_w W = s_p P + s_w (Y - P) = (s_p - s_w)P + s_w Y$$

which is the same as equation (5) from which we derived Kaldor's profit share equation.

But what about the *material* side of Boulding's explanation? As we said before, he puts all the emphasis on business decisions with regard to the division of receipts between dividends, self-finance, liquid holdings, etc. Even if we accept for the moment that these decisions possess central significance, a 'full' theory would have to tell us by what behaviour rules they are shaped. Here, however, Boulding lets us down. When he deals with long-term growth, this is what he has to offer:

> What emerges ... from the analysis is a concept of long-run dynamics which is much less deterministic than that of the classical, the Marxist, or the marginal school. The historical movement of the relative shares is determined by how people behave and is not predetermined by any iron physical laws.[25]

Now, this seems to me to be (a) too defeatist, and (b) rather hard on the Classics and Marx. It is defeatist because it seems to draw too sharp a line between physical laws and (purely volatile?) human behaviour. Of course, income distribution will depend on people's behaviour (within a certain physical and institutional environment). But to find the regularities of this behaviour − call them 'social laws', if you want − is the task of a useful distribution theory. The nineteenth-century macroeconomic theories were based on some definite and simplified assumptions with regard to people's behaviour in the production process and not just on 'physical laws'. These (and the capitalist mode of production) only circumscribe the radius of action open to the individuals and groups participating in the economic game.

If Boulding had tried to delve a bit deeper into the forces that influence the business decisions he regards as decisive, his theory would link up with most of the other recent attempts in this field. Take, for instance, the decision on dividend policy. This will obviously be strongly influenced by factors like trade union action, market structure, role of managers, ideas about 'normal' profits, all of which loom largely in one or the other of the modern distribution theories.

VII

Let me now turn to two further distribution models which are in the 'Kaldor' category. The first one is by Schneider.[27] It is interesting, because a comparison of this model with Kaldor's shows how slight differences in the underlying assumptions can focus attention on quite different adjustment processes in the economy.

Basically (and after some manipulation) the structure of Schneider's model resembles closely that of Kaldor. He distinguishes between non-entrepreneurs receiving contractual incomes and entrepreneurs who receive residual incomes. In line with our previous notation we shall call the former W and the latter P. Savings and consumption of both groups will again depend on their incomes, and ex-post savings will be necessarily equal to ex-post investment. Schneider distinguishes in this context between intended and unintended savings and investment.[28] As long as unintended savings and investment exist the economy will be in a state of disequilibrium. Only when they disappear will equilibrium be reached. On the path to equilibrium investment will change and this will have some distributional aspects. These are also dealt with in Schneider's paper, but we shall neglect them here and advance directly to the equilibrium position where the sum *intentionally* saved from wages and profits (i.e. in accordance with the saving propensities of the two income groups[29]) equals intended investment ($= I_0$). This position is contained in the following formula

$$s_p P + s_w W = I_0 \tag{15}$$

which is again equivalent to formula (5) which we encountered in Kaldor's and Boulding's system.

There is, however, a significant difference between Kaldor and Schneider with regard to the use to which this formula is put. In Kaldor's model not only I_0 but also $Y(= P + W)$ is taken as given (the latter at full employment level). With given departmental saving propensities this yields a unique distribution, since there is only one division between W and P that will make total savings equal to I_0. Schneider, however, does not tie his saving-investment equality to a given income level. Different combinations of profits and wages (each combination yielding a different level of total income) will secure savings equal in size to the given investment volume (I_0).

This case is best illustrated with the help of a simple diagram. In Figure 17.2 profits are depicted on the abscissa and wages on the ordinate. If *only* profits were earned, total income would have to be equal to OB, where OB is given by the equation $s_p \cdot OB = I_0$. Similarly total income would have to be equal to OA, if only wages were earned, OA being given by $s_w \cdot OA = I_0$. OA has to be greater than OB because we have assumed that the non-entrepreneurial savings propensity is smaller than the entrepreneurial propensity ($s_w < s_p$). To reach a given level of savings ($= I_0$), a higher income is, therefore, required if it consists of wages than if it consists of profits. If we now connect the points A and B by a straight line, then each point on this line represents a combination of wages and profits out of which an amount of I_0 will be saved.[30] This line is an 'iso-savings' line, but not an 'iso-income' line. On the contrary: each of the 'possible' points represents a different total income ($Y = P + W$) whose size lies between the values OA and OB.

By letting income fluctuate Schneider, therefore, does not obtain a determinate solution for income distribution, even when the investment level is (exogenously) given. To make the system determinate he introduces a further (behavioural) relationship. He says that *at a given wage level* the employment and wage bill created by entrepreneurs will depend on the intended (or expected) profits. If we denote the intended entrepreneurs' income by P^*, then we can write

$$W = \phi(P^*) \tag{16}$$

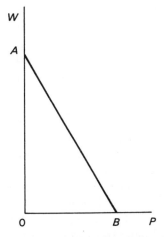

Figure 17.2   An 'iso-savings' line between wages and profits

When we combine this relationship with equation (15) we get a determinate solution for W, P and Y (given I_0, s_p and s_w). If the form of the functional relationship expressed in equation (16) is known, this solution can be worked out. As a special simplified relationship Schneider introduces the assumption that the wage bill created by employers is *proportional* to expected profits. If we further concentrate our attention on the equilibrium position where actual profits are equal to expected profits ($P = P^*$), we can rewrite equation (16) in the following form

$$W = \alpha P \qquad (16a)$$

α being a constant. Together with equation (15) this gives us

$$I_0 = s_p P + s_w W \qquad \text{(equation 15)}$$
$$= s_p P + s_w \alpha P \qquad \begin{array}{l}\text{(substituting for } W \\ \text{from equation 16a)}\end{array}$$
$$= (s_p + s_w \alpha) P$$

or

$$P = \frac{1}{s_p + s_w \alpha} \cdot I_0 \qquad (17)$$

W is obtained from (16a)

$$W = \frac{\alpha}{s_p + s_w \alpha} \cdot I_0 \qquad (18)$$

This solution can be easily illustrated in diagrammatical terms. In Figure 17.3 the axes and the line AB have the same meaning as in Figure 17.2. The line OZ represents the functional relationship between expected profits (measured on the abscissa) and wages paid out by employers (measured on the ordinate). In the diagram the simplified assumption of proportionality is depicted. With given saving propensities and a given investment volume the equilibrium solution is given by the intersection of AB and OZ at R. At this point expected and actual profits ($O\bar{P}$) will coincide and the wages paid out ($O\bar{W}$) will therefore appear 'justified.' Savings out of $O\bar{P}$ and $O\bar{W}$ will be equal to the desired level of investment (I_0). Total income will be equal to $O\bar{P} + O\bar{W}$ – not necessarily a full employment income.

We can now see that the Kaldor and Schneider models, though starting from similar assumptions, work in rather different ways. What they have in common is the introduction of (more or less constant) separate saving propensities in the profit and wage sectors. Kaldor then works at a given total income level (full employment income) so that the *sum* of profits and wages is exogenously determined (size of population, capital stock, production function). Investment or changes in investment will determine the *relative* shares of profits and wages in total income. More investment, for instance, requires a higher savings ratio out of total income, and this comes about by a shift from wages to profits.

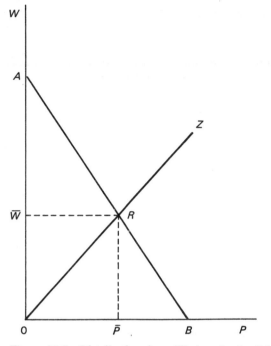

Figure 17.3 Distributional equilibrium in the Schneider model

Schneider, on the other hand, does not take total income as given. With the given saving propensities of capitalists and workers, total income (both wages *and* profits) will rise or fall with increases or decreases in investment. This mechanism of rising and falling incomes ensures the adjustment of savings to investment. The *relative* distribution between the two income types is given by a behaviour–technical relationship. Distributional equilibrium is reached when the wages employers are willing to pay with respect to an expected income, lead to that expected income. As can be seen from equation (16a), in the case of a proportional relationship, where

$$W = \alpha P$$

or

$$\frac{W}{P} = \alpha$$

the relative distribution (*in times of equilibrium*) will be constant, quite irrespective of the volume of investment.

At the danger of tiring the reader, I want to illustrate the difference between the two models with the aid of a simple numerical example. Using the same symbols as before, let us assume that

$$s_p = 0.2, \qquad s_w = 0.1$$

We want to compare two periods: in period 1 investment (I_1) equals 100, in period 2 (I_2) it rises to 110. In both periods savings must equal investment.

Let us start with the Kaldor model. Here we must make a further assumption about the size of total income. Let us set it at 750. In period 1 we have, therefore, the following relationship

$$S = s_p P + s_w (Y - P) = I_1$$

or

$$0.2P + 0.1(750 - P) = 100$$

Solving for P this gives

$$P = 250$$

and consequently

$$W = 500$$

The share of profits in total income is

$$\frac{P}{Y} = \frac{250}{750} = \frac{1}{3}$$

In a similar way we obtain for period 2

$$S = 0.2P + 0.1(750 - P) = I_2 = 110$$

$$P = 350; \qquad W = 400$$

The share of profits has risen to

$$\frac{P}{Y} = \frac{350}{750} = 0.47$$

And now to Schneider. Here we make no assumption about total income, but assume that in the relationship

$$W = \alpha P$$

$\alpha = 2$ (in equilibrium).

From equations (17) and (18) we know that for the savings-investment equality we require

$$P = \frac{1}{s_p + s_w \alpha} \cdot I_1 \text{ and } W = \frac{\alpha}{s_p + s_w \alpha} \cdot I_1.$$

Substituting our numerical values in these equations we obtain

$$P = 250, \qquad W = 500.$$

Total income $(Y_1) = 750$, and the share of profits

$$\frac{P}{Y} = \frac{250}{750} = \frac{1}{3}$$

When investment rises to 110, substitution in the profit and wage equations yields the following values

$$P = 275, \qquad W = 550.$$

Income has risen to 825, but the share of profits (275/825) is 1/3 as before. [31]

In a way, one could say that Schneider's model is more 'Keynesian' than Kaldor's, because it leaves room for those fluctuations in income with investment which have been such an outstanding characteristic in the Keynesian debate. [32] But however one views this aspect of Schneider's theory, in its present form it, too, does not extend far beyond a purely formal statement. The assumed constancy and independence of the two saving propensities it shares with Kaldor's theory; and the crucial relationship between profit expectations and wage payments remains rather unexplained. What we are told, in fact, is that the more employment and wages entrepreneurs are prepared to offer in relation to expected (and in equilibrium realized) profits the higher will be the share of wages in income. To make this rather obvious statement more useful, one would have to find out more about the actual determinants of business policy with regard to wages and employment. This would soon lead to the appearance of some of the categories we have met before, like 'normal' profits, market structure, trade unions, banking policy.

VIII

Of the several models that show some resemblance to the 'Kaldor' approach[33] I want to present one more as an example of a rather different 'split-up' of the macroeconomic aggregates. In an essay on the determinants of income distribution in the modern economy[34] Wilhelm Krelle takes as his starting point the division of total income into income from property and income from work. This is not the same as profits and wages, as he splits the income of entrepreneurs into a property part and a reward for the labour they perform. This distinction is not only introduced at the conceptual level but also maintained − with the aid of some estimates − in the statistical investigation that accompanies his theoretical considerations.

Krelle wants to explain the forces determining the relative shares of property and labour income. This explanation is hooked on to the following simple identity

$$\frac{P'}{Y} \equiv \frac{P'}{K} \cdot \frac{K}{Y} \tag{19}$$

Where P' stands for income from property and K for capital.

The two components on the right-hand side of (19) are readily recognized as the real rate of interest and the capital–output ratio. By concentrating attention on these two factors Krelle wants to shed light on the movements of income shares. As far as the trade cycle is concerned we have an increase of the capital–output ratio in times of depression (because of unused capacity) accompanied by a fall in the real return to capital (and vice versa for the boom). These divergent movements tend to stabilize income shares during the cycle.

For the long run Krelle stipulates a gradual decline of the capital–output ratio as a consequence of technical progress. It is not quite clear how far Krelle here just projects tendencies of the first half of this century into the future, or how far there is a more solid foundation for such a forecast. In any case, as far as the capital–output ratio is concerned he would expect a long-run tendency towards a lower property share. But the final outcome also depends on the behaviour of the real rate of interest. Krelle does not believe in a uniquely determined interest rate (given the relative quantities of labour and capital). Rather he offers a number of factors which will influence its level. Attention is focused on four such factors: the relative strength of trade unions and employers' federations, banking policy, market structure, and the 'Prinzip des rekurrenten Anschlusses' ('Principle of Recurring Links') which refers to the influence of the historically grown income shares. Like Kaldor, Krelle adds absolute lower limits for property and labour incomes that must be observed if the system is to function at all.

Krelle's theory displays the same 'open' character which we observed in Kalecki's case. A formal identity is established and taken as the basis for throwing out suggestive hints about some of the forces moulding the income structure without, however, providing a complete or definite picture of the probable future course of these forces and their effect on income shares.

IX

All the theories mentioned so far have one thing in common. They start from a simple analytical framework (a few identities and behaviour equations) and then try to clothe these structures by 'going behind' the chosen strategic coefficients and ratios. This usually brings them into contact with sociological and institutional factors whose influence, however, is usually only lightly sketched. Even when explicitly named they remain normally somewhat in the shadow.

In contrast to this stands the new 'French school' which quite determinedly puts sociological and institutional considerations right into the centre of its search for a new macroeconomic distribution theory. Although several French writers take part in this theoretical development,[35] the driving force and the main representative is without doubt Jean Marchal. Marchal has laid down his main ideas in several articles,[36] but the magnum opus in which it will get its final touches is still under way.[37]

The 'French' approach takes its initial inspiration not from the Keynesian model but from the sociological and institutional changes that have taken place since the nineteenth century. Several factors have contributed to change the distribution process from a microeconomic event into a nation-wide bargaining affair. Technical change has resulted in bigger-sized firms and this has led to greater labour solidarity and closer employer relationships. Greater mobility and closer contacts have increased the scope for coordinated action. Further, incomes are no longer regarded purely as a 'price', but also as a 'proper' payment signifying one's status in society; also, their function in the maintenance of an adequate total purchasing power is taken into account.

All these factors make for a 'national' policy. In this nation-wide bargaining process several groups can be distinguished which are differentiated by type of income and by their behaviour in the struggle for income and income shares. A macroeconomic distribution theory should study the (interdependent) division of total income between these selected groups. Marchal, therefore, does not stop at the two-way split-up we met in the previously discussed theories. Nor does he restrict himself to the classical trinity of rent, profits and wages. Where socio-economic observations demand new subdivisions, they are introduced; a distinction is made, for instance, between industrial and agricultural profits.

The study of the distribution of national income has to concern itself with the behaviour of these more or less homogeneous groups. They will try to maintain their absolute and relative standards, both by economic *and* political action. This means that market structures and institutional data can no longer be taken as given (which they were in the days of purely individualistic action) but must be seen as variables which can be changed in the course of the group struggle for higher income shares.

A very important rallying point for group action are standards acquired in the past. When they are threatened a state of social tension arises. This can set up various economic and social processes: inflation, changes in output, migration between groups, etc. Gradually adjustment is achieved either because the group manages to reconquer its former standard, or because the idea about what represents a 'proper' standard is revised after some members have left the group and the rest has accepted the deterioration.

It will be clear that this theory is not necessarily contradictory to the models we described in earlier sections. It is true, the various propensities and coefficients we met there do not appear explicitly in the basic structure of Marchal's theory. But with a clearer outline of the economic and sociological rules for group behaviour we could follow up their consequences and this could probably be translated into degrees of monopoly, saving propensities, real rates of interest and the like. This would provide a link between the various types of theories and show up their points of contact and their differences.

X

I hope to have given a general outline of some of the macroeconomic distribution theories that have cropped up so rapidly in the past decade. The main task of this essay was to inform. Though a few critical remarks were added here and there no full critical evaluation was attempted. If I now conclude by adding some general observations, these, too, should be regarded more in the nature of suggestions than as a final verdict.

What is obvious is that there is a definite demand for a macroeconomic distribution theory. The almost complete neglect of macroeconomic aggregates and inter-relationships in the neoclassical marginal productivity theory is felt as a serious shortcoming. By turning attention to group incomes and to income shares a link to the classical and Marxist tradition is established. This link may be conscious or unconscious. Boulding, for instance, regards himself as heir to Mill's wage-fund theory. With others the points of contact with their ancestors may have to be discovered by the student of economic doctrines.

In contrast to classical theory, however, there is today no 'recognized' classification of main income groups. On the whole there is a preference for two groups. But this seems to stem more from a wish to obtain a simple theoretical structure than from any deep conviction that this is the 'proper' division. Exceptions are perhaps Kalecki, whose distinction between wages of manual labour on the one hand and gross profits on the other may have been deliberately chosen in line with Marx's theory of value and surplus value; and Boulding, who explicitly stated that in his opinion the division of non-labour income into profits, interest and rent does not present 'many serious theoretical problems'.[38] A special case is the 'French' theory which introduces as many income groups as the special period 'requires' and in fact uses a larger number of income groups for the present age than did the classical and neoclassical schools in their days.

While the demand for a macroeconomic approach to distribution problems is obvious, the lack of a sure foundation for the new theories is similarly evident. What we experience now is the groping for relevant and theoretically fruitful subdivisions of total income and other macroeconomic aggregates. A 'splitting-up' activity is in process which reminds one of the work of atomic scientists. (Distribution theorists are, however, of less immediate danger for mankind.) The consequence is that the number of models is rapidly increasing. Soon we may have the same situation as in trade cycle theory, viz. that we suffer from an embarrassement de richesse rather than from a shortage of formal models.

What is at present most needed is a stronger empirical and theoretical underpinning for the behaviour of the chosen aggregates. In this process the traditional economic categories will obviously have to be supplemented by sociological and institutional factors. In the 'Keynesian' theories these factors are often disguised behind the economic variables of the model and are usually only introduced in a vague and uncertain manner. The French, on the other hand, have clearly made the plunge into sociology, but have not yet managed to give their theory sufficient shape and formal strength.

The consolidation of the theoretical development would be much easier if the empirical evidence were not so weak and inconclusive. Here we have to deal with long-term developments in a field where reliable statistics have only been recently (and intermittently) available[39] and where even now the statistical and theoretical categories are hopelessly at variance. Under these circumstances it is not surprising that so far empirical tests have not been able to give much help in judging the explanatory efficiency of the various models. Using American figures and comparing the periods 1900–9 and 1949–57, I. B. Kravis[40] shows that taking Kaldor's assumptions[41] he obtains very unlikely saving propensities (0.6 for profit earners, slightly negative ones for wage earners!).[42] But apart from the considerable role played by error margins for the earlier data, this calculation suffers from the fact that the profit and investment shares moved irregularly between 1900 and 1957, which makes the choice of periods rather crucial. Melvin W. Reder[43] – also using American data but in a different arrangement – thinks that the variations in labour's share in the period 1909–56 could be adequately explained with the help of Kaldor's theory. He himself prefers, however, a marginal productivity approach coupled with a Cobb-Douglas type of production function. Kravis, too, offers an explanation of income shares in 'pre-Keynesian' (mainly Hicksian) terms, resting his analysis on supply conditions of labour and capital, elasticity of substitution, and nature of technical progress. But both of them are aware of the incompleteness and crudity of the factual material. 'The data are not such,' writes Reder,[44] 'as to guarantee that the results bear the interpretation placed upon them.' And Kravis[45] refers 'to the possibly important pieces of the share puzzle that lie within realms of the social mechanism other than the purely economic.'

Thus it seems that the renewed interest in distribution theory has still a wide field of action in front of it. There will probably be more experimentation in the model sphere and it may turn out that a higher degree of disaggregation and a more dynamic approach to 'propensities', coefficients and structures is required. On the empirical side much remains to be done to improve the quality of the data and to achieve a higher correspondence between theoretical concepts and statistical categories. Finally, there will be no room for artificial barriers keeping out the sociological, political, and institutional factors and their influence on the distribution process.

NOTES

1 Based on a paper read before members of the Economics Departments at Glasgow and Manchester University in 1960.

2 Kalecki, M. (1938) 'The Determinants of Distribution of the National Income', *Econometrica*, April.

3 Harrod, R. (1939) 'An Essay in Dynamic Theory', *Economic Journal*, April.

4 Fellner, William J. (1953) 'Significance and Limitations of Contemporary Distribution Theory', *American Economic Review*, Papers and Proceedings (May).

5 With regard to Kalecki this criticism can be found, for instance, in Bauer, P. T. (1941) 'A Note on Monopoly', *Economica*, 8, p. 201; Mitra, A. *The Share of Wages in National Income* (Rotterdam, 1954), pp. 29 f.; and to some extent also in Kaldor, N. 'Alternative Theories of Distribution', *Review of Economic Studies*, Vol. XXIII, pp. 92 f.

6 In what follows I am not using Kalecki's original formulation of his theory, but the revised form which he used in his *Theory of Economic Dynamics* (1954).

7 In an article 'The Concept of Monopoly and the Measurement of Monopoly Power', *Review of Economic Studies*, Vol. I, pp. 157 ff., A. P. Learner defined the 'degree of monopoly' by the ratio $p - m/p$, where p is the price and m the marginal cost of the product. In the Kalecki case the margin created by k is $p - a$, where a equals average prime cost. But since Kalecki assumes constant average prime costs, average and marginal costs coincide and $p - a = p - m$. Thus, at least when the firm is in equilibrium (marginal revenue = marginal cost) and has a cost structure as stipulated by Kalecki, Kalecki's k will be directly connected with Lerner's 'degree of monopoly'.

8 *Theory of Economic Dynamics*, p. 38. See also my article (1957) 'Der Lohnanteil am Gesamteinkommen', *Weltwirtschaftliches Archiv*, 78, 2, p. 166, footnote 4.

9 Dunlop, J. T. (1950) *Wage Determination under Trade Unions*, Oxford.

10 Phelps Brown, E. H. and Hart, P. E. (1952) 'The Share of Wages in National Income', *Economic Journal*, 62. See also Phelps Brown, E. H. 'The Long-Term Movement of Real Wages' in Dunlop, J. T. (ed.), (1957) *The Theory of Wage Determination*, London.

11 In his later essay, mentioned in the previous note, Phelps Brown suggests that the trend of raw material prices has a decisive influence on the market environment. Falling raw material prices lead to a hard, rising raw material prices to a soft market environment.

12 Kaldor, N. (1955–6) 'Alternative Theories of Distribution', *Review of Economic Studies*, XXIII, 2, p. 100.

13 Boulding, K. (1950) *A Reconstruction of Economics*, New York, Ch. 14. Boulding produced a slightly modified version of his model in 'The Fruits of Progress and the Dynamics of Distribution', *American Economic Review*, Papers and Proceedings (May, 1953), and in McCord Wright, D. (ed.) (1951) *The Impact of the Union*, New York. Hahn, F. H. (1951) 'The Share of Wages in the National Income', *Oxford Economic Papers* (June).

14 Kaldor's distribution theory was developed in two stages. A first exposition appeared in 'Alternative Theories of Distribution', *Review of Economic Studies*, XXIII (2). It was then adapted and incorporated in his 'Model of Economic Growth', *Economic Journal* (December 1957).

15 The shifts come about by changes in the price–wage relationship. Higher investment expenditure will send up prices. This will mean higher profits and therefore a greater savings ratio out of a given total real income. The process will continue until total savings equal the new and higher investment level. The opposite movement would apply when investment is reduced.

16 And also in relation to the income level. This assumption enables him to equate the average and marginal propensities to save.

17 The influence would be brought about via the choice of different techniques of production.

18 The capital–output ratio together with the full employment assumption and an investment function yields a unique value for the 'equilibrium' volume of investment.

19 I have offered some doubts in this respect in (1959) 'The Limitations of Economic Growth Models', *Kyklos*, XII, 4.

20 Externally financed investment corresponds to savings by households.

21 We assume for simplicity's sake that all the capitalists' savings are made via undistributed profits and that dividend and interest payments are used for consumption.

22 Which Boulding largely regards as transfer payments.

23 See Reder, Melvin W. (1959) 'Alternative Theories of Labor's Share' in *The Allocation of Economic Resources*, Essays in Honor of B. F. Haley, Stanford.

24 Equations (13) and (14) on p. 246.

25 Boulding, Kenneth (1953) 'The Fruits of Progress and the Dynamics of Distribution', *American Economic Review*, Papers and Proceedings, May, p. 480.

26 In his *Reconstruction of Economics* (p. X) Boulding writes: 'The distribution structure is thus seen to be the result not of wage bargaining (except in so far as wage bargains react on the prime determinants) but of various decisions in regard to investment, consumption, finance, and liquidity.' Why the decision about investment should be more *prime* as a determinant than the wage bargain influencing this decision I fail to see, unless we take the formal construction of Boulding's model as an absolute standard for classifying the real world.

27 Erich Schneider. 'Einkommen und Einkommensverteilung der makroökonomischen Theorie', *L'Industria*, 1957, No. 2. (An English translation appeared in *International Economic Papers*, No. 8, 1958).

28 Unintended savings and investment arise mainly among entrepreneurs. Unintended investment in the form of changing stocks, unintended savings as part of an uncertain residual which is left over after consumption has been geared to the *expected* income level. Since gaps between unintended and intended quantities are mainly seen in the entrepreneurial sector, it is from this sector that the adjustment process in times of disequilibrium will start.

29 Schneider – like Kaldor – works on the assumption of stable saving propensities, with marginal and average values being equal.

30 The combinations lie on a straight line because we have assumed constant saving coefficients.

31 The difference between the two models could also be shown by letting the saving propensities vary, investment remaining unchanged. Here again, Kaldor's case would lead to a change in the equilibrium distribution, Schneider's model to a change in total income.

32 Or at least we should say that Schneider's model has a more familiar ring in connection with Keynes' 'General Theory'. The 'Keynesianism' of Kaldor's model is partly related to the 'Treatise on Money' and the 'widow's cruse' theory of distribution indicated there.

33 Their number is rapidly growing. Here is a random selection of some recent contributions. Robinson, Joan (1958) *The Accumulation of Capital*, London; Weintraub, Sidney (1958) *An Approach to the Theory of Income Distribution*, Philadelphia; Stobbe, Alfred (1960) 'Kurzfristige und langfristige Bestimmungsgründe der Einkommensverteilung', *Schweizerische Zeitschrift für Volkswirtschaft und Statistik*, 96, 2; Bombach, G. (1959) 'Preisstabilität, wirtschaftliches Wachstum und Einkommensverteilung', *Schweizerische Zeitschrift für Volkswirtschaft und Statistik*, March; Findlay, R. (1960) 'Economic Growth and the Distribution Shares, *The Review of Economic Studies,* June.

34 Krelle, W. 'Bestimmungsgründe der Einkommensverteilung in der modernen Wirtschaft' contained in Hoffmann, W. G. (ed.) (1957) *Einkommensbildung und Einkommensverteilung* (Schriften des Vereins für Socialpolitik, Gesellschaft für Wirtschafts-und Sozialwissenschaften, Bd. 13), Berlin.

35 Some of the literature is surveyed in Hosmalin, G. (1960) 'Der soziologische Ansatz und die ökonomische Theorie der Einkommensverteilung in Frankreich', *Jahrbücher für Nationalökonomie und Statistik*, 172, 4 (July).

36 See, for instance, Marchal, J. 'Contribution à la construction d'une theorie de la distribution du revenue', *Economia Internazionale* (1954); 'Wage Theory and Social Groups' in Dunlop, J. (ed.) (1957) *The Theory of Wage Determination*, London.

37 The work in question is a many-volume affair: Marchal J. and Lecaillon, J. (1958) *La Repartition du revenu national*, Paris. Three volumes have appeared so far: I. Wage-earners and Salaried Employees, II. Entrepreneurs, Farmers, Rentiers and Recipients of Transfer Incomes; III. The Classical and the Marxist Model. A later volume or volumes will deal with the neoclassical, the modern macroeconomic and Keynesian models and the authors' own theory.

38 *A Reconstruction of Economics*, p. 246.

39 As far as profits are concerned this is still too optimistic a statement.

40 Kravis, I. B. (1959) 'Relative Income Shares in Fact and Theory', *American Economic Review*, December.

41 Investment playing the *active* part in changing income shares, constant saving propensities of wage and profit earners.

42 Kravis *op. cit.*, p. 939, footnote.

43 Reder, M. W. (1959) 'Alternative Theories of Labor's Share' in *The Allocation of Resources. Essays in Honor of Bernard Francis Haley*, Stanford.

44 *Op. cit.*, p. 200.

45 *Op. cit.*, p. 947.

18 Different approaches in distribution theory

A note on Mr Ferguson's two-sector variant of Kaldor's distribution model

In the course of examining macroeconomic distribution theories in his recently published work *The Neoclassical Theory of Production and Distribution* Professor Ferguson introduces a simple variant of Mr Kaldor's model, containing in addition to two income groups and two saving propensities also two commodity groups with different prices. In the present paper Mr Ferguson's model is introduced in order to indicate the different approaches used and the different questions asked by some basic distribution theories. First the model is given a concrete form by making specific assumptions about production functions and the pricing behaviour on factor and commodity markets. Then three cases are compared: the Ferguson (neoclassical) and the Kaldor assumptions, and a 'truly' Keynesian approach, where full employment is not taken for granted. For each case the crucial assumptions and the typical problems arising in comparative statics are pointed out and illustrated with the aid of numerical examples.

I

Present-day distribution theory is characterized by a few competing basic approaches which differ from each other by laying particular stress on some special factors of the distribution process while neglecting others or regarding them as constants. The different theories − being as they are neoclassical marginal productivity theories, degree of monopoly, Keynesian, sociological and institutional approaches − must therefore be regarded as intensive investigations of limited aspects of the distribution puzzle rather than as complete theories of the distributive process as a whole.

This being the case it is not surprising that the past ten years have seen a growing number of attempts to link together certain aspects and considerations of the various distribution theories in order to get a fuller view of the distributive process in a capitalist market economy. This has led to a great variety of models combining the basic elements in different ways. The variability was further increased by the desire to connect the long-term distribution theory with growth theory which in its turn had quite a number of variants to offer.

Early and ambitious steps towards an all-embracing distribution theory were the suggestive ideas put forward by Preiser[1] or the very involved theoretical structure which Krelle presented.[2] These models − and Krelle's in particular – show that attempts towards including a large number of the factors, which may possibly affect distribution and growth, lead to a rapid complication of the theoretical structure. This in itself would be no argument against such attempts, were it not for the fact that many relations which have to be introduced are by necessity extremely simplified or purely formal ingredients.[3] The lack of transparency which such intricate constructs display is thus not compensated by a guarantee that their results are particularly reliable when it comes to decide on practical policies.

While a lot is to be said for continuing on this line in the hope for steady improvements in the realism and generality of such wide-cast theories, there will be room for simpler models for some time to come. By highlighting only a few of the basic relationships it is possible to point out certain important connections which should be kept in mind while at the same time leaving the theoretical structure sufficiently transparent and flexible to make it adaptable to different situations. Thus both from the viewpoint of exposition and as a minor aid in policy discussions the development of simple models and model combinations has a certain part to play.

It has been recognized that one way of bridging the gulf between the seemingly unconnected supply-orientated and demand-orientated theories of distribution[4] is the construction of two-sector models containing not only two factors of production but also two commodities (consumption and investment goods) with different production functions. A simple model of this kind based on previous writings by Meade and by himself was presented by Solow at the IEA conference on income distribution.[5] Solow's main attempt is to show that the marginal productivity and the Keynesian (demand) approach by themselves are not complete, but that they can be reconciled in a two-sector model taking account of differing production functions and saving propensities.[6]

There is, however, no need to aim directly at the reconciliation of a *specific* supply theory (resting, for instance, on competition, marginal productivity, as for Cobb-Douglas) with a *specific* demand theory (e.g. Kaldor's technically determined investment ratio). For a simple first approach it may be useful to have a model which just indicates what cross effects there may be between demand, production, and income distribution without – to begin with – putting too many constraints on these relations. Such a 'model', if it is sufficiently flexible, can then be used for a confrontation of various alternative situations.

A useful two-sector model of this kind has recently been presented by Ferguson, though merely as a side-thought in connection with his intensive analysis of neoclassical distribution theory.[7] The following section contains a short account of Ferguson's model while in section III it will be shown how this model can be used – in connection with some simple assumptions about productive and distributive relations – for a comparison of the different approaches to the distribution problem.

II

Ferguson's model – like most current distribution models – is a two factor model comprising wage and profit earners. The model is static and it is assumed that (in spite of some saving activity) wage earners obtain *only* wage incomes, profit earners *only* profit incomes. Full employment is assumed and the saving propensities of wage and profit earners are taken as constants.

All these assumptions tally with those which Kaldor employed in his 'Keynesian' distribution model.[8] Accordingly, we get the well-known equilibrium relationship between income distribution and the investment ratio stemming from the fact that in equilibrium intended savings and intended investment must be equal. A merely *formal* difference between Kaldor and Ferguson exists in so far as Kaldor expresses distribution as the share of profits in total income, while Ferguson uses the ratio of wages to profits.

Starting off with this relationship we can write (Y: national income, P: total profits, W: total wages, S: total savings, I: investment, s_p and s_w: saving propensities of profit and wage earners respectively, $s_p > s_w$):

$$Y \equiv P + W \tag{1}$$

$$S = s_p P + s_w W \tag{2}$$

Considering that in equilibrium $S = I$ we obtain after some regrouping

$$\frac{I}{Y} = (s_p - s_w)\,\frac{1}{1 + W/P} + s_w \tag{3}$$

This is the basic Kaldorian relationship and also the core of his distribution theory because he introduces a causal chain leading from a *given* investment ratio (determined through factors not considered here) to the corresponding equilibrium distribution. In the present context, however, equation (3) is only to be seen as a necessary equilibrium condition between I/Y and W/P.

W/P itself is determined in the factor market. Writing P_L and P_K for the prices of labour and capital respectively, we have by definition

$$\frac{W}{P} \equiv \frac{P_L}{P_K} \cdot \frac{L}{K} \tag{4}$$

In contrast to Kaldor's one-good model we introduce two commodity groups: consumption goods (G) and investment goods (I). The monetary demand for consumption goods (D_G) in equilibrium is $Y - s_p P - s_w W$, and the demand for investment goods (D_I) is equal to $s_p P + s_w W$. This gives us (considering that $Y = W + P$):

$$\frac{D_G}{D_I} = \frac{Y - s_p P - s_w W}{s_p P + s_w W} = \frac{W + P}{s_p P + s_w W} - 1$$

Dividing by P we obtain

$$\frac{D_G}{D_I} = \frac{(W/P) + 1}{s_w(W/P) + s_p} - 1 \tag{5}$$

i.e. the relative demand flows depend on the income distribution and the saving propensities. (This is merely the complementary aspect to the relationship between I/Y and W/P in a two-commodity world. The higher the profit share, the higher I/Y and the lower D_G/D_I.)

Since – with factor supplies given and fully employed – we cannot assume that the supply elasticities of the commodities are completely elastic we allow for a change in relative prices when the relative demand flows change. Prices will increase relatively in the sector in which relative demand rises. Writing P_G and P_I for the commodity prices in the two sectors we can introduce a price function[9]

$$\frac{P_G}{P_I} = g\left(\frac{D_G}{D_I}\right), \quad \frac{dg}{d(D_G/D_I)} > 0 \tag{6}$$

We have now five ratios to be 'explained' (I/Y, W/P, D_G/D_I, P_G/P_I, P_L/P_K), but so far only four equations (equations 3–6) to 'explain' them. To close the system Ferguson introduces an equation securing equilibrium in the factor markets. Given factor ratios imply a certain equilibrium price ratio adjusting demand to the given supplies. Relative prices of scarce factors will tend to rise:[10]

$$\frac{P_L}{P_K} = h\left(\frac{L}{K}\right), \quad \frac{dh}{d(L/K)} < 0 \tag{7}$$

This system of equations is used by Ferguson to show in a formal way the equilibrium interrelationship between income distribution and relative prices in the factor and commodity markets. His 'causal' chain runs like this. From a given and fully employed supply of factors of production we obtain, at first, a certain factor price ratio in the factor market. This leads immediately to a certain income distribution whence we derive the investment ratio and the relative demand flows in the commodity markets. These in turn determine relative commodity prices. In schematic form this can be depicted as follows[11] (the figures in brackets refer to the equations determining the specific relationship):

$$\frac{L}{K} \text{ (given)} \xrightarrow[(7)]{} \frac{P_L}{P_K} \xrightarrow[(4)]{} \frac{W}{P} \underset{(5)}{\overset{(3)}{\lessgtr}} \begin{array}{c} \dfrac{I}{Y} \\[2mm] \dfrac{D_G}{D_I} \xrightarrow[(6)]{} \dfrac{P_G}{P_I} \end{array}$$

III

We shall now make use of the structure of Ferguson's model in order to compare in a very simple manner some basic approaches in distribution theory. In doing this we shall (a) cast some of the general Ferguson relationships into specific forms using simplified assumptions; (b) apply numerical values in the comparative-static examples.

We introduce the following assumptions about conditions in the factor and commodity markets. In the factor market the following form is chosen for equation (7):

$$\frac{P_L}{P_K} = a + b\,\frac{K}{L} \tag{8}$$

The interpretation of equation (8) rests on the idea that the factor market is influenced by market and sociological-institutional forces. Changes in relative factor supplies react (economically) on their prices, but – especially in the short run – there is strong pressure by the income groups to maintain traditional price- (income-) relations. The lower the value of b, the stronger is the sociological-institutional influence. [12]

In the field of commodity production we introduce the assumption – again not *too* unrealistic in the short run – that production in both sectors is carried on under conditions of fixed (but sectorially different) factor proportions. Denoting the output of consumption and investment goods with x_G and x_I respectively, and writing a_{KG}, a_{LG}, a_{KI}, a_{LI} for the (given) input coefficients of capital and labour in the consumption and investment good sectors, we obtain the following two equations:

$$a_{KG}x_G + a_{KI}x_I = K \tag{9}$$

$$a_{LG}x_G + a_{LI}x_I = L \tag{10}$$

where K and L are the quantities of capital and labour used in the production process. If we take these quantities as given and stipulate full employment of both factors [13] then the real output of both consumption and investment goods (and thus total real output) is uniquely given. Substitution of capital for labour *within* each production process is excluded, but in the total economy substitution (and therefore adjustment to different capital/labour ratios) is possible by shifts *between* the sectors.

While thus – under our assumptions – full employment and given technical conditions determine completely *real* output and its division, there remains variability in the *value* composition of total output. In fact, it is through prices that the (monetary) consumption and investment demands, flowing from the income distribution process on the factor market, are brought into line with the real outputs determined by productive conditions. [14] We must have: monetary demand for consumption goods equals monetary supply of consumption goods and equally for investment goods, i.e.

$$
\left.\begin{aligned}
D_G &= P_G x_G \\
D_I &= P_I x_I
\end{aligned}\right\}
\tag{11}
$$

In this way we obtain a concrete expression for the price equation (6):

$$
\frac{P_G}{P_I} = g\left(\frac{D_G}{D_I}\right) = \frac{D_G/x_G}{D_I/x_I} = \frac{D_G}{D_I} \cdot \frac{x_I}{x_G}
\tag{12}
$$

We have now cleared the ground for the illustrative comparisons we want to present.

The Ferguson (classical) case

The stress in this approach lies on conditions in the factor and commodity markets, on price and income formation which in turn influences consumption and saving (and thus investment). The main interest in comparative statics is concentrated on changes in (relative) factor supplies and on changes in the technical process. [15]

For our illustration we introduce the following numerical values. The symbols have been previously introduced and will not be newly explained. Another point to be noted is that in contrast to Ferguson we shall not only work with ratios but also with absolute values (e.g. we take not only K/L, but K *and* L as given).

The following values are exogenously given:

$$
\begin{aligned}
K &= 360 \\
L &= 200
\end{aligned}
\qquad \therefore \frac{K}{L} = 1.8
$$

$$
s_w = 0.2; \; s_p = 0.5
$$

$$
a_{KG} = 0.2; \; a_{KI} = 0.5; \; a_{LG} = 0.15; \; a_{LI} = 0.2
$$

Furthermore, we introduce the assumption that P_K is fixed at the value 1. This means that we introduce a 'numeraire' in order to move from relative to absolute prices. [16]

Next we assume that equation (8) has the following parameters:

$$
\frac{P_L}{P_K} = 3.46 + 0.3 \frac{K}{L}
\tag{8a}
$$

This gives us $P_L/P_K = 4$ and correspondingly:

$$
P_K = 1, \; P_L = 4
$$

Combining this with the data for K and L we obtain the money incomes:

$$
W = 800, \; P = 360, \; Y = 1160
$$

Income distribution is indicated by the ratio $W/P = 2.22$. Using the saving propensities we get

$$S = s_w W + s_p P = 160 + 180 = 340$$

$$C = Y - S = 820$$

Saving decisions determine the nominal investment ratio[17]

$$\frac{I}{Y} = \frac{S}{Y} = 0.293$$

We now turn from the factor markets, factor incomes and spending decisions to the production sectors. Substituting our numerical input coefficients into equations (9) and (10) we obtain

$$0.2\, x_G + 0.5\, x_I = 360 \tag{9a}$$

$$0.15\, x_G + 0.2\, x_I = 200 \tag{10a}$$

resulting in $x_G = 800$ and $x_I = 400$ as the full employment real output.

Finally, with the aid of equations (11) we establish the equilibrium prices (i.e. the prices that will clear the market)[18]

$$P_G = \frac{D_G}{x_G} = 1.025$$

$$P_I = \frac{D_I}{x_I} = 0.85$$

We now move into 'comparative statics' appropriate to this approach. What changes follow from a change in (relative) factor supplies? As a concrete example we assume that the supply of labour increases from 200 to 220, while capital, saving propensities, and technical conditions remain unchanged. Following the same course as before we obtain the following results.

$$\text{From } \frac{K}{L} = 1.64 \text{ we obtain } \frac{P_L}{P_K} = 3.95$$

Since we stick to a capital price of 1 it follows that P_L falls from 4 to 3.95. This small reduction in the nominal wage rate in spite of a 10 per cent rise in the labour force is a consequence of our assumption that the parties in the factor markets will strongly resist a relative deterioration in their pay. This behavioural assumption also implies that the nominal share of the increased factor expands.[19]

Taking into account the changed factor quantities and prices we obtain

$$W = 869, \ P = 360, \ Y = 1229$$

$$\frac{W}{P} = 2.41$$

Income has grown from 1160 to 1229 in consequence of the increased factor supply, and distribution has shifted to wages (from 2.22 to 2.41).

Out of the higher money income more is saved and consumed than before. Savings rise from 340 to 354 (174 out of wages, 180 out of profits), consumption expenditures from 820 to 875. The relative shift to wages reduces the share of savings in income. The change in income distribution has changed the savings ratio *and this reduces* the (nominal) investment share from formerly 29.3 per cent to 28.8 per cent.

The increased supply of labour also affects real output. If full employment is maintained it leads (a) to a higher aggregate output (using some sensible index number), and (b) to a shift to the more labour-intensive type of production (for only in this way can a full employment combination of the factors be preserved). Inserting the new value of L in equation (10a) and solving equations (10a) and (11a) we obtain[20]

$$x_G = 1086$$

$$x_I = 286$$

with the corresponding equilibrium prices

$$P_G = 0.81$$

$$P_I = 1.24$$

The increase in labour supply has led to a 36 per cent increase in the output of labour intensive consumption goods, while the output of investment goods, which relies heavily on the (now) relatively scarce capital, has to be sharply reduced. The glut in the consumption goods market leads to a drop in prices (by 21 per cent), even though the monetary demand for these goods has risen more than that for investment goods. The scarce investment goods, on the other hand, become much more expensive.

The full employment adjustments in the real field mean that the real distribution is shifted still further in favour of labour. In addition to the well maintained money income they also benefit from the fact that the goods which are predominantly wage goods are labour intensive and, therefore, become cheaper as a consequence of the increased labour supply.

It will be clear that all the *special* consequences for distribution which have just been derived from the change in labour supply depend decisively on the chosen assumptions regarding the working of the factor markets and the production function. With different assumptions the distribution effects may be quite different. What should, however, emerge quite clearly are the basic relationships characteristic for this type of approach, and the strong dependence of distribution on the pricing and production processes in all markets.

The Kaldor case

The central place in the Kaldorian approach is occupied by the exogenously given investment decision. As before, full employment is assumed, but no longer do pricing processes determine distribution, saving *and thus* equilibrium investment; rather, investment 'demands' a certain equilibrium savings volume *which implies* certain factor prices.

Let us start with an initial position where all quantities take the same values as in the initial position of case 1. In particular, we start off with an investment ratio

$$\frac{I}{Y} = 0.293$$

The 'typical' question for comparative statics in a Kaldor model is concerned with the adjustments following a change in the investment ratio (L and K remaining unchanged).

Now let us assume that the investment ratio falls – for some reasons – to 0.288.[21] In the new equilibrium the saving ratio has also to fall to this level. With L and K remaining unchanged and fully employed this can only be achieved through a change in income distribution. With fixed saving propensities there is only one income distribution, and – with L and K given – only one factor price ratio which will yield voluntary savings equalling the investment decisions. To achieve equilibrium the factor price ratio must, therefore, be flexible. This means that equation (7) which relates factor prices in some unique way to relative factor supplies is no longer applicable. In place of $P_L/P_K = f(L/K)$ in case 1 we now have to introduce $P_L/P_K = f(I/Y)$. A decisive part of marginal productivity and related theories of distribution (which can be accommodated in section 1) linking relative factor prices to relative factor scarcities has to be thrown out.[22]

Fitting the Kaldorian case into the modified Ferguson structure we find the following values. Equation (3)

$$\frac{I}{Y} = (s_p - s_w) \frac{1}{1 + W/P} + s_w$$

can be turned into

$$\frac{W}{P} = \frac{s_p - s_w}{I/Y - s_w} - 1 \tag{3b}$$

Putting $I/Y = 0.288$ and using the given saving propensities we obtain

$$\frac{W}{P} = \frac{0.3}{0.088} - 1 = 2.41 \tag{11}$$

The reduced investment ratio plus the full employment assumptions 'demand' a shift in income distribution (W/P) from the initial 2.22 to 2.41. This can be achieved if (and only if) the factor price ratio is flexible. We assume here that P_L is rigid but that P_K can change in response to market conditions.

With $P_L = 4$, $K = 360$, $L = 200$ as before we get:

$$W = 800$$

$$\frac{W}{P} = 2.41 \qquad\qquad \text{from (11)}$$

$$\therefore P = 332$$

$$Y = W + P = 1132$$

$$P_K = \frac{P}{K} = 0.92$$

This is as far as the usual Kaldor model goes. The reduction in investment 'demands' reduced savings, and this is achieved through a shift in income from profits to wages. With wage rates fixed this can only come about through a fall in P_K (from 1 to 0.92). This 'deflationary' solution is mirrored in the reduced market value (1132 as against 1160 in the initial position) of the (unchanged) full employment real product.

This 'backward' reaction of the change in the (nominal) investment ratio can now be supplemented by looking at the 'forward' reaction on commodity prices. Real production remains – by assumption – unchanged at its full employment level: [23]

$$x_I = 400, \quad x_G = 800$$

The monetary demand flow in the investment sector is given by

$$D_I = \frac{I}{Y} \cdot Y = 0.288 \cdot 1132 = 326$$

Consumption expenditure is

$$D_G = Y - D_I = 806$$

Thus we obtain

$$P_G = \frac{D_G}{x_G} = \frac{806}{800} = 1.008$$

$$P_I = \frac{D_I}{x_I} = \frac{326}{400} = 0.815$$

Our 'deflationary' solution leads to a fall in both consumption good (from 1.025 to 1.008) and investment good prices (from 0.85 to 0.82), and it is through this fall in prices that – with wages remaining constant – the reduction in P_K and profits is brought about.

Again it must be stressed that the structure of the interrelationships is important, but not their *special* form in this example. Thus we could just as well have assumed that P_K stays fixed. Then the adjustment would have been brought about in an 'inflationary' way with profits staying at their old level, while wages and prices would go up.

The 'truly' Keynesian case

Kaldor-type distribution models are frequently called 'Keynesian' models because – like Keynes's employment model – they rest their case on the macroeconomic adjustment of savings to a given investment level or ratio. But in another respect they are – like the classical case – quite un-Keynesian; viz. in their *assumption* of full employment. To remain fully in the Keynesian spirit we should admit the possibility of less-than-full-employment conditions.

If we do this the sequence of events once again changes. The central place is now taken by the decision on the absolute level of real investment (not the investment ratio). This determines factor employment in the investment goods sector and via the multiplier total employment. Depending on the pricing mechanism in both factor and commodity markets employment and distribution are determined *uno actu*. The central question for comparative statics in this model refers to the effects of changes in real investment.[24]

Let us look at this case in terms of our simple 'model'. Obviously, our assumption that the *productively employed* quantities of L and K are given (and equal to their total supplies) can no longer be maintained. L and K now become variables to be determined within the system. To solve it we must, therefore, introduce two other exogenously given quantities. We do this by introducing price rigidities. This is also in the Keynesian spirit and certainly not unrealistic in an imperfectly competitive world with under-employment equilibria.

In addition to our original assumption of $P_K = 1$ we now also assume that P_L and P_I are kept constantly at $P_L = 4$ and $P_I = 1$. This means that we assume that in the factor market both social groups maintain their supply price, independent of the market situation, and that similarly administered prices prevail in the investment goods industry.

Let us now start with an initial position where entrepreneurs want to invest to the extent of $I = 300$. (Since P_I is fixed at 1 investment in the following discussion can always be seen in nominal *and* real terms. We have $D_I = x_I = 300$.) To obtain the equilibrium values for L, K and x_G we first note that in equilibrium planned savings must equal the given investment volume:

$$s_w W + s_p P = 300 \tag{12}$$

But $P_L = 4$ and $P_K = 1$ are given, so that

$$W = 4L, \; P = K$$

Using the values for $s_w(= 0.2)$ and $s_p(= 0.5)$ equation (12) becomes

$$0.8L + 0.5K = 300 \tag{13}$$

We now turn to the production sector. With $x_I (= 300)$ and the production coefficients being given we obtain from equations (9) and (10):

$$0.2 \, x_G + 150 = K \tag{9b}$$

$$0.15 \, x_G + \ \ 60 = L \tag{10b}$$

From equations (13), (9b) and (10b) we obtain:[25]

$$L = 180.7; \, K = 310.9; \, x_G = 805$$

Using the values for P_L and P_K (4 and 1 respectively) we get:

$$W = 722.8; \ P = 310.9; \ Y = W + P = 1{,}033.7$$

$$D_G = C = Y - I = 733.7; \ P_G = \frac{D_G}{x_G} = 0.91$$

The income distribution is characterized by the ratio $W/P = 2.32$.

Next we assume that investment is raised by 10 per cent to a level of 330. Substituting this value for the previous value of 300 in equations (13), (9b) and (10b) we obtain:

$$0.8 \, L \ + 0.5 \, K = 330$$

$$0.2 \, x_G + 165 \quad = K$$

$$0.15 \, x_G + \ \ 66 \quad = L$$

which yields:[26]

$$L = 198.8; \, K = 342; \, x_G = 885$$

$$W = 795.2; \ P = 342.0; \ Y = 1137.2; \ C = D_G = 807.2$$

$$P_G = 0.91; \ \frac{W}{P} = 2.32$$

The normal Keynesian employment mechanism is quite clearly visible. The increase in investment from 300 to 330 leads to increased employment (L: $+ 18$, K: $+ 31$) and consumption demand which raises the output of consumption goods from 805 to 885 and total (nominal and real) income from 1,034 to 1,137. Prices in both markets remain stable with factor and commodity supplies being expandable at the ruling values.

What is important in our context is that this change in investment and income is not accompanied by any change in income distribution (W/P remains unchanged at 2.32). This is a consequence of the special conditions we have assumed in the sphere of production where fixed coefficients rule in both sectors.[27] Under different assumptions in this respect or with regard to price behaviour different results would emerge. But the simple example brings out with sufficient clarity the difference in assumptions and distributive consequences of the standard Keynesian approach[28] as compared with the previously discussed Ferguson and Kaldor cases.

NOTES

1 Preiser, E. (1961) *Wachstum und Einkommensverteilung*, Heidelberg, 2nd revised edn 1964.
2 Krelle, W. (1962) *Verteilungstheorie*, Tübingen. A compressed version of this theory – though marred by several misprints – can be found in Marchal, J. and Ducros, B. (eds) (1968) *The Distribution of National Income*, London and New York, ch. 16.
3 Thus, for instance, Krelle's theory depends very much on the special investment functions he chooses. Again, the influence of bargaining strength of trade unions and employers' organizations is taken care of by introducing a variable μ to indicate its importance, but which otherwise is more or less suspended in mid-air (see Marchal and Ducros, *op. cit.*, p. 426).
4 This is a broad classification to show that some theories – e.g. marginal productivity – take the production side (combined with other assumptions) as the basic explanatory factor, while others – e.g. Kaldor's approach – stress the role of demand factors.
5 Solow, R. M. 'Distribution in the Long and Short Run', in: Marchal and Ducros (eds), *op. cit.*, ch. 17.
6 For Solow and others it seems desirable to show that marginal productivity theory and 'Keynesian' theory are not contradictory. This can indeed be shown in their two-sector models where relative prices of goods enter in addition to the general price level. Another question is whether this really elevates marginal productivity theory to the same status of generality as Keynesian theory. Keynesian theory, after all, starts from certain truisms arising from definitions (which are adjusted to the requirements of distribution theory) and then provides fairly free play to all sorts of assumptions. It only stresses certain circular interdependences which must not be neglected. Marginal productivity theory, on the other hand, is hemmed in by its dependence on certain not necessarily realistic assumptions, like a high degree of competition in labour and commodity markets, fairly short-period profit maximization under flexible conditions, and the like.
7 The model is contained in ch. 15, section 3.2 ('A Two-sector Variant of Kaldor's Model') in Ferguson, C. E. (1969) *The Neoclassical Theory of Production and Distribution*, Cambridge. Ferguson introduces this section mainly in order to expose 'the weaknesses of Kaldor's model' (p. 322) which neglected production conditions and the facts of a multi-commodity world, but his ideas can be interpreted as a useful extension of the Keynesian approach.
8 Kaldor, N. (1955–6) 'Alternative Theories of Distribution', *Review of Economic Studies*, XXIII, pp. 83–100.
9 The actual form of the price function will depend on pricing behaviour, production conditions, etc.
10 Again, nothing in particular is said about the concrete form of this relationship. Marginal productivity theory has, of course, a special answer. A different assumption will be used in section III. Ferguson writes in this context (p. 320): 'Explicit reference to the conditions of production has so far been avoided; and it may still be avoided, although most neoclassical economists are likely to read an implicit productivity concept into the equation now to be introduced.'

11 A neat diagrammatic exposition is given by Ferguson, *op. cit.*, p. 319. It should be noted that though Ferguson calls his model a variant of Kaldor's model *the actual way* in which he presents it (and which is reproduced in the above paragraph) is classical in its reasoning and not Kaldorian. For in the above scheme income distribution (determined in the factor market) determines saving intentions and they in turn determine investment expenditure. With Kaldor it is the other way round; investment intentions determine the (flexible) income distribution. Both approaches, however, share the equilibrium condition between income distribution and the investment ratio.

12 The introduction of equation (8) implies, of course, specific expressions for some of the other ratios. Thus

$$\frac{W}{P} = \frac{P_L}{P_K} \cdot \frac{L}{K} = a\,\frac{L}{K} + b \text{ and } \frac{D_G}{D_I} = \frac{a(L/K) + b + 1}{s_w(a \cdot L/K + b) + s_p} - 1$$

13 This may be secured through government intervention, e.g. by taxing the high-profit sector and subsidizing the other sector, or by some other means. Later on we shall drop the assumption of full employment.

14 Since we assume that technical conditions and full employment do not permit a shift in commodity composition, it is clear that the investment share in real terms is given (at least in the short run). Income distribution can, therefore, only influence the nominal investment share. But while the amount of consumption (and investment) goods remains the same, changes in income distribution will still be important by determining how much of the given supply of consumption goods can be appropriated by wage earners and how much by profit earners.

15 Only the first case will here be illustrated. The second case can easily be introduced by varying the value of the input coefficients in equations 9 and 10.

16 This is a purely formal procedure and leaves the original Ferguson model unimpaired. One could, of course, also give a material interpretation to this procedure by saying, for instance, that P_K is institutionally fixed, at least in the short period.

17 This can also be directly calculated by substituting the value of W/P in equation (3). Similarly, the value of $D_G/D_I = 820/340 = 2.41$ can be derived from equation (5).

18 If these prices are compared with unit costs it will be seen that conditions in the two sectors are rather different. Taking the input coefficients and the factor prices we find that labour and capital costs per unit of production are 0.6 and 0.2 in the consumption good sector and 0.8 and 0.5 in the investment good sector. While, thus, profits arc earned in the consumption good sector there are losses in the capital good sector. This situation is, however, not incompatible with short-run conditions where capital is 'frozen' in each sector. Capital costs can be taken as fixed costs (e.g. in the form of interest payments). Since the price in the investment goods sector still lies above labour costs production will be continued even though total costs are not covered.

19 Other assumptions about the mechanism of the factor markets are of course possible and will lead to different results. In this context, however, it is only important to show *where* crucial assumptions are made in the different approaches, and not necessarily *what sort* of assumptions.

20 Here and elsewhere rounded figures are given. Where values are obtained through division there may be slight divergences, since the divisions were originally carried out before rounding the individual items.

21 This is the ratio we obtained *as a result* in case 1 after L was increased. Here the change is exogenous. The same value was only taken in order to point out quite clearly the differences in the direction of relationships and in the results.

22 Hence the well-known exclamation of surprise in Kaldor's pioneer article: 'I am not sure where "marginal productivity" comes in in all this' (Kaldor, N. (1955–6) 'Alternative Theories of Distribution', *Review of Economic Studies*, XXIII, 2, p. 100).

23 It will be remembered that our production functions do not permit a change in the product mix if both factors are to be fully employed. The 'real' investment ratio can, therefore, not be altered. Changes in the nominal ratio can only affect the commodity price ratio.

24 In case 1 and 2 real investment was a fixed quantity because of our assumption of full employment and fixed production coefficients. Without changes in factor supplies only nominal investment and the nominal investment ratio could vary. Now, with factors being not necessarily fully employed, real investment can also change.

25 If we assume that total labour and capital supplies are as before, these results imply an 'unemployment' of 19 labour units and 49 capital units.

26 Unemployment of labour falls from 19 to 1 unit, of capital from 49 to 18 units.

27 Formally the results of this case resemble those which Erich Schneider obtains in his 1957-model (Schneider, E. (1957) 'Einkommen und Einkommensverteilung in der makro-ökonomischen Theorie', *L'Industria*, 2; English translation in *International Economic Papers*, 8, 1958). But the constancy of distributive shares in Schneider's model is due to his special assumptions about entrepreneurial profit expectations (desired profits are a function of wage payments) while in the present context the constancy is connected with the production function (which leads to proportional expansion of factor requirements) and the (fixed) pricing conditions in the factor market.

28 This approach is here extended in a Kaldorian direction by explicitly recognizing the existence of two income groups with different saving propensities.

19 Theme and variations – remarks on the Kaldorian distribution formula

Kaldor's famous 'Keynesian' distribution formula is very useful when considered as a tautological formulation of the coherence between investment, saving and income as circulatory components. But Kaldor puts the formula in a theoretical model in which full employment and a constant propensity to save were assumed. Furthermore, since he considered real investment as an 'active' factor, then consequently income distribution is only a dependent variable.

In the author's opinion, sociological and socio-psychological factors are neglected by Kaldor. Two main cases are treated in the present paper. First, in a short-term model the income-political aims of employees must additionally be taken into account, because through this factor investment plans of enterprises are realizable only to a certain degree. Therefore the connections between investment and income distribution are not unilateral, but reciprocal.

On the other hand, to assume a constant propensity to save in a long-term model is unrealistic. One can suggest, for example, that this propensity may be changed by wage policies. Consequently, not only investments but also labour market policies can change the long-term income distribution.

I

Kaldor's well-known formula for a 'Keynesian' approach to income distribution[1] is, of course, an identity. Its contents follow directly from our definitions of income, saving, investment, saving propensities, wages and profits in a Keynesian equilibrium system. The following Keynesian identities are used:

$$Y = P + W \tag{1}$$

and

$$I = S \tag{2}$$

where Y stands for national income, P for profits, W for wages, I for investment, and S for saving. Writing s_p and s_w for the (average and marginal) saving propensities of profit and wage earners respectively, we can express total savings as

$$S = s_p P + s_w W \tag{3}$$

Substituting (3) and (2) and making use of (1) we obtain

$$I = s_p P + s_w(Y - P) \tag{4}$$

Dividing by Y and regrouping the items we get the Kaldorian distribution formula:

$$\frac{P}{Y} = \frac{1}{s_p = s_w} \cdot \frac{I}{Y} - \frac{s_w}{s_p - s_w} \tag{5}$$

To call a formula an 'identity' has ceased to be an offending remark. We know that well-chosen identities, bringing together economically and statistically relevant concepts in a novel manner can have extremely stimulating effects on economic theorizing. The quantity formula has played a role of this sort in monetary theory.[2] I think that Kaldor's formula has already proved its capacity of acting as a stimulant (or 'irritant' to some people) in distribution discussions and it will continue to be useful as a peg on which to hang diverse considerations.[3] In this way it is also regarded in the following pages where it serves as a basis for a few tentative considerations on some aspects of short-term (section III) and long-term (section IV) distribution problems. But at first a few words on Kaldor's distribution *theory* may be in order.

II

Kaldor does, of course, not rest content in presenting his distribution identities. With them he delivers an outline of distribution theory.[4] Though this theory is not developed very systematically, it does imply some ideas which are not easily acceptable. It is not pure coincidence that Kaldor shapes equations (1) to (3) into the special form of equation (5). In presenting an identity in a certain way one does already suggest a certain interpretation of the sequences in the real world. By writing P/Y on the left-hand side of his equation Kaldor signifies that he regards the income distribution in a full employment economy more or less as the 'dependent' variable, 'determined' by the saving propensities and by investment activity (in relation to total income) which are gathered on the right-hand side. From what Kaldor says in connection with his formula it is clear that he regards the saving propensities as rather fixed so that I/Y becomes the prime mover in the distribution puzzle.[5] As long as wages or profits do not fall below a certain 'absolute' minimum (indicated by the subsistence wage and the minimum risk-premium), investment behaviour 'determines' the – more or less malleable – income distribution.

From Kaldor's system emerges, therefore, a somewhat Schumpeterian entrepreneur whose investment behaviour (influenced by technical and growth factors) leaves its unmistakable imprint on the social and income structure. While Kaldor, looking at his results, noticed with some surprise that he was 'not sure where "marginal productivity" comes in all this,'[6] others have been missing the influence and effects of group action (Marx's class struggle) on the distributional problem in Kaldor's exposition. Some have tried to repair this short-coming by constructing predominantly socio-logical and institutional models, in which group pressures take a prominent place,[7] some — remaining within the orbit of predominantly economic models — have changed or supplemented Kaldor's approach;[8] I shall try to sketch some thoughts on these aspects within the framework of Kaldor's useful distribution identity.

III

In this section we shall look at investment and distributional changes in the short and medium period. The 'sociological' fact we want to introduce into the Kaldor system is the reluctance of workers and trade unions to accept a deterioration of their acquired incomes in the face of rising investment.[9]

In expansionary periods of full employment, slight inflation, and rapid economic progress the desire to invest among entrepreneurs will be strong. With the necessary credits forthcoming I and I/Y could rise considerably if the entrepreneurial wishes were fulfilled. But workers and trade unions have become rather sensitive against downward changes of their wages and diminutions in their share of the national income. Their aspiration levels will be decisively influenced by the standards acquired in the past.[10]

Let us assume that for some time past the share of wages in national income has been W_0/Y_0. We also assume that in the short and medium run the trade unions will offer strong resistance against any reduction of their 'traditional' share by more than k per cent. Under these circumstances the problem is no longer how investment behaviour affects the income distribu-tion, but rather what limitations distribution behaviour sets to investment plans.

Let us express this idea in a slightly modified Kaldor formula. Instead of deriving formula (4) from equations (1) to (3),[11] we can take the following path:

$$I = s_p(Y - W) + s_w W = s_p Y - (s_p - s_w)W \qquad (6)$$

Dividing by Y and using the suffix 0 to denote the 'equilibrium' situation which has ruled for some time we can write

$$\left(\frac{I}{Y}\right)_0 = s_p - (s_p - s_w)\left(\frac{W}{Y}\right)_0 \qquad (7)$$

This can be simplified by assuming that $s_w = 0$:

$$\left(\frac{I}{Y}\right)_0 = s_p - s_p\left(\frac{W}{Y}\right)_0 \qquad (8)$$

We now denote the percentage decrease in labour's share where trade union resistance sets in with full force by k. This sets an upper limit to the investment share for the next few periods. We can write

$$\left(\frac{I}{Y}\right)_{max} = s_p - s_p\left(1 - \frac{k}{100}\right)\left(\frac{W}{Y}\right)_0$$

$$= s_p\left[1 - \left(1 - \frac{k}{100}\right)\left(\frac{W}{Y}\right)_o\right]$$

(9)

In other words, in the medium period and starting with a 'traditional' base situation, investment will within certain limits – between $(I/Y)_0$ and $(I/Y)_{max}$ – determine distributional shares, while distributional behaviour will stop investment at a certain limit. If entrepreneurs tried to push the investment (and profit) share beyond $(I/Y)_{max}$ the wage pressure of the trade unions will be strong enough to prevent this. The higher wages will either destroy the entrepreneurial desire to go on with their investment plans or – more likely under our full employment assumptions – the ensuing wage price spiral will prevent that the growing investment expenditure leads to a further increase in real investment and investment shares.

To the distributional determinants introduced by Kaldor (investment and saving propensities) we have now added the variable k. $1/k$ is an expression for the militancy of the trade unions. If they are prepared to accept quite a large reduction in wage shares, $1/k$, the measure of their fighting strength, will be small. With more resistance to downward revisions it will be greater.

A short numerical example may be useful as an illustration of the above ideas. Let us assume that in the base period the share of wages in income (W/Y) equals 0.6 and $s_p = 0.4$ $(s_w = 0)$. If we further assume that $k = 5$ per cent, i.e. that trade unions will not accept a reduction of the wage share below 57 per cent, then – according to equations (8) and (9) – the investment share can only move from 16 per cent in the base period to 17.2 per cent in nearby subsequent periods. Up to this point it will have a Kaldorian distributional effect.

The level of 17.2 per cent will, however, present an absolute limit only if we assume – with Kaldor – that the saving propensities are absolutely fixed in the medium period.[12] It is, however, not unlikely that a tough behaviour of the trade unions coupled with credit restrictions may raise s_p. Particularly, big companies with a strong urge to invest can increase the undistributed portion of profits.[13] If we assume in our example that s_p is raised from 0.4 to 0.45, then I/Y can be further raised (with W/Y kept at 0.57) to 19.3 per cent. With an unchanged s_p an increase of I/Y to this level would require a reduction of W/Y to 51.7 per cent! It seems obvious, therefore, that taking I/Y as the independent variable and letting income distribution take the full weight of adjustment can only be realistic for small deviations from the traditional level. When greater changes are attempted distributional behaviour and induced changes in savings behaviour have to be introduced into the discussion.

The above 'model' implied that trade unions will direct their attention to labour's *share* in the national income. If other targets are chosen, they can be easily assimilated by suitable adaptations of the basic Kaldor model. Let us assume, for instance, that trade union policy does not defend labour's share but rather a certain 'traditional' wage level. If we denote the wage per worker with w and the labour force with L, we can rewrite equation (8) as

$$\frac{I}{Y} = s_p - s_p \frac{wL}{Y} \tag{10}$$

Writing $p\ (= Y/L)$ for labour productivity and denoting with the suffix 0 prevailing conditions, we obtain

$$\left(\frac{I}{Y}\right)_o = s_p - s_p \frac{w_0}{p_0} = s_p\left(1 - \frac{w_0}{p_0}\right) \tag{11}$$

To realize what 'range of freedom' Kaldor's independent variable, the investment share, possesses in the short run we must specify the bargaining policy of the trade unions. Assuming that they are not prepared to accept any reduction in the acquired real wage, I/Y could in a subsequent period only be expanded to

$$\left(\frac{I}{Y}\right)_{max} = s_p\left(1 - \frac{w_0}{p_1}\right) \tag{12}$$

where p_1 stands for labour productivity in the respective period. If we start with the assumptions of our previous numerical example and let labour productivity rise (from period 0 to period 1) by 2 per cent, then the investment share can move freely (in the Kaldorian manner) from 16 per cent in the initial situation to 16.5 per cent in the following period, changing distributional shares in the interval (labour's share would fall from 60 to 58.8 per cent). Any attempt to move beyond that stage without further increases in productivity would flounder on the wage demands of the trade unions. Rising wages would prevent investment to increase its share in national income. Here, of course, we may again find that trade union resistance increases s_p and, in this way, creates additional room for investment.

In the formulation of equation (12) the distributional aspirations of the trade unions do not show up directly as in equation (9) where they are indicated by $1/k$. But they are implied in the value of w in equation (12). A strong trade union policy will try to let w not fall far behind changes in p, a weak one may even allow a drop from acquired standards.

Our discussion has so far only circled round the question how investment and distribution influence each other in the short run when the investment share is revised upwards. With regard to downward revisions the mechanism is probably somewhat different. Small reductions in I/Y will lead (via falling prices and profits) to an increase of W/Y in the 'prescribed' Kaldorian manner. But it is doubtful whether this process can go very far. With prices being rather rigid it is unlikely that investment can be reduced to any great extent without endangering full employment. The Kaldorian distributional mechanism finds, therefore, also a fairly narrow downward limit. Heavier falls in investment will either end the full employment assumption and will land us in a Keynesian downward spiral with Y falling together with I; or – because this may be politically unacceptable – the government will step in and will supplement private investment through public investment. In both cases I/Y will be provided with a floor. Only down to this limit can the investment ratio be the main determinant of income distribution.

IV

We have shown that in the relatively short run the Kaldorian mechanism of investment shares determining income distribution works within certain narrow limits. The limits in their turn are determined by institutionally and sociologically circumscribed distributional behaviour. These limits may continue to apply in the longer run, if trade union policy with regard to income shares or government intervention policy (in the case of falling investment) remain fairly rigid over the years and decades. But on the whole we would expect the range over which I/Y can move and influence income distribution to be wider in the long run. Accepted standards can be constantly nibbled at until the notion as to what is 'normal' has changed. This is the more true since in a growing economy deteriorations in income shares (or in the growth rate of one's income) can be accompanied by considerable increases in absolute living standards. The limits which occupied our attention in the previous section will, therefore, tend to be somewhat more flexible in the long run.

But when we allow sufficient time for the establishment of changed standards, we have to consider a new element. While the assumption of fairly rigid saving propensities may have some justification over short periods, it can hardly be maintained for the long period. The following considerations are an attempt to indicate some possible relations in this field and to trace their effect on income distribution.[14] Again the discussion is carried out within the framework of Kaldor's formula.

The basic idea from which we start is that saving and consumption propensities are not just given psychological magnitudes, but are shaped by sociological and economic influences. In particular, we believe that the longer-run development of saving and consumption standards among entrepreneurs will not be independent of the conditions they meet in the labour market. If wages can always be set at a low level, this will probably encourage waste and carefree consumption among capitalists. This is not untypical for many underdeveloped countries. Constant wage pressure, on the other hand, will make entrepreneurs more concerned about their position in the business world and will encourage higher saving appropriations out of income. If wage demands are continuously very high[15] a countereffect may set in: saving and investment may now be discouraged in some cases in face of such high odds.

The considerations of the previous paragraph lead us to the assumption that in the longer run the saving propensity of profit earners is a function of wages: $s_p = f(W)$. The shape of the function may approximate the curve in Figure 19.1, where W_0 and W_1 represent the limits for changes in W. These limits are set by the resistance of workers' and employers' organizations against further changes and by the policy of the monetary authorities. Between these limits s_p would somewhat rise and then fall as wages are pressed beyond the minimum level.

The savings of workers, on the other hand, will be somewhat influenced by the consumption standards of the upper classes. If profit earners consume less and save more out of their incomes this will also encourage savings among wage earners; high consumption standards in the capitalist group will lead to higher consumption propensities among the workers.[16] Workers' saving propensities can, therefore, be regarded as a function of profit earners' saving propensities: $s_w = F(s_p)$. As a simple assumption we can take s_w to be a constant fraction of s_p. This relation between s_w and s_p is shown in Figure 19.2.

Since s_p is a function of W, s_w – a function of s_p – can also be

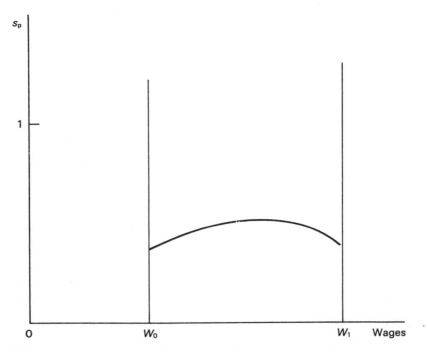

Figure 19.1   The influence of wage levels on the saving propensity of profit earners

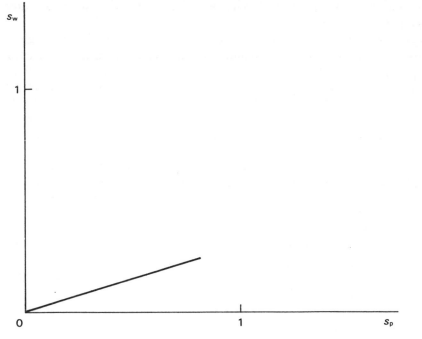

Figure 19.2 The influence of saving propensities of profit earners on workers' saving propensities

expressed as a function of W:

$$s_w = F(s_p) = F[f(W)] = g(W)$$

Using Kaldor's original distribution formula[17] we can, therefore, write for long-run conditions[18]

$$\frac{P}{Y} = \frac{1}{f(W) - g(W)} \cdot \frac{I}{Y} - \frac{g(W)}{f(W) - g(W)} \tag{13}$$

The income distribution is still influenced by the investment share; but wage policy (through its long-run effect on saving propensities) has also a say in the final result. Whatever the investment share may be, there will be a certain wage policy which will yield a minimum long-run equilibrium value for P/Y and give the best attainable distribution (within a functioning capitalist framework) to the workers. If we assume that full employment is secured by government policy and that the volume of investment is not dependent on the size of the profit share,[19] then I/Y is an exogenous magnitude and the workers' distributional 'optimum' will also secure that the absolute level of wages is kept at the maximum path. If, however, wage and profit levels have repercussions on investment, a 'better' distribution now may impair economic growth and thus depress the absolute level of wages in later periods.[20]

Let us review the considerations of the last few paragraphs in a slightly more concrete form. We shall assume that the s_p and s_w functions have the shape indicated in Figures 19.1 and 19.2. Instead of relating s_p directly to certain wage levels we shall link them to increases above the minimum acceptable wage. The minimum wage sum we have denoted with W_0.[21] Wage payments below that level will not be tolerated by the workers' organizations or public opinion. Trade unions can, however, raise money wages beyond W_0 by a certain percentage.[22] Let this percentage addition be called x. Then s_p will be a function of x. We have assumed[23] that s_p will take an approximately parabolic course, first rising and then falling as x increases. We can thus write:

$$s_p = a - b(x - c)^2, \qquad \begin{array}{l} 0 < a < 1 \\ b, c > 0 \end{array} \qquad (14)$$

This means that s_p increases when the wage sum is raised beyond W_0 and reaches a maximum a when the percentage increase amounts to c, further wage increases will reduce s_p.

For s_w we take – again in accordance with our previous considerations – the simple relation

$$s_w = m s_p, \qquad 0 < m < 1 \qquad (15)$$

By substituting (14) and (15) in the Kaldorian distribution equation (5) we obtain (after some simplifying)

$$\frac{P}{Y} = \frac{1}{(1 - m)[a - b(x - c)^2]} \cdot \frac{I}{Y} - \frac{m}{(1 - m)} \qquad (16)$$

If a maximum shift of national income to wages is desired, P/Y must be made a minimum. We have

$$\frac{d(P/Y)}{dx} = \frac{2b(1 - m)(x - c)}{(1 - m)^2 [a - b(x - c)^2]^2} \cdot \frac{I}{Y} \qquad (17)$$

Setting the right-hand side of (17) = 0, we obtain $x = c$ as the condition of a minimum P/Y or a maximum W/Y (I/Y being given). That is to say, aiming at high wages and wage shares trade unions should raise wages beyond the minimum as long as the wage increases stimulate greater saving attitudes among the entrepreneurs. Within this range wage rises will be accompanied by less than proportionate price rises and the wage share will increase. When wages are raised beyond the maximum s_p-point, the reduced saving of the entrepreneurs will mean that (with a given I/Y) prices begin to rise faster than wages so that their real level and their share in income declines.

It is not unlikely that by instinct or experience 'militant' trade unions have come near an 'optimum' course, as described in the last paragraph.

They usually demand higher wages than would rule without interference, but seldom try to press for the last ounce of wage concessions that may be obtainable even within the traditional capitalist framework.

In our example the 'optimum' distribution from the workers' point of view is only dependent on c, i.e. on the shape (viz. the maximum point) of the s_p function. This is so, because the linear dependence of s_w on s_p, which we have assumed, means that the saving propensity of the wage earners will reach its maximum together with the profit earners' maximum. The 'optimum' wage rise is, therefore, independent of m, which indicates the strength by which workers' savings habits are influenced by capitalist savings. But while m does not influence the 'optimum' wage policy, it does contribute to the effect of that policy. The higher m, i.e. the higher s_w for any given s_p, the greater will be the share of income going to wage earners. [24]

In conclusion we want to illustrate the 'model' of the previous paragraphs by using some not too implausible concrete numbers. For the long-run saving propensity of profit earners we write

$$s_p = 0.35 - 0.000347(x - 12)^2$$

where x has the same meaning as before. This assumes that the saving propensity of profit earners is 0.30 when wages are at W_0 − the acceptable minimum − rises to 0.35 when wages are 12 per cent above the minimum and declines thereafter.

The profit share will be at a minimum (and the wage share at a maximum) when wages are raised to W_0 plus 12 per cent. The distributional effects of this and some other wage levels under the assumption of an investment share of 20 per cent is shown for different assumptions regarding s_w in Table 19.1. It can be seen that even the comparatively slight response of capitalists' saving propensities to wage changes assumed in our example can lead to considerable distributional effects. Also a shift of m − the factor of workers' adjustment to capitalist savings − can have noticeable effects.

Table 19.1 Distributional equilibria with varying wages and saving propensities

x (increase of money wages beyond minimum) in %	s_p	$\dfrac{P}{Y}$ in % under the assumption $I/Y = 20\%$		
		$s_w = 0.3 s_p$	$s_w = 0.2 s_p$	$s_w = 0.09$
0	0.300	52.4	58.3	52.4
6	0.338	41.8	49.1	44.4
12	0.350	38.8	46.4	42.3
16	0.344	40.2	47.6	43.3
20	0.328	44.3	51.1	46.2

In the last column a constant saving propensity for workers has been assumed.

It shows that in this case the changes in distribution owing to wage changes are considerably damped, because the variations in profit savings are no longer intensified by parallel swings in wage savings.

V

To summarize: We have tried to instil some institutional and sociological elements into the Keynesian-Kaldorian distribution equilibrium. It was shown that in the short run investment activities will influence distribution within narrow limits, while on the other hand distributional aspirations will set definite limits to the size of the investment share. In the longer run the investment share may range over wider intervals. But over the longer period we must cease to regard the saving propensities as given magnitudes. They will be influenced by wage policy and by social imitation. When this is taken into account there is no longer a single full employment distributional equilibrium connected with a given investment share. Different equilibria can be established depending on the relations between income policy and the saving propensities of entrepreneurs and wage earners. Some simple ideas about these relations have been advanced in the final part of the paper.

NOTES

1 See Kaldor, N. (1955–6) 'Alternative Theories of Distribution', *Review of Economic Studies*, XXIII, 2, (1957) 'A Model of Economic Growth', *Economic Journal*, December 1957.

   Kaldor was not the only one to push the distribution approach in this direction. Similar ideas were evolved by various authors: Boulding, J. Robinson, E. Schneider. (See my paper 'Some Recent Contributions to a Macroeconomic Theory of Income Distribution', *Scottish Journal of Political Economy*, October 1961.) But there is no doubt that Kaldor's presentation of the new ideas had a greater influence on the subsequent discussion than any of the other contributions.

2 That the quantity formula has often created more confusion than illumination was a consequence of the failure of some earlier economists to distinguish between identities on the one hand and hypotheses or theories on the other. See in this context the remarks by Brunner, K. (1955) 'Ein Ausblick auf die ökonometrische Forschungsarbeit', *Schweizerische Zeitschrift für Volkswirtschaft und Statistik*, 91, p. 172f.

3 Thus G. Bombach, who in some ways is rather critical of the Kaldor proposals (he doubts, for instance, the advisability of throwing together the profits of small business and the undistributed earnings of big companies), points out quite correctly: 'The advantage of the model consists without doubt in its simple construction which shows up the decisive influence of sectoral saving propensities on the distribution of income among the sectors. We said earlier that the theorist requires not only highly efficient systems which, by necessity, are also rather complicated, but also handy and transparent models. In the present case a model of this kind is put at our disposal.' (Bombach, G. 'Die verschiedenen Ansätze

der Verteilungstheorie' in Schneider E. (ed.) *Einkommensverteilung und technischer Fortschritt*, Berlin.)

4 Kaldor, *op. cit.*, passim.

5 That the Kaldor theory tends in this direction has been criticized by several writers. Thus A. K. Sen writes: 'The chief difficulties with the Neo-Keynesian model seem to be its assumptions of (a) fixed propensities to save independent of price changes, (b) fixed *real* investment irrespective of price changes, and (c) lack of any feed-back mechanism when entrepreneurial expectations are unfulfilled.' (Sen A. K., 1963, 'Neo-Classical and Neo-Keynesian Theories of Distribution', *The Economic Record*, 39, March, pp. 53 ff.)

Another example is C. E. Ferguson: 'In Kaldor's theory, investment is a completely exogenous variable whose behaviour is not determined by the model. In fact, the Kaldor model simply determines the profit share that is consistent with full employment, given an exogenous level of investment and the unequal propensities to save. This is a far cry from a theory of distribution...' (Ferguson, C. E. 1964, 'Theories of Distribution and Relative Shares', *Jahrbücher für Nationalökonomie und Statistik*, February, S.34f.)

In the discussions following his first article Kaldor has been quite outspoken on this point. In 'A Rejoinder to Mr Atsumi and Professor Tobin' (*The Review of Economic Studies*, XXVII, 2, February 1960) he writes (on p. 122): 'The basic assumption of all Keynesian theory is that Investment − i.e. expenditure charged to capital account, and not on income account − is determined independently of current savings. But since in equilibrium, savings must be equal to investment, it is the decisions concerning capital expenditure which will determine the level and/or the distribution of incomes, and not the other way round... Assuming "full employment", and hence a given real income, an increase in Investment (which also involves in this case a higher *ratio* of Investment to Consumption) will cause profit margins to increase until the savings−investment equilibrium is restored.'

The problem is, of course, whether the parties affected by the investment decisions will necessarily accept all consequences flowing from them, and whether and to what extent entrepreneurs will be able to carry out their planned real investment. In dealing with this question I shall be mainly concerned with the assumptions regarding distributional adjustment and saving propensities. The full employment assumption will not be questioned, since it can be taken as a good first approximation in the present-day European economy. This was not so in pre-war days and may not apply at some future date. I shall also disregard the problem of substitution between capital and labour which has bothered many participants in the discussion.

6 Kaldor, 'Alternative Theories...', *op. cit.*, p. 100.

7 Here one has to mention above all the French 'sociological' school (J. Marchal and others) and several contributions by American labour economists (J. Dunlop, A. Ross and others).

8 A very interesting example in this direction is E. Preiser's *Wachstum und Einkommensverteilung* (Heidelberg, 2nd ed., 1964), where he marries the Kaldorian method with a 'degree of monopoly' approach of Kalecki origin. The Kaldor equation is used to ensure the fulfilment of macroeconomic flow-equilibrium. The degree of monopoly is introduced 'in order to bring out the essence of the distribution problem. All recent attempts in the field of distribution theory have similar aims, but in so far as they lean exclusively on Keynesian macroeconomic equilibrium the very essence of the distribution process moves out of sight. The relative shares of profits and wages are solely derived from investment demand and saving propensities and are, therefore, only a

bye-product of decisions which have no direct connection with the distribution problem. This is in direct contradiction to experience. We know that people plan for a certain distribution: a definite real wage, a rate of profit, and more recently, in collective bargaining, even a share in the social product' (p. 49).

I agree with the sentiments expressed in this quotation. My approach, however, differs from that of Preiser.

9 I shall present my argument mainly in static terms to make the exposition as simple as possible. The ideas can easily be adapted to a growing economy where not present incomes but traditional rates of income increase are demanded and defended.

10 This influence of past data on the present situation has received increasing attention in German literature on distribution problems (Krelle, Preiser), and has found expression in the term 'das Prinzip des rekurrenten Anschlusses'.

11 See section I, pp. 276–7.

12 Changes in saving propensities in the longer run are dealt with in the next section.

13 But also non-corporate business may increase its savings in such a situation. We should not overlook that this does not necessarily mean a reduction in the private consumption of entrepreneurs. In many cases savings can be achieved by cutting down unnecessary and unproductive expenditure within the firm. The strong stand of the trade unions will then be a lever for organizational improvements. This argument gains force in a *growing* economy where an active wage policy can force firms to channel productivity gains into new investment rather than into wasteful 'costs' or into consumption.

14 Krelle and Weintraub belong to the very small group of economists who mention changes in saving propensities. But they are mainly concerned with short-run Duesenberry effects when income fluctuates or with once-and-for-all changes in psychological attitudes. (See Krelle, W., 1962, *Verteilungstheorie*, Tübingen pp. 128 ff., 181; Weintraub, S., (1958), *An Approach to the Theory of Income Distribution*, Philadelphia.) The sociological long-term influences discussed above are of a different nature.

15 Correctly speaking, this entire discussion of long-run distribution should be conducted in terms of *changes* in wage rates, profits, income, etc. We can, however, simplify the treatment by speaking of wage levels, profits, and income without loss of meaning as long as we keep in mind that all these magnitudes grow over time so that relative deteriorations can go hand in hand with absolute improvements.

16 J. S. Duesenberry (*Income, Saving, and the Theory of Consumer Behaviour*, Cambridge, Mass., 1949) makes the saving propensity dependent on an individual's relative station in the income distribution. But surely, what will even be more decisive than relative income levels will be visible consumption standards.

17 Equation (5) on p. 277.

18 Ignoring the *rise* in wages, profits, and incomes.

19 Various investment functions (autonomous investment, an accelerator function, etc.) would meet this requirement. This assumption also implies that the growth of the economy is not influenced by the wage policy.

20 The *immediate* effect of a depression in investment would be a still further relative shift of incomes from profit to wage earners.

21 What is important for the single worker is, of course, not the wage sum but the wage rate. If we, however, assume that there is just one single wage rate *or* that the wage structure moves proportionately upwards and downwards, then changes in the wage sum are equivalent to changes in individual wage rates.

22 Since we are dealing with longer run developments we must consider W_0 as changing slowly with time. The trade union action leads to a certain percentage addition to the historically grown 'minimum' level.

23 See pp. 281–2 and Figure 19.1.

24 With s_p and I/Y being given and $s_w = ms_p$, we have

$$\frac{P}{Y} = \frac{1}{(1-m)s_p} \cdot \frac{I}{Y} - \frac{m}{(1-m)}$$

and

$$\frac{d(P/Y)}{dm} = \frac{s_p}{(1-m)^2 s_p{}^2} \cdot \frac{I}{Y} - \frac{1}{(1-m)^2}$$

which can be simplified to

$$\frac{d(P/Y)}{dm} = \frac{I/Y - s_p}{(1-m)^2 s_p}$$

The denominator on the right-hand side of the last equation is positive so that the sign of $d(P/Y)/dm$ coincides with the sign of the numerator. Since equilibrium in the Keynesian-Kaldorian system depends on $s_p > I/Y > s_w$, this sign is necessarily negative. With growing m, therefore, P/Y declines and W/Y increases.

20 Some notes on Weintraub's eclectic theory of income shares

(*Journal of Post Keynesian Economics*, Summer 1985, Vol. 7, No. 4.)

INTRODUCTORY REMARKS

One reason which made Sidney Weintraub such a powerful force in economic thinking was his strongly motivated presentation of original and hard-hitting theoretical structures dealing with highly relevant issues. One may be surprised, convinced or provoked, but one cannot easily ignore his 'attacks'. This is amply proved by the many discussions which his various publications have elicited. It also became visible when he returned to one of his age-old pet subjects, income distribution, round about 1980. After some preparatory thoughts in related writings (Weintraub 1978; 1979) he brought various strands of his thinking together in an 'Eclectic Theory of Income Shares' (1981). Within a short time the article met with a considerable echo.[1] His views were subjected to various remarks, extensions and criticisms. The present article is written in the same spirit: to take up the challenge of Weintraub's views and to discuss some of the points which are raised by his essay.

DISTRIBUTION THEORIES AND ECLECTICISM

Disregarding 'old' theories of income shares (Ricardian, Marxian etc., which are anyway partly incorporated in more recent models) we are faced in 'modern' times by three dominant approaches: neoclassical marginal productivity theory, Kaldor-Keynesian types of $I = S$ origins, and Kalecki-type 'degree of monopoly' schools. Is there a need for an eclectic approach? After all, since each of them deals with the same specific item — the wage or profit share — one might expect that a *decision* for the 'right' theory is what is needed rather than an eclectic combination which in any case 'will be interpreted by each side as denying their claim' (Weintraub 1981: 23).

But things are not as simple as that. There are, of course, fundamental differences regarding certain basic assumptions (e.g., neoclassics and Kalecki) which make combinations difficult even if they are regarded as desirable. But when 'Kaldor' and 'Kalecki' (names being used for families of theories) are compared Weintraub rightly stresses that they are complementary rather than competitive. Each is biased in one direction: Kaldor looks at demand-side factors (propensities to consume) while Kalecki is orientated towards factors which have to do with the production side (capital intensity, materials input, etc.) and with social power relations (this is where Marx peeps in).

Why this one-sidedness? And why have there been so few attempts to bring at least these two sides together?[2] Quite apart from the general tendency in economics and other social sciences to let differing theories exist side by side in a multi-paradigm world there is here, I believe, an additional, special factor at work. A theory of distributive shares should show what it is that determines their size and changes in their size. Just as the theory of prices asks where a price settles down and when and by how much it changes in the course of time, so the same question could be asked about the wage (profit) share. But for more than fifty years theoretical research in this field has been dominated by a different kind of question: 'How is the observed constancy of the wage share to be explained?' The relative constancy of the wage share was (and is?) assumed to be established by empirical research. We shall later − when dealing with the *k*-factor − discuss briefly what one has to think about this assumed constancy. Here it suffices to point out that from the days of Douglas and Cobb via Keynes and Kalecki right up to Kaldor and later writers the 'puzzle' of constant shares was a motivating force in distributional research. Behind the question why the wage share is what it is, there was the 'deeper' and dominating question why the share is constant.

This promoted a search for *the* factor which keeps the share near its constant level while other factors whose influence might be acknowledged were relegated to a secondary position. They may cause temporary divergencies, but they are not decisive for the normal trend. Now each of the three approaches I have mentioned found an explanatory structure which could account for the constancy of the wage share. Marginal productivity theory, resting its case on the full employment maximizing behaviour and market clearance assumptions of neoclassic reasoning, found an answer in a special macroeconomic (Cobb-Douglas) production function whose substitution elasticity of one would guarantee constant shares in equilibrium. For Kaldor the Keynesian ex post identity of $I = S$ would − with given but differing marginal consumption propensities of wage and profit earners − fix definite shares in full employment equilibrium whose size would be determined by the equilibrium investment share (determined in turn by growth theoretical analysis). Finally, Kalecki rested his argument on an imperfectly competitive, underemployed world and a markup price assumption where a comparatively stable (or only slowly changing) 'degree of monopoly' keeps the markup and with it the distributional shares at a near-constant level.

Once each of these theories had found its 'anchor-point' for an explanation of constant wage shares there was no strongly felt need to take into account other factors (or theories). But as soon as we begin to question (a) the fact of constant shares and/or (b) the assertion that constant shares are always due to only one and the same factor, and once we want to know more about actual levels and variations, this asceticism is no longer justifiable. Eclecticism, 'deciding that everyone is a "little right" in share theory' (Weintraub 1981: 23), becomes a promising adventure.

THE *k*-FACTOR AND THE CONSTANCY OF THE WAGE SHARE

The 'older' Weintraub (meaning the 'younger' Weintraub as against the 'newer' Weintraub) certainly should have had (and did have) a certain inclination towards a predominantly Kaleckian distribution approach, particularly if the wage share should prove to be fairly constant – because then distribution *and* inflation could both find their main explanation in Weintraub's WCM-theory (wage-cost markup theory) in which price formation through a markup procedure is of central importance – just as in the case of Kalecki.

In Weintraub's formulation we have for GBP (gross business product)[3]

$$Y = PQ = kwN \qquad k > 1 \qquad (1)$$

where Y = nominal GBP, P and Q the corresponding price level and real output, w average nominal wage, and N employment. Then wN is the wage and salary bill (in the business sector) and k = average markup of prices over unit labour costs w/A (where $A = Q/N$ = average labour product). This k of Weintraub is not exactly the same as Kalecki's degree of monopoly, which is a markup on unit *production* labour costs (wages without salaries) plus unit material costs and which 'explains' the share of *wage* labour's income in GBP. But the k of equation (1) is near enough to Kalecki's thinking (under certain simplifying assumptions) to permit Weintraub's calling his WCM equation quite rightly 'close . . . to a Kalecki-type formulation'.[4]

From equation (1) one obtains – for a fairly stable k – simultaneously a meaningful theory of inflation and of distribution. For inflation the reformulation of (1) is

$$P = \frac{kwN}{Q} = k \cdot \frac{w}{A}$$

and for distribution (represented by the wage share, with W standing for the total wage and salary bill)

$$\frac{W}{Y} = \frac{wN}{PQ} = \frac{w/A}{P} = \frac{1}{k} \qquad (2)$$

If k is stable we can then deduce that inflation 'is due' to money wages rising faster than labour productivity and that income distribution remains more or less constant.

It is obvious that these results can only be regarded as 'causal' and meaningful theories if the constancy of k can be taken for granted. This could be assured in either of two ways. One way is to analyse the various elements which influence the multi-dimensional k-factor (as there are: capital intensity, depreciation charges, monopoly power in the narrow sense, market conditions, social power, collective bargaining, etc.) and to find reasons why these elements should tend to remain stable over the cycle and in the longer run or why their movements will neutralize each other. The other, less ambitious way is to look at the available statistics and see whether in fact they yield fairly constant k-values. If this is the case, one can rely provisionally on this observed fact (committing the sin of induction) even if one cannot deduce the reasons for it from an underlying hypothesis.

Kalecki argued his case for a fairly constant (Kaleckian) k by both methods albeit in a somewhat impressionistic way. The Weintraub who argued for a constant k and consequently for a constant wage share relied predominantly on the second method.[5] He pointed out that k in the GBP of the United States exhibits remarkable constancy as compared with the 'wild' dynamics of wages, productivity and prices. Between 1929 and 1974, k showed very small year-to-year changes though it followed a downward trend. From slightly below 2.2 in the years before the Second World War it fell gradually to values around 1.8 in the 1970s (Weintraub 1978: 47).

The question is: how satisfactory is this evidence to rest a theory of income distribution on a *constant k*? That is, do these data suffice for the assumption of constancy? Before going into this question let me supplement Weintraub's US findings by data from Austria.[6] Column 1 in Table 20.1 shows the k-values for Austria (nominal GDP divided by total wages and salaries) for the years 1964 to 1982. The picture is remarkably similar to Weintraub's story. There are comparatively small year-to-year variations but the same gradual downward trend appears as before: from about 2.1 in the mid-1960s to roughly 1.8 by 1980.

The downward trend (in both cases) hardly fits the idea of a constant k (or wage share). But in fact an important reason for this downward trend can be easily found – at least for Austria – in the steady decline in the proportion of self-employed persons and the increase in the proportion of dependent employees (wage and salary earners). Such movements from self-employment into wage status must increase the wage share (reduce the *calculated k*) even if the markup in the wage-paying firms remains unchanged.[7] Column 2 in Table 20.1 represents k-values which have been corrected for this structural change. They are calculated on the basis of a standardized (unchanged) proportion of wage earners in the total labour force. The trend is now almost gone and the k-values fluctuate between 2.25 and 2.05.[8] But even a rapid inspection reveals that these fluctuations are not

Table 20.1 k-values for Austria, 1964–82

	(1) k-values[a]	(2) Corrected[b] k-values, k'	(3) Annual growth rate (%) of real GDP (prices of 1976)
1964	2.14	2.14	6.2
1965	2.11	2.14	3.0
1966	2.09	2.14	5.1
1967	2.05	2.12	2.8
1968	2.08	2.16	4.1
1969	2.08	2.17	5.5
1970	2.13	2.25	6.4
1971	2.06	2.21	5.1
1972	2.06	2.24	6.2
1973	2.01	2.23	4.9
1974	1.96	2.20	3.9
1975	1.86	2.10	− 0.4
1976	1.86	2.11	4.6
1977	1.85	2.12	4.4
1978	1.78	2.05	0.5
1979	1.82	2.10	4.7
1980	1.83	2.12	3.0
1981	1.80	2.09	− 0.1
1982	1.86	2.16	1.1

Notes:
[a] GDP (gross domestic product) divided by the sum of wages and salaries.
[b] Corrected for changes in the labour force structure. See note 7.

purely accidental. Looking at the growth rates of real GDP in column 3 of Table 20.1 and at Figure 20.1 we see that the corrected k-values fluctuate pro-cyclically and, particularly, that in all the years exhibiting strong recessionary tendencies (1967, 1975, 1978, 1981) there is a decisive dip in k-values denoting a drop in profit shares which is reversed when recovery sets in.

In addition to these systematic, market-determined fluctuations in the 'degree of monopoly' we should take note of the fact that even small variations in k are not without significance. With W, the wage and salary bill, taking an important place in both the numerator and denominator of the wage share, a high stability of k is to be expected and it is further fortified by the sociological fact that *big* distributional changes would cause an upheaval in normal times. A numerical illustration can show what is involved. Let us take a GDP of 100 and k-value of 2 involving a wage share of one-half. Consequently $W = 50$ and so is R, gross profits. Taking depreciation (D) at 10 per cent of GDP and denoting net profits R' we get

$$\frac{W}{Y} = \frac{1}{k} = \frac{W}{W + D + R'} = \frac{50}{50 + 10 + 40} = 50\%; \qquad k = 2.$$

Now we assume that a *considerable* redistribution takes place: wages are

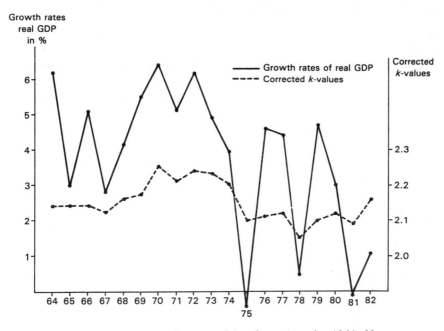

Figure 20.1   Growth rates and corrected k-values, Austria, 1964–82

increased by 10 per cent at the cost of net profits so that net profits fall by 12.5 per cent and the wage–profit ratio (W/R') rises from 1.25 (50/40) to 1.57 (55/35). The wage share changes to

$$\frac{W}{Y} = \frac{55}{55 + 10 + 35} = 55\%; \qquad k = 1.82$$

Thus even such a big change in distribution registers as a fairly small change in k; the question whether one can regard the observed k-values as an example of one of the 'great constants' in economics becomes more than questionable.[9]

Once k itself becomes a variable to be explained it is no longer possible to rest a distribution theory firmly on the degree of monopoly (or the markup). In his article of 1981 Weintraub acknowledges this fact. This leads him towards eclecticism. The article still presents the constant markup case (Weintraub 1981: 17–18), but it is now a *special* case. When it prevails, then the demand factors can indeed be neglected as far as the distribution side is concerned. Demand only determines (in Keynesian fashion) the *level* of production and employment. Distribution is completely determined by given supply side factors: labour unit costs, markups and the power relations behind them.[10] But once the markup is variable and not independent of the state of production and markets the demand side has to be brought in. This leads to Weintraub's *general* case.

THE 'NEW' WEINTRAUB AND THE STRATEGIC FACTORS

In macroeconomic theories definitions and definitional equations though being tautologically 'true' can play an important part. By proper arrangement of 'necessary' relations between different elements (as defined) research can be helped to sort out strategic factors for theoretical explanation. The equation of exchange in the Fisherian or Cambridge formulation or the $I = S$ formulation of Keynesian vintage are cases in point. In macroeconomic distribution theory such formulations always had and have their place, and Weintraub has often proved to be a master in the apt handling and transformation of such 'truisms'. I am not so sure, however, whether he has chosen the most promising roads in his eclectic theory.

We know what the 'strategic' elements are in the *ruling* distribution paradigms. In neoclassical equilibrium theory with factor supplies (or supply schedules) given marginal productivities take the central place. In Kaldorian theory, with full employment assumed, investment (I, exogenously given or derived from growth equilibrium) together with the consumption propensities of wage and profit earners defines the distribution. And in Kalecki's case the markup in an imperfectly competitive world running below capacity determines the distributional equilibrium irrespective of the volume of production.

In Weintraub's case – as behoves an eclectic theory – all these elements appear but they do so in a partly disguised form. Stressing that a full distribution theory must pay attention to 'both blades of the scissors' Weintraub reshapes the demand and the supply aspects of the distribution problem. Let us take the supply side first. Starting with the Kaleckian-type markup theory we have the previously derived equation (2).

$$\frac{W}{Y} = \frac{w/A}{P} = \frac{1}{k} \tag{2'}$$

with A (average labour productivity) and k (markup) as typical supply side elements. This formulation is changed by Weintraub in such a way (Weintraub 1981: 13) that a link with neoclassical theory is established.

In neoclassical theory the real wage in every firm will equal the marginal product which we denote by M. We have, therefore, in a firm under full competitive equilibrium

$$\frac{w}{P} = M \tag{3}$$

If monopoly elements are present the real wage will lie below the marginal product

$$\frac{w}{P} = nM, \text{ with } 0 < n < 1 \tag{4}$$

Aggregating over all firms and substituting equation (4) in equation (2) we obtain

$$\frac{W}{Y} = \frac{nM}{A} \left(= \frac{1}{k} \right)$$ (5)

Now k as the 'degree of monopoly' is replaced by n, with smaller values of n denoting a higher degree of monopoly. We shall return to this reformulation later on.

On the demand side Weintraub diverges from Kaldor's well-known split of saving (or consumption) behaviour by income types [11] and introduces the 'consumption-to-wage ratio' a [12] which (in analogy to the supply side formulation $Y = kwN$) links total consumption to wage earnings

$$C = awN$$ (6)

where C = total consumption expenditure. What determines the size of a? By splitting up consumption we get (Weintraub 1981: 15)

$$C = c_w wN + c_r \lambda R + \Theta = awN$$ (7)

where c_w, c_r = average consumption propensities out of wages and distributed profits respectively, λ = corporate payout ratios, and Θ = transfer incomes (which are fully used for consumption). It follows that

$$a = c_w + c_r \lambda R' + \Theta'$$ (8)

where $R' = R/W$ and $\Theta' = \Theta/W$.

Without going further into various and interesting details of Weintraub's article we have here the bare bones of what he regards as the strategic elements for distributional equilibrium. Thinking in terms of a 'causal chain' running from investment over changing profits and employment to variations in consumption and the 'degree of monopoly' he comes to the conclusion that 'the eclectic thesis has isolated I, a, n, and A as the proper items for theoretical focus' (Weintraub 1981: 23).

But has it? One can, of course, quite easily quarrel about what is 'proper'. But I have serious doubts whether the introduction of n and a as strategic elements is an improvement over the more traditional formulations. Indeed it is difficult to see why they were introduced. My suspicion is that they were chosen because they can serve as indicators of *limiting* cases which have played an important (*too* important!) role in distribution theory: the perfect competition model and what Weintraub calls the K-K-R (Kalecki-Kaldor-Robinson) or the 'all and nothing' model, i.e. the classical-Kaleckian model where workers only consume and capitalists only save (invest). For the former case we have $n = 1$, for the latter case $a = 1$. [13] But since both cases are extreme theoretical abstractions these 'standardizations' seem to me to be of little value.

When we evaluate the elements from the point of view of economic interpretation (this section) and the problem of relevant factors in disequilibrium situations (to be dealt with in the following section) one begins to doubt whether Weintraub's changes represent an improvement. The replacement of k by n could be seen as an advantage if one really believes that the model of perfect equilibrium *with all its assumptions* can serve as a useful and relevant point of departure. Then the idea of full equality between real wages and marginal productivity (with $n = 1$) has a clear meaning and deviations from it would be an appropriate measuring rod for 'degrees of monopoly'. But if one doubts the possibilities of perfect competition and maximizing behaviour in the fundamentally oligopolistic environment of modern capitalism, if one looks for a more adequate post-Keynesian price theory, then the factor k – with all its weaknesses and ambiguities – is probably a better guide to fruitful research than n because it focuses attention on markup influences rather than on marginal cost conformity.[14]

But the real question arises in connection with the factor a. It is, of course, no problem to extract a from statistics (C/W) and to follow its course. It is also easy to establish a 'truistic' relation between distribution and a, for the wage share can be written (Weintraub, 1981, p. 15) as

$$\frac{W}{Y} = \frac{c}{a} \qquad (9)$$

since $a = C/W$ and $C = cY$, where $c =$ average overall propensity to consume.

But can a be accepted as a meaningful parameter? Logical and behavioural objections arise. As Dixon (1982a) points out quite correctly a cannot 'explain' distribution because it itself is a function of distribution.[15] As equation (8) shows a is a function of R' (R/W) which is a distributional variable. Any change in distribution leads via the change in R/W to a change in a and consumption just in the same way as depicted by Kaldor. But the Kaldorian formula has the theoretical advantage of picking out the consumption propensities as sectorial *behavioural* factors which can be studied in a meaningful sense while no such basic meaning can be attached to a. In fact, if Weintraub had stuck to his consumption equation (7) he would have singled out as his strategic elements on the demand side c_w, c_r, λ, and Θ. This would have eased economic interpretation and would have enhanced the eclectic links of his approach. Thus c_w and c_r form the bridge to Kaldor's theory, λ links up with the pioneer macroeconomic distribution theory of Boulding (1950) where the dividend policy of corporate business plays a decisive role, and Θ can be seen as a Keynesian policy element with redistribution affecting distribution and consumption *uno actu*.

DISEQUILIBRIUM: WHAT GIVES WAY?

The list of strategic elements used by or derived from Weintraub's eclectic theory can act as a guide to research; it also indicates what distribution will be if these (interdependent) factors are 'in equilibrium'. What happens when equilibrium is disturbed? Weintraub touches this point only perfunctorily (1981: 20–1). When demand and supply side factors are not consistent the solution is 'indeterminate': either the supply side and monopoly (k) determine the picture with distribution remaining unchanged and demand being forced to adjust (the Kalecki case), or demand predominates and markups and distribution change (the Kaldor case), or anything between these two limits may happen.

Here, of course, lies the real challenge of Weintraub's article for research. If we want to say something about actual variations in income shares we must at least try to get beyond equilibrium formulations, for 'the economist's refuge for a priori futility carries "indeterminate" as the password' (1981: 21). The following remarks are meant as an indication of what might be done.

First, we should be aware that the meaning of 'equilibrium' and 'disequilibrium' – always a precarious one – is particularly shaky when we deal with income distribution. While a macroeconomic full employment equilibrium can easily be reconciled with the idea of mutually consistent and stable desires in the fields of production, consumption, and markets, there can be no such 'peaceful' stability in the distribution field. Eclectic theory in particular must take into account that *discontent* over shares belongs to the essence of capitalist (if not any) societies. As Weintraub properly states: 'Share theory lays bare the Ricardo-Marx-Sraffa judgement of *conflict* over income shares, despite the lulling marginal productivity harmonies by the many reincarnated J. B. Clarks' (1981: 23).

In a way, then, 'disequilibrium' in a wider sense is an almost 'natural' state in the distribution sphere. Even if we have an equilibrium situation as far as the parameters of the theoretical frame are concerned, it will always be a precarious balance of social and economic forces with each side on the look-out for achieving (aggressively) or preventing (on the defence) changes in the situation. Since in normal times the socioeconomic distribution of power is unlikely to undergo dramatic changes these fluctuations in shares around the 'equilibrium' value will, however, be fairly limited.

When this aspect is considered the variable calling for special attention is obviously the degree of monopoly (markup) represented by k. Employers who want to increase their share will try to enforce a higher markup, while workers will tend to demand higher wages hoping that prices will stay put, which would result in a decline of k. Whether and when such attempts towards changing the 'equilibrium' distribution can be successful in view of countervailing power depends on the surrounding circumstances. Post-Keynesian theorizing, having left the comforting shelter of general equilibrium with its nice solutions, cannot provide easy general answers. In the same way as Keynes had to conclude that changes in money wages can have different effects on employment depending on the market situation at home and abroad, on monetary policy, etc., we must realise that there are several scenarios for distributional conflicts. Whether and for how long k can be increased through deliberate action on the part of employers will obviously depend on the possibilities of increasing prices without heavy sales losses and on the lags in wage demands in the face of rising prices and profits. Similarly, money wage advances on top of productivity changes will only change distribution if employers cannot uphold k because a restrictive monetary policy or competitive markets prevent them from shifting the higher labour costs onto prices. But even in that case, if employers insist on their markup and relative position they might stick to their k and raise prices proportionately to wages. The result will then be an unchanged distribution combined with lower output and employment. [16]

This interplay between distributional attempts and conditions in goods and factor markets plays a major explanatory role in Phelps Brown's interpretation of long-term distributional variations round the trend. He distinguishes between 'vigorous' and 'restrained' unions in the factor markets and between 'soft' and 'hard' market environments in the sphere of goods. When vigorous unions coincide with hard market environments where price rises cannot be easily achieved (e.g., in recession or on competitive foreign markets) the wage share rises somewhat, while the opposite is true when restrained unions and a soft market environment enable employers to raise k. The other two combinations – restrained unions plus hard markets and vigorous unions plus soft markets – will leave distribution at its 'equilibrium' level though the two cases will have quite different repercussions on the course of inflation. [17]

As soon as we leave the limited field of variations of distribution around the 'equilibrium' caused by the endogenous conflict of interests the set of possible 'scenarios' increases considerably. The source of disequilibrium and the concomitant circumstances become relevant. When an exogenous shock upsets the 'equilibrium' and a new one has to be found, *all* the strategic elements of the distributional puzzle may come into play. Although in the last resort *any* change in distribution will – for definitional reasons $(W/Y = 1/k)$ – be mirrored in k, it will not necessarily be the markup as such which is *directly* involved. Other elements may have to diverge from their intended course and their movements will determine the ultimate effects on distribution and k. The decisive *and situationally conditioned* question to be answered in 'true' disequilibrium situations is therefore: What stays put and what has to give way? Or, in the words of Weintraub (1981: 23), we must look for the 'mover and shaker', the volatile elements. The following concluding remarks are meant to give an indication of possible processes which could be relevant. They are only meant as illustrations and are neither exhaustive nor do they go into great detail.

Let us start with some sort of distributional 'equilibrium', which gets disturbed by a desire of entrepreneurs to increase investment. [18] When we try to sketch various scenarios we have to distinguish whether the economy works at or near full employment or whether there is widespread underemployment and unused capacity. Further, we must take into account whether the monetary policy under which the adjustment process takes place is accommodating or restrictive. In the first four of the following scenarios we assume full employment and an accommodating monetary policy. These assumptions are later relaxed.

1 The increased investment expenditure financed with additional credit leads to increased pressure on markets and to a decumulation of inventories. This favourable market situation induces firms to increase their markup and prices rise. If trade unions do not react quickly and fully wages will lag behind. Real investment and k have increased; distribution shifts towards profits as a consequence of the increased investment expenditures. This is more or less the Kaldorian case, but also fits neoclassical reasoning if the price rises are interpreted as demand-determined and a wage lag is accepted.

2 An alternative scenario can be based on Eichner's megacorp theory (1976). Here oligopolistic firms have some leeway in their markup. It is increased in advance of an investment expansion to provide the necessary internal finance.[19] With wages passive or lagging, k will again rise and distribution will change to profits, but this time in *advance* of investment. The statistical picture could also be given another interpretation: a rising profit share leads to investment.

3 Instead of securing the necessary internal finance through an increased markup the firms can also reduce the proportion of profits paid out in dividends. Instead of an increase in k we get an increase in λ. Prices, wages and distribution remain unchanged; the rise in real investment is not financed out of workers' forced savings but out of additional capitalists' savings ('enforced' through reduced dividends). This picture would fit Boulding's approach.

4 When we assume that the trade unions are strong and share conscious they will try to defend the traditional wage share. The wage lag disappears. Any rise in prices is immediately followed by proportional rises in wages: k $(= PA/w)$ becomes a constant. Distribution does not change while prices and wages rise in an inflationary spiral. What has to give way are the intended changes in *real* investment.

5 If the monetary policy is not fully accommodating the attempts to shift the distribution via a higher k (cases 1 and 2) and higher prices will come up against the limits of money and credit. If a certain price rise can be effected production will go down and unemployment will rise. The reduction in quantities demanded and an upward tendency of interest rates might put a break on I and k so that the change in distribution may stay within narrow bounds. In case 3 the monetary policy is irrelevant. In case 4 the steady upward pressure on wages and prices in the fight for and against a changed k will – under a restrictive monetary policy – lead to stagflation: a certain amount of inflation will be accompanied by rising unemployment.

6 If we finally abandon the assumption of full employment in the initial situation a new dimension is added. Higher intended investment

expenditure (and real investment) is no longer dependent on redistribution within a given real income but can also be realized through an expansion of income. Depending on leads and lags each of the foregoing cases may still ensue but we can now also have a successful increase in I with all the strategic distributional variables (c_r, c_w, λ, Θ, n) and with distribution itself remaining unchanged. This fits both the pure Keynesian case with I determining Y and distribution being neglected (and neglectable), or the case of Kalecki and Preiser where socio-economic forces (case 4) keep distribution stable while I and Y fluctuate in an oligopolistic world of underutilized capacities. One factor that becomes important with output variations is average labour productivity (A). If prices and (hourly) wages remain fixed because of short-term rigidities or because of the depressed market situation, the course of A will be the decisive distributional influence. Depending whether – with rising output – A falls (the neoclassical case and Keynes's original position), stays stable (Kalecki), or rises (Verdoorn's Law) we shall have a rising, stable, or falling wage share.

It will be obvious that this enumeration of adjustment scenarios following a disturbance of 'equilibrium' is anything but exhaustive. Not only could one find other plausible and realistic 'stories'; one also obtains further cases by combining the above 'pure' processes so that one may get adjustments in I, k, λ, A, and Θ which are partly offsetting. One might also speculate whether the consumption propensities are necessarily constants without longer-term trends.

All that was intended was to show with the aid of simple illustrations that an eclectic distribution theory à la Weintraub can do more than just point out the limits in disequilibrium situations. What it *cannot* do is to give simple answers which will hold without respect to concrete situations and circumstances; but that is true of all disequilibrium theory. It is this what makes it so 'sloppy' compared with pure equilibrium theory.

NOTES

1 See, for instance, Dixon (1982a; 1982b), Brosnan (1983), Ferri (1983), Hedlund (1983) and Watanabe (1982–83).
2 An early attempt towards a 'marriage' of Kaldor and Kalecki with interesting parallels and differences *vis-à-vis* Weintraub's approach was performed by Erich Preiser (1961). More recently Jan Pen (1981) has advocated an eclectic approach bridging the gap between neoclassical and post-Keynesian approaches by taking a fairly broad view of neoclassical reasoning i.e., abandoning strict maximizing (marginal productivity) decision rules but permitting *some* elasticity of demand for labour even in less-than-full employment situations. Factor scarcities and effective demand are then both assigned some role with neoclassical or post-Keynesian (Kaldor-Kaleckian) elements in the foreground depending on the cyclical and general economic situation.
3 For this and the immediately following paragraphs see Weintraub (1978), pp. 44 ff. and Ch. 11.

4 See Weintraub (1981), p. 12.

5 See Weintraub (1978) pp. 46–56. 'Practically, k changes very little year-to-year or over the long run' (p. 46); 'Compared to the other "great ratios" of economics, k (or its reciprocal) has been most nearly constant' (p. 47).

6 Lack of suitable data makes it necessary to calculate k for Austria for gross domestic product (GDP) instead of GBP in Weintraub's case.

7 Let GDP be produced by a labour force L. Some of these work as employees in firms (N) and are wage and salary earners; others (N') produce for the market on their own. The proportion of employees in the total labour force is denoted by α. We thus have

$$L = N + N'$$
$$N = \alpha L$$

Using the same symbols as before we can calculate k from macro-statistics

$$k = \frac{PQ}{wN} = \frac{PQ}{w\alpha L}$$

With unchanged output, prices and wages a shift from self-employed to wage earners (an increase in α) reduces k and increases the wage share. The corrected k-value in Table 20.1 (k') has been obtained by multiplying the original k by α/α' where α are the current values of the N-share and α' is the proportion of employees in 1964. We thus obtain

$$k' = k \cdot \frac{\alpha}{\alpha'} = \frac{PQ}{w\alpha L} \cdot \frac{\alpha}{\alpha'} = \frac{PQ}{w\alpha' L}$$

i.e., k' is standardized for all years on the basis of the 1964 proportion of wage and salary earners in the total labour force.

8 A slight trend remains. The average value of k drops from 2.17 for the period 1964–72 to 2.13 in 1973–82. This adds to the doubts about k-constancy which are mentioned below.

9 See on this Rothschild (1957).

10 Similar results are derived – though by different assumptions and routes – by Preiser (1961) and Schneider (1957). For Kaldor the problem looks different: production is fixed at the full employment level so that only the demand side (consumption propensities) determines the equilibrium distribution once the level of investment is given.

11 The formulation being

$$\frac{R}{Y} = \frac{1}{s_r - s_w} \cdot \left(\frac{I}{Y} - s_w \right)$$

where R = profits and s_r, s_w are the marginal and average propensities to save out of profits and wages respectively.

12 This appeared as α in Weintraub (1978), pp. 50–1.

13 But though the K-K-R case involves $a = 1$ the reverse is not true. A value of 1 for a also arises when workers' savings are exactly balanced by capitalist consumption.

14 If one *does* want to establish a relevant (eclectic) link to neoclassical distribution theory it can probably best be achieved by accepting *some* consequences of neoclassical models in a somewhat watered-down fashion, in particular by permitting some influence for factor scarcities and demand elasticities in factor markets (see Pen 1981). This does not require the introduction of marginal productivity as a benchmark.

15 This fact is slided over by Weintraub (1981) when on p. 16 he writes $a = a(R)$ instead of $a = a(R')$.

In the articles following Weintraub only Ferri (1983) and Hedlund (1983) try to utilize *a*. The fruitfulness of this attempt remains doubtful. One advantage seems to be that one can work with an overall Keynesian *average* propensity to consume – see equation (9). But this is achieved by hiding the differential propensities in the distribution-determined *a*.

16 Since we have $PQ = kwN$ a restrictive monetary policy will keep $PQ = \bar{Y}$ constant. With *k* also kept constant (by price setting behaviour) *P* will rise proportionately with *w*; *Q* and *N* will adjust downwards to $\bar{Y}$.

17 See Phelps Brown (1968), Ch. 2.

18 Alternatively, there could be an increase in other (exogenous) non-consumption demand like government spending or export demand. As far as the latter is concerned it must be noted that this article deals (like Weintraub's exposition) with a closed economy. When we allow for external transactions new variables enter and the analysis must be expanded. For a modification of Weintraub's model in this direction see Brosnan (1983).

19 Weintraub (1981: 14) asks why such firms did not increase their *k* before, if this opportunity for raising profits is available. I am not sure whether this objection is fully tenable. Price-setting is not the same thing as profit-maximizing. Though *high* profits remain the decisive target, the decision process is based on (historical) habit, aspiration levels, and X-efficiency. The latter two can vary when investment plans come up.

REFERENCES

Boulding, Kenneth E. (1950) *A Reconstruction of Economics*. New York: John Wiley.

Brosnan, Peter (1983) 'The Wage Share in an Open Economy', *Journal of Post Keynesian Economics*, Fall, 6, 1, pp. 65–72.

Dixon, Robert, (1982a) 'Relative Shares: A Comment', *Journal of Post Keynesian Economics*, Fall, 5, 1, pp. 120–4.

—— (1982b) 'The Rate of Exploitation and the Wage-Share as Weighted Sums of Sectoral Measures', *Australian Economic Papers*, December, pp. 421–4.

Eichner, A. S. (1976) *The Megacorp and Oligopoly. Micro Foundations of Macro Dynamics*, Cambridge: Cambridge University Press.

Ferri, Piero (1983) 'The Consumption-Wage Gap', *Journal of Post Keynesian Economics*, Summer, 5, 4, pp. 579–89.

Hedlund, Jeffrey D. (1983) 'Distribution Theory Revisited: An Empirical Examination of the Weintraub Synthesis', *Journal of Post Keynesian Economics*, Fall, 6, 1, pp. 73–81.

Pen, Jan (1981) 'On Eclecticism, or We Are (Almost) All Neo-Classical Neo-Keynesians Now', *De Economist*, 129, 1, pp. 127–50.

Phelps Brown, E. H. (1968) *Pay and Profits*, Manchester: Manchester University Press.

Preiser, Erich (1961, 3rd edn 1970) *Wachstum und Einkommensverteilung*, Heidelberg: Carl Winter Universitätsverlag.

Rothschild, Kurt W. (1957) 'Der Lohnanteil am Gesamteinkommen', *Weltwirtschaftliches Archiv*, 78, 2, pp. 157–202.

Schneider, Erich (1957) 'Einkommen und Einkommensverteilung in der makroökonomischen Theorie', *L'Industria*, April–June, pp. 3–15.

Watanabe, Ken-ichi (1982–3) 'An Adaptation of Weintraub's Model', *Journal of Post Keynesian Economics*, Winter, 5, 2, pp. 228–44.

Weintraub, Sidney (1978) *Capitalism's Inflation and Unemployment Crisis: Beyond Monetarism and Keynesianism*, Reading, MA: Addison-Wesley.

Weintraub, Sidney (1979) 'Generalizing Kalecki and Simplifying Macroeconomics', *Journal of Post Keynesian Economics*, Spring, 1, 3, pp. 101–6.

—— (1981) 'An Eclectic Theory of Income Shares', *Journal of Post Keynesian Economics*, Fall, 4, 1, pp. 10–24.

21 Inequality: is income distribution an adequate measure?

INTRODUCTION

Hand in hand with the growing refinement and sophistication in the methods used in economic analysis there is an increasing uneasiness about the relevance and appropriateness of traditional economic theory. The criticisms come from different angles. There is, for instance, the warning that economics in its search for deterministic, closed models has taken the wrong roads of abstraction and can contribute little towards explaining the causes and courses of actual economic events.[1] Another important criticism points out that traditional economic theory bypasses some of the most important socio-economic issues, partly because of theoretical one-sidedness, partly because ideological blinkers narrow the view.[2]

These criticisms do not just refer to some side-issues of economic theory; they touch its very core. Growth theory, the favourite child of economic analysis in the 1950s and early 1960s, has come under specially heavy attack. The problems of the developing countries had revealed the inadequacy of the purely economic framework for explaining differences in growth rates, and the pressing problems of pollution and environmental quality showed up the limited relevance of growth definitions and growth measures in relation to the needs and aspirations of the population.[3]

Next to growth of income the distribution of income is one of the most important fields in economic theory as far as human aspirations and human welfare is concerned.[4] Here, it seems to me, a critical look at traditional ways is just as necessary as in the field of growth theory. To some extent there has already taken place some fruitful rethinking, particularly in the dominant sphere of income distribution by factor shares. The artificial and narrow assumptions of the neoclassical marginal productivity theory – still ruling the field almost undisturbed some twenty years ago[5] – have come under heavy attack for their neglect of important influences in the process of factor price determination. The criticism has partly taken the form of offering plausible alternative economic models which can do without marginal productivities (Kalecki 1954; Kaldor 1955; Sraffa 1960), partly it has added realism by leaving the artificial confines of 'pure' economic theory and stressing the force of sociological and institutional influences. In this latter direction Jean Marchal has played a pioneering part (Marchal and Lecaillon 1958).

I do not intend to deal with these problems of factor shares, but want to throw up some questions and suggestions with regard to the use of personal income distribution (or income distribution by households) as a measure of inequality. The remarks will not be concerned with the adequacy or inadequacy of *theories* of personal income distribution. This side of the problem can be largely neglected, because there are so few genuine theories in this field. What we have are a few ingenious, but certainly incomplete attempts which either regard existing distributions as empirical 'laws' (Pareto 1897; Gini 1936), or as the outcome of certain plausible stochastic processes (Gibrat 1931; Champernowne 1953), or as the result of the combined influence of a few decisive factors like home environment, talent, schooling and hierarchical position (Lydall 1968). What we would need in this context is a careful elaboration of the existing theoretical beginnings, and a search for new explanatory roads, which should certainly include a large share of sociological and institutional factors.

My remarks have a more modest aim. I want to point out that the usual economists' and statisticians' analysis of the shapes of actual income distributions and of their changes does not suffice to give full information on inequality and inequality trends, though the latter are usually discussed in the light of those statistics. Herein lies the parallel to the present criticism of growth percentages, where it is pointed out that they do not provide − by themselves − the hoped-for index of economic progress and economic welfare.

SHORTCOMINGS OF INCOME DATA AND CONCENTRATION MEASURES

Inequality and particularly inequality in living standards is an important social and political problem. Economists and other social scientists should be able to sift and interpret material which has some bearing on this question. The point is whether the concentration on measuring (by various methods) the shape and development of income distribution has been sufficient to fulfil this task.

Let us first consider the fact that a large number of income analysts believe to have discovered a levelling in the distribution of personal incomes in many advanced industrial countries. Somewhat dramatically A. F. Burns announced more than twenty years ago that the levelling of American incomes since the 1930s has been 'one of the great revolutions in history' (Burns 1951: 3). Now, if such a long-term, 'revolutionary' trend has been going on in the USA and other developed countries, we should expect that

– if levelling means more equality – this should show up in a much greater awareness of equality among the populations, and in a decline of tensions arising from inequality. To find out whether such a change has taken place (apart from the abolition of unemployment!) would be a very difficult research assignment indeed. But we can certainly say that there is no sign that feelings about inequality have declined continuously and in a 'revolutionary' manner. The question of one's relative income is still a widely discussed topic in spite of much higher absolute standards, strikes show no tendency to disappear, and the structure and incidence of taxation remains a much-debated issue.

The fact that feelings about inequality remain strong in spite of the alleged tendency towards a more egalitarian income distribution[6] can have different causes. To begin with there is the possibility that the levelling tendency which most economists have deduced from published data is more apparent than real because of the inherent weaknesses of official income statistics. There are considerable differences between tax return data and actual incomes, partly dependent on the definition of income adopted. Without going into detail one may point out such factors as the treatment of capital gains and undistributed profits, the transformation of personal expenses into business expenses, the changing estimates of depreciation, losses and imputed income, the tax-evading income arrangements within families, foundations and trusts, etc.

All these methods of tax avoidance are more accessible to higher and non-wage incomes than to the lower income groups. This leads to a continuous underassessment of the incomes of persons in the higher income brackets. Moreover, this bias is growing. The advancing progressive taxation strengthens the incentive to keep income off individual tax returns: we have a growing erosion of the tax base, particularly among the higher income groups. The consideration of these influences has led to estimates which cast doubt on the assertion that there has been a distinct and continuous levelling in the income distribution.[7]

Leaving aside the possibility of 'wrong' data there is still room for divergencies between what economists say about changes in the degree of income inequality and what people 'feel' about it. There is no single, 'authorized' measure for characterizing the degree of income inequality. Stark (1972: 41) mentions fifteen well-known measures of income dispersion. Now, if the levelling tendency over the years were very strong, probably all the measures would indicate a long-term levelling trend. But there is no such very strong tendency; and – as Stark shows for the British data – not all measures point all the time in the same (levelling) direction.

The widespread agreement about levelling tendencies rests partly on the favoured usage of accepting the income share going to the top 5 per cent of income receivers as a good measure of income concentration. This share has – at least as far as published statistics go – declined significantly. This has also brought down the Gini concentration coefficient. But there is no guarantee that events affecting mainly the top income receivers are the socio-political decisive aspect of inequality assessment.[8]

There is, however, a more fundamental consideration which affects *all* the usual measures of income concentration. All of them – be it a percentile analysis, Gini's concentration ratio, indicators of dispersion, of curtosis, etc. – try to work out an absolute statistical index which summarizes in one way or other the divergence of actual income distributions from an 'ideal' or 'optimal' distribution. (Normally the standard is absolute equality of incomes.) By comparing such indices over time conclusions are drawn about changes in inequality. But what one really measures describes the chosen index, and not necessarily the socially relevant phenomenon of income equality. In times of rapid changes in average income levels and in income structures (over the whole range) probably no uniformly designed statistical measure will all the time catch exactly those aspects of distributional change that seem important to certain groups of the population or to policy-orientated welfare analysts.

Even if we take income distribution as the sole indicator of inequality it would, therefore, be necessary to devise *socially* orientated measures, which can contribute to a politically relevant discussion about changes in inequality. Since ideas about equality and inequality differ among persons and classes, a multitude of such measures are imaginable and desirable. There would be room for choice among various *socio-political* indices, each laying stress on particular aspects of the distribution problem, just as in the case of the existing *statistical* measures. The traditional statistical measures would, of course, not become obsolete: they would provide the basic information about changes in distributional patterns without, however, deciding whether this has meant a change in 'inequality'. Thus, a given shift of incomes from the eighth to the seventh, and from the second to the third percentile of income receivers would be reflected in different, but well-defined ways in the various statistical indices. The 'social' indices would then show how such a shift is considered – with regard to the inequality problem – by different reference groups among the politicians and the population.

To be a bit more concrete I want to refer to a proposal made by Thomas Stark in a study on income distribution in Great Britain.[9] He introduces a measure of inequality based on the ideas about 'poor' and 'wealthy' as expressed in the welfare and taxation system of the nation. This index can take account of changing attitudes about inequality over time. The calculation of this 'high/low income inequality index', as Stark calls it, is very simple. He adopts for his base year (1949) a definition of low and high incomes for different family sizes[10] and then calculates the proportion of income units (families) falling into these two groups. The addition of the two percentages gives his 'inequality index', which is thus insensitive to distributional regrouping in the in-between range. In comparisons over time inequality increases when the proportion of low plus high income units increases, and vice versa.

The decisive point, however, is that over time the question of what constitutes 'low' and 'high' incomes props up and has to be (subjectively) decided. Stark, for instance, advances two solutions. In one estimate ('average income method') he raises the low and high income limits in subsequent years by the same percentage as per capita incomes have gone up. In another estimate ('trend method') he extends the range of lower incomes in later years by taking into account the fact that assistance payments had risen faster than per capita incomes. In this way he wants to capture the changed 'national' attitude towards poverty and an equitable distribution.

In Table 21.1 I reproduce some of Stark's calculations for the income distributions in the years 1949, 1954, 1959 and 1963. The first three indices are examples of objective, statistical indices. It can be seen that their development does not always point in the same direction. But they all show a shift towards greater equality between 1959 and 1963. This is not true for the two 'subjective' indices in the last two columns. The de-concentration of the income distribution had not been sufficient to reduce the proportion of those who remained in the low income brackets when the rising income level and − in the last column − rising aspirations with regard to equality standards are taken into account. It is not suggested that Stark's specific proposal is necessarily the best or the only possible one. But something on these lines seems justified if measurements of income distribution are not only meant for formal discussions of inequality, but also as an instrument for discussing the social and dynamic aspects of the problem.

Table 21.1 Values of different measures of inequality for changes in the distribution of British incomes, 1949−63

	Relative mean difference	Gini concentration ratio	Gibrat coefficient (log-normal coefficient)	High/low income inequality index	
				Average income method	Trend method
1949	0.561	38.73	85.983	19.24	19.24
1954	0.561	39.21	95.600	22.57	22.85
1959	0.549	38.99	100.974	16.54	18.40
1963	0.547	38.31	100.550	17.24	21.65

Note: For all indices a higher value implies a less equal distribution. The distribution under consideration refers to families. The official data were adjusted to cut out double-countings and other errors. (The data refer to Stark's type 1 distribution.)
Source: Stark (1972), pp. 47, 48, 143.

SUBSISTENCE AND EXCESS INCOME

The discussion so far has pointed out the ambiguity and weaknesses in the statistical treatment of income distribution data where questions of inequality and its trend are concerned. The rest of this essay will indicate that the normal income statistics by themselves are an insufficient basis for the inequality discussion under present-day conditions in developed countries.

In his once famous book on the inequality of incomes Dalton said that such inequalities become relevant when 'the less urgent needs of the rich are satisfied, while the more urgent needs of the poor are left unsatisfied. The rich are more than amply fed, while the poor go hungry' (Dalton 1929: 10). The fact that people could not satisfy their most urgent needs while others could go beyond them was certainly the most pressing problem in Europe in those days and still is in the major part of the world. Every slight redistribution of incomes which permits the needy to cover a little bit more of their most pressing natural requirements must – under these circumstances – be regarded as a reduction in inequality in a stark and obvious sense.

The situation becomes less clear-cut once technical progress, capital accumulation and social policy (including employment policy) permit society to cover the most urgent needs of the major part of the population. Disregarding the pockets of poverty, which persist even in the most advanced industrial nations, a rigid application of Dalton's dictum to these countries would result in the surprising conclusion that income inequalities have ceased to be a relevant problem. But this is – socially and politically – obvious nonsense. Rather, it follows that inequality acquires different meanings in different stages of development. The fact that people's minimum requirements are more or less generally covered means that the problem of inequality in developed 'welfare states' starts to become relevant at a different level. The differences in the economic status of households become interesting where the command over goods beyond the 'survival needs' is concerned. This means that for measurements of inequality and its changes it might be better not to look at the distribution of total incomes but rather at the distribution of 'excess income' i.e. of that income which remains disposable after the survival requirements have been covered.

For those who regard this proposal as abstruse let me add two remarks. First, all discussions of inequality contain conventional elements which decide where the line is to be drawn between things that should be included or excluded. If we include free goods (sunshine), public goods and merit goods (parks, schools), we reach a higher degree of equality than if we regard market incomes only. One important question is, which goods are normally considered as relevant or irrelevant in public discussions about inequality. The course of this inequality is then worth studying. In wealthy societies minimum living requirements tend increasingly to be regarded as the basis on which the different material standards of life are built; they are not part of these differences.

The second point is that the proposed idea has its roots in classical and socialist thinking where the subsistence minimum (physical or traditional) was often regarded as the 'necessary' basic income for maintaining the population (labour force) intact. Just as in the case of property income, where income and its distribution are measured on a net basis, i.e. after deduction of maintenance and depreciation costs, we can quite meaningfully speak of a net income of persons. It covers the 'excess income' which remains available after the maintenance costs have been met.

To show the distributional picture is influenced by such a modification I want to present a simple concrete example. Its data are taken from a sample survey of household expenditures in Austrian towns (with a population of more than 2000) in 1964. The investigation unit was the household and information was only obtained about *expenditure* in the reference year; the level of *income* was not asked for (because there were doubts, whether reliable answers would be obtained). To cut out the problems of different household sizes with their different 'minimum requirements', I have chosen for my illustration a subgroup of all households, viz. households with two grown-ups and one child below the age of fourteen.

Table 21.2 presents the distribution of these households by expenditure classes as given by the survey.[11] In Table 21.3 'modified expenditures' have been calculated for all households. This was done by subtracting uniformly from each household's expenditure that sum (1,406.09 AS[12]), which the average household in the lowest expenditure class (monthly expenditure below 2,000 AS) spent on food, rent, heating and lighting, and clothing

Table 21.2 Sample distribution of three-person-households[a] by expenditure classes in Austrian towns, 1964 (monthly averages, Austrian shillings)

Expenditure class (AS)	Number of households	Average expenditure per household (AS)	Total expenditure per class (AS)	Cumulative percentage of households (%)	Cumulative percentage of total expenditure (%)
Under 2,000	28	1,678.08	46,986.24	3.09	0.98
2,000–2,999	139	2,578.76	358,447.64	18.41	8.44
3,000–3,999	197	3,498.88	689,279.36	40.13	22.80
4,000–4,999	188	4,482.28	842,668.64	60.86	40.35
5,000–5,999	118	5,480.28	646,673.04	73.87	53.82
6,000–6,999	80	6,509.18	520,734.40	82.69	64.66
7,000–7,999	49	7,433.41	364,237.09	88.09	72.25
8,000 and over	108	12,338.00	1,332,504.00	100.00	100.00

Note:
[a] 2 adults, 1 child under 14.
Source: Österreichisches Statistisches Zentralamt, *Der Verbrauch der städtischen und bäuerlichen Bevölkerung Österreichs*, Vienna 1966, p. 70, and calculations by the author.

Table 21.3 Distribution of the households from Table 21.2 on the basis of modified expenditure estimates[a] (monthly averages, Austrian shillings)

Expenditure class (total expenditure) (AS)	Number of households	Modified Expenditure Average per household (AS)	Total per class (AS)	Cumulative percentage of households (%)	Cumulative percentage of total modified expenditure (%)
Under 2,000	28	271.99	7,615.72	3.09	0.22
2,000–2,999	139	1,172.67	163,001.13	18.41	4.84
3,000–3,999	197	2,092.79	412,279.63	40.13	16.53
4,000–4,999	188	3,076.19	578,323.72	60.86	32.93
5,000–5,999	118	4,074.19	480,754.42	73.87	46.57
6,000–6,999	80	5,103.09	408,247.20	82.69	58.14
7,000–7,999	49	6,027.32	295,338.68	88.09	66.52
8,000 and over	108	10,931.91	1,180,646.28	100.00	100.00

Note:
[a] Expenditure of *all* households reduced by the expenditure of households in the lowest expenditure group for food, rent, heating, lighting, and clothing (purchases, repair, cleaning). The reduction is 1,406.09 AS per household.
Source: As for Table 21.2.

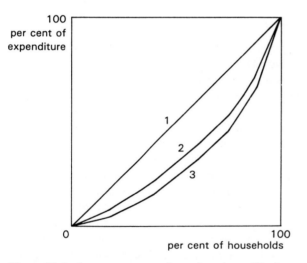

Figure 21.1 Lorenz curves of total and modified expenditures of three-person households in Austrian towns, 1964

Notes: 1: Line of equal expenditure
2: Distribution of total expenditure (see Table 21.2)
3: Distribution of modified expenditure (see Table 21.3)

(purchases, repair, cleaning). This sum is taken as a rough indicator of the
– physically and traditionally determined – minimum basic costs of a three-
person-household at the time of the inquiry. It is realized that some of the
non-covered items (part of the expenditure for transport, health, furniture,
etc.) could easily be included in the 'basic sector'. However, for a rough
estimate it will suffice to assume that the neglected sums are more or less
compensated by the inclusion of expenditure above 'basic requirements' in
the covered items.

The distributional implications of the two estimates are illustrated by the
Lorenz curves in Figure 21.1. A glance at the curves shows clearly that
'feelings' about inequality will differ according to which of the two expenditure (income) types are regarded as relevant. The question can also be
important when changes in inequality over time are discussed. If in the past
years the prices of food and housing have risen more sharply than the prices
of 'less essential' industrial goods then our modified expenditure (income)
approach may very well show an increase in inequality even when the
inequality index declines for the normal income distribution. This will be
a fortiori true when we allow for a rising minimum standard over time.

SOCIAL AND ENVIRONMENTAL INDICATORS

So far we have dealt with possible pitfalls resulting from an uncritical use
of income statistics and concentration measures as a guide to judgements
about inequality and its changes. We now come to a different and fundamental point: the insufficiency of income-derived information, be it modified or not.

In recent years there has developed a growing uneasiness about the
relevance of 'success reports' derived from national income data and
growth rates. The facts about environmental deterioration, pollution and
other external effects accompanying economic growth, about the changes in
occupational requirements and working conditions caused by rapid technical progress, are not reflected in national income figures, but they are certainly highly relevant when the progress of material well-being is to be
judged. The traditional and exclusive use of national income accounts for
this purpose seems questionable.[13] This new trend of looking at things has
found expression in a growing concern for the 'quality of life', and has contributed to the development of 'social indicators' which are regarded as
necessary supplements to the information derived from national income
analysis.[14]

Similar doubts about the significance of traditional indicators seem justified where inequality considerations are derived solely from income distributions. The fact that more and more by-products of economic growth
become decisive for the welfare of people on this limited planet should
induce us to pay more attention to their distribution.[15] The important point
to note is that owing to the absolute scarcities and indivisibilities with which

we are frequently confronted in environmental situations, slight changes in the distribution of incomes may have no significance for the distribution of important welfare factors.

Let me illustrate this with a simple example. As long as food and clothing were the main items in living standards any slight redistribution of incomes from rich to poor implied a comparable reduction in real inequality: the poor could now have a little bit more of the things which the rich could afford all the time. But take as a contrasting example the question of living in a comparatively noiseless zone, or of having access to nature (at reasonable levels of travel time and travel expenditure). Economic growth which may have led to a more equal income distribution, has created conditions which limit the number of people who can obtain such living conditions. While income distributions indicate a trend towards greater equality, the distribution of the non-covered items (*arising from the same development process*) may move in a different direction.[16] What is more, many of these inequalities cannot be influenced by slight changes in income distribution. The number of people who can have a garden at the lakeside is absolutely limited. The need of people to move out of unhospitable towns may increase, but the chance to do so will not change in the same piecemeal fashion as income structures. In many cases a reduction of inequality in these spheres can only be achieved by public action turning private goods into public or merit goods.

What I want to stress is that the problem of inequality is only partly covered by information on changes in income distribution. This information has to be supplemented by numerous environmental and social distributional indicators. This is particularly important, (1) because the environmental debate has shown that the items not covered by income statistics are rapidly increasing in their relevance for welfare, and (2) because there is no reason to assume that these additional items[17] show parallel tendencies to income patterns as far as changes in inequality are concerned. In fact, from the distributional angle two different questions could be asked. First, with regard to each item (e.g. housing space, housing conditions, access to hospital accommodation, exposure to noise or smoke, etc.) we could draw up separate statistics showing the distribution of this particular item by persons or households and study their development over time; second, and more interesting in the light of the general inequality debate, we should attribute these non-income items to the households arranged by income classes in order to see how far the other distributional aspects reinforce or alleviate the income picture (both at a given moment and in the course of time).

As far as the first aspect is concerned there exist already a number of useful statistics in several countries showing the distribution of size of houses, equipment of houses, education of persons, and of some other important welfare indicators. But we have practically no information as far as the second aspect is concerned. Social indicators are available and are used for comparisons between regions and countries, showing their uneven equipment and changes over time. But there is very little indeed to supplement income distribution data by matching distributional information about other important social and environmental welfare factors.[18] What Freeman says about the distribution of pollution applies to most of these factors:

'Does the degradation of environmental quality tend to increase or decrease the degree of inequality of welfare among individuals?', he asks. 'Is pollution the great leveler? Or does it tend to increase the disparities among individuals caused by differences in money income or wealth? We cannot answer this question conclusively for two reasons. The first is the problem of defining and measuring welfare where non-marketed environmental services are central to the question at hand. Here in particular, money income is a totally inadequate surrogate for welfare. The second reason is that as yet we do not have sufficiently detailed information to present a comprehensive picture of the patterns of distribution of environmental services' (Freeman 1972: 243–4).

Just in order to show what kind of information would be required I want to present the results of an investigation drawn from the above-quoted essay by Freeman. Using data from the US Censuses of Population and Housing in 1960 and from various investigations on air pollution carried out for the US Department of Health and the Public Health Service, Freeman calculated the exposure (at their place of residence) of different families to air pollution.[19] The investigation was carried out for three Metropolitan Areas. In Table 21.4 I show the distributional results for Washington, DC. The distributional picture is the same in the two other areas, though the absolute levels differ.

A glance at Table 21.4 shows that the distribution of air pollution reinforces the pattern arising from income distribution. This is worth stressing, because the opinion has been voiced that air pollution – like death – may

Table 21.4 Air pollution exposure by income size class,[a] Washington, DC, 1960

Income Class ($)	Suspended Particulates ($\mu gms/ml$)	Sulfation (mg.SO_3/100 cm^2 per day)
Under 3,000	64.6	0.82
3,000–4,999	61.7	0.82
5,000–6,999	53.9	0.75
7,000–9,999	49.7	0.69
10,000–14,999	45.5	0.64
15,000–24,999	43.2	0.58
25,000 and over	42.0	0.53

Note:
[a] At the place of residence.
Source: Freeman (1972), p. 265.

after all be the great leveller, affecting rich and poor alike. That this is not so at present – whatever the future may hold – is indicated by the above American figures.

But the table was not presented in order to deal with this particular question; it should show what sort of additional data we require to supplement income distribution data, especially when we discuss changes in inequality over time. Has the levelling in income distributions (if any) been 'paid for' by growing inequality in other welfare factors?[20] Or has inequality decreased in most fields? To answer these questions we would require a whole programme of well-conceived sample investigations to be carried out in regular intervals. If the problem of distribution and inequality were accorded that measure of urgency, which to my mind it deserves, then statistical offices and private research organizations would have to apply far more attention and resources to the provision of this type of social and environmental distributional information

EQUALITY IN CONSUMPTION?

In this final section I want to touch a point which lies a bit outside the usual discussion of income inequality but has a definite bearing on it. When speaking of inequality people often think first and foremost of differences in the possession of and in the command over goods and services.[21] In fact, the wish to have such a greater command over goods is regarded as the main motive for people to be worried about distributional issues.

Now, there is a widespread feeling – and that feeling may not be quite erroneous – that with growing national income and considering the limited capacities and time for consumption the real inequalities in the sphere of *consumption* tend to lose their significance. (There remains, of course, an unlimited range for inequalities in wealth and power. This is a major economic and political problem; but it does not concern us here.) These feelings often find expression in middle- or upper-class parties where one can hear exclamations like these (sometimes expressed with pleasure, sometimes with dismay): 'Nowadays everybody owns a car', or 'Almost everybody can afford a holiday nowadays', or 'Even the woman who comes for cleaning has a fur coat', etc.

I do not want to examine the 'truth value' of such statements; I do not want to point out that poverty still exists, that some households have two or more motor cars, that there are new products, different qualities etc. I rather want to discuss the above-mentioned tendencies towards a greater ubiquity of consumption goods and services, *in so far as they exist*, in the light of our discussion of inequality trends. In fact, I want to discuss the extreme case where all households, those with high, and those with low incomes, consume the same classes of consumption goods in equal quantities. There would, of course, remain the inequality in the possession of assets. But would we have equality in the realm of consumption? I believe not, and that for reasons which are already visible and relevant in our present-day not-quite-so-rich societies.

Inequality arises – as we said – first and foremost because people desire to have more goods (and wealth, and power). But inequality is also desired for its own sake: as a status symbol. This can be and is expressed in the consumption sphere by the possession and display of goods which others cannot afford. We may mention such things as diamonds, helicopters, hunting grounds, etc. This has been the 'classical' case of inequality in consumption: the enjoyment of types of goods which are not available to others and Veblen's 'conspicuous consumption'. This still plays a large part in our world, even in the wealthiest countries, but it may lose in importance.[22]

In a world of heterogeneous goods inequality can, however, persist even if all *types* of consumption goods and services can be found in every single household. The desire for status and for class exclusiveness can be satisfied by pricing *specific forms* of these goods and services out of reach of the lower income groups. The differentiated product will usually also possess higher qualities. But they may not be decisive and they may not be sufficient to account for the price differential whose main function may be to secure the separation of purchasers, i.e. economic and social inequality.[23]

Let me use an extremely simplified example to drive home the point I want to make. Assume that there are only two types of (consumption) commodities, each produced in one factory owned by one capitalist employing ten workers. We further assume that in each factory 21 units of the respective commodities (say A and B) are produced every week. To skim the wealthy market each entrepreneur differentiates *one* unit of his weekly output in some discernible way and sells it at a much higher price to the other entrepreneur.[24] We may then have the following situation. Suppose the weekly wage per worker is 2, i.e. the total wage bill in our 'economy' is 40. The price charged for the 'ordinary' form of commodities A and B is in both cases 1, and the 40 'ordinary' units produced in both factories are sold to the 20 workers. The price for the differentiated product is then set much higher. In fact, it does not matter how high it is set, as long as the ratio to the ordinary price is the same in both industries, and both entrepreneurs are willing to buy the expensive variation. Setting the high prices yields the high profits which enables the wealthy to exchange the differentiated products among themselves.[25] We may have equality in types of consumption goods, but – helped partly by genuine, partly by fake differentiation – two separate price levels and income circulations which could maintain the inequality problem as a social phenomenon even in the dream world of saturated consumption requirements.

I have mentioned this case, first because I believe that such separate price–income circuits due to and enforcing socio-economic stratifications have already some significance in our days, and second because I wanted to stress that economic inequality and its trend cannot only be regarded as a problem of 'natural' needs and requirements, but must also be seen as a sociological phenomenon.

NOTES

1 'Most economists live almost in a dream-world. They are a kind of sect engaging in mental gymnastics – impressive on occasion – in their own cabalistic language. They lose sight of the fact that what is important is the analysis and interpretation of the real world'. (Meerhaeghe 1971: XXVI). The full references are given at the end of the essay.

2 See for instance, Robinson (1972).

3 See Bombach (1973), particularly Section II, 'Qualitatives oder quantitatives Wachstum?'

4 It is a well-known fact that Ricardo gave pride of place to the problem of distribution. 'Political Economy', he wrote to Malthus, 'you think is an enquiry into the nature and causes of wealth. I think it should rather be called an enquiry into the laws which determine the division of the produce of industry among the classes who concur in its formation' (P. Sraffa and M. H. Dobb (eds) *Works of David Ricardo*, Vol. VII. Cambridge 1955. p. 278).

5 'By contemporary distribution theory we presumably mean a qualified marginal productivity theory; that is to say, a combination of the marginal productivity theory with other analytical elements' (Fellner 1953).

6 This refers exclusively to income distribution within advanced industrial countries. In developing countries and for the world as a whole the facts and problems are quite different.

7 See, for instance, the studies by Brittain (1960) and Titmuss (1962) for Great Britain, and by Kolko (1962) for the USA.

8 According to Brittain's (1960: 595–6) estimates the decline in top shares in the UK between 1938 and 1955 benefited the groups *above* the median. Leaving out the top 5 per cent of income receivers he finds an increase in the Gini concentration ratio both for pre-tax and post-tax incomes.

9 Stark (1972: ch. 3).

10 Low income limits are calculated – with some modifications – on the basis of assistance payments by the National Assistance Board. High incomes are those which are liable to surtax.

11 As to the source see the reference in Table 21.2. When looking at the figures it should be noted (a) that the number of income earners in the different households may be 1 or 2, and (b) that distribution by incomes instead of expenditures would yield a more uneven distribution since savings rise with rising income. Both factors are, however, irrelevant for our *comparison*, because they affect the data in Table 21.3 in the same way as in Table 21.2.

12 AS = Austrian shillings.

13 The doubts about the significance of the usual economic indices are very strongly expressed by Mishan (1967). Thus, he writes (p. 171): 'The notion of economic expansion as a process on balance beneficial to society goes back at least a couple of centuries, about which time, however, the case in favour was much stronger than it is today when we are not only incomparably wealthier but also suffering from many disagreeable by-products of rapid technological change... The general conclusion of this volume is that the continued pursuit of economic growth by Western Societies is more likely on balance to reduce rather than increase social welfare.'

14 See Bombach (1973: 47 ff.); also Sheldon and Moore (1968).

15 The neglect of this type of analysis is stressed by Ida C. Merriam in Sheldon and Moore (1968: 780).
16 It may, of course, also go in the same direction. This will be specially the case, where scarce facilities are provided as public goods by the state.
17 The number of items can be very large. There is yet no clear convention about the 'right' coverage. The French system of social indicators includes 21 groups, each of which is subdivided into further items.
18 Lest it be objected that these other factors should not concern the economist (why not, by the way?), let us stress once more that these other factors and their distribution spring from the same technical-economic process which influences the size and distribution of measured income. A general discussion of inequality has to take them into account if we do not want to give a one-sided and distorted picture.
19 Only two aspects of air pollution could be covered: suspended particles and sulfation.
20 On the basis of some rather simple and general theoretical considerations Freeman concludes that environmental improvement measures tend to benefit the wealthy more than the poor. See Freeman (1972: 250–8).
21 Savings raise some special problems which we shall neglect.
22 The decline in the importance of this type of inequality is stressed – to my mind over-stressed – in the chapter on Inequality in Galbraith (1958).
23 A good example might be restaurant services. The high-priced restaurant may have better food (but not necessarily so) and it will certainly have all sorts of nick-nacks and frills in order to *justify* the higher prices charged. But the *function* of the higher prices is to differentiate the good so that an unequal society can consume the 'same 'things in separate and unequal forms. The same goes for certain species of motor cars and other durable consumption goods, for first class and economy flights etc. If competition (in the sense of entry to the sector) is strong, extra profits from the sale of differentiated products to the rich will disappear through the addition of so many 'unnecessary' embellishments until the 'extras' eat up the price differential. Where firms can establish a reputation for producing the 'exquisite' product, they will reap a permanent monopoly profit from selling to the rich.

The whole problem can, of course, be made to disappear by refusing to define commodities functionally and by taking each differentiated item as a special commodity. Then we are back at the 'classical' case of inequality (see the previous paragraph). But the type of talk mentioned at the beginning of this section 'Nowadays everybody owns a car' would be meaningless.
24 In our case, with two monopolistic producers, this price need not have any relation to the additional costs of differentiation.
25 In the above example we have also to allow each capitalist the retention of one unit of the luxury edition out of his own output. I have cut this out from the production and income side.

REFERENCES

Bombach, G. (1973) 'Konsum oder Investionen für die Zukunft?' in Friedrichs, G. (ed.) *Qualität des Lebens. Vol 7: Qualitatives Wachstum*, Frankfurt.
Brittain, J. A. (1960) 'Some Neglected Features of Britain's Income Levelling', *American Economic Review*, 50, Papers and Proceedings.
Burns, A. F. (1951) *Looking Forward*, 31st Annual Report of the National Bureau of Economic Research, New York.

Champernowne, D. G. (1953) 'A Model of Income Distribution', *Economic Journal*, 63.

Dalton, H. (1929) *The Inequality of Incomes*, London and New York.

Fellner, W. (1953) 'Significance and Limitations of Contemporary Distribution Theory', *American Economic Review*, 43, Papers and Proceedings.

Freeman, A. M. III (1972) 'Distribution of Environmental Quality' in Kneese, A. V. and Bower B. T. (eds) *Environmental Quality Analysis*, Baltimore and London.

Galbraith J. K. (1958) *The Affluent Society*, London.

Gibrat, R. (1931) *Les Inégalités Economiques*, Paris.

Gini, C. (1936) 'On the Measure of Concentration with Especial Reference to Income and Wealth', Cowles Commission.

Kaldor, N. (1955) 'Alternative Theories of Distribution' *Review of Economic Studies*, 23.

Kalecki, M. (1954) *The Theory of Economic Dynamics*, London.

Kolko, G. (1962) *Wealth and Power in America. An Analysis of Social Class and Income Distribution*, New York.

Lydall, H. F. (1968) *The Structure of Earnings*, Oxford.

Marchal, J. and Lecaillon, J. (1958) *La Répartition du Revenu National*, Paris.

van Meerhaeghe, M. A. G. (1971) *Economics, A Critical Approach*, London.

Mishan, E. J. (1967) *The Costs of Economic Growth*, London.

Pareto, V. (1897) *Cours d'Economie Politique*, Lausanne.

Robinson, J. (1972) 'The Second Crisis of Economic Theory', *American Economic Review*, 62, Papers and Proceedings.

Sheldon, E. B. and Moore, W. E. (eds) (1968) *Indicators of Social Change*, New York.

Sraffa, P. (1960) *The Production of Commodities by Means of Commodities*, London.

Stark, T. (1972) *The Distribution of Personal Income in the United Kingdom, 1949–1963*, Cambridge.

Titmuss, R. M. (1962) *Income Distribution and Social Change*, London.

22 A just distribution of incomes: a dilemma between ethics and economics?

(Translation of 'Verteilungsgerechtigkeit: Ein ethisch-ökonomisches Dilemma?' in Pappi, F. U. (ed) (1989) *Wirtschaftsethik – Gesellschaftliche Perspektiven*, Kiel: Universität Kiel, pp. 75–85)

When quotations regarding income distribution are discussed bishops and professors of economics are not always in harmony. Their ideas and opinions point in different directions; there are irritations, misunderstandings and frictions. Is this problem inherent in the question and therefore unavoidable or is it a failure in communication due to different 'language systems' or could it be a clash of temperaments between 'cool' economists and 'blue-eyed' moralists? The following attempt to disclose some of the sources of the frictions might be useful for finding a basis for peaceful coexistence or – better still – for a fruitful and complementary cooperation between ethics and economics. We shall also be able to discover some of the difficulties existing in current dialogues.

One possible scenario for a coexistence free of problems and frictions could be a clear separation of the two disciplines. Each could be restricted to its own clearly defined specialized sphere without meddling in the neighbour's affairs. This idea which corresponds to the widely accepted picture of a highly specialized and departmentalized scientific establishment seems particularly attractive in the problem under discussion. On the one side one could have a positive economic science which would 'explain' – avoiding all value judgements – the mechanisms of the real economy including the existing income distribution[1] whose results would be recorded quite unemotionally ('is'-statements); on the other side there would be the normative statements of ethical 'experts' who would have to provide reasons why certain distributions should be regarded as desirable ('ought'-statements) without having to pay attention to the possibilities of such 'ideal' distributions and their realization.[2]

In such a situation each side could be interested in what the other side is doing but there would be few or no overlappings or contradictions. A moral philosopher who is interested in possibilities or realization would respect the information obtained from economists, while the latter would accept the ethical ranking of alternative distributions given by the 'moralist' (short for moral philosopher, student of ethics). But things are not as simple as that. Even if one regards such a strict separation as desirable, experience shows that it is hardly practicable.

An objective difficulty derives from the fact that neither economists nor moralists have a unified viewpoint within their own discipline. Economists do not all subscribe to the same theories and there is no basic ethical consensus about the shape of a just income distribution.[3] No unequivocal answers can be obtained from the neighbouring discipline so that one is forced to form an opinion of one's own. More decisive, however, is another factor. Income distribution is socially and politically such an important and explosive theme that a strict abstinence from looking at certain of its aspects is very difficult in practice and it is frequently not even accepted by persons who in methodological discussions favour a strict departmentalization. As we shall see, the economic profession has some very outspoken ideas about the evaluation of alternative distributions and moralists are seldom contented with an isolated explication of ethical qualities; they argue that their ideas are realizable and demand their application. The transgression of frontiers is pervasive. This can be stimulating and fruitful but it also leads to misunderstandings and irritations which are caused by an insufficient acknowledgment of differences in the initial position. This problem will occupy us later on.

A special – and occasionally proposed – constellation where the separation discussed above seems to have a better chance of survival, but which also comes up against severe barriers in practice, demands that economists and moralists accept a division of labour in attacking a common problem from two different sides. The task of the economists would be to see to it that the economy produces as big a cake as possible, and ethics would have to decide about its just distribution. Both, economists and moralists, would be motivated by the same target – an increase in 'welfare'[4] – but each would be responsible for a special aspect of it. Ideas like this lie behind some considerations about tax systems as a means of 'secondary distribution' or behind the German concept of a '*Soziale Marktwirtschaft*'. The difficulty with this approach lies in the limited separability of the two partial targets. The size of total output is not independent of the way in which this output is ultimately distributed, and distribution patterns are not independent of the way in which the national cake is produced. The potential conflicts between efficiency and distributional targets prevent a simple division of tasks between economists and moralists. Difficult factual questions regarding economic processes and social welfare as well as the trade-off between the two would tend to be neglected.

There is a third variant of a conflict-free relationship between ethics and economics. It exists when the positive statements of the economists are in full agreement with the normative judgements of the moralists. This will, for instance, be the case when economists find that the market process results in an income distribution which corresponds very closely to the performance of the income receivers (or to their contribution to 'social welfare') *and* when moralists regard performance-related incomes as a 'just' basis for distribution. Such a combination, which is not unknown in the real world,[5] can provide legitimacy and apologetics for a system, but it is certainly not always and everywhere acceptable. Neither economists nor moralists are always of the opinion that we live in a Pangloss world with the best possible institutions and circumstances. As far as reality is concerned one can have doubts about the performance-conformity of incomes when one looks at differences in (initial) wealth, natural and artificial monopolies, external effects, etc. And the ethical discourse shows that a majority of people seem to favour a reduction of income differentials[6] – both for persons and for nations – and/or the consideration of criteria like needs, family, etc. which find no reflection in market payments.

This sketch of 'peaceful' scenarios and their difficulties should suffice to indicate why differences in opinion and conflicting views between economics and ethics are not an exceptional phenomenon. Existing differences cannot be completely eliminated: the subject is too complicated and the emotional engagement on both sides too different. But it can certainly be useful to look a bit more closely at the core of the economic-ethical dilemma; this might help to narrow down areas of disagreement and to find a clearer definition of the possible contributions from each side. In dealing with this problem it will be necessary to look at factual contexts on the one hand and at valuation problems on the other.

But before turning to these questions I want to draw attention to the extreme complexity of the subject which burdens all discussions in this field. It has already been pointed out that neither economists nor moralists are of one opinion about the mechanisms and norms of the distribution process. In addition, the distribution itself is a multi-faced phenomenon which can be viewed from different angles. Should we deal with personal or household incomes, with income and/or wealth, should we include other factors like working conditions, opportunities, access to public goods or even climate (in international comparisons)? Even when one has agreed on one definition, say personal incomes, there still remain difficult questions regarding the measurement of equality and inequality which affect the evaluation of different distributions.

All these questions, which are the subject of many discussions, will not be treated here. They must be discussed *within* the economic and ethical communities in order to arrive at clear definitions and alternatives which will ease the path towards a more precise communication. Since I am only concerned with the essentials of the economic-ethical controversy I can restrict myself to the central question of the distribution of net incomes (incomes after tax and including transfers) and I shall assume that expressions like 'more equality', 'less equality', 'levelling', etc. are self-explaining and need not be further defined. The centre of our considerations is occupied by the economic-ethical dilemma 'efficiency vs. justice'.

Let us begin with the factual aspects of the problem. The question is whether it is possible (or impossible) to combine the aim of economic efficiency and as big an output as possible with ethical ideas about a just distribution. The valuation criteria which we shall discuss later become relevant as soon as an ideal combination of the two aims proves to be unattainable and a 'proper' trade-off between them has to be found. The factual question becomes topical in economic-ethical discussions when the moral philosophers are not contented to discuss 'ideal' distributions *in abstracto* (including pure utopias) but have an understandable urge to influence practical affairs (institutions and behavioural patterns) so that a just distribution of incomes (here treated in the sense of more equality) can be accomplished.

The core of the problem lies – as James Meade has shown very convincingly (Meade 1964) – in the double function of prices (including wages as prices for labour services). On the one hand prices serve as market signals to indicate scarcities and demand pressure so that resources can be 'optimally' allocated, on the other hand they constitute income for the owners of production factors (labour, capital, land). A conflict arises because these two functions may not point in the same direction when satisfactory solutions are desired. High prices may be useful in some cases in order to attract resources and services into certain activities which yield high returns, but the primary incomes so created may go to persons which have already a high income and a high standard of living (and vice versa). Redistribution through taxes and transfers and social policy can mitigate such divergencies (secondary distribution), and this has been the historical compromise between economics and ethics; but there are limits to this process in so far as the supply of productive services depends on disposable income. It is this incentive effect of net wages which commands the interest of economists while moralists lay more stress on needs and the status aspects of income.

When *factual* questions about the existence and extent of this conflict in targets are under discussion economists will normally be in a stronger position than moralists, since they are professionally concerned with the analysis of economic mechanisms and effects. It is understandable that economists are sometimes irritated by well-meaning proposals for a fairer income distribution (nationally or internationally) when these are only looking at the immediate redistribution effects neglecting the longer-term consequences on incentives and behaviour which can lead to a lower growth of the social product. As far as such negative consequences exist they should at least be declared as 'costs' of the redistribution proposal. What decision is then taken is a question of valuation. This aspect will be treated later.

However, even in the factual sphere the situation is not quite so simple. It is not just the case that knowledgeable economists are confronted with naive ethical demands. First of all it has to be remembered that over a considerable range the conflict between economics and ethics does not arise. Almost since its beginning economic theory has used the (economic) concept of 'rent' to denote an income which is sheltered against competition by monopolistic or other institutional barriers and which is neither performance-conditioned nor required as an incentive. The 'pure' rent income going to the owner of scarce land is the classical example, but elements of rent can be found in many prices and incomes. Their elimination would have – by the very definition of rent elements – no influence on the supply of productive services. In these spheres action can be taken without bringing economic and ethical considerations into conflict. Anti-monopoly legislation is an obvious example. It should be added, however, that while economists argue against rents quite generally (for efficiency reasons), the moral argument applies only when rents accrue to comparatively high incomes.

Leaving the rent case behind and turning to the competitive sector we have to face the confrontation between efficiency and justice (in the sense of less inequality). Their relationship is an empirical question which has been a well-known problem in the theory of public finance for a long time. It finds its extreme expression in the so-called Laffer curve which points to the trivial fact that when the tax level becomes too high individual economic efforts will decline and ultimately fall to zero when the tax rate reaches 100 per cent. But in practical cases we are not concerned with extreme cases or with demands for absolute income equality (which might not even be regarded as 'ideal' on purely ethical grounds). The problem is that one might plan to take *a few steps* in the direction of a more equal income distribution and wants to know whether and to what an extent this will have negative effects on incentives and output. This requires a more differentiated approach.

One thing is certain: moralists tend to take an optimistic view with regard to this problem while economists frequently display a more sceptical or pessimistic attitude. This is partly due to differences in the human prototype underlying the two disciplines. Most moral philosophers have hopes and ideas of a gradually progressing humanity, while economists look at people as they have become conditioned in modern market- and profit-orientated societies. But there are also some more concrete reasons which can be held against the economists' bias to stress the inevitability of efficiency losses whenever redistribution is considered.[7] Behind this bias lies the assumption of economic theory that the '*homo oeconomicus*' always regards goods as a positive item while work enters his/her utility function as a negative element (i.e. leisure time is always regarded as a positive good).

But there are types of work which are experienced as a positive contribution to welfare by some persons, in particular in relation to forms and contents of alternative activities. One *wants* to perform certain activities and their supply is – within limits – not dependent on the income one receives. Tinbergen (1975) has suggested the possibility that only so much should be paid to a person as is actually necessary to induce him/her to remain in the chosen (market-orientated) occupation instead of moving to another job.

A further element which does not receive sufficient attention under the economic perspective is connected with the methodological individualism of mainstream economic theory. The motivations and preferences of the isolated individual take centre-stage with the consequence that individual income and possibly the disutility of work become the prime movers of action. If we look, however, at people as socially related human beings, then it becomes necessary to pay more attention to social traditions and targets. Utilities and motivations are then not only a function of one's own income but are also dependent on its relation to other incomes. The adoption of a 'fair' income distribution can increase utility and foster incentives, first of all, of course, among low-paid people who benefit directly, but also among better-paid persons who accept 'fairness' as a social standard. It is significant that experiences in this direction made by business economists and psychologists have found practically no reflection in the work of economic theorists. To some extent this is due to the 'dehumanization' and 'depsychologization' of economic theory in whose models people are frequently 'factors of production' which react more or less mechanically to the price signals of the market.[8]

These considerations show that it is not permissible to assume quite generally that proposals for a more even income distribution must always come into conflict with the aim of a plentiful production of goods. Whether and to what extent such a conflict exists will depend on a number of circumstances such as form and extent of the redistribution process, social ideas and values, economic policy, etc. The fact is that there is no clear empirical evidence for a negative relationship between economic growth and income levelling[9] though it must be admitted that it is not easy to isolate this relationship in international comparisons.

But whatever the decisive conditions may be in individual instances the fact remains that conflicts between efficiency and justice targets *can* arise and have to be considered. This brings us to the question of evaluation, to a weighing of targets and target combinations.

Before turning to this question a short diversion is necessary to point towards a possible limitation of the problem under discussion. Economists have always made it clear that their idea of an efficient economic system implies the achievement of the highest possible level of *utility* (under the constraints of a given structure of purchasing power). A higher volume of goods and services is a desirable target because one assumes that an increase in material goods leads to increased utility. As long as we look at a Robinson economy this perspective creates no problem. But as soon as we admit the existence of social structures with ideas of fairness, justice, solidarity, etc. we have to take into account that more justice in the distribution of incomes can enter as a positive element in individual utility functions (typical example: the family) and can compensate to some extent a reduction in output.

Two consequences follow from this. First, when efficiency is defined in terms of utility maximization, economics and ethics (justice) can to some extent march in the same direction even if some negative incentive effects exist. The second remark points towards a possible 'productive' contribution on the part of ethics. In analogy to the economic stress on the value of occupational education for the formation of human capital which helps to increase productivity and production, ethical education can be regarded as valuable when it contributes to a wider utility-increasing acceptance of just distributions. This would offer more room for redistribution measures without leading to efficiency losses (in the above sense).

We can now turn to the decisive dilemma which has to be faced when a choice has to be made between a higher output and more distributional justice (however defined). This is clearly a problem of values and it would seem that for such problems the main responsibility lies with the moral philosophers. Economists could accept the role of 'experts' who could provide factual knowledge in order to show what material sacrifices the various distribution proposals imply. If they could stick to this pure informational task no conflict would arise. But just as moralists feel an urge to give practical advice and to demand certain actions, economists are obviously unable or unwilling to refrain from passing normative judgements – often pretty strong ones – about alternative possibilities. The list of sins in this field is a long one.

The existence of this valuation problem has been known for a long time. Conflicting targets including growth and income distribution are a well-known subject and it is usually acknowledged that the resolution of the conflicts cannot be achieved by scientific methods but is a political task (hopefully to be supplemented by 'ethical' considerations). But while these views are accepted in principle and can be found in the introductory chapters of economic textbooks, theoretical economics and economists do not hesitate to express very outspoken valuations about alternative possibilities. This finds its expression not only in the frequent use of such adjectives as 'good', 'bad', 'advantageous', 'detrimental' and so on but also in a semi-scientific, semi-normative vocabulary which contains emotionally coloured words like 'optimality', 'welfare', 'maximum utility', etc.

The problem is, of course, not that economists have certain standards of value – ethical or otherwise – and want to express their views. As long as they follow Myrdal's demand to make it quite clear what their personal standards are which they introduce into a discussion of real processes and alternatives no problem arises. In fact such a procedure is preferable to a seemingly 'objective' analysis which will almost unavoidably contain some implicit value elements. Nothing can be said against personal opinions of economists on normative aspects. These cannot be left to moral philosophers as an exclusive privilege.

The roots of the problem lie in the fact that a number of normative and emotionally coloured elements are already 'built in' to the traditional economic theory and its interpretations giving them a 'theoretical' and 'objective' dignity which is the more effective because the normative character is hidden behind an impressive formal structure. Normative judgements can thus obtain the character of objective necessities. This problem is particularly relevant in the conflict between size and distribution of the national income. This is so because economists do not restrict their treatment of this subject to an analysis of the effects of alternative distributions on 'allocative efficiency' – a problem which is their proper concern; too often they tend to use 'allocative efficiency' not only as an explicative technical term but also as an obvious and binding norm in judging alternative proposals and conditions.

This would, of course, cause no problem if efficiency and economic growth were the only target. In medical research nobody could possibly object to the practice to couple the proof of the harmfulness of a medicine with a strong advice to stop the use of it. No problem arises because health is a clear and generally desired common target. In so far, however, there is a conflict between economic growth and a just income distribution the uniqueness of the efficiency target is lost; it has no longer a claim to priority. Decisions have now to be made under a wider perspective and on a broader level where economists should certainly have their say but should not have the right to set the imperatives.

I shall now give a brief account of the mechanisms (or should one say the 'tricks'?) which have been and are used by considerable portions of economics to create a seemingly objective framework for an 'economic ethics' which permits a rather unreflected 'theoretical' practice to equate 'economically more efficient' with 'generally better'. This tendency finds already an expression in the obvious practice to attach far greater weight to questions regarding the level and growth of production than to those concerning a 'just' distribution. This may be partly justified in view of the 'softness' of the concept of 'justice'; but a general tendency to regard the size of the cake as the measure of success irrespective of the way it is distributed cannot be denied. The efficient allocation of the factors of production obtains highest priority without further questions being asked. In this context the incentive problem is particularly important.

The normative problem gains weight when economic theory deals with such questions as 'welfare' or 'optimality' which have an obvious affinity to value. How is it possible for an 'objective' scientist to arrive at 'objective' statements and conclusions in this sphere? Put rather sharply and rudely the answer is that one can achieve this only by clearing the decisive terms of all their delicate aspects so that one obtains a structure which looks and sounds like a purely objective representation in which, however, the decisive ethical aspects have been lost. [10]

Let us start with the concept of 'welfare' which has obvious normative connotations. Who would object to an increase in welfare, who does not prefer more welfare to less? The consensus regarding this simple question provides the basis for the preferences and recommendations of economists. This would create no problem if 'welfare' were a clear and unequivocal concept for an individual and for society. This is, however, certainly not the case. 'Welfare' itself needs closer psychological and ethical scrutiny. Economics reduces the complexity of this question first by assuming (probably quite realistically) that a greater volume of goods and services implies – *ceteris paribus* – a higher level of welfare; and second by admitting that economists only deal with *material welfare* and cannot pass judgement on *total welfare* which depends on a number of further factors (which, however, may not be independent of the way in which production is organized). Though, therefore, the partial character of the economic approach is acknowledged in principle we find that this insight is often neglected when it comes to recommendations regarding practical alternatives. Then the ranking of alternatives often relies exclusively on economic criteria (level of output, efficiency) without any consideration of other influences and possibilities. The reasonable proposal by Little (1950) that economic theorists should talk of 'ecfare' instead of 'welfare' in order to draw attention to the limited validity of their welfare statements has found no permanent echo.

But even when we neglect this question and restrict ourselves to material welfare we are not rid of the conflict which is connected with the efficiency–distribution dilemma which economists have to face when they turn to the real world. If they did not want to escape into the simple prescription 'First bake as big a cake as possible (responsibility of economists), then distribute it (responsibility of moralists)' which neglects the interdependence of the two aspects, economists had to find other means which would allow them to develop 'objective' economic judgements. Three elements paved the way to a 'solution': Impossibility of interpersonal comparisons of utility, Pareto-optimality and compensation principle.

As long as only total output serves as a standard of valuation one has some problems of aggregation but on the whole it is clear what one has to measure and it is usually not difficult to agree about the meanings of 'more' or 'less'. As soon as the distribution question is added things become more complicated. Not only does one need a welfare-relevant standard for measuring distribution aspects, this standard must also be somehow comparable with the output standard so that it is possible to find the welfare-optimal trade-off between a reduction of goods and an increase in justice (or vice versa). It can hardly be expected that an 'exact' formulation of such a standard is possible[11] (which by the way is also true for the output standard as such). But this does not mean that the two aspects cannot be subjected to arguments which can offer help in practical decisions, difficult as such a task may be.

This difficult problem is eschewed in economics by falling back on the postulated impossibility of interpersonal comparisons of utility. Building on the undeniable fact that individual utilities and satisfactions can hardly be measured and compared, modern welfare economics jumps to the conclusion that no 'reasonable' statements can be made in redistribution debates. This is a strange purism if we remember that economists are the main users of the concept of individual utility and do not hesitate to make utility maximization (how measured?) an important aspect of their behavioural axioms. In practice some sort of interpersonal comparisons are unavoidable in real world debates on welfare and distribution and they can be supported by personal experience, by biological, physiological and psychological knowledge and other relevant arguments. [12]

With the denial of a 'scientific' basis for comparative statements about income distributions the logical step for economics would be to withdraw completely from any debate about welfare aspects. Economic theory could analyse the output consequences of alternative distribution arrangements; but the final decision would have to be left completely to moral philosophers, politicians and the society at large. But economists have an understandable yearning to do more than to give only such background information. This dilemma between a 'scientific' impossibility of and a practical wish for giving advice was circumvented in the so-called 'New Welfare Economics' with the aid of Pareto-optimality and the compensation principle.

Pareto-optimality opened a path to normative statements without getting involved in distributional judgements. The quickest way to explain Pareto-optimality is by giving a definition for situations which are *not* Pareto-optimal. They are said to exist if there are possibilities of increasing total output (or utility) in such a way that *no* individual is worse off in the alternative situation than in the existing one. Such situations are valued – explicitly or implicitly – as 'worse' than Pareto-optimal situations because they permit material improvements without any 'sacrifice' on the part of some people. Once a Pareto-optimal position is reached such opportunities are no longer available; increases in the social product (or utility) cannot be achieved without making at least some persons worse off than before. This creates a distribution problem which prevents a 'scientific' evaluative comparison of different (Pareto-optimal) distributions. To overcome this obstacle the compensation principle is introduced. A transition from one Pareto-optimum to another one with a higher total output is regarded 'objectively' as an 'improvement' if the people who benefit from the change would still support it even if they were forced to pay sufficient compensation to those who are injured so that they are at least as well off as before.

This modified standard for ranking situations as 'better' and 'worse' ones, 'welfare-optimal' or 'sub-optimal' ones, does however not yield a real solution for an 'objectivization' of the normative problem when we want to make distribution an essential ingredient of welfare. Two serious problems have to be considered.

The first deals with the Pareto-aspect. If we take the social aspects of distribution seriously it is no longer certain that Pareto-optimal situations are always 'superior' to non-optimal ones which they could replace. If *relative* income enters into the utility function (in addition to its absolute level) it can easily happen that a somewhat lower total income which is 'justly' or 'fairly' distributed may create more welfare than a Pareto-optimal higher income where everybody is better off but where relativities are regarded as 'unjust'. It is difficult to lay down a concept of 'welfare' which takes no account of distribution.

Even more questionable is the attempt to get rid of the difficulties of distributional judgements with the help of the compensation principle. It is obviously not sufficient to stop at the recommendation of Pareto-optimal situations if one wants to offer (normative) advice in real world situations. This would make it impossible to distinguish – as far as 'welfare' is concerned – between a situation where everybody is near the average income and a situation where one half of the population is very well off and the other half starves; in both cases no redistribution is possible without harming some persons. The stipulated impossibility of interpersonal comparisons of utility excludes any meaningful 'objective' comparison.

But choices between alternative Pareto-optimal situations are the typical problem in distributional conflicts. To be able to enter this debate the compensation principle has been created. If a change of the Pareto-optimal situation *A* to the Pareto-optimal situation *B* permits full compensation for the damaged persons *in principle* then *B* can be seen as a 'welfare-improvement' as compared to *A*. This sounds very much like an 'objective' standard (provided Pareto-optimality is accepted) which avoids interpersonal comparisons of utility. But quite apart from the problems of measurement which this concept involves, the principle of a *hypothetical* possibility of full compensation makes this method irrelevant for *practical* valuation problems. In real world conflicts about alternative distributions the decisive question is whether and to what extent compensations will *in fact* flow from the winners to the losers, be it directly or via the state. Situations with a high *hypothetical* compensation potential can then be inferior – with regard to distribution and welfare – to less productive situations with a higher chance for *realizable* compensations.

What conclusions can be derived from all these considerations? Alternative income distributions and particularly the confrontation of efficiency and justice give rise to a number of difficult economic and ethical problems which are hotly debated within the disciplines of economics and ethics and are only partly 'solved'. To some extent the research programmes and perspectives of the two disciplines are complementary: economics is more concerned with the positive aspects of the problem, ethics with the normative aspects. A knowledge of the work and results of the opposite discipline can help both sides to get a better understanding of the possibilities and limitations of their own analyses. Dilemmas between economic and ethical approaches have different causes. There is a purely factual difficulty arising from the lack of sufficient data which would allow to clear up some of the areas where economic 'necessities' and ethical 'imperatives' come into conflict. Additional frictions are created through the 'violation of frontiers' when moral philosophers advance demands on the basis of rather 'naive' ideas about economic relationships or when economists try to turn their theoretically favoured norms into a decisive standard for evaluation.

NOTES

1 Here and in what follows I shall deal exclusively with income distributions which usually occupy the main interest. But the distribution of wealth is also a subject for ethical considerations. This will not be considered. To some extent it is of course connected with inequalities in income.
2 Such a 'departmentalization' is regarded – at least in principle – as a desirable arrangement by many economists. See, for instance the 'classical' essay by Robbins (1932).
3 In his book on income distribution the Dutch economist Jan Pen presents a list of twenty-one different (not necessarily contradictory) norms for a 'just' income distribution which have been proposed at one time or another (Pen 1971: ch. VII). Sen who has given more thought to questions of income distribution and distributional justice than almost any other economist quite rightly complains: 'Apart from the complexity of the moral concepts involved, their abundance is really remarkable' (Sen 1984: 302). A considerable variety in economic approaches must also be admitted.
4 Always assuming that a growing output is an accepted target. Ecologists and ascetics may not agree.
5 A typical early example is J. B. Clark who at the end of last century put forward the idea that the marginal productivity theory is both an explanation of reality and an ethical norm (Clark 1899).
6 See the remarks and references in Sen (1973: 2).
7 We are dealing here only with losses in efficiency due to a reduction in incentives. Efficiency losses as a consequence of 'bad' tax systems (e.g. high marginal taxes) are not treated because they are avoidable (at least in principle).
8 This should not be seen as a fundamental criticism of such models which can be quite useful in some contexts. But it is a warning that they should not be applied uncritically and without the necessary modifications to complicated real situations.
9 See, for instance, the results in Fields (1984) who compares the developments in seven developing countries over the period 1960–80.
10 For an ethical and philosophical perspective see Ulrich (1986), chapters 4.3 and 5.5.
11 An account of the considerable formal problems which arise even on a very general and abstract level can be found in Ebert (1987) particularly chapter 7 and in the literature noted there.
12 The problems connected with interpersonal comparisons of utility are extensively treated in Möller (1983).

REFERENCES

Clark, J. B. (1899) *The Distribution of Wealth*, New York: Macmillan.

Ebert, U. (1987) *Beiträge zur Wohlfahrtsökonomie. Effizienz und Verteilung*, Berlin: Springer.

Fields, G. S. (1984) 'Employment, income distribution and economic growth in seven small open economies', *Economic Journal* 94, 1, pp. 74–83.

Little, I. M. D. (1950) *A Critique of Welfare Economics*, Oxford, Oxford University Press.

Meads, J. E. (1964) *Efficiency, Equality and the Ownership of Property*, London: Allen & Unwin.

Möller, R. (1983) *Interpersonelle Nutzenvergleiche. Wissenschaftliche Möglichkeiten und politische Bedeutung*, Göttingen: Vandenhoeck & Ruprecht.

Pen, J. (1971) *Income Distribution*, London: Allen Lane.

Robbins, L. (1932) *An Essay on the Nature and Significance of Economic Science*, London: Macmillan.

Sen, A. (1973) *On Economic Equality*, Oxford: Clarendon.

—— (1984) 'Ethical issues in income distribution' in Sen, A. *Resources, Values and Development*, Oxford: Blackwell.

Tinbergen, J. (1975) *Income Distribution. Analysis and Policies*, Amsterdam: New Holland.

Ulrich P. (1986) *Transformation der ökonomischen Vernunft. Fortschrittsperspektiven der modernen Industriegesellschaft*, Bern: Haupt.

Index

Numbers in italics refer to figures or tables where these are separate from the textual reference.